Praise from Job Seekers for the *Knock 'em Dead* Books

"I was sending out hordes of resumes and hardly getting a nibble—and I have top-notch skills and experience in my field. I wasn't prepared for this tough job market. When I read your book, however, I immediately began applying some of your techniques. My few nibbles increased to so many job interviews I could hardly keep up with them!"

—C.S., Chicago, Illinois

"Every time I've used your book, I've gotten an offer! This book is incredible. Thanks for publishing such a great tool."

—W.Z., Columbia, Maryland

"I read and used your book, *Resumes That Knock 'em Dead*, as I searched for a job. I was called for an interview and was up against ten applicants. To make a long story short, I interviewed on Monday morning, and by Monday afternoon knew I had the job."

—E.H. (no address given)

"I've used *Knock 'em Dead* since 1994 when I graduated. It's the reason I've made it to VP—thank you!"

—P.L., Norfolk, Virginia

"After reading your book, *Resumes That Knock 'em Dead*, I rewrote my resume and mailed it to about eight companies. The results were beyond belief. I was employed by one of the companies that got my new resume, and received offers of employment or requests for interviews from every company. The entire job search took only five weeks."

—J.V., Dayton, Ohio

"My son called me from college last night, desperate to help a friend on her first interview. My advice? Tell her to drop everything and head to the nearest bookstore to get *Knock 'em Dead*. The book is a godsend and helped me obtain the job of my dreams eight years ago. It is by far THE best book on interviewing out there. I highly recommend it to everyone I know who asks me for help. As a Director of HR now, I know. No one should go to an interview without reading, re-reading, and re-re-reading this informative, absorbing, tremendously helpful book. It is utterly amazing. Thank you!"

—S.D., Philadelphia, Pennsylvania

"I am very grateful for your *Knock 'em Dead* series. I have read the trio and adopted the methods. In the end, I got a dream job with a salary that is almost double of my previous! By adopting your methods, I got four job offers and had a hard time deciding!"

—C.Y., Singapore

"I rejigged my resume exactly as you outlined in your book and one employer said, 'You can tell this person has a real love of PR from his resume.' Within three weeks I had three job offers and was able to pick and choose the perfect job for myself."

—M.W., Detroit, Michigan

"Your book is simply fantastic. This one book improved my yearly income by several thousand dollars, and my future income by untold amounts. Your work has made my family and myself very happy."

—M.Z., St. Clair Shores, Michigan

"I cannot tell you what a fabulous response I have been getting due to the techniques you describe in your books. Besides giving me the tools I needed to 'get my foot in the door,' they gave me confidence. I never thought I could secure an excellent position within a month!"

—B.G., Mountainview, California

"My job search began a few months ago when I found out that I would be laid off because of a corporate buyout. By following your advice, I have had dozens of interviews and have received three very good job offers. Your excellent advice made my job hunt much easier."

—K.C., St. Louis, Missouri

"I heard of your book right after I bombed out on three interviews. I read it. I went on two interviews after reading it. I have been told by both of those last two interviewers that I am the strongest candidate. I may have two job offers!"

—B.V., Albuquerque, New Mexico

"I read your book and studied your answers to tough questions. The first interview that I went on after doing this ended up in a job being offered to me! The interviewer told me that I was the best interviewee she'd seen! Thanks a million for writing your book. I am so thankful that I had heard about you!"

—K.P., Houston, Texas

"I just finished writing the letter I have dreamed of writing for three years: my letter of resignation from the Company from Hell. Thanks to you and the book *Knock 'em Dead*, I have been offered and have accepted an excellent position with a major international service corporation."

—C.C., Atlanta, Georgia

"After having seen you on television, I decided to order the *Knock 'em Dead* books. Your insights into selling myself helped me find opportunities in my field that would not have been attainable otherwise."

—E.M., Short Hills, New Jersey

"I just received the offer of my dreams with an outstanding company. Thank you for your insight. I was prepared!"

—T.C., San Francisco, California

"I got the position! I was interviewed by three people and the third person asked me all the questions in *Knock 'em Dead*. I had all the right answers!"

—D.J., Scottsdale, Arizona

"Thank you for all the wonderfully helpful information you provided in your book. I lost my job almost one year ago. I spent almost eight months looking for a comparable position. Then I had the good sense to buy your book. Two months later, I accepted a new position. You helped me turn one of the worst experiences of my life into a blessing in disguise."

—L.G., Watervliet, New York

"I was out of work for four months— within five weeks of reading your book, I had four job offers."

—S.K., Dallas, Texas

"I followed the advice in *Knock 'em Dead* religiously and got more money, less hours, a better hospital plan, and negotiated to keep my three weeks vacation. I start my new job immediately!"

—A.B., St. Louis, Missouri

RESUMES

K*THAT*NOCK 'EM *DEAD*

7TH EDITION

Martin Yate, C.P.C.

Adams Media
Avon, Massachusetts

Acknowledgments

In nineteen years of publication around the world, the *Knock 'em Dead* books owe their success to millions of satisfied readers who spread the word, and three generations of dedicated professionals at Adams Media. Thank you all for your support, and through it that greatest of honors: making a difference with one's life.

Copyright © 1993, 1995, 2001, 2002, 2003, 2004, 2006 by Martin John Yate.
All rights reserved. This book, or parts thereof, may not be reproduced in any form without permission from the publisher; exceptions are made for brief excerpts used in published reviews.

Published by Adams Media, an F+W Publications Company
57 Littlefield Street
Avon, MA 02322
www.adamsmedia.com

ISBN 10: 1-59337-748-7
ISBN 13: 978-1-59337-748-9
J I H G F E D C B A

Library of Congress Cataloging-in-Publication Data
Yate, Martin John.
Resumes that knock 'em dead / Martin Yate. -- 7th ed.
p. cm.
Includes index.
ISBN-13: 978-1-59337-748-9
ISBN-10: 1-59337-748-7
1. Résumés (Employment) I. Title. II. Title: Resumes that knock them dead. III. Title: Knock 'em dead.

HF5383.Y38 2007
650.14'2--dc22
2006019730

This publication is designed to provide accurate and authoritative information with regard to the subject matter covered. It is sold with the understanding that the publisher is not engaged in rendering legal, accounting, or other professional advice. If legal advice or other expert assistance is required, the services of a competent professional person should be sought.
—From a *Declaration of Principles* jointly adopted by a Committee of the American Bar Association and a Committee of Publishers and Associations

Many of the designations used by manufacturers and sellers to distinguish their product are claimed as trademarks. Where those designations appear in this book and Adams Media was aware of a trademark claim, the designations have been printed with initial capital letters.

This book is available at quantity discounts for bulk purchases.
For information, please call 1-800-872-5627.

CONTENTS

INTRODUCTION

Most books on writing resumes haven't adjusted to accommodate today's changing work environment, or the way that corporations now store, access, and review resumes. The goal of this book is to help you accelerate your job search with an understanding of the world in which your resume must compete, and the tactics that will enable it to compete most effectively.

No one wants to write a resume. On the list of things we "want" to do, it comes just above hitting yourself in the head with a hammer; and in part that is because of the self-analysis involved. Although we know ourselves better than anyone else does, actually taking that knowledge and packaging it for public consumption is always an extremely difficult task.

In *Resumes That Knock 'em Dead*, I explain the ins and outs of putting a resume together as painlessly as possible. I'll show you the best ways to look at your background and present it to the public in your resume. You'll understand why certain things should be in your resume and how they should look, and why other things should never appear. Today's world of work is complex, and your circumstances are unique, so there will be situations when what is right for one person's resume is wrong for another's. In these cases, I'll always share with you what the experts think on the topic; and whenever industry experts disagree, I'll give you both sides of the argument, along with my reasoned solution to the dispute. That way you can make a prudent decision based on the factors that affect your particular situation. In addition, you will see a wide variety of styles and approaches that can be used within these practical guidelines to help you create a truly individual resume.

You'll get to read real resumes from real people. Each of the resumes in this book is based on a "genuine article" that opened the doors of opportunity for its writer. Resumes are included for today's and tomorrow's in-demand jobs, as defined by the U.S. Bureau of Labor Statistics and confirmed by the professionals on the front lines: corporate recruiters and other employment industry professionals from across the country. You are quite likely to find a resume that reflects exactly the kind of job you are after; if not, you can still learn lots from the examples, and you can lift and adapt key phrases and use their layouts as templates for your work.

You will also find a number of resumes from people with special challenges. These reflect the pressures and needs of a modern, profession-oriented society struggling into the information age. Like the resume that got a six-dollar-an-hour factory worker a $70,000-a-year professional sales job; or the one that helped a recovering alcoholic and drug-abuser get back on his feet again. Included here are winning resumes of people who are recovering from serious emotional challenges, re-entering society after prison time, starting over after a divorce, and sometimes changing careers. What's more, these examples have proved themselves effective in every corner of the nation; their writers landed both interviews and jobs.

A powerful, on-target resume, properly distributed, is only one element in a successful job search; for this reason, *Resumes That Knock 'em Dead* is part of an integrated series of books crafted to help you land jobs and prosper in them. This book will at times touch on subjects that are handled in greater depth elsewhere in the series. In these instances, I will refer you to the appropriate work. For example, the self-knowledge you develop in preparing your resume will also help you prepare for job interviews; when I touch on this topic I will refer you to the nearly 200 pages on interviews and offers in the companion volume, *Knock 'em Dead: The Ultimate Job Seeker's Guide*.

The wide range of resume examples here, and the nuts-and-bolts advice about resume production and distribution, will give you everything you need to create a distinctive, professional resume—and get it in front of the people who count! You will find something on every single page that you can put to work in your job search right now, today.

THE POWER OF A GREAT RESUME

WHO NEEDS A resume? Everyone, unless you are so well known that your reputation proceeds before you to all potential employers.

You didn't come to a book like this for a good read; you came because you are facing serious challenges in your professional life, which you realize will impact the quality of your life outside of working hours. Maybe you are a seasoned pro who has discovered that your current resume no longer does the job. You are probably right; after adding job after job since those long-ago college days, your document now probably looks more like a patchwork quilt than a focused resume. Perhaps you are fresh out of school and are wondering how you can create a professional resume that will catapult you from paper-hat-and-name-tag jobs into the professional world. Or perhaps you have been struggling along without a resume and simply filling out application forms, but have finally made the commitment to do it right this time.

Whatever your reason for reading this book, the following pages will help you get your act together. By the end of the process you will not only have a knock 'em dead resume, you will also have a much firmer grasp of the job search process along with some crucial lifetime career management skills.

The person who is better organized and more focused will be viewed more favorably than his or her competition—and that is exactly what the development of your resume will do for you. Creating a resume helps you in your job search way beyond opening doors. It will help you understand what employers need and what you have to offer; as a result, it will give you ammunition to handle those tough interview questions. Furthermore, an effective resume is a staunch friend who speaks well of your candidacy long after you leave the interview.

No one ever gets added to the payroll for the love of humanity. Management never gets up and collectively sighs, "Ah, it's a loverly day in the neighborhood . . . let's hire us some accountants." People get added to the payroll to make money, and to save money or save time for the company; and they all do this at some level by anticipating and preventing problems from arising, and solving them in a timely manner when they do arise.

No resume ever gets read, and no one ever gets interviewed or hired, unless someone somewhere is trying to solve a problem. That problem may be finding a quicker way to manufacture silicon chips, or it may be getting the telephone calls answered now that the receptionist has suddenly quit. As disparate as these examples might seem, both are still concerned with problem solving. And invariably, the problem that needs a solution is the same: productivity. The simple question is, "How on earth are we going to get things done quicker/cheaper/ more efficiently without a _____ ?" Resumes that get acted upon are those that position the writer as someone knowledgeable enough about the job to anticipate, prevent, and solve its problems, thus contributing positively to the bottom line.

Your resume's job is to speak loudly and clearly about your value as a potential on-staff problem solver in a specific functional area. And this value must be clearly expressed in a few brief seconds, because that's all the attention your resume will get in its first perusal. *Initially* your resume just helps get your foot in the door, and because you can't be there to answer questions, it has to stand on its own.

A Strong Focus Leads to Positive Results

Many people make the mistake of thinking that a resume is a simple recitation of all you have done in your professional life. They're wrong—this will result in a resume that will lack focus, punch, and ultimately results. The most productive resumes start with a clear focus on the target job, looking at the job's responsibilities from the point of view of the hiring team.

Let's start with this exercise for determining what is worth focusing on in your efforts to obtain your target job:

1. Develop your own job description of the target job by looking at job postings and recruitment advertisements.
2. Under each bullet point you enter, ID your skills, achievements, and contributions in this area.
3. Think of the best people you have ever seen doing this job and what made them stand out.
4. Think of the worst people you have ever seen doing this job and what made them stand out.

On completion of this simple exercise you will not only have a clear idea of whether or not you can do the job, you'll have

- The clear focus on the target job that will make your resume truly productive.
- Knowledge of what employers want to hear about in your resume, and examples that will do the job.
- A selection of the critical keywords that need to appear within your resume to insure that it gets selected from the resume databases by headhunters and hiring managers.

So the most productive resumes are focused on what has happened in your business life, as it relates to your ability to shine in the job you have targeted as the next logical step in your career. It speaks of the actions you took to make things happen, and what supportive professional behaviors you brought to the task; and it pictures (you hope) a professional who understands the small yet necessary role that the job plays in the overall deliverables of the department and the company.

The Short and the Long of It

Now given the choice, you'd never be writing a resume (or reading this book, in fact), but as you don't really have a choice in the matter, you might as well learn how to do it right. Resumes evolved as a solution to a productivity problem. Can you imagine what would happen to a business if everyone who applied for a job was given even a cursory ten-minute interview? The nation would simply grind to a halt, then topple into bankruptcy, because employers would do nothing but interview. The solution: Find a way to get a glimpse of applicants' potentials before meeting them face-to-face. Thus the resume evolved as a screening and timesaving tool for the corporation.

Now look at the realities of being on the receiving end of a resume. You may think that *writing* a resume is a tough job, but consider for a moment the plight of the person who has to read them. In the world of enjoyable reading, resumes are pretty far down the list; they offer little competition to murder mysteries, tales of international intrigue, or love stories.

Nevertheless, resumes are a required part of every manager's reading, and, because they are usually deadly dull and appear in such vast numbers, they are avoided like the plague. To combat this deep-seated avoidance, you should follow this general rule that will help your resume get read and acted upon in the quickest possible time: It needs to be both short and long. Short on words, but long on promise and an energy that reflects the real you. It needs to be specifically vague: specific enough to whet the reader's appetite to know more, vague enough that the reader needs to get in communication with you.

Good resume writing focuses attention on your strengths as they relate to the deliverables of a specific target job. At the same time, it draws attention away from those areas that lack definition or vigor. Writing a good resume requires that you first focus on the job you want, and then makes you analyze your work history in support of that goal. The entire process is one where you take the time to look at and then package yourself as a desirable product, and this does an awful lot to help you prepare for job interviews. In a very real sense, putting a resume together is the foundation for succeeding at the job interview. Preparation for one is preparation for the other. With a resume focused on a specific target job and built from the ground up with the employer's likely needs in mind, you will be far more likely to grab a reader's attention and gain an invitation to interview.

For example, the interviewer's command to "tell me about yourself" is one of those tough interview questions that almost all of us have difficulty answering without sounding like a snake oil salesman. Were you totally satisfied with your response the last time it came up? I doubt it. You can only answer this question well if you have taken the time to analyze and package all your strengths and weaknesses in an organized fashion. It is the only way you will ever learn to speak fluently about your background and skills in a fashion guaranteed to impress the interviewer. For this reason, *Resumes That Knock 'em Dead* will kill two birds with one stone—it will help you prepare a resume that will open all the right doors for you, and it will give you a real understanding of what you have to offer when those tough questions start flying.

Many interviewers base their questions on resume content: This means that, to a certain extent, you can guide the course of your interviews by preparing an appropriately focused resume. Without one, you are obliged to deliver your work history on a job application form, which rarely allows a perfect representation of skills, and which gives the interviewer no flattering starting point from which to base the interview questions.

In addition to helping you get your foot in the door and easing the course of the interview, your resume will be your last and most powerful advocate. After interviewing all the candidates, interviewers review all the contenders by going over their notes, and the candidates' resumes. Your resume becomes your spokesperson long after you have left that last interview, and it has the final word on your candidacy. You can begin to see why having a resume focused on a target job makes so much sense.

The preparation of a good resume also has the benefit of personal discovery. You may find that your job experience is deeper than you imagined, that your contributions to previous employers were more important than you thought, or you may discover some areas for professional growth. In any case, you'll gain a realistic awareness of the kind of performance that will allow you to shine at the interview and in your next job—and that's a powerful awareness to possess.

No sane person will tell you that resume writing is fun, but I will show you the tricks of the trade that make the process easier.

What makes this book truly different is, first, the understanding that comes from my thirty years in the career management business and, second, that the resume examples are all real resumes from real people, resumes that landed them jobs within "in-demand" professions. They were all sent to me by employment specialists, professional resume writers, and headhunters from around the nation. These are the pros on the firing line, the ones who know what works and what doesn't in the professional marketplace.

You will find everything you need to make resume writing fast, effective, and painless. Just follow my instructions, and you'll have a knockout resume and never have to read another word about the damn things as long as you live.

With that in mind, do it once and do it right—you'll generate a topflight resume without knocking yourself out!

So now, for your delight and edification, we'll review the marks of a great resume: What type of resume is right for you, what goes in (and why), and what always stays out (and why), and what might go in depending on your special circumstances. This will be followed by countless resume examples and a "paint-by-numbers" guide that makes resume writing easy for anyone!

THREE WAYS TO SUM YOURSELF UP

"GIVE ME A moment of your busy day! Listen to me. I've got something to say!"

That's what your resume must scream—in a suitably professional manner, of course. Not in the manner of the would-be retail clothing executive who had his resume "hand-delivered" . . . attached to the hand and arm of a store window mannequin.

As it happened, that was only the first surprise in store for the personnel director who received the delivery: The envelope was hand-decorated in Gothic script; the cover letter inside was equally decorative (and illegible); the resume writer had glued the four-page resume to fabric, and stitched the whole mess together like a child's book. The crowning glory, however, was yet to come: All the punctuation marks—commas, colons, periods, and the like—were small rhinestone settings. Yes, it got noticed, but its success had to depend entirely on the recipient's sense of humor—which in this case was, unfortunately, most noticeable for its absence.

Here's the point: trying to do something out of the ordinary with any aspect of your resume is risky business indeed. For every interview door it opens, at least two more may be slammed shut. The best bet is to present a logically displayed, eye-appealing resume that will get read. That means grabbing the reader right away—on that first page. And that's one big reason for short, power-packed resumes.

We all have different backgrounds. Some of us have worked for only one company, and some of us have worked for eleven companies in as many years. Some of us have changed careers once or twice, and some of us have maintained a predictable career path. For some, diversity broadens our potential, and for others concentration in one area deepens it. We each require different vehicles to put our work history in the most exciting light. The goals, though, are constant:

- To show off achievements, attributes, and accumulation of expertise to the best advantage
- To minimize any possible weaknesses

Resume experts acknowledge just three essential styles for presenting your credentials to a potential employer: Chronological, Functional, and Combination (Chrono-Functional). Your particular circumstances will determine the right format for you. Just three styles, you say? You will see resume books with up to fifteen varieties of resume style. Such volumes are, alas, merely filling up space; in the final analysis, each additional style that such books mention is a tiny variation on the above three.

The Chronological Resume

This is the most common and readily accepted form of presentation. It's what most of us think of when we think of resumes—a chronological listing of job titles and responsibilities. It starts with the current or most recent employment, then works backward to your first job.

This format is good for demonstrating your growth in a single profession. It is suitable for anyone with practical work experience who hasn't suffered too many job changes or prolonged periods of unemployment. It is not always the best choice if you are just out of school or if you are changing careers, where a chronological format could then draw attention to your weaknesses (i.e., your lack of specific experience in a field) rather than your strengths.

The exact content of every resume naturally varies depending on individual circumstances. A chronological resume typically incorporates these basic components:

- Contact Information (always)
- A Career Objective (sometimes) or Career Summary (sometimes)
- A Chronological Description of Work History (always)
- Education (almost always)

The Work History is the distinguishing characteristic of the chronological resume, because it ties your job responsibilities and achievements to specific employers, job titles, and dates.

There are also optional categories determined by the space available to you and the unique aspects of your professional experience. These will be discussed in Chapter 3.

Chronological Resume

Jane Swift, 9 Central Avenue, Quincy, MA 02169. (617) 555-1212. jswift@careerbrain.com

SUMMARY: Ten years of increasing responsibilities in the employment services industry. Concentration in the high-technology markets.

EXPERIENCE: Howard Systems International, Inc.   2004-Present
Management Consulting Firm
Personnel Manager

Responsible for recruiting and managing consulting staff of 250. Set up office and organized the recruitment, selection, and hiring of consultants. Recruited all levels of MIS staff from financial to manufacturing markets.

Additional responsibilities:
- Coordinated with outside advertising agencies.
- Developed P.R. with industry periodicals—placement with over 20 magazines and newsletters.
- Developed effective referral programs—referrals increased 32%.

EXPERIENCE: Technical Aid Corporation   1995–2004
National Consulting Firm. MICRO/TEMPS Division

Division Manager   2000–2004
Area Manager   1997–2000
Branch Manager   1995–1997

As Division Manager, opened additional West Coast offices. Staffed and trained all offices with appropriate personnel. Created and implemented all divisional operational policies responsible for P & L. Sales increased to $20 million dollars, from $0 in 1992.

- Achieved and maintained 30% annual growth over 7-year period.
- Maintained sales staff turnover at 14%.

As Area Manager, opened additional offices, hiring staff, setting up office policies, and training sales and recruiting personnel.

Additional responsibilities:
- Supervised offices in two states.
- Developed business relationships with accounts—75% of clients were regular customers.
- Client base increased 28% per year.
- Generated over $200,000 worth of free trade-journal publicity.

As Branch Manager, hired to establish the new MICRO/TEMPS operation. Recruited and managed consultants. Hired internal staff. Sold service to clients.

EDUCATION: Boston University
B.S. Public Relations, 1994.

10

The Functional Resume

This format focuses on the professional skills you have developed over the years and bring to a specific target job, rather than on when, where, or how you acquired them; it also de-emphasizes employment dates. Job titles and employers can likewise play a minor part with this type of resume. The attention is always focused on the skill rather than the context or time of its acquisition.

This functional format is suited to a number of different personal circumstances, specifically those of:

- Mature professionals with a storehouse of expertise and jobs
- Entry-level types whose track records do not justify a chronological resume
- Career changers who want to focus on skills rather than experience
- People whose careers have been stagnant or in ebb, who want to give focus to the skills that can get a career under way again, rather than on the history in which it was becalmed in the first place
- Those returning to the workplace after a long absence
- People closer to retirement than to the onset of their careers

For any resume to be effective, it must be conceived with a specific target job in mind, and this is especially true for a functional resume. Because it focuses so strongly on skills and the ability to contribute in a particular direction, rather than on a directly relevant work history, you must have an employment objective clearly in mind.

Though a functional resume is more free-form than a chronological one, there are certain essentials that make it work.

- *A Functional Summary.* Different skills are needed for different jobs, so the functional summary is where you make the tough decisions to determine what goes in to strengthen the focus of your resume.
- *Accomplishments/skills/professional behaviors.* Based on your target job, this is where you identify relevant accomplishments, along with the skills and behaviors that made them possible.
- *Dates.* Strictly speaking, a functional resume needn't give dates, but a resume without dates waves a big red flag. So if your employment history lacks stability, a functional resume allows you to de-emphasize dates somewhat by their placement.
- *Education.* This is always included.

Inclusion of other optional categories is determined by the space available and the unique aspects of your background.

Functional Resume

Here's an example of a functional resume. It reflects the same work history as the prior chronological example, to help you by comparison.

Jane Swift
9 Central Avenue
Quincy, MA 02169
(617) 555-1212
jswift@careerbrain.com

OBJECTIVE:	A position in Employment Services where my management, sales, and recruiting talents can be effectively utilized to improve operations and contribute to company profits.
SUMMARY:	Over ten years of Human Resources experience. Extensive responsibility for multiple branch offices and an internal staff of 40+ employees and 250 consultants.
SALES:	Sold high-technology consulting services with consistently profitable margins throughout the United States. Grew sales from $0 to over $20 million a year. Created training programs and trained salespeople in six metropolitan markets.
RECRUITING:	Developed recruiting sourcing methods for multiple branch offices. Recruited over 25,000 internal and external consultants in the high-technology professions.
MANAGEMENT:	Managed up to 40 people in sales, customer service, recruiting, and administration. Turnover maintained below 14% in a "turnover business."
FINANCIAL:	Prepared quarterly and yearly forecasts. Presented, reviewed, and defended these forecasts to the Board of Directors. Responsible for P & L of $20 million sales operation.
PRODUCTION:	Responsible for opening multiple offices and accountable for growth and profitability. 100% success and maintained 30% growth over seven-year period in 10 offices.
WORK EXPERIENCE:	
2004 to Present	HOWARD SYSTEMS INTERNATIONAL, Boston, MA National Consulting Firm Personnel Manager
1995–2004	TECHNICAL AID CORPORATION, Needham, MA National Consulting & Search Firm Division Manager
EDUCATION:	B.S., 1989, Boston University
REFERENCES:	Available upon request.

The Combination Chronological-Functional Resume

For the upwardly mobile professional with a track record, this is becoming the resume of choice. It has all the flexibility and strength that come from combining both the chronological and functional formats, and it allows you to clearly demonstrate your thorough grasp of the job and its deliverables.

- *A Career Summary.* The combination resume, more often than not, has either a career summary, where you spotlight yourself as a professional with a clear sense of self, and a history of relevant contributions. It might include a power-packed description of skills, achievements, and professional behaviors that fairly scream "Success!"

Alternatively, it may contain a "job objective" that doesn't so much announce what you want in a job, but rather showcases your thorough understanding of the target job and its contribution to the target endeavor. Ideally, whichever heading you choose, your copy will embrace both these concepts, as the resume is not a document that you use to outline your demands, but one that positions you as a desirable solution to an employer's challenges.

- *A Description of Functional Skills.* This is where the combination of styles comes into play. Following the summary, the combination resume starts out like a functional resume and highlights achievements in different categories relevant to the job/career goals, without any reference to employers.
- *A Chronological History.* Then it switches to the chronological approach and names companies, dates, titles, duties, and responsibilities. This section can also include further evidence of achievements or special contributions.
- *Education.* Then come the optional categories determined by the space available to you and the unique aspects of your background.

In the next chapter, we are going to take a look at all the component parts that, given your unique experiences, might have a place in your resume. As you read this chapter, continue to think which format is best suited to your primary resume. As a practical matter, you may well develop resumes in several different formats just as the professional in this chapter did. If you are not sure what is best, start by creating a chronological resume.

Combination Chronological-Functional Resume

Jane Swift
9 Central Avenue
Quincy, MA 92169
(617) 555-1212
jswift@careerbrain.com

OBJECTIVE:

Employment Services Management

SUMMARY: Ten years of increasing responsibilities in the employment services market-place. Concentration in the high-technology markets.

SALES: Sold high technology consulting services with consistently profitable margins throughout the United States. Grew sales from $0 to over $20 million a year.

PRODUCTION: Responsible for opening multiple offices and accountable for growth and prof-itability. 100% success and maintained 30% growth over seven-year period in 10 offices.

MANAGEMENT: Managed up to 40 people in sales, customer service, recruiting, and adminis-tration. Turnover maintained below 14% in a "turnover business." Hired branch managers and sales and recruiting staff throughout the United States.

FINANCIAL: Prepared quarterly and yearly forecasts. Presented, reviewed, and defended these forecasts to the Board of Directors. Responsible for P & L of $20 million sales operation.

MARKETING: Performed numerous market studies for multiple branch opening. Resolved feasibility of combining two different sales offices. Study resulted in savings of over $5,000 per month in operating expenses.

EXPERIENCE: Howard Systems International, Inc.   2004-Present
Management Consulting Firm
Personnel Manager

Responsible for recruiting and managing consulting staff of five. Set up office and organized the recruitment, selection, and hiring of consultants. Recruited all levels of MIS staff from financial to manufacturing markets.

Additional responsibilities:
• Developed P.R. with industry periodicals—placement with over 20 maga-zines and newsletters.
• Developed effective referral programs—referrals increased 320%.

Combination Chronological-Functional Resume page 2

Technical Aid Corporation   1995–2004
National Consulting Firm. MICRO/TEMPS Division

Division Manager	2000–2004
Area Manager	1997–2000
Branch Manager	1995–1997

As Division Manager, opened additional West Coast offices. Staffed and trained all offices with appropriate personnel. Created and implemented all divisional operational policies. Responsibilities for P & L. Sales increased to $20 million dollars, from $0 in 1992.

- Achieved and maintained 30% annual growth over seven-year period.
- Maintained sales staff turnover at 14%.

As Area Manager, opened additional offices, hiring staff, setting up office policies, and training sales and recruiting personnel.

Additional responsibilities:
- Supervised offices in two states.
- Developed business relationships with accounts—75% of clients were regular customers.
- Client base increased 28% per year.
- Generated over $200,000 worth of free trade journal publicity.

As Branch Manager, hired to establish the new MICRO/TEMPS operation. Recruited and managed consultants. Hired internal staff. Sold service to clients.

EDUCATION: B.S., 1994, Boston University

15

THE BASIC
INGREDIENTS

IT USED TO be that there were just a few set rules for writing a great resume. Now, however, many of the jobs for which those rules were made no longer exist—so many of these traditional rules no longer apply.

Technology continues to create new professions overnight, and, with them, new career opportunities. The content of these new professions and careers has made the employment world dramatically different from that of just a few years ago. What used to be strictly off-limits in all resumes is now acceptable in many and required in some. One example that comes to mind: the increasing need for technical jargon to explain skills. Elements that were often included, like a photograph, are now frowned upon in most instances; exceptions would be models and actors whose appearance is deemed relevant to the job. So what are the rules?

Writing a resume is a bit like baking a cake. In most instances, the ingredients are essentially the same; what determines the flavor is the order and quantity in which those ingredients are blended. There are certain ingredients that go into almost every resume. There are others that rarely or never go in, and there are those that are added as special touches (a pinch of this, a dash of that), depending on your personal tastes and requirements.

Sound complicated? It really isn't. If a certain ingredient must always go in, you will soon understand why. In circumstances where the business world holds conflicting views, I will explain the divergence so that a reasoned judgment can be made.

First, let's look at the ingredients that are part of every successful resume.

What Must Always Go In

You should create a template for your resume, so that as you proceed and read that an item must go in, go right ahead and add it as you read, making any changes necessary for your particular circumstances. Don't worry about the whole thing looking like a bit of a mess; the biggest challenge in any creative process, especially writing, is capturing the initial idea in some concrete form. Once you have something on paper, the editing process is relatively simple.

Name

We start with the obvious, but there are other considerations about your name besides remembering to put it on your resume. Give your first and last name only. It isn't necessary to include your middle name(s). My name is Martin John Yate—but my resume says simply Martin Yate, because that is the way I would introduce myself in person. Notice also that it isn't M. J. Yate, because that would force the reader to play Twenty Questions about the meaning of my initials. Even if you are known by your initials, don't put them on your resume. If you use quotation marks or parentheses, those on the receiving end might think it a little strange. Better that it comes out at the interview when the interviewer asks you what you like to be called: At the very least you'll have some small talk to break the ice.

It is not required to place Mr., Ms., Miss, or Mrs. before your name, unless yours is a unisex name like Gayle, Carroll, Leslie, or any of the other names that are used for members of either sex. In such instances it is acceptable to write Mr. Gayle Jones, or Ms. Leslie Jackson.

Finally, if you are the IInd, IIIrd, Junior, or Senior holders of your name: If you always add "Jr." or "III" when you sign your name or if that is the way you are addressed to avoid confusion, go ahead and use it. Otherwise, it is extraneous information on the resume, and therefore not needed.

Address

Always give your complete address. Do not abbreviate unless space restrictions make it absolutely mandatory. If you do abbreviate—such as with *St.* or *Apt.*—be consistent. The state of your residence, however, is always abbreviated to two capitalized letters (for example, MN, WV, LA), according to post office standards. The accepted format for laying out your address looks like this:

Maxwell Krieger
9 Central Avenue, Apartment 38
New York, NY 23456

Notice that the city, state, and zip code all go on the same line, with a comma between city and state. If space is an issue you can put your contact information on a single line; use your judgment.

Telephone Number

Always include your telephone number: Few businesses will send you an invitation for an interview in the mail. Including your area code is important even if you have no intention of leaving the area. In this era of decentralization, your resume might end up being screened in another part of the country altogether!

Unless your current employer knows of your job search and approves, leave your work number off the resume, but, if your circumstances dictate, put it in your cover letter. Good cover letters do this with a short sentence that conveys the information and demonstrates you as a responsible employee. For example, something like this can work very well:

"I prefer not to use my employer's time by taking personal calls at work, but with discretion you can reach me at 202/555-5555, extension 555, to initiate contact."

If you are employed, it is entirely acceptable to replace the name of your current employer with something more generic; I will show you how best to do this in a few pages.

E-Mail

Your e-mail address is an integral part of your contact information; if you have an e-mail address, use it. If you don't, get one—because without it you are stating that you are disconnected from the communications technology that impacts every job on the planet.

Never use your work e-mail address. It increases the odds of your boss learning that you are looking at broader horizons, because e-mails leave a trail that employers can and do follow. Nowadays, it is common for an IT worker to be assigned to monitor appropriate use of company computers, and that always includes tracking Internet and e-mail usage. Using company e-mail outside regular working hours won't work either; the trail is still there for prying eyes to see. Please stay away from company telephone and e-mail usage for your job search. It can be and often is regarded as theft of company time and services; as such, it's not only cause for dismissal from your current job, but it also sends the wrong message to potential employers.

Job Objective

This section can appear on resumes with any of these headings:

Job Objective
Employment Objective
Career Objective

All are acceptable. Regardless of the heading, your objective is not so much about what you want in a job, as it is a definition of what employers want when hiring this type of person and how your skills and background will allow you to contribute to the company in such a position. A job objective paragraph with an easily visible target job title and a couple of sentences summarizing your value proposition (skills, achievements, credentials, and behaviors) can be a powerful way to open your resume: It gives the reader a clear focus and summary of who you are and what you bring to the table. Remember that the functional resume in particular, almost demands such an objective.

Even so, feelings run strong about whether or not to include a job objective in the resume. Let's review the cases for and against, and then reach a considered conclusion.

The case for inclusion: Without a job objective, a resume can have no focus, no sense of direction. The resume revolves around your objective like the earth around the sun. And if you don't know where you are going, you can't write a resume, because the body copy has nothing to support. Additionally, overworked resume screeners are given a ready focus for their evaluation.

The case for exclusion: A job objective is too constricting and can exclude you from consideration from countless jobs you might have been interested in, and for which you are qualified. And after creating a resume with the intent of opening as many doors as possible, you wouldn't want to have half of them slammed shut. Besides, employers are not generally believed to be overly concerned about what you want from them until they have a damn good idea about what they can get out of you.

The solution: It's a personal judgment call, but objectives that give the reader focus and which demonstrate what you bring to the table rarely do harm and often do good.

Traditionally, these objectives appear at the top of a resume, as a headline and attention grabber. They focus on skills, achievements, and relevant personal behaviors that support the argument.

Including job objectives, and the like, has as much to do with storage and retrieval systems and computers as it does with people. On the one hand, the resume reader is looking for a problem solver. By seeing that you fit into a general area, he or she will want to rush on to the rest of the resume (where there are more specifics). Then what happens? In the best-case scenario, you will get a call asking you to interview right away. But what happens when there isn't a need for your particular talents that day? Your resume gets filed or logged onto the company's database. They will file your resume according to what you include in it. And unless you give it the right help, it may never see the light of day again. The more your objective describes the target job and uses the right keywords to describe such work, the greater frequency with which it will be retrieved and reviewed in the future.

The same argument holds true for resumes sent to employment agencies and executive recruiters. Such considerations are encouraging many job seekers to include brief and nonspecific job objectives in their resumes.

Employment Dates

Resume readers are often leery of resumes without employment dates. If you expect a response, you can increase your odds dramatically by including them—in one form or another.

With a steady work history and no employment gaps you can be very specific (space allowing) and write:

January 11, 2002 to July 4, 2004 or 1/11/02 to 7/4/04

or, to be a little less specific:

January 2002–July 2004

But if there are short employment gaps, or the occasional job with short duration, you can improve the look of things:

2001–2002

instead of

December 12, 2001–January 23, 2002

There is no suggestion here that you should lie about your work history, but it is surprising just how many interviewers will be quite satisfied with such dates. There seems to be a myth that everything written on twenty-pound rag paper needs no further inquiry.

While this technique can effectively hide embarrassing employment gaps, and it may get you in for an interview, you should of course be prepared with an adequate answer to questions about your work history. Even if such questions are posed, you will have the opportunity to explain yourself in person, and that is a distinct improvement over being peremptorily ruled out by some faceless nonentity before you get a chance to speak your piece. The end justifies the means, in this case.

If you abbreviate employment dates, be sure to do so consistently. It is acceptable to list annual dates, rather than month and year, but be aware of the potential penalties if you intend to do more. When references get checked, the very first things verified are dates of employment, and leaving salary. Untruths in either of these areas are grounds for dismissal with cause, and that can dog your footsteps into the future.

Keywords

Just as computers have helped streamline your job-search activities, they have done the same for the recruitment work of many human resource departments. One of the changes gaining ground in corporate America is the use of resume screening and tracking systems. Understanding how this technology affects the way your resume is stored and retrieved will dramatically affect your chances for success in your job hunt.

While electronic resume distribution makes your life easier, it has created an avalanche of electronic paper on the other side of the desk. If a company once had to deal with 100 resumes a day, it now probably sees 1,000 or more. With the high cost of human handling, the wholesale adoption of resume screening and tracking systems by businesses is a given. When computer screening replaces human judgment, the whole game changes. The computer program can't use human logic (although it is already getting pretty close); instead, the computer searches for keywords that describe the position and the professional skills needed to execute the duties effectively.

It works like this: the company representative sits down at the keyboard and opens the storage and retrieval program and keys in a job title into a dialogue box, the program then offers an extensive selection of words that can be used to describe that job. The user scrolls through the list clicking on the keywords that best describe the current needs. At the end of the sequence the user hits a "search" button and the program goes to work. It searches the resume bank for any resumes that mention any of the keywords; then when this is done it weights the list of resumes with the resumes with the greatest frequency of the selected keywords ranked first.

Your resume—and a thousand like it—can be scanned for the necessary keywords in seconds. The user receives a weighted list of the resumes that contain the appropriate keywords. The greater the number of relevant keywords in your resume, the higher your ranking. The higher your ranking, the greater the likelihood that your resume will be rescued from the avalanche and passed along to human eyes for further screening. This has led directly to the denser resumes that we are seeing today and the increasing prevalence of keyword sections.

In some of the resume examples later in the book you'll see a section that lumps a string of keywords together. This is often referred to as Core Competencies, Special Knowledge, Keyword Preface, Keyword Section, or Areas of Expertise. Here's what the keyword section of a taxation specialist's resume looks like:

AREAS OF EXPERTISE

SBT, C-Corporation and S-Corporation State Income Tax Returns • Vehicle Use Tax Returns • State Income Tax Budgeting and Accrual • Multistate Property Tax Returns • Federal, State, and Local Exemption Certificates • State and Local Sales, Use and Excise Tax Management • Tax Audit Management • Tax License and Bonding Management • Certificates of Authority and Annual Report Filing Maintenance • State Sales and Use Tax Assessment • Federal Excise Tax Collection and Deposits • Determination of Nexus • Tax Amnesty Programs

A keyword section not only dramatically increases your chances of getting the computer's attention, but HR people appreciate them as a brief synopsis of the whole resume. A keyword/core competencies section also allows you to succinctly identify skill sets that might not otherwise make it into your resume, and demonstrate that you obviously have more to offer than that discussed in detail within the body of the resume.

One last point. This approach also allows you to repeat highly important keywords that appear in the body of your resume. This repetition of keywords that speak to especially relevant competencies can improve the ranking of your resume in the weighted list, because the search programs count the frequency with which keywords are used as part of the weighting process.

Job Titles

The purpose of a job title on your resume is not to reflect exactly what you were called by a particular employer, but rather to provide a generic identification that will be understood by as many employers as possible. So if your current title is "Junior Accountant, Level Three," realize that such internal titling may well bear no relation to the titling of any other company on earth.

To avoid painting yourself into a career corner, you can be "specifically vague" with job titles like:

Administrative Assistant
instead of
Secretary

Accountant
instead of
Junior Accountant Level II

It is imperative that you examine your current role at work, rather than rely on your starting or current title. Job titles within companies change much more slowly than the jobs themselves, so a job change can be the opportunity for some to escape stereotyping and the career stagnation that accompanies it. This approach is important because of the way titles and responsibilities vary.

This obviously doesn't apply when you apply for a job in certain specific professions, such as health care: a cardiologist wouldn't want to be specifically vague by tagging herself as a Health Aide.

Company Name

The names of your employers should be included. There is no need to include the street address or telephone number of past or present employers, although it can be useful to include the city and state.

When working for a multiple-division corporation you may want to list the divisional employer: "Bell Industries" might not be enough, so you would perhaps add "Computer Memory Division." By the way, it is quite all right to abbreviate words like Corporation (Corp.), Company (Co.), Limited (Ltd.), or Division (Div.) but remember to be consistent in your editing process.

Here is how you might combine a job title, company name, and address:

Design Engineer
Bell Industries, Inc., Computer Memory Div., Mountain View, CA

The information you are supplying is relevant to the reader, but you don't wish it to detract from space usable to sell yourself. If, for instance, you live in a nationally known city, such as Dallas, you need not add "TX," if space is at a premium.

There is a possible exception to these guidelines. Employed professionals are justified in omitting current employers when their industry has been reduced to a small community of professionals who know, or know of, each other, and where a confidentiality breach is likely to have damaging repercussions. This usually happens to professionals on the higher rungs of the ladder. Of course, if you don't quite fit into this elite category but are still worried about identifying your firm, you are not obliged to list the name of your current employer.

One approach is simply to label a current company in a fashion that has become perfectly acceptable in today's business climate.

A National Retail Chain
A Leading Software Developer
A Major Commercial Bank

A company name can be followed by a brief description of the business line:

A National Retail Chain: Women and junior fashions and accessories
Established Electronics Manufacturer producing monolithic memories

This further description is unnecessary when the writer can get the company's function into the heading.

A Major Commercial Bank

Being succinct in your resume can save precious space for more valuable information and keywords.

Responsibilities

The area where you address your responsibilities and achievements is the meat, or *body copy*, of the resume; it's the area where not only are your responsibilities listed, but your special achievements and other contributions are also highlighted. This is a crucial part of the resume, and it will be dealt with in detail in Chapters 4 and 5.

Endorsements

Remember when you got that difficult job finished so quickly, and all the good things the boss said about your work? Well, in a resume you can very effectively quote him, even if the praise wasn't in writing (though of course it is best to quote directly). A line such as "Praised as 'most innovative and determined manager in the company'" is a nice plus to be able to add.

These third-party endorsements are not necessary, and they most certainly shouldn't be used to excess. But, used sparingly, an endorsement or two can be very impressive.

Such endorsements become especially effective when the endorsements support your quantified achievements.

Accreditation and Licenses

Many fields of work require professional licensure or accreditation. If this is the case in your line of work, be sure to list everything necessary. If you are close to a particular accreditation or license (a C.P.A., for example), you would want to list it with information about the status:

Passed all parts of C.P.A. exam, September '06
(expected certification March '07)

Professional Affiliations

Your affiliation with associations and societies related to a profession demonstrates a commitment to your career. Membership is also important for networking, so if you are not currently a member of one of your industry's professional associations, give serious consideration to joining. Note the emphasis on "professional" in the heading. An employer is almost exclusively interested in your professional associations and societies. Omit references to any religious, political, or otherwise potentially controversial affiliations, unless your certain knowledge of that specific company assures that such affiliations will be positively received.

An exception to this rule is in those jobs where a wide circle of acquaintances is regarded as an asset. Some examples would include jobs in public relations, sales, marketing, real estate, and insurance. In these cases, include your membership/involvement with community organizations, charities, and the like, as such involvement demonstrates a professional involved in the community, a fact that speaks to having a wide circle of contacts.

By the same token, a seat on the town board, charitable cause involvement, or fundraising work are all activities that show a willingness to involve oneself and can often demonstrate organizational abilities through titles held in those endeavors. Space permitting, these are all activities worthy of inclusion because they show you as a force for good in your community.

These activities become more important as companies who take their community responsibilities seriously look for staff who feel and act the same way.

As for method of inclusion, brevity is the rule.

American Heart Association: Area Fundraising Chair

Civil Service Grade

If you have a civil service job in your background, you will have been awarded a civil service grade. So, in looking for a job with the government, be sure to list it. In transferring from the government to the private sector, you are best advised to translate it into generic terms and ignore the grade altogether, unless you are applying for jobs with government contractors, subcontractors, or other specialized employers familiar with the intricacies of civil service ranking.

Publications and Patents

Such achievements are usually found at the end of the resume. While their importance varies from profession to profession, they make a powerful statement about creativity, organization, determination, and follow-through on any resume. They tell the reader that you invest considerable personal time and effort in your career and are therefore a cut above the competition. Publication carries more weight in some industries and professions (where you hear phrases like "publish or perish"), while patents are a definite plus in the technology and manufacturing fields. You will notice in the resume examples in this book how the writers list dates and names of publications, but do not include copyright information.

"Radical Treatments for Chronic Pain." 2002. *Journal of American Medicine.*
"Pain: Is It Imagined or Real?" 2000. *Science & Health Magazine.*

Languages

Technology allows all companies the opportunity to become global in their activities and many companies have a vibrant international presence; a linguistic edge might give you just the edge you need. If you are fluent in a foreign language, don't hide your light under a bushel. If you understand a foreign language, but perhaps are not fluent, still mention it.

Fluent in French   Read German
Read and write Serbo-Croatian   Understand Spanish

Education

Educational history is normally listed wherever it helps your case the most, although the exact positioning of the information can vary according to the length of your professional experience, the relative strength of your academic achievements, and your profession.

If you are recently out of school with little practical experience, your educational credentials, which probably constitute your primary asset, will appear near the beginning of the resume.

As you gain experience, your academic credentials become less important in most professions, and gradually slip toward the end of your resume. The exception to this is found primarily in certain professions where academic qualifications dominate a person's career—medicine, for instance. This does not mean that your educational efforts are unimportant in any way; on the contrary, the educational section of your resume can show a commitment to ongoing professional education. This makes a powerful statement about both your competency and commitment, finishing your resume on a high note.

You will notice that all examples for education are in chronological order: The highest level of attainment always comes first, followed by the lesser levels. In this way, a doctorate will be followed by a master's degree, then a bachelor's. For degreed professionals, there is no need to go back further into educational history; it is optional to list your prestigious prep school.

Those who did not achieve the higher levels of educational recognition will list their own highest level of attainment. A word on attainment is in order here. If you graduated from high school, attended college, but didn't graduate, you may be tempted to list your high school diploma first, followed by the name of the college you attended. That would give the wrong emphasis: it says you are a college dropout and focuses on you as a high school graduate. In this instance you would in fact list your college and omit any reference to earlier educational history.

While abbreviations are frowned on in most circumstances, it is normal to abbreviate degrees (Ph.D., M.A., B.A., B.Sc., etc.).

Those with scholarships and awards should list them, and recent graduates will usually also list majors and minors (space and relevancy permitting). The case is a little more confused for the seasoned professional. Many human resources professionals say it makes life easier for them if majors and minors are listed, so they can further sift and grade the applicants. That's good for them, but it might not be good for you. All you want the resume to do is get you in the door, not slam it in your face. So, as omitting these minutiae will never stop you from getting an interview, I urge you to err on the side of safety and leave 'em out, unless they speak directly to the target job.

If you are a recent entrant into the workplace, both your scholastic achievements and your contributions have increased importance. List your position on the school newspaper or the student council, memberships in clubs, and recognition for scholastic achievement—in short, anything that demonstrates your potential as a productive employee. As your career progresses, however, prospective employers care less about your school life and more about your work life.

Technology is rapidly changing the nature of all work, so if you aren't learning new skills every year, you are being paid for an increasingly obsolescent skill set. At some point this will affect your employability. Employers really appreciate people who invest in their future, and here's some proof from the U.S. Department of Education:

Of postsecondary students who enrolled in any A.A. degree program but didn't graduate, 48 percent received better job responsibilities and 29 percent received raises! If they actually graduated, it gets even better: 71 percent gained improved job responsibilities and 63 percent got raises. Clearly being enrolled in ongoing education looks good on a resume; you have nothing to lose and everything to gain by committing to your career.

Avoid exaggerations of your skills, accomplishments, and educational qualifications. Research has now proven that three out of every ten resumes feature inflated educational qualifications. Consequently, verification, especially of educational claims, is on the increase. If, after you had been hired, you were discovered to have exaggerated your educational accomplishments, it could cost you your job.

Changing times have also changed thinking about listing fraternities and sororities on resumes. A case could be made, I think, for leaving them off as a matter of course: If such organizations are important to an interviewer he or she will ask. My ruling, however, is that if the resume is tailored to an individual or company where membership in such organizations will result in a case of "deep calling to deep," then by all means, list it. If, on the other hand, the resume is for general distribution, forget it.

Military

If you have a good military record, include it with your highest rank, especially if you are applying for jobs in the defense sector. Military experience speaks to your determination, and your understanding of teamwork, policies, and procedures. Always list your military experience—it's a plus.

Professional Training

Under the educational heading on smart resumes, you will often see a section for continuing professional education, focusing on special courses and seminars attended. For example, if you are computer literate, list the programs you are familiar with.

Summer and Part-Time Employment

This should only be included when the resume writer is either just entering the work force or re-entering it after a substantial absence. The entry-level person can feel comfortable listing dates and places and times. The returnee should include the skills gained from part-time employment in a fashion that minimizes the "part-time" aspect of the experience—probably by using a functional resume format.

What Can Never Go In

Some information just doesn't belong in resumes. Make the mistake of including it, and at best your resume loses a little power, while at worst, you fail to land the interview.

Titles: Resume, Fact Sheet, Curriculum Vitae, etc.

It should not be necessary to use any of these variations on a theme as a heading. Their appearance on a properly structured resume is redundant: If it isn't completely obvious from the very look of your document that it is a resume, it needs further work. Such titles take up a whole line, one which could be used more productively. You can either use the space for information with greater impact, or buy yourself an extra line of white space to help you with more accessible formatting.

Availability

All jobs exist because there are problems that need solutions, and interviewers rarely have time for interviews that don't potentially help them solve the problem at hand. Statements about your availability for employment on a resume are redundant. If you are not available, then why are you wasting everyone's time? The only justification for including this item (and then only in your cover letter—see Chapter 8, in *Cover Letters That Knock 'em Dead*) is if you expect to be finishing a project and moving on at such and such a time, and not before. In such a case, your enlightened self-interest demands that you always have your eyes and ears open for better career opportunities. You aren't forced to act on those opportunities, but you are best advised to at least know about them. If leaving before the end of a project could affect your integrity and/or references, okay. There's a lot to be said for not burning your bridges, and as careers progress, it's surprising how many of the same people you bump into again and again.

As a rule of thumb, let the subject of availability come up at the face-to-face meeting. After meeting you, an employer is more likely to be prepared to wait until you are available. He or she will probably appreciate your integrity, but will usually pass on an interview if you are not available now.

Reason for Leaving

There is no real point to stating your reasons for leaving a job on a resume, yet time and again they are included—to the detriment of the writer. The topic is always covered during an interview anyway; if the employer isn't interested, why should you raise an issue that could turn into a negative? You can usually use the space more productively; however, if you have been caught in a couple of downsizings, there is an argument for listing the reason to countermand any perception of willful job-hopping.

Salary

Leave out all references to salary, past and present—it is far too risky. Too high or too low a salary can knock you out of the running even before you hear the starting gun. Even in responding to a help-wanted advertisement that specifically requests salary requirements, don't give them. A good resume will still get you the interview, and in the course of the discussions with the company, you'll certainly talk about salary anyway. If you somehow feel obliged to give salary requirements, simply write "competitive" or "negotiable," and then only in your cover letter—never put salary on a resume.

Charts and Graphs

Even if charts and graphs are part of your job, they make poor use of the space available on a resume—and they don't help the reader. The same goes for other examples of your work. If you are a copywriter or graphic artist, for example, it is all right to say that samples are available, but only if you have plenty of resume space to spare; in such instances it is a given that you will bring a portfolio to the interview.

Mention of Age, Race, Religion, Sex, and National Origin

Government legislation was enacted in the 1960s and '70s forbidding employment discrimination in these areas. It is wisest to avoid reference to these unless they are deemed relevant to the job.

Photographs

In days of old when men were bold and all our cars had fins, it was the thing to have a photograph in the top right-hand corner of the resume. Today, the fashion is against photographs; including them is a waste of space that says nothing about your ability to do a job. Obviously, careers in modeling, acting, and certain aspects of the media require photos. In these instances, your face is your fortune.

Health/Physical Description

You are trying to get a job, not a date. Unless your physical health (gym instructor, for example) and/or appearance (model, actor, media personality) are immediately relevant to the job, leave these issues alone.

Early Background

I regularly see resumes that tell about early childhood and upbringing. To date, the most generous excuse I can come up with for such anecdotes is that the resumes were prepared by the subject's mother.

Weaknesses

Any weakness, lack of qualifications, or information likely to be detrimental to your cause should always be avoided. Never tell resume readers what you don't have or what you can't or haven't had the opportunity to do yet, they might never ask.

Demands

You will never see demands on a good resume. Don't outline what you feel an employer is expected to give or to provide. The time for making demands is when the employer extends a job offer with a salary and job description attached. That is when the employer will be interested and prepared to listen to what you want. Until then, concentrate on bringing events to that happy circumstance by emphasizing what you can bring to the employer. In your resume you should, to paraphrase John F. Kennedy, ask not what your employer can do for you, but rather what you can do for your employer.

Judgment Calls

Here are some areas that fall into neither the do nor the don't camp. Whether to include them will depend on your personal circumstances.

Career Summary

A Career Summary, when it is included in a resume, comes immediately after an Objective. Or it can replace the Objective. The goal is to encapsulate your experience and perhaps highlight one or two of your skills and/or contributions. You hope, in two or three short sentences, to grab the reader's attention with a power pack of the skills and attributes you have developed throughout your career. Good summaries are short; you don't want to show all your aces in the first few lines! (You can see examples of resumes with strong summaries in the sample resume section of this book.)

On the other hand, many experts feel that the content of the summary must be demonstrated by the body of the resume, and that therefore summaries are pointless duplication and a waste of space. The choice is yours. Used wisely and well, they can help give the reader a ready focus.

Personal Flexibility, Relocation

If you are open to relocation for the right opportunity, make it clear. It will never in and of itself get you an interview, but it won't hurt. On the other hand, never state that you aren't open to relocation. After all, that factor usually comes into play only when you have a job offer to consider. Let nothing stand in the way of a nice collection of job offers! You can always leverage a job offer you don't want into an offer you do; you can learn how in Chapter 21 of *Knock 'em Dead: The Ultimate Job Seeker's Guide*.

Career Objectives

These are okay to include at the very start of your career, before your general direction has been confirmed by experience and track record. Inclusion is also acceptable if you have very clearly defined objectives and are prepared to sacrifice all other opportunities. If that is the case, state your goals clearly and succinctly, remembering not to confuse the nature of long-term career objectives with short-term job objectives.

Beware, though, of the drawbacks. First of all, resume readers aren't famous for paying much attention to objectives; that's why in talking about Job Objectives I emphasized the desirability of reflecting real-world job descriptions. Second, I have seen these used on many occasions to make a hiring decision between two candidates. The resumes are compared: A has no objective; B has an objective that doesn't match the initial expectations. Result? A gets the job. Another consideration is that your resume may be on file for years, during which time your objectives are bound to change.

References

It is inappropriate and unprofessional to list the names of references on a resume. You will never see it on a top example. Why? Interviewers are not interested in checking them before they meet and develop a strong interest in you—it's too time-consuming. In addition, the law forbids employers to check references without your written consent (thanks to the 1970 Fair Credit and Reporting Act), and they have to meet you first in order to obtain your written permission.

You typically grant this permission when you fill out an application form; in fact, it is usually the reason you are given an application form to complete when you already have a perfectly good resume. There at the bottom of the backside of the form is the space for your signature and above it a block of impossibly small type. Your signature below that type is granting permission for the reference check. This is why companies frequently require that you fill out an application form even though you have a perfectly good resume. What they really want is permission to check your references when the time comes, which won't be until immediately before or after the offer is made.

One further note on this: If you have a good resume, you can usually get away with filling in the employer information and writing "see resume" for other information. As long as they have your signature, most potential employers will be quite happy with this.

Employers assume that references are available anyway, and if they aren't available, boy, are you in trouble! For that reason, there's an argument to be made for leaving that famous line—References Available Upon Request—at the end of your resume, but only if space allows; if you have to cut a line anywhere this would be one of the first to go. It may not be absolutely necessary to say that references are there for the asking, but those four extra words certainly don't do any harm and may help you stand out from the crowd. Including the phrase sends a little message: "Hey, look, I have no skeletons in my closet."

A brief but important aside: If you have ever worked under a different surname, you must take this fact into account when giving your references. A recently divorced woman I know of wasted a strong interview performance because she was using her maiden name on her resume and at the interview. She forgot to tell the employer that her references would, of course, remember her by a different last name. The results of this oversight were catastrophic. Three prior employers denied ever having heard of anyone by the name supplied to the references by the interviewer. She lost the job.

Written Testimonials

It is best not to attach written testimonials to your resume. Of course, that doesn't mean that you shouldn't solicit such references for your files. Instead you might consider using them as a basis for those third-party endorsements we talked about earlier, then you can produce the written testimonials at the interview with the comment that they will support the claims made on your resume; this way you get to use them twice to good effect. This will be especially helpful to you if you are just entering the work force, or re-entering after a long absence, because the content of the testimonials can be used to beef up your resume significantly.

Marital Status

If you think mention of your marital status will enhance your chances (if you are looking for a position as a long-distance trucker, marriage counselor, or traveling salesperson, for example), include it. In all other instances leave it out. Legally, your marital status is of no consequence.

Personal Interests

A Korn Ferry study showed that executives with team sports on their resumes were seen to be averaging $3,000 a year more than their more sedentary counterparts. Now, that makes giving a line to your hobbies worthwhile, if they fit into certain broad categories. These would include team sports, determination activities (running, climbing, bicycling), and "brain activities" (bridge, chess). The rule of thumb, as always, is only to include activities that can in some way contribute to your chances of being hired.

Personal Activities

Here and there throughout the resume section of this book you will see resumes that include—often toward the end—a short personal paragraph that gives you a candid snapshot of the resume writer as a person. Done well, these can be exciting, effective endings to a resume, but they are not to everyone's taste. Typically, they refer to one or two personal traits, activities, and, sometimes, beliefs. These are often tied in with skills required for the particular job sought.

The idea is to make the reader say, "Hey, there's a real person behind this piece of paper, let's get him in here; he sounds like our kind of guy." Of course, as no one can be all things to all people, you don't want to go overboard in this area.

RESUMES THAT KNOCK 'EM DEAD

IT HAS BEEN theory up to now: this is where the rubber hits the road.

his is the part of the book that requires you to do some thinking. I will ask questions to jog your memory about your practical experience. The outcome will be a smorgasbord of your most marketable professional attributes. Whether you are a fast tracker, recent graduate, work force re-entrant, career changer, or what-have-you, if you are considering new horizons, you must take stock before stepping out.

People change jobs for a multitude of reasons. Perhaps your career isn't progressing as you want it. Perhaps you have gone as far as you can with your present employer, and the only way to take another career step is to change companies. Maybe you have been in the same job for three or more years, without dramatic salary increases or promotions, and you know that you are going nowhere, your having been stereotyped, classified, and pigeonholed.

You need to know where you've been, where you are, and where you're headed. Without this stocktaking, your chances of reaching your ultimate goals are reduced, because you won't know how best to use what you've got to get where you want to go.

Believe it or not, very few people have a clear fix on what they do for a living. Oh, I know; you ask a typist what he or she does, and you get, "Type, stupid." You ask an accountant, and you hear, "Fiddle with numbers, what do you think?" And that is the problem. Most people don't look at their work beyond these simplistic terms. They never examine the implications of their jobs in relation to the overall success of the company. Most people miss not only their importance to an employer as part of the business, but also, their importance to themselves. Preparing your resume will give you a fresh view of yourself as a professional and your role in your chosen profession.

Employers all want to know the same thing: How can you contribute to keeping their ship afloat and seaworthy? Everyone who ever gets hired for any job gets hired because they are a problem solver. Look at your work in terms of the problems you solve in the daily round, as well as the problems that would occur if you weren't there.

The Secret of Resume Writing

As a resume writer, you are going to have a lot in common with journalists and novelists. Beginners in each field usually bring some basic misconceptions about how writing is done: a novice writer may assume that Stephen King or John Grisham just sits down, writes "Page 1," and then three weeks later writes "The End," placidly returning the quill to the inkwell. In fact, many professional writers have a lot in common with the creative process employed by sculptors, who create beauty from a block of stone. Writers start the creative process by creating a mass of notes. This great mass is the raw material, like the sculptor's block of stone, at which they chip away to reveal the masterwork that has been hiding there all along.

The key is that the more notes you have, the better. Just remember that whatever you write in the note-making part of your resume preparation will never suffer public scrutiny; it is for your private consumption only. Don't let the "need to get it done," or the fear of others' judgment cramp the creative process of capturing information: the final product can only ever be as good as the components from which you assemble it.

This process will help you

- Get a focus for your job search
- Prepare an effective resume
- Open doors for interviews
- Provide interviewers with a road map of your choosing
- Act as a positive spokesperson long after you have left the interview

On top of all these benefits, this information-gathering process will also help you properly prepare for telephone and in-person interviews, as you will see over the following pages.

Questionnaire, Part One: Raw Materials

First, set up a document titled "Resume Questionnaire" and save it to a resume subfolder within your career management folder. Add each of the following Steps into the document and then steadily work your way through them.

Step #1: Identify Your Target Job

It's a misconception to think that a productive resume is a simple recitation of what you have done with your professional life. On the contrary, such a resume will seem unfocused and may well demand more effort on the part of the reader to determine if you are a worthwhile candidate.

Your resume will be incalculably more productive if you begin with defining a clear focus on a target job that you can land and in which you can be successful. Start with identifying this target job title.

Step #2: Research the Target Job

Go surf the Web for an hour and collect as many job descriptions as you can with this target job title. Once you have a selection, deconstruct them into a series of bullets here as your answer for Step #2.

You should realize that:

- No one is ever added to the payroll for the love of humanity.
- At some level all employees are hired to do the same job: Problem solution and problem avoidance within a specific area of expertise.
- No one ever reads resumes for fun.

- Resumes are always read with job titles in mind.
- Resumes are always read with a job description in mind.

You can see the absolute necessity of beginning the evaluation of your background with an understanding of what potential employers will be looking for when they come to your resume.

Step #3: Go Through Your Recent Work History

With the focus you have gained from Steps 1 and 2, understanding the sort of information those resume readers are going to be looking for, it is time to start working through your work history. In this process you'll not only be gathering all the information necessary for your resume, but reminding yourself of all kinds of data employers are likely to require at different stages of the selection cycle. This is a time when you are going to get completely immersed in your work history.

A. Current or Last Employer

Identify your current or last employer by name and location, follow it with a brief description (5–6 words) of the company's business/products/services.

> *Note:* This includes part-time or voluntary employment if you are a recent graduate or about to re-enter the work force after an absence. Try looking at your school as an employer and see what new information you can reveal about yourself.

For your current or most recent employer, write down the following:

Starting Date: _____
Starting Title: _____
Starting Salary: _____
Leaving Date: _____
Leaving Title: _____
Reason for Leaving: _____
Potential References for this Job: _____
Leaving Salary: _____

B. Deliverables

Make a bulleted list of the duties/responsibilities/deliverables in this position. Then arrange the elements from most important to least.

C. Skills and Special Knowledge

Now, for each of your identified deliverables, answer the following questions:

- What special skills or knowledge did you need to perform this task satisfactorily?
- What educational background and/or credentials helped prepare you for these responsibilities?
- What are your achievements in this area?

For each of your major areas of responsibility you should consider both the daily problems that arise and also those major projects/problems that stand out as major accomplishments. Think of each as a problem-solving challenge, and the analytical processes and subsequent actions you took to win the day. There is a four-step technique you will find useful here called PSRV:

P. Identify the *project* and the problem it represented, both from a corporate perspective and from the point of view of your execution of duties.

S. Identify your *solution* to the challenge and the process you implemented to deliver the solution.

R. What was the *result* of your approach and actions?

V. Finally, what was the *value* to you, the department, and the company? If you can, define this in terms of time saved, money saved, or money earned. This is not always possible, but it is very powerful whenever you can.

Step #4: Consider Teamwork and Your Professional Profile

Next within your information-gathering document, ask yourself the following questions:

- What verbal or written comments did peers or managers make about your contributions in each area of your job?

- What different levels of people did you have to interact with to achieve your job tasks? What skills and methods did you use to get the best out of superiors? Coworkers? Subordinates?
- What aspects of your personality were brought into play when executing this duty?

Professional Behaviors

To help you address that last question in Step #4, we're going to take a little break from the questionnaire (you've earned it, haven't you?). In order to identity which traits and abilities enabled you to perform well at your work in the past, look over the following list of twelve professional behaviors. These are behaviors that are in demand by all employers for all jobs at all levels. Going through the list, you will probably recognize that you already apply some or many of these behaviors in your work. As you read, come up with examples of your own using each particular behavior in the execution of each of your major duties at this job. The examples you generate can be used in your resume, in your cover letters, and as illustrative answers to questions in interviews.

#1: Communication & Listening Skills: This covers your ability to communicate effectively to people at all levels in a company, and refers to verbal and written skills along with technological adeptness, dress, and body language. This is an especially important consideration when it comes to your cover letter and resume, because these written documents are the first means an employer has of judging your communication skills. You should demonstrate that you have to take the time to craft and edit, and re-edit your resume until it communicates what you want it to, and at the same time demonstrates that you have adequate communication skills.

Communication embraces *Listening Skills:* Listening and understanding, as opposed to just waiting your turn to talk; there is a big difference between the two. Consciously develop your "listening to understand" skills and the result will be improved persuasive communication abilities.

#2: Goal-Orientation: All employers are interested in goal-oriented professionals: those who achieve concrete results with their actions and who constantly strive to get the job done, rather than just filling the time allotted for a particular task. Whenever possible, you should try to use an example or reference to this behavior in your letters and resume.

#3: Willingness to Be a Team Player: The highest achievers (always goal-oriented) are invariably Team Players: employers look for employees who work for the common good and always with the group's goals and responsibilities in mind. Team players take pride in group achievement over personal aggrandizement; they look for solutions rather than someone to blame.

#4: Motivation & Energy: Employers realize a motivated professional will do a better job on every assignment. Motivation expresses itself in a commitment to the job and the profession, an eagerness to learn and grow professionally, and a willingness to take the rough with the smooth.

Motivation is invariably expressed by the energy someone demonstrates in their work, always giving that extra effort to get the job done and to get it done right.

#5: Analytical Skills: Valuable employees are able to weigh the short- and long-term benefits of a proposed course of action against all its possible negatives. We see these skills demonstrated in the way a person identifies potential problems and so is able to minimize their occurrence. Successful application of analytical skills at work requires understanding how your job and the role of your department fits into the company's overall goal of profitability. It also means thinking things through and not jumping at the first or easiest solution.

#6: Dedication & Reliability: We are speaking here of dedication to your profession, with an awareness of the role it plays in the larger issues of company success, and of the empowerment that comes from knowing how your part contributes to the greater good. Dedication to your professionalism is also a demonstration of enlightened self-interest. The more you are engaged in your career, the more likely you are to join the inner circles that exist in every department-and company-enhancing opportunities for advancement; this dedication will therefore repay you with better job security and improved professional horizons.

Your dedication will also express itself in your *Reliability:* Showing up is half the battle; the other half is your performance on the job. To demonstrate reliability requires following up on your actions, not relying on anyone else to ensure the job is done well, and keeping management informed every step of the way.

#7: Determination: Someone with this attribute does not back off when a problem or situation gets tough; instead, he or she is the person who chooses to be part of a solution rather than standing idly by and being part of the problem. Determined professionals have decided to make a difference with their presence everyday and are willing to do whatever it takes to get a job done, even if that includes duties that might not appear in a job description.

#8: Confidence: As you develop desirable professional behaviors, your confidence grows in the skills you have and in your ability to develop new ones. With this comes confidence in taking on new challenges. You have the confidence to ask questions, the confidence to look at challenges calmly, the confidence to look at mistakes unflinchingly, and the confidence to make changes to eradicate them. In short, you develop a quiet confidence in your ability as a professional who can deliver the goods.

#9: Pride & Integrity: Pride in yourself as a professional means always making sure the job is done to the best of your ability; paying attention to the details and to the time and cost constraints. Integrity means taking responsibility for your actions, both good and bad; it means treating others, within and without the company, with respect at all times and in all situations. With pride in yourself as a professional with integrity, your actions will always be in the best interests of the company, and your decisions will never be based on whim or personal preference.

#10: Efficiency: Working efficiently means always keeping an eye open for wasted time, effort, resources, and money.

#11: Economy: Most problems have two solutions—and the expensive one usually isn't the best. Ideas of efficiency and economy engage the creative mind in ways other workers might not consider; they are an integral part of your analytical proficiency.

#12: Ability to Follow Procedures: You know that procedures exist to keep the company profitable, so you don't work around them. Following the chain of command, you don't implement your own "improved" procedures or organize others to do so.

Employing these learnable behaviors is the key to long-term career success. If you can recognize the role each of these learnable behaviors play over the course of a successful career, you'll not only craft a better resume and land a better job, but you'll also be more successful in your new job and in all future ones.

And now, let's head back to the questionnaire.

Step #5: Add Your Previous Work History

It is not unusual to have held a number of different titles with a specific employer. If this applies to you, such professional progression needs to be identified on your resume, as it speaks to your competency and promotability. For each different intermediary title, repeat Steps 3 and 4. Do not skimp on this process. All you write may not go into the final version of your resume, but all your effort will reward you at some point during the selection process and lead to more and better job offers.

Next (and this may take some time), repeat Steps 3 and 4 for each of your previous employers. Most finished resumes place greatest emphasis on the last three jobs, or last ten years' experience. In this developmental portion of the process, however, you must go back in time and cover your entire work history. Remember that you are doing more than preparing a resume here: You are preparing for the heat of battle. The work you do in a careful analysis of your career to date will help prepare you for interviews down through the years. One of the biggest complaints interviewers have about job candidates, and one of the major reasons for rejection, is unpreparedness: "You know, good as some of this fellow's skills are, something just wasn't right. He seemed slow somehow. You know, he couldn't even remember when he joined his current employer!" You won't have that problem.

Step #6: Compile Endorsements

Looking at each of your major areas of responsibility, come up with whatever verbal or written commentary on your performance you can.

Questionnaire, Part II: Details, Details, Details

The hard work is done, and it's all downhill from here. Step #7 (the last one!) of the questionnaire is to fill in the details concerning your abilities and experience in the following areas.

Military History

Include branch of service, rank, and any special skills that could further your civilian career.

Educational History

Start with highest level of attainment and work backward. Give dates, schools, majors, minors, grade-point averages, scholarships, and/or special awards.

List other school activities, such as sports, societies, and social activities. Especially important are leadership roles: Any example of how you "made a difference" with your presence could be of value to your future. Obviously, this is most important for recent graduates with little work experience, and those in the very early stages of a career.

Technological Literacy

In this new era of work, every potential employer is concerned about your ability to work with new technologies. If you are technologically literate, let's hear the details. If not, it's time to catch up with today's technology—before you get left behind with the industrial-era dinosaurs.

Ongoing Professional Development

Identify all the classes and courses you have pursued during your career, including certification and accreditations; they all speak to your professional commitment and to employers' belief in your potential.

Languages

The ability to read and write foreign languages is always a plus; specify your fluency in each.

Personal Interests

List interests and activities that could be supportive to your candidacy. For example, an internal auditor who plays chess or bridge would list these on a resume, because they support the analytical bent so necessary to that field. Activities that challenge you physically, analytically, or as a member of a team are all regarded positively in the selection process.

Patents and Publications

Include patents that are both pending and awarded. If you have published articles, list the name of the publication, title of article, and the publication date. If you have had books published, list the title and publisher.

Professional Associations

Include membership and the details of any offices you held.

Civic Affiliations and Volunteer Work

It isn't only paid work experience that makes you valuable, so include membership in civic groups and any volunteer work you performed. Involvement in such activities has a variable value depending on the company and individual hiring manager; regardless it is always regarded as a positive commentary on your achievements.

Miscellaneous Areas of Achievement

All professions and careers are different. Use this section to itemize any additional aspects of your history where you somehow "made a difference" with your presence.

Do Your Credentials Warrant the Target Job?

We started the information-gathering process by focusing on a target job title and then researching recruitment advertising to come up with a clear idea of what employers are typically looking for under that job title. There is a simple check-and-balance step you can take here that will benefit you in some powerful ways. You'll remember that I advised you to make a bulleted list of the desired requirements from all the recruitment postings you discovered. Now go back to that list and reading each bullet, go through your answers in the question-naire and proceed to cut and paste relevant information beneath each bullet. At the end of the process you can read the composite job description and your answers; you'll very quickly get a picture of your relative strengths and weaknesses. Hopefully this will tell you:

- I can do the job.
- I have a picture of what employers are going to ask me about.
- I have a blueprint for what I can talk about in response.

Being able to do 70 percent or more of the job will usually get you in the running for the interview cycle. Less than this and you may need to re-evaluate your target job title. Most people don't get promotions to the next step up the professional ladder when they change jobs, because they are coming onboard as an unknown quantity. Typically, most professionals accept a position similar to the one they have now, one that offers the opportunity for growth once their mettle is proved. An exception might be when they are already doing that higher-level job but without the title; another might be the executive who is combining experience and credentials from a number of jobs into a new in-demand configuration.

CHAPTER · CHAPTER · CHAPTER · CHAPTER · CHAPTER · CHAPTER

5

WRITING THE RESUME

RESUMES DEPART FROM the rules that govern all other forms of writing.

First and last they are an urgent business communication that no one really likes to read, so they must be succinct and to the point.

You can assume that the potential employer has a position to fill and a problem to solve, and that he or she is buried in an avalanche of resumes.

For the next fifteen minutes, imagine yourself in one of your target companies. You are in the HR department on resume detail, and the morning mail has just landed thirty resumes on your desk to be read. Go straight to the example section now and try to read thirty resumes without a break, and then return to this page.

Now you have some idea of what it feels like. Except that you had it easy—the resumes you read were all well put together; they were, as I've mentioned, resumes that got real people real jobs. Even so, you probably felt a little punch-drunk at the end of the exercise. But you also learned a very valuable lesson: Brevity and focus are to be desired above all other things.

Choose a Layout

You have seen the basic examples of chronological, functional, and combination resumes in Chapter 2, and you have browsed through the resumes. If you didn't do so before, now is the time to find one that strikes your fancy and fits your needs, and use it as your model. It need not reflect your field of professional expertise. Obviously your template will need work; you will need to put in your own contact information and job objective, add the details of each of your jobs, and make other changes as necessary.

This first step is just like painting by numbers. Go through the template and fill in the obvious slots—name, address, telephone number(s), e-mail address, employer names, employment dates, educational background and dates, activities, and the like. Shazam! You immediately have a document that is beginning to look like a resume.

Filling in the Picture: Chronological Resumes

Objectives

You can have a simple nonspecific objective, one that gives the reader a general focus, such as, "Objective: Data Processing Management." It gets the message across succinctly; and if there is no immediate need for someone of your background, it encourages the employer to put your resume in the file where you feel it belongs. That's important, because even if you are not suitable for today's needs, it increases the odds that your resume will be pulled out when such a need does arise.

If you choose to use an expanded, detailed objective, you will of course focus the objective on what you can do for the company and avoid mention of what you want in return. You can use the job description you developed in your information-gathering process (as described in Chapter 4) to craft an objective in the language that employers use to describe your target job. This will help both human eyes and database spiders to find your resume attractive.

The Company's Business

Now, for each employer, edit your response from the Questionnaire in Chapter 4 to outline that company's services or products. Make it one short sentence: This is not necessary if the company name, like Microsoft, is a household name.

Job Titles

Remember what we said in Chapter 3. There is nothing intrinsically wrong with listing your title as "Fourth-Level Administration Clerk, Third Class," as long as you are prepared to wait until doomsday for it to be considered by someone who understands what it means and is able to relate it to current needs. Make sure that you use job titles that will be commonly understood.

Responsibilities

In a chronological resume, the job title is sometimes followed by a short sentence that helps the reader visualize you doing the job. If you choose to do this, get the information from the completed questionnaire and do a rough edit, getting it down to one short sentence; don't worry about perfection now, you can polish it later.

The responsibilities and contributions you list here are those functions that best relate to the needs of the target job; if you have focused on a target job in which you can be successful, this should not pose a problem. They do not necessarily correspond with how you spent the majority of your working day, nor are they related to how you might prefer to spend your working day. It can perhaps best be illustrated by showing you part of a resume that came to my desk recently. It is the work of a professional who listed her title and duties for one job like this:

> Sales Manager: Responsible for writing branch policy, coordination of advertising and advertising agencies. Developed knowledge of IBM PC. Managed staff of six.

Is it any wonder she wasn't getting responses to her e-mailing campaign? She has mistakenly listed everything in the reverse chronological order, not in relation to the items' relative importance to a future employer. Let's look at what subsequent restructuring achieved:

Sales Manager: Hired to turn around stagnant sales force. Successfully recruited, trained, managed, and motivated a sales staff of six. Result: 22 percent sales gain over first year.

Notice how this is clearly focused on the essentials of a sales manager's job:

Hired to turn around stagnant sales force. (*Demonstrates her skills and responsibilities.*)

Successfully recruited, trained, managed and motivated a consulting staff of six. Result: 22 percent sales gain over first year. (*Shows what she subsequently did with the sales staff, and just how well she did it.*)

By doing this, her responsibilities and achievements become more important in the light of the problems they solved.

A important word about "contributions": Business has very limited interests. In fact, those interests can be reduced to a single phrase: making a profit. Making a profit is done in just three ways: By saving money in some fashion for the company; by saving time through some innovation at the company, which in turn saves the company money and gives it the opportunity to make more money in the time saved; or by simply making money for the company. That does not mean that you should address only those points in your resume and ignore valuable contributions that cannot be quantified. But it does mean that you should try to quantify as much as you can.

Achievements

Pick two to four accomplishments for each job title and edit them down to bite-size chunks that read like a telegram. Write as if you had to pay for each entry by the word—this approach can help you pack a lot of information into a short space. The resulting abbreviated style will help convey a sense of immediacy to the reader.

Responsible for new and used car sales. Earned "Salesman of the Year" awards, 2004 and 2006. Record holder for: Most Cars Sold in One Year.

Here's another example from a fundraiser's resume:

- Created an annual giving program to raise operating funds. Raised $2,000,000.
- Targeted, cultivated, and solicited sources including individuals, corporations, foundations, and state and federal agencies. Raised $1,650,000.
- Raised funds for development of the Performing Arts School facility, capital expense, and music and dance programs. Raised $6,356,000.

Now, while you may tell the reader about these achievements, never explain how they were accomplished; the key phrase here is "specifically vague." The intent of your resume is to pique interest and to raise as many questions as you answer. Questions mean interest, and getting that interest satisfied requires talking to you!

You may have plenty of accomplishments to share with the reader that will tempt you to add a second page to your resume—and third and fourth pages. Describing your achievements succinctly will not only leave room for further discussion at the hoped-for interview, but it will also make it easier to scale down your resume to the preferred length of one page, or at most two.

Next, prioritize the listing of your accomplishments as they relate to your target job, and be sure to quantify your contributions wherever possible and appropriate.

If you can, now is the time to weave in some of those laudatory quotes. Put in all that you have right now, but when you come to the final editing phase you will want to cut it back; one or two will be fine, although I have seen resumes where each job entry is finished with a complimentary quote. For example:

- Sales volume increased from $90 million to $175 million. Acknowledged as "the greatest single gain of the year."
- Earnings increased from $9 million to $18 million. Review stated, "always has a view for the company bottom line."

Functional or Combination Resumes

In a functional or combination resume, you will have identified the skills and attributes necessary to fulfill the functions of the target job, and will highlight the appropriate attributes you have to offer. In this format, you will have headings that apply to the skill areas your chosen career path demands, such as:

Management, Training, Sales, etc. Each will be followed by a short paragraph packed with selling points. These can be real paragraphs, or an introductory sentence followed by bullets. Here is an example of each style.

COLLECTIONS:
Developed excellent rapport with customers while significantly shortening payout terms through application of problem-solving techniques. Turned impending loss into profit. Personally salvaged and increased sales with two multimillion-dollar accounts by providing remedial action for their sales/financial problems.

COLLECTIONS:
Developed excellent rapport with customers while significantly shortening payout terms:

- Evaluated sales performance; offered suggestions for financing/merchandising, turned impending loss into profit.
- Salvaged two multimillion-dollar problem accounts by providing remedial action for their sales/financial problems. Subsequently increased sales.

Keep each paragraph to an absolute maximum of four lines. This ensures that the finished product has plenty of white space so that it is easy on the reader's eye.

Editing and Polishing

Sentences gain power with verbs that demonstrate an action. For example, a woman with ten years at the same law firm in a clerical position had written in her original resume:

I learned to use a computer database.

After discussion of the circumstances that surrounded learning how to use the computer database, certain exciting facts emerged. By using action verbs and an awareness of employer interests, this sentence was charged up, given more punch:

I analyzed and determined the need for automation of an established law office. Responsible for hardware and software selection, installation, and loading. Within one year, I had achieved a fully automated office.

Notice how the verbs show that things happen when you are around the office. These action verbs and phrases add an air of direction, efficiency, and accomplishment to every resume. They succinctly tell the reader why you did it and how well you did it.

Now look at the above example when a third-party endorsement is added to it:

I analyzed and determined need for automation of an established law office. Responsible for hardware and software selection, installation, and loading. Within one year, I had achieved a fully automated office. Partner stated, "You brought us out of the dark ages into the technological age, and in the process neither you nor the firm missed a beat!"

Now while the content is clearly more powerful, the presentation is still clunky and it takes up too much space. Read on, and in the next few pages you will see how you can speed up and shorten paragraphs like this further.

Keywords

With the advent of electronic resume screening tools, it's become more and more important to use specific keywords in your resume. Internal job descriptions are usually built of nouns and verbs that describe the skill sets required for the job. Your resume should be built the same way, with nouns that identify the skill sets and verbs/action phrases that describe your professional behavior and achievements with these skill sets.

This is an important distinction in the initial screening process. Screening software focuses on the skill sets, which invariably are nouns. If you are a computer programmer the screening device might search for words like "HTML"; if you are an accountant it might search for words like "financial analysis." Only when the computer has identified those resumes that include matching skills do human eyes enter into the picture; and only then can the verbs/action phrases that describe your competencies and achievements have the desired impact. With an electronic resume, the nouns/skill sets are the skeleton, while the verbs/action phrases are designed to put flesh on the bones for human eyes hungry for talent.

For our purposes the keyword nouns are the words commonly used to describe the essential skill sets and knowledge necessary to carry out a job successfully. They are likely to include:

- Skill sets/abilities/competencies
- Application of these skill sets
- Relevant education and training

You may also want to study the keywords that appear frequently in recruitment postings; if you have been following the program outlined here, you have already collected these for your job description.

You'll want to weave the nouns and verbs describing your professional competencies into the main body of your resume as much as possible. However, that won't always be possible. The logical flow of your resume—or insufficient space—might prevent you from using the keywords in place. That's where a separate keyword section comes in handy. It is the perfect spot to list the technical acronyms and professional jargon that you can't fit into the body copy.

Here's an example of a core competencies/keyword section from a sales management professional:

SPECIFIC KNOWLEDGE AND SKILLS

Market Trend Analysis • Profit & Loss • Multi-Site Management • Needs Analysis • Budget • Employee Motivation • Business Savvy • Sales • Performance Evaluations • Contract Negotiation • Technical Expertise • Team Training

---

This innovation in resume writing allows you to add a host of additional information to your resume in a space-efficient way—usually in 20 to 60 words.

Using a core competencies/keyword section will increase the odds of an electronic screening agent making multiple matches between your resume and an open job requisition. Human eyes will view the list of for topics for discussion.

This compels me to offer you a warning: Don't use keywords to extend the "reach" of your resume. You must have real experience in each of the areas you include. Including keywords for areas where you have no professional expertise may get you a telephone conversation with an employer, but it will also quickly reveal you as an impostor. End of story.

Where does the core competencies/keyword section go? As far as the computer is concerned it doesn't matter. The computer doesn't care about the niceties of layout and flow. However, human eyes will also see this section, so there is a certain logic in putting it front and center, after any summary or objective or immediately after the contact information. This section acts as a preface to the body copy, in effect saying, "Hey, here are all the headlines. The stories behind them are immediately below." To put it another way, the keyword section acts as a table of contents for your resume, with the body—and its action words and phrases—explaining and expanding on the list of topics.

Your keyword section can be as long as you require, though they typically don't run longer than 60 items and usually are a little shorter. There's no need to use definite or indefinite articles or conjunctions. Just list the word, starting with a capital—"Forecasting," for example—or a phrase, such as "Financial modeling."

You can also think of your core competencies section as an electronic business card that allows you to network with computers!

Action Verbs

Here are over 175 action verbs. See which ones you can use to give punch to your resume writing.

accepted	assisted	completed	decreased
accomplished	attained	composed	defined
achieved	audited	computed	delegated
acted	authored	conceptualized	demonstrated
adapted	automated	conducted	designed
addressed	balanced	consolidated	developed
administered	budgeted	contained	devised
advanced	built	contracted	diagnosed
advised	calculated	contributed	directed
allocated	cataloged	controlled	dispatched
analyzed	chaired	coordinated	distinguished
appraised	clarified	corresponded	diversified
approved	classified	counseled	drafted
arranged	coached	created	edited
assembled	collected	critiqued	educated
assigned	compiled	cut	eliminated

emended	influenced	performed	restructured
enabled	informed	persuaded	retrieved
encouraged	initiated	planned	revamped
engineered	innovated	prepared	revitalized
enlisted	inspected	presented	saved
established	installed	prioritized	scheduled
evaluated	instigated	processed	schooled
examined	instituted	produced	screened
executed	instructed	programmed	set
expanded	integrated	projected	shaped
expedited	interpreted	promoted	solidified
explained	interviewed	proposed	solved
extracted	introduced	provided	specified
fabricated	invented	publicized	stimulated
facilitated	launched	published	streamlined
familiarized	lectured	purchased	strengthened
fashioned	led	recommended	summarized
focused	maintained	reconciled	supervised
forecast	managed	recorded	surveyed
formulated	marketed	recruited	systemized
founded	mediated	reduced	tabulated
generated	moderated	referred	taught
guided	monitored	regulated	trained
headed up	motivated	rehabilitated	translated
identified	negotiated	remodeled	traveled
illustrated	operated	repaired	trimmed
implemented	organized	represented	upgraded
improved	originated	researched	validated
increased	overhauled	resolved	worked
indoctrinated	oversaw	restored	wrote

Use these words to edit and polish your work, to communicate, persuade, and motivate the reader to take action.

Varying Your Sentences

Most good writers are at their best when they write short punchy sentences. When writing a resume, where space is especially limited, this dictum is particularly true. Keep your sentences under about twenty words, and if it is longer try to shorten it by editing out unnecessary words, or make two sentences out of the one.

At the same time, you don't want the writing to sound choppy, so vary the length of sentences when you can. You can also start with a short phrase and follow with a colon:

- Followed by bullets of information
- Each one supporting the original phrase

These techniques are designed to enliven the reading process. Here's the example from a few pages back that we have gradually been improving:

I analyzed and determined need for automation of an established law office. Responsible for hardware and software selection, installation, and loading. Within one year, I had achieved a fully automated office. Partner stated, "You brought us out of the dark ages into the technological age, and in the process neither you nor the firm missed a beat!"

Now let's take this "punching up" process a step further and see what the result looks like:

Analyzed and determined need for automation of an established law office:

- Responsible for hardware and software selection.
- Coordinated installation database and workstations.
- Operated and maintained equipment, and trained users.
- Achieved full automation in one year

Partner stated, "You brought us out of the dark ages, and neither you nor the firm missed a beat!"

Just as you use short sentences, you should also use common words, They are easy to understand and communicate efficiently. Remember:

Short words in short sentences help
make short, gripping paragraphs:
Good for short attention spans!

Voice and Tense

The voice for your resume depends on a few important factors: getting a lot said in a small space, being factual, and packaging yourself in the best way.

The voice you use should be consistent throughout the resume. There is considerable disagreement among the experts about the best voice.

Sentences can be truncated (up to a point) by omitting pronouns—*I, you, he, she, it, they*—and articles—*a* or *the*. In fact, many authorities recommend the dropping of pronouns as a technique that both saves space and allows you to brag about yourself without seeming boastful. It gives the impression that another party is writing about you. Many people feel that to use the first-person pronoun—"I automated the office"—is naive. These experts suggest you use either the third person, as in "He automated the office," or leave the pronoun out altogether—"Automated office."

At the same time, there are others who feel that writing in the first person makes you sound well, personable; and I have seen the occasional resume like this that really does work. Use whatever style works best for you. If you do use the personal pronoun, try not to use it in every sentence—it gets a little monotonous and takes up valuable space on the page.

A nice variation I have occasionally seen used is a third-person voice used through the resume and then a final few words in the first person appended to the end of the resume, to give an insight into your values. Here are examples:

Regular third person:
James Sharpe is a professional who knows Technical Services from the ground up. He understands its importance in keeping a growing company productive, and takes pride in creating order in the chaos of technology.

First person:
I am accustomed to accepting responsibility and delegating authority, and am capable of working with, and through people at all levels. Am able to plan, organize, develop, implement, and supervise complex programs and special projects. All of this requires sound communication and people management skills and a commitment to timely, cost-effective results.

Many people mistake the need for professionalism with stiff-necked formality. The most effective tone is one that mixes the conversational and the formal, just the way we do in our jobs. The only overriding rule is to make it readable, so that another person can see the human being shining through.

Length

The accepted rules for length are one page for every ten years of your experience. If you have more than twenty years under your belt, many of the skills from those early days are now irrelevant; so on the whole the "two-page maximum" rule is still a sensible guideline.

Now while the advent of electronic databases and the consequent tilt toward data heavy resumes (to maximize the keyword registers) is leading toward two-page resumes as the norm for all but entry-level professionals, never pad your resume to make it longer.

A note on executive resumes is necessary here. In my private consulting practice I work with executives around the world who are typically both seasoned professionals and earning over a quarter of a million dollars a year; they are relatively few in number, and they hold unrelentingly complex jobs.

With the increased complexity of these modern management jobs, the need to demonstrate competence, and the exigencies of electronic database manipulation, makes exceeding the traditional two-page mark not only necessary but often desirable. Now while brevity and focus are still the very soul of a productive resume, that $350,000-a-year EVP of Marketing resume is going to have to be read by someone in a position to hire you. So squeezing everything onto two pages for the sake of accepted norms defeats your purpose. Assuming that the first page clearly demonstrates a thorough understanding and competency in the target job, you can feel comfortable taking that third and sometimes fourth page. In the chapter of sample resumes, you'll see two examples of justifiably longer executive resumes, starting on page 258.

You'll find that thinking too much about length considerations while you write will hamper you. Think instead of the story you have to tell, and then layer fact upon fact until it is told. When that is done, you can go back and ruthlessly cut it to the bone. Ask yourself the following questions:

- Can I cut out any paragraphs?
- Can I cut out any superfluous words?
- Can I cut out any sentences?
- Where have I repeated myself?

If in doubt, cut it out—leave nothing but facts and action words!

The Proofreading Checklist for Your Final Draft

There are really two proofing steps in the creation of a polished resume. The first is one you do at this point, to make sure that all the things that should be in are there—and that all the things that shouldn't, aren't. In the heat of the creative moment, it's easy to miss critical components or mistakenly include facts that give the wrong emphasis. Check your resume against the following points:

Contact Information

- Is the pertinent personal data—name, address, personal telephone number, and e-mail address—correct? You will want to make sure that this personal data is on every page.

Objectives

- If you use an objective, does it briefly state your employment goals without getting too specific and ruling you out of consideration for many jobs?
- If you gave a detailed objective, does it focus on what you can bring to the employer, rather than what you want from the employer?
- Is your stated objective supported by the facts and accomplishments stated in the rest of your resume?

Summary

If you choose to include a summary:

- Is it no more than five lines long, so that the block of type remains accessible?
- Does it include at least one substantial accomplishment that supports your employment goals?
- Does it include reference to some of your personality or behavioral traits that are critical to success in your field?

Keywords/Core Competencies

If you include a keyword section/core competencies section:

- Do you have experience in each of the areas you've listed?
- Can you illustrate your experience in conversation?

- Does it include commonly used synonyms for your skill sets that you have not already used in the body of the resume?
- Is the spelling and capitalization correct? (It's easy to make mistakes here, especially with acronyms.)
- Are there any other justifiable keywords you should add?

Body of Resume

- Is your most relevant and qualifying work experience prioritized throughout the resume to lend strength to your application?
- Have you avoided wasting space with unnecessarily detailed employer names and addresses?
- Have you been suitably discreet with the name of your current employer?
- Have you omitted any reference to reasons for leaving a particular job?
- Have you removed all references to past, current, or desired salaries?
- Have you removed references to your date of availability?

Education

- Is education placed in the appropriate position? It should be at the beginning of the resume if you have little or no work experience, and, in most professions, at the end if you are established in your field and your practical experience now outweighs your degree.
- Is your highest educational attainment shown first?
- Have you included professional courses that support your candidacy?

Chronology

- If you've done a chronological resume, is your work history stated in chronological order, with the most recent employment coming at the head of the resume?
- Within this chronology, does each company history start with details of your most senior position?
- Have you avoided listing irrelevant responsibilities or job titles?
- Does your resume emphasize contributions and achievements?
- Can your body copy include one or more third-party endorsements of your work?
- Have you avoided poor focus by eliminating all extraneous information? This includes anything that doesn't relate to your job objective, such as captaining the tiddlywinks team in kindergarten.

- Have you included any volunteer or community service activities that can lend strength to your candidacy?
- Is the whole thing long enough to whet the reader's appetite for more details, yet short enough not to satisfy that hunger?
- Have you left out lists of references and only included mention of the availability of references if there is nothing more valuable to fill up the space?
- Have you avoided treating your reader like a fool by highlighting the obvious—i.e., heading your resume, "RESUME"?

Writing Style

- Have you substituted short words for long words? And one word where previously there were two?
- Is your average sentence no more than twenty words? Have you made sure that any sentence of more than twenty words is shortened or broken into two?
- Have you kept every paragraph under five lines, with many paragraphs considerably shorter?
- Do your sentences begin, wherever possible, with powerful action verbs and phrases?

Crossing the T's, Dotting the I's

Before your resume is finished, you have to make sure that your writing is as clear as possible. Incorrect spelling and poor grammar are guaranteed to annoy resume readers. Go back and check all these areas. If you feel uneasy about your resume, get a third party involved; and always use your spell and grammar checker.

It simply isn't possible for even the most accomplished professional writer to go directly from final draft to print, so don't try it. Your pride of authorship will blind you to the blemishes, and that's a self-indulgence you can't afford.

You need some distance from your creative efforts to gain detachment and objectivity. There is no hard-and-fast rule about how long it takes to come up with the finished product. Nevertheless, if you think you have finished, leave it alone as long as you can—at least overnight. Then you can come back to it fresh and read it almost as if it were meeting your eyes for the first time.

More Than One Resume?

Do you need more than one type of resume? Probably. With just a few years experience, most people have a background that qualifies them for more than one job. If this applies to you, the process is as simple as changing your target job focus, developing and objective job description, as discussed, and then rewriting the document along the lines explained in this chapter. You will already have a layout and even with a different focus much of the information will remain the same, so it shouldn't feel like you are back to square one.

To be maximally effective you can't rely on a "one size fits no one" approach; you will have to create new resumes to go after those jobs that ask for skills that didn't make it into your prime version. With a computer-based template this shouldn't be too much of a headache; you will also need an e-mail version for each print resume.

There is also a case for having resumes in more than one format. I was once engaged in an outplacement experiment for a group of professionals. With a little work, we developed chronological, functional, and combination resumes for everyone. The individuals sent out the resume of their choice. Then, in those instances where there was no response, a different version of the resume was sent. The result from just a different format: 8 percent more interviews. So if your chronological resume isn't getting results, maybe try a little reformatting and send it out as a combination style resume.

THE FINAL PRODUCT

WHEN IT COMES to clothes, style has a certain feel that everyone recognizes but few can define. Fortunately, with resumes, there are definite rules to follow.

By some counts, upward of 80 percent of resumes are stored in and retrieved from electronic databases. Even if this number is unscientific, we can still accept that the percentage is substantial indeed. Your resume may be an aesthetic marvel, but if it goes into the computer as gobbledygook, it won't do you much good. This chapter will cover the "traditional" resume—the resume designed for human eyes. The other kind, the "computer-friendly" resume, is designed to get through a computer scanner with data intact. It is so vital in today's job market that I have devoted a separate chapter to it. The two kinds of resumes do have certain basics in common.

Avoiding the Circular File

The average resume arrives on a desk with dozens of others. Your resume will get only thirty to forty seconds of initial attention, and then only if it's laid out well and looks accessible to a tired pair of eyes. What are the three biggest complaints about those resumes that reach the trash can in record time?

1. *Impossible to read.* They have too much information and run too long or they have too much information crammed into too little space with too small a font.
2. *No coherence.* Their layout is unorganized, illogical, and uneven. They look shoddy and slapdash.
3. *Typos.* They are riddled wiht misspelings. (See how annoying that last sentence is?)

Here are some tips that will help your resume rise above the rest.

Fonts

Business is rapidly coming to accept the likes of Bookman, New York, Times New Roman, and Palatino as the norm. When choosing your font, stay away from heavy and bold for your body copy (although you may choose to take a more dramatic approach with keywords or headlines). Bold type takes space, so use it sparingly to begin with. You should bold those things you want to jump out, and that would certainly include any words the company may have used in recruitment advertising. Avoid "script" faces similar to handwriting; while they look attractive to the occasional reader, they are harder on the eyes of people who read any amount of business correspondence. Capitalized copy is tough on the eyes too; many people think it makes a powerful statement, when all it does is cause eye strain and give the reader the impression that the writer is shouting at him or her.

How to Brighten the Page

Once you decide on a font, stick with it, because more than one on a page looks confusing. You can do plenty to liven up the visual impact of the page within the variations of the font you have chosen.

You will notice from the examples that the clearest and most successful resumes use just a couple of typographic variations and stick with them.

Proofing

When you have the printed resume in hand, you must proofread it.

- Is everything set up the way you want it?
- Are there any typographical errors?
- Is all the punctuation correct?
- Has everything been underlined, capitalized, bolded, italicized, and indented, exactly as you desire?

Once you read the resume, get someone else to review it. A third party will always provide more objectivity, and can catch errors you might miss.

Appearance Checklist

- The first glance and the first feel of your resume make a powerful impression. What's your immediate reaction to it?
- Have you used only one side of the page?
- If more than one page, did you paginate your resume ("1 of 2" at the bottom of the first page, and so on)?
- Does the first page of the resume clearly announce that you understand and can do the job?

Choosing Your Paper

While you should not skimp on paper cost, neither should you be talked into buying the most expensive available. Indeed, in some fields (health care and education come to mind), too ostentatious a paper can cause a negative impression. The idea is to create a feeling of understated quality.

Every resume should be printed on standard, 8½" x 11" (letter-size) paper. Paper comes in different weights and textures. Good resume-quality paper has a weight designation of between 20 and 25 pounds. Lighter, and you run the risk of appearing nonchalant and unconcerned. Heavier, and the paper is unwieldy. Most office supply stores carry paper and envelopes packaged as kits for resume and cover letters.

As for color, white is the prime choice. Cream is also acceptable, and I'm assured that some of the pale pastel shades can be both attractive and effective. Personally, I think that most professionals don't show up in the best light when dressed in pink—call me old-fashioned if you will. White and cream are straightforward, no-nonsense colors.

Cover letter stationery should always match the color and weight of your resume. To send a white cover letter—even if it is written on your personal stationery—with a cream resume looks uncoordinated, and detracts from the powerful statement of attention to detail you are trying to make.

It is a good idea to print some cover-letter stationery when you produce your resume. The letterhead can be in a different font but on the same kind of paper, and it should have the same contact information as your resume.

The Final Checklist

- Have you used good-quality paper?
- Does the paper size measure 8½" x 11"?
- Have you used white, off-white, or cream-colored paper?
- If your resume is more than one page, have you stapled the pages together (one staple in the top left-hand corner)?
- Is your cover letter written on stationery that matches your resume?

How to Use the Internet for Your Job Search

CHAPTER · CHAPTER · CHAPTER · CHAPTER · CHAPTER · CHAPTER

7

THE INTERNET OFFERS you an array of opportunities to get your resume on the desks of thousands of companies and recruiters. This communication medium makes research and contact easier than it has ever been, but you shouldn't rely on the obvious online approaches exclusively.

The Internet is especially effective in identifying all the target employers in a specific geographical area—whether it is where you live today or where you want to live as soon as possible. Its usefulness diminishes somewhat when you are only looking for jobs in your immediate area, and that area is a small town; even then there are still many useful ways you can use the medium.

From the corporate perspective, Internet recruitment serves a dual purpose: a company's personnel openings are cost-effectively advertised to attract candidates, and the technologically challenged potential applicants screen themselves out

How can the Internet benefit your job search? It allows you to:

- Research your industry and identify companies.
- Create customized electronic documents and communicate with potential employers and recruiters pretty much instantly.
- Find job openings through job banks and employers' job sites.
- Have potential employers find you, whether you are currently looking for a position or just maintaining visibility for career growth opportunities.
- Use database and networking sites to identify names and titles.
- Pick up useful job search and career management advice, especially at knockemdead.com.

You can post your resume on the Internet so that companies and recruiters can find you; you can surf for job openings and you'll have access to more information about prospective employers, making you a better-informed candidate. The Internet offers you access to millions of job openings, and tens of thousands of companies and recruiters. Of course, they are not all going to be in your town, so the wider your geographical parameters, the more useful the tool will become.

The Electronic Resume

Whether electronic or a paper, companies increasingly store resumes received in electronic databases. You need to create a database-compatible resume—one that can be stored in a public job site or corporate database, where Human Resources people and recruiters can have quick access to it.

Due to competition and the growth of the Internet, resume scanning and searching capabilities are now available to virtually all companies and recruiters. When an employer needs to sort through resumes for likely job candidates, they go to the keyboard, type in a job title, and are presented with a list of descriptors and choose those most relevant to the job being filled (*descriptors* are keywords describing different aspects of a particular job). The selection of keywords having been chosen, the software program searches in the company's database and ranks the documents containing any of the selected keywords. The more keywords your resume matches the better your chances are of having it read, because the program not only looks for resumes that contain those keywords, it also ranks the generated list and puts the most keyword-heavy resumes at the top. As you use the Internet and recruitment ads from newspapers and professional publications to find open positions, pay attention to the keywords that you see repeated. If you see keywords in job descriptions for positions that interest you and fit your qualifications, add these keywords to your resume.

Making Your Resume Scannable

In today's electronic world, you need both a "keyword conscious" paper resume that is scannable as well as an electronic resume that can be sent via e-mail and is database compatible. When you mail your resume to a company it is a paper document. In order for a company to quickly and effectively transform your resume to an electronic format they can scan, or digitize, it.

Here's what happens behind-the-scenes: a company receives your paper resume and they place it in a scanner that takes a picture of your resume. When you fax your resume to a company, the fax machine will act just like a scanner and create a file with a picture of your resume. A software program called OCR (optical character recognition) is then applied to that picture of your resume. The OCR software tries to identify parts of that picture that represent letters, numbers, and symbols. Knowing that recruiters and employers use this technology means that you must create your print resume to operate within the technical capabilities of the software. The software capability improves almost monthly, but that doesn't mean that every company always has the latest version of the best program, so we will err on the side of conservatism. Here are some general rules to follow to assure that your print resume is indeed scannable:

- Always avoid paper with a dark or even medium color, a colored border, heavy watermark, or graining—plain white paper is best.
- Be circumspect about adding borders around a document or around a section of text in the resume. The OCR software could identify the outline as a single character and omit the entire content of that section.
- Do not use columns—when scanned, the order of words will be out of sequence and that could hurt the effectiveness of your keyword sections.
- Do not use fonts smaller than 10 point; 12 point is ideal. If the employer experiences difficulty in scanning your resume you will not receive a polite phone call asking you to resubmit it.

When Should You Use a Scannable Resume?

Anytime you are mailing or faxing your resume to a company, assume that it will be scanned. Always use the "fine mode" setting when faxing your resume.

This will result in better resolution and allows the OCR to optimize the digital conversion. Many companies do not print faxed resumes, but instead convert them directly to digital. Also, most PCs now come with standard software that allows the user to fax and receive documents without ever having to print them.

The Difference Between Scannable and Electronic Resumes

An electronic resume is one built solely on a computer, sent via e-mail to the recipient, and, once received, usually downloaded directly into an employer's resume database. Whereas an electronic resume is only digital, a scannable resume is a paper resume that is converted to digital. There are three different ways you can send your resume electronically:

1. ASCII or plain text
2. Formatted, usually as an Microsoft Word document
3. Web-based/HTML

You may not need all three, but you will definitely need at least the first two. Here are descriptions of all three:

1. *Plain text or ASCII:* This is the simplest version of the three. We're talking just the basics: only text; letters, numbers and a few symbols found on your keyboard. ASCII (American Standard Code for Information Interchange) resumes are important because this is the only format that any computer type, whether PC or Macintosh, can read. The reader will not need a word-processing program such as Microsoft Word or Word Perfect, and their software or printer compatibility needn't be considered.
   An ASCII resume looks like the average e-mail message you receive.
2. *Formatted Electronic Resume:* This is a resume that is also sent via e-mail, but as an attachment. A formatted electronic resume is usually your resume as created in a word-processing document, most often in MSWord, which has become the standard WP format. It is normal when sending resumes, without a prior conversation to determine that the recipient expects the attachment, to paste your resume into the body of your e-mail with a notation that a copy is also attached. You paste yoru resume into the body of the e-mail and attach it as an MSWord document because many employers will not open attachments from people

they do not know, for fear of viruses. It is sensible to work with Microsoft Word, which is the world's word-processing program of choice.

3. *Web or HTML Resume*: A Web resume is not a "must have" for everyone. Essentially, a Web resume is an electronically formatted resume housed on the Internet. There are some advantages; for example, you can include audio and video clips, music, and pictures. If you are in a creative profession and would typically have a portfolio, a Web resume can allow access to your work samples. Likewise, if you are a Web page design professional or HTML guru, then, by all means, use the Internet to show your creative and electronic abilities. Otherwise, a web-based or HTML resume is a nice thing to have but not mandatory. My advice is to get your MSWord resume completed along with a text version, get your job search up to speed, and then decide if you need to develop this third variation.

How to Convert Your Formatted Resume to ASCII

Converting your resume into a text or ASCII version is simple. To start the ASCII conversion process, go to your "My Documents" or "My Briefcase" folders and create a series of new folders to store the various documents you will be creating.

Job search folders

As you can see, our typical job seeker, Susan O'Malley, has created a section within the "My Documents" folder and then created a series of folders within that to hold her "Resumes," "Cover Letters," "Job Descriptions," etc. Within each of these folders, she will need to name her documents appropriately—even creating additional subfolders.

Next, open your resume using your word-processing program. The most widely used is Microsoft Word, so that's what we'll use in our example. Copy the entire document by choosing "select all" from the "edit" pull-down menu, then, by choosing "copy" from the "edit" pull-down menu or Ctrl+C for Windows.

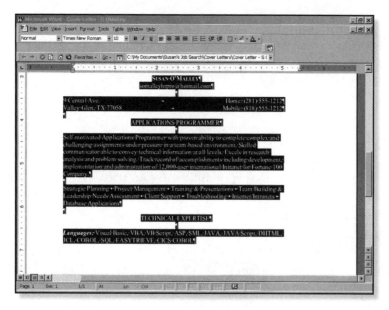

Converting your resume

Then, open a new document in your word processor. Set the margins to 1.5 inches on both right and left sides, which equates to about 60 characters per line depending on type size and font. The number of characters in each line must be limited because electronic screens are restricted to that viewing width; consequently you do not want text to "wrap off the screen."

Setting margins

Next you are going to paste the resume you just copied into this new document. Simply choose "paste" from the "edit" pull-down menu, or Ctrl+V for Windows. Initially, the document will look very similar to your previous resume, but we will modify it further. Do not panic if your one-page resume just became two pages. If you had small margins, the shorter line length will create a longer resume.

Go to the "edit" pull-down menu and choose "select all." Now you are going to change the font type and size. To do this, choose "font" from the "format" pull-down menu and change the font type to Times New Roman or Courier. Change the size to 12 point.

Changing the font

Now, we need to save this new document using the "save as" command. Select the document type as "text only," and rename the document. Let's call it "Text Resume 1" and even put it in a new folder—let's use Susan's resume folder.

Pay attention: you will get a message box saying that you will change your formatting that asks if you want to continue. Answer "yes." An ASCII or text-based resume strips out formatting that could make your document difficult to read. Notice that the file name of the resume no longer ends with *.doc*; it now ends in *.txt*, meaning text-based document.

The document has lost many of its features and "pretty looks." Spacing is also altered considerably. You will want to spend time proofreading this new document, and making necessary adjustments. Any tabs, tables, or columns that you used in your formatted version may wreak havoc on your new text version. In order to prevent lines from wrapping or flowing down to the next line, you need to make your document flush left by removing empty spaces and tabs.

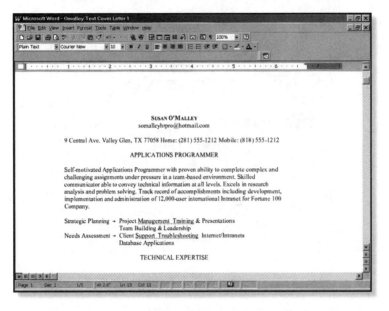

A text-only resume

You will need to use ALL CAPS for section headers and to replace things that were bolded or underlined. Likewise, all of your bullets will be gone and you will have to adjust the spacing to create a new type of emphasis, or use characters on your keyboard such as "*". Remember that the goal is to get your resume downloaded into the databases of potential employers and then retrieved by the software. A better-looking paper resume can be sent after your first electronic contact with the manager, Human Resource professional, or recruiter.

Once properly edited, Susan's resume looks like this:

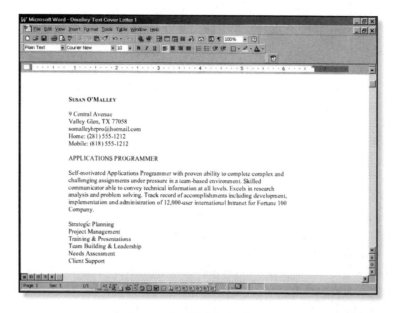

A properly edited text resume

Before you send your resume, take time to save and proofread it carefully. Send your electronic cover letters and resume attachments to yourself, and to a friend, or your family member. Ask them for printouts of your practice e-mail messages and resumes to ensure that what you intended to send is actually what was received. Often this exercise will help you find mistakes, bloopers, or larger problems incurred during the conversion process; you shouldn't be finding spelling errors at this stage, and if you do, reward yourself with a smack up the side of the head for being sloppy.

Posting Your Resume, and Tricks to Online Questionnaires

Job sites have evolved tremendously over the last few years. There are literally thousands of job boards on the Internet, from mega sites to very focused sites that cater to a specific geographical location or profession.

Most of the larger sites offer free job delivery and resume posting services. You just select a few criteria, and job listings matching your specifications are automatically sent to your inbox. With the resume banks, your resume goes into a database for employers and recruiters to search by keywords, when there is a match you will be notified. If you are already employed, these sites allow you to stay on top of your career by keeping abreast of available opportunities in your direction of choice.

If you are currently in a full-blown job search, spend plenty of time browsing the job site itself. Keep your search criteria broad-based; you might even eliminate salary or geographical requirements when you begin. This enables you to uncover the maximum number of companies and recruiters in your industry. Even if the specific job opening isn't a great match or you aren't planning to relocate, you'll be able to check your resume against the requirements being advertised and the keywords being used to describe them; additionally, you'll become aware of these companies for future reference.

Internet resume posting allows an employer to find you while you are sleeping, playing, or working—it never sleeps. It sounds great and it works—if you understand the rules of the game.

Not all job sites and resume banks work the same way. On some sites, you simply copy and paste your resume like we've done in the prior examples. On other sites, you'll have to complete a proscribed profile or questionnaire that creates your online presence at that site.

These sites are usually free for job hunters, though an exception would be the executive sites, which typically charge a monthly membership fee. The job sites work with prospective employers to develop better screening tools, since the employers are the paying clients. By making job seekers fill out very specific profiles and questionnaires, employers have more specific data with which to screen.

When filling out a profile or questionnaire, keep these two things in mind:

1. What is my audience? Who will be reading this?
2. What are they really asking me?

When a site or a company does not want your resume, but does want you to complete a registration or profile process, they are looking to provide employers with effective screening tools. Let's take a closer look at the Monster resume builder as an effective screening tool, and what you can do to make it work to your benefit.

Once on the site, Susan follows the buttons for new users, and begins to set up her free "My Monster Account," filling out her name, address, career level, and degree, which are all required fields. When a field is required, it must be completed or your enrollment process stops. These are the hardest fields to complete, as they can force you to divulge more information than you want.

Setting up a new account at Monster.com

As with most "free" sites, Susan is immediately asked to sign up for newsletters and advertisements.

One of the nice features of Monster.com is that it allows you to maintain five different resumes/profiles; this is particularly useful when you have a broad background and can do a number of different jobs. Use this opportunity! Make some of your profiles very specific, and make others very broad in order to increase your visibility.

The Monster resume builder is typical in that it breaks up the resume, and, in this case, a profile, into a number of specific topics. Topics include things like Career Objective, Target Job, Target Location, Salary, Work Status, Skills, References, and Education. These are all common topics covered in most online profiles and registrations.

One of the very first screens Susan is asked to complete includes her "Title" and "Career Objective." The site offers examples to help you fill in answers to these questions—but their advice is not in your best interest. Remember, the employer pays the job sites for advertising space and they are trying to help the employer screen you out. Monster advises you to list a specific position title and, in the "Career Objective" field, write out a short professional profile and list your career goals.

If you want to increase your visibility, then you need to think beyond these questions. This is all about keywords. Instead of completing the "Title" field, Susan, noticing that this field holds up to 60 characters, has the opportunity to add another 37 characters besides her actual title. The best way for her to make use of that space is to list the computer languages, software, and systems that she knows.

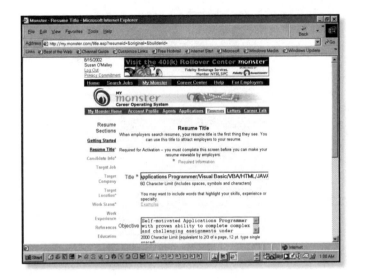

A Monster.com online resume

According to the comments under the "Objective" field, Monster tells us that it holds up to 2,000 characters. That's half of Susan's resume! Following the site's examples by listing a two- or three-sentence objective would be wasting an opportunity to inundate employers with favorable keywords. Remember, it is not just the mention of a keyword that is counted by the software; the number of times keywords are repeated counts into the grand total. So, from her resume, Susan copied her professional profile, her language, software, and systems expertise into this field, and still had room for a list of all her accomplishments with past employers. When answering these questions, you are building your resume all over again, so use your keywords and highlight past successes that will attract the attention of database search software and, consequently, prospective employers.

As Susan continues to complete her profile, she comes to a section that breaks down her "target job." The important element to notice here is that you are not always limited to one answer—even in the case of checkboxes. For her desired job type, Susan can select both *Employee* and *Temporary/Contract/Project*, and even *Intern* if she wanted. It's a good idea to test the site to see if you can select more than one answer. Never assume you are limited—not even if the directions on the screen indicate that you are.

Choosing a target job

Susan was also asked about her salary requirements. We all dread this question in a pre-employment screening. Although the salary question is sandwiched between "required" fields, it is not required. So Susan can, and should, leave it blank. In instances where you are forced to answer the question, answer in terms of a range as you would in an interview situation.

The last question on this screen allows Susan 500 characters to describe her ideal job. This is not a space to really answer that question; it is more an opportunity to use keywords to describe the kind of job you can land and in which you can succeed. Remember that the more keywords that appear in your profile, the higher on the list it will appear; and the more likely it is to be read by a human being.

Now the dreaded relocation question—check to make sure that this is a required field. If it isn't, don't answer it. If it is, keep your answer broad. Any company or recruiter only interested in local candidates will use the address on your resume as the search parameter.

Here's the rule: you can always say "no," but you can't say "yes" unless you've been asked. For the right job, the right opportunity, and the right money, we all might move to Timbuktu. Besides, what isn't right for your career today may be tailor-made for your situation a year from today; you never know what the future may hold and you need to be prepared.

Choosing a company

Notice that while the page is optional, the "Company Category" field is designated "required" by the red asterisk. Most people have probably completed this screen assuming that it is required. Read every word to distinguish between what is optional and required and how much information can be included or excluded.

You are most likely to come across online questionnaires and profiles in these situations:

- Registering with a job site
- Posting with a job site
- Applying for a job within a company
- Registering with a recruitment firm

In each case, you must always consider who is asking you the question and why. They are trying to screen you in or out, so consider your responses carefully. Always read the instructions, avoid questions on salary and relocation if possible, and add as many keywords as possible. Proofread and spell-check everything you enter, and only post to sites that allow editing and updating.

Sending Your Resume Directly to Companies and Recruiters

The third way to distribute your resume via the Internet involves direct contact with companies and recruiters. There are a number of ways to use the Internet to help you locate companies and recruitment firms and appropriate executives within them; you'll find a wide range of Internet research resources at knockemdead .com. Once you are aware of a company in your industry or a recruitment firm that makes placements within your profession, why not make contact? You do not need a help-wanted ad to have a reason to get your credentials in front of hiring eyes.

The Internet is a particularly useful information resource—provided you know where to look. Luckily, sites and services exist to simplify our search.

If a Health Care/Medical Insurance Sales Manager went to *www.6figurejobs. com* and did a simple search for the keyword "insurance" he or she would get hundreds of results. The vast majority of hits would be for jobs of limited interest. However, just because you do not see a job advertised with your name on it where you happen to be looking today, that does not mean that particular company is not looking for someone like you. You can look at job postings simply as a way of identifying companies so that you can apply to them directly whether or not you have seen a relevant job posting. Instead of replying directly to the job postings, visit the company Web sites and browse there. Send a cover letter and your resume to specific individuals, or, failing that, send one blind into the HR department. Add this contact information to your database for future job-search efforts.

Many job sites offer pages listing all companies posting jobs with them. Usually, these lists link to those companies' job openings, or directly to their home pages. Look for this feature on every job site you enter; it can help you build your job search database and will serve to stop you relying solely on visible job postings.

There are many database sites that exist to help develop corporate intelligence, allowing you to search entire industries and develop long lists of companies and their executives. Free lists of recruiters can be found at Recruiters Online *(www.recruitersonline.com)* and at i-Recruit.com *(www.i-recruit.com)*.

A second use of this data is accumulating e-mail addresses in an address book or even in a Word document. Assemble an electronic cover letter suitable for a mass distribution to go with it, and "blast" your resume out there yourself. By utilizing the bcc (blind copy) feature on your e-mail software, you can e-mail 100 letters at a time—far more productive than individually.

A third option is hiring a company to do it for you. Several years ago, "resume blasting" services came into being. Their results are not too bad. Companies like ResumeBlaster *(www.resumeblaster.com)* will distribute your resume electronically (via e-mail). The cost depends on the number of people you intend to contact. It is important to receive a copy of the list of addresses being sent to, even if it adds to the cost of the service. This list allows you to follow up after the "blast," and you can enhance your career management database with it.

Keep in mind that whether you do the research on your own, or purchase it from another company, either process involves time or money—probably a bit of both. Treat it as an investment in your career management. While resume blasting companies were hot news when they first appeared, the promise hasn't always lived up to the hype; consider the option carefully. To my mind, just blasting resumes and cover letters out blind to companies doesn't provide a worthwhile return on the time and cost involved. The only situation where this is viable is mass e-mailing to the headhunting community.

Internet Job Search Strategies

The Internet is a powerful job search tool, and your approach in using it will make a difference in your success. No single job search method guarantees this success. The best approach is one that integrates networking, online job search, and all the other effective techniques addressed in *Knock 'em Dead: The Ultimate Job Seeker's Guide.*

The following list is a brief overview of strategies for Internet-based resume distribution.

- *The Blitz*—just like in football, send everyone to make the tackle. You are unemployed (or soon to be unemployed or graduating) and need a job ASAP. In this case, you have no concern for confidentiality and want maximum exposure and results. You should visit and post your resume to a selection of job sites including the majors, and also professional association and profession specific sites. You should "blast out" resumes to all the companies and recruiters on the databases you have accumulated from your research or purchase.
- *Focused Attack*—a much more focused version of the Blitz. Employed or unemployed, you will want to use a couple of the major job boards with more specialty sites, associations, and specific company site research. The focused attack could be as confidential as you decide to make it. It can also work well for those pursuing multiple potential career paths, or for those

interested in a career/industry change. If you are still employed but have informed your employer that you are looking for a change, then this is the perfect strategy for you.

- *Stealth Mode*—There are two types of job seekers fitting this strategy. The first is the employed seeker who understands the value of keeping a pulse on the job market. Only post confidential resumes, if any, and only utilize sites that deliver jobs to you. The second type of job seeker using this strategy is one who has identified his or her dream company or geographic area to work in. You are employed, and are using the Internet to monitor sites that this dream company posts to, in order to send them confidential resumes, research their executive bios, association members, and like information, in order to find an open door.

Whichever strategies you use, make the commitment and follow through. Remember, no single strategy is an absolute, surefire way to find a suitable job. Always use an integrated approach employing all of your online and offline resources.

The Internet encourages three primary methods of resume distribution:

1. Responding to help-wanted ads (job postings)
2. Posting your resume and credentials
3. Sending your resume directly to companies and recruiters

Any time you can grab human attention before the electronic system takes over, it is to your advantage. Two elements will help to get you there: the ability to use your cover letter and the subject line to garner attention, and circumventing the electronic system by sending your documents to specific individuals.

Since all e-mail messages you send are electronic versions of your cover letter, you may want to take a look at the companion book *Cover Letters That Knock 'em Dead*. Electronic cover letters are similar, but don't take the availability of unlimited space to make them longer, just as you would limit a paper cover letter to one page or three to five paragraphs, do the same with your e-mail cover letter.

Use keywords that illustrate your potential and examples of your accomplishments to prospective employers in this document as well. With a little practice, you can write short, powerful sentences, which will get your e-mail messages and attached resumes read. It's a smart idea to create cover letter templates that you can easily customize for each response (again, see *Cover Letters That Knock 'em Dead*).

The subject line is your first, and possibly only, chance to interest the initial reader enough to read your resume instead of forwarding it directly to a database. The key is to focus on a clear message stating the nature of your contact, hopefully giving them some incentive for interest. If you are responding to a job posting or print advertisement state the job posting number or job title, and where possible take an extra step to get yourself noticed.

Susan O'Malley has been using the Society for Human Resource Management career site and has found an appealing job posting in California. A vacation resort developer is seeking a Regional Human Resources Manager.

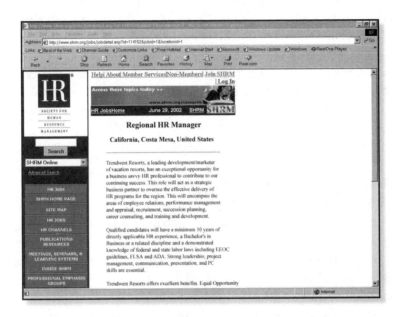

The job posting

This position requires ten years of experience, and the job description indicates that knowledge of employment laws such as EEOC, FLSA, and ADA are important. Susan is a good match.

This position has requested that correspondence be sent in the following manner:

"Candidates may apply by sending their resume to Trendwest Resorts, 9805 Willows Road, Redmond, WA 98052 or by e-mail to *pamelae@trendwestresorts.com*."

Responding by e-mail suggests technological adeptness, while a regular mail response offers another opportunity to get your resume brought to the top of the pile. You should do both.

Since the employer did not provide any additional directions, it is best for Susan to paste it into the body of the e-mail and attach also it as an MSWord document.

We want our electronic cover letter example to do three things: identify the purpose of sending this resume; emphasize why it deserves to be read; and get you an interview or next contact. Notice in the next figure how Susan has accomplished these things with her cover letter.

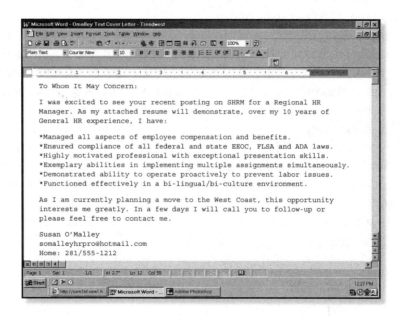

An e-mail compatible cover letter

She succinctly stated the purpose of her e-mail, hit her "hot points" to get the reader's attention, and requested the follow-up information. Before closing this document, Susan needs to copy the entire letter. She does this by choosing "select all" from the "edit" pull-down menu, then, by choosing "copy" from the "edit" pull-down menu or Ctrl+C for Windows.

The next step is to create the e-mail, insert the cover letter text and the text only version of her resume, and then attach the formatted MSWord resume. From her inbox, Susan will create a new message by choosing "compose" from the tabs along the top of the page. By placing her cursor within the message of the newly created e-mail, Susan can then paste the contents of her custom electronic cover letter in the message box. Simply choose "paste" from the "edit" pull-down menu or Ctrl+V for Windows.

With the cover letter safely pasted, turn your attention to addressing the e-mail to the proper recipient and establishing your subject line. From the job posting, you can copy and paste the e-mail to the address provided by the company. The subject line needs to be factual, professional, and intriguing. How about "Your next Reg HR Manager-EEOC, FLSA, & ADA exp" or "Reg HR Candidate-10 yrs exp w/EEOC, FLSA, & ADA." Remember, the subject line may get your resume an immediate review instead of automatic computer upload. Give it adequate thought; subject lines usually accommodate about thirty characters, so take advantage of this as Susan did.

Keep copies of all your correspondence. It's a good idea to keep track of exactly what you've sent out to avoid unnecessary repetitions. It also allows you to move messages from a general folder to a specific company-named folder once you have started a communication stream with an interested corporation.

Under the subject line of the new e-mail Susan created, there is a button for "Add/Edit Attachments." All programs will have a menu choice to insert documents; for example, in Microsoft Outlook, the paper clip icon designates the button for this function. Once you select this menu choice, you need to find the document that you want to attach. Follow the instructions on the screen. Once you have "browsed" to locate the file, it may have you select "open." In Hotmail, once you've browsed and found the file you must then select "attach." The name of your file will then appear in the attachment box.

Attachments

Before you send a message, recall the two points made earlier when Susan came across this job posting. First, the employer did offer a suggested resume format. The most popular format is the one we have chosen, but it is not 100 percent effective in the rare instances when an employer doesn't use Microsoft Word, or for some reason, cannot open the attachment. The sensible precaution you can always take is to paste your ASCII resume into the body of the e-mail, and attach your formatted Microsoft Word document, noting that you have done both in your e-mail cover letter.

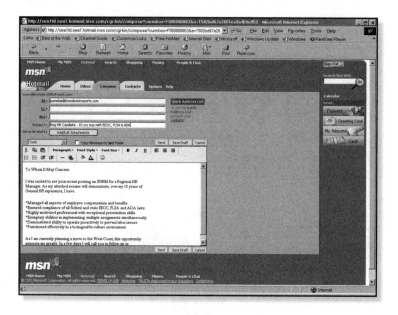

Sending the message

Your goal is not so much to get your resume launched into cyberspace, but to get it read by a human being. With company e-mail addresses, the Web site name of the company is often the part that comes after the person's username and the "@" symbol. In this case it is safe to assume that if we break up the e-mail address of *pamelae@trendwestresorts.com*, we can probably find the company's home page at *www.trendwestresorts.com*. If that doesn't work, you can use Google or another search engine to look for "Trendwest Resorts" (putting it in quotes will work best). You can then surf the site to look for a company career center, the bios and contacts for company executives, and press releases about their business.

Your mission here is finding other potential inroads, other people to whom you can pitch yourself. With a little effort, you could make a direct connection to your next potential boss, gather information that will help you ace an interview, and garner you your dream job. As they say, luck comes to those who make it happen.

Now if you see a job posting that requires you to blindly respond to the HR department, but through your research have been able to identify specific executives likely to be involved in the hiring cycle: you can approach them directly. When you do this, it is best not to note that you are attempting to circumvent established procedures. You can achieve your ends by any number of ways you will find in my cover letter book, and you'll see an example in just a couple of paragraphs.

COVER LETTERS

DO YOU EVER receive junk mail? Of course, you do. Who doesn't?

When the envelope is opened, your cover letter is the first thing seen. It can make an indelible first impression. Of course, your cover letter sets the tone for your candidacy, and done properly it will get your resume a careful examination.

Tons of junk mail arrives in your house mailbox over the years. Now, what do you do with the stuff marked "Occupant"? Either junk it without reading, or junk it after a quick glance. If you don't want this to be the fate of your resume, your cover letter is the best preventative tool you can employ.

Your cover letter is the personalizing factor in the presentation of an otherwise essentially impersonal document—your resume. A good cover letter sets the stage for the reader to accept your resume as something special.

The best way to start a cover letter is with someone's name, which alone dramatically increases the chances of it being read. It shows you have focus, and you can obviously do at least some degree of investigation. It also means you have someone to ask for by name when you do your follow-up—something important when you are interview hunting.

Your target is someone who can either hire you or refer you to another who can; a management title always offers you a more direct contact with the ultimate decision maker, but an HR name is just as good, for different reasons. The HR contact can't make the hiring decision (although he or she can have a strong influence), but their pivotal position makes them aware of other areas of the company that could use your skills. The moral is that any name is better than no name.

Your cover letter will either be sent to someone as a result of a prior conversation, or sent "cold"—with no prior conversation. You will see how to handle both these eventualities as we progress through the chapter. You can find a wealth of practical advice on all the different letters you can use in an effective job hunt in the companion volume *Cover Letters That Knock 'em Dead*.

Cover Letter Rules

The following four steps will help you create the body of the letter:

Step One

There are four basic building blocks to creating a productive cover letter, and the underlying rules of effective written communication embodied in these four steps can be applied to any memo or business letter you ever write.

Your first step is to grab your reader's ATTENTION. You do this with the appearance of your letter: the type is large and legible enough for others to read, it is free of misspellings and it is well laid out so that it is easy on the eye; and if that letter is going by mail rather than e-mail you grab attention by using quality stationery, and matching envelopes. This way your letter and resume will match and give an impression of balance and continuity (see Chapter 6, "The Final Product," for details on paper choice). When your message is crafted with this attention to detail, and convenience for the reader, it reflects the kind of professional who just might have something to say. Here is an example:

Recently I have been researching the leading local companies in data communications. My search has been for companies that are respected in the field, and who provide ongoing training programs. The name of DataLink Products keeps coming up as a top company.

I am an experienced voice and data communications specialist with a substantial background in IBM environments. If you have an opening for someone in this area you will see that my resume demonstrates a person of unusual dedication, efficiency, and drive.

My experience and achievements include:

- The complete redesign of a data communications network, projected to increase efficiency companywide by some 12 percent.
- The installation and troubleshooting of a Defender 1V callback security system.

I enclose a copy of my resume, and look forward to examining any of the ways you feel my background and skills would benefit DataLink Products. While I prefer not to use my employer's time taking personal calls at work, with discretion you can reach me on my cell phone at (213) 555-5555 to initiate contact. Let's talk!

Yours,

[SIGNATURE]
[TYPED NAME]

Step Two

Your second step is to generate INTEREST with the letter's content. The first opportunity you have to do this is by addressing the letter to someone by name (I explain research approaches to achieve this in *Knock 'em Dead: The Ultimate Job Seeker's Guide.* The first couple of sentences grab attention, and the rest of the paragraph introduces your candidacy. The secret is to introduce yourself with conviction, if you don't believe in the professional product that is you, how can you expect anyone else to believe?

Use research to get your letter off to a fast start; with Google and other search engines, anyone can search the Web for articles and visit the employer's own site. For example:

"I came across the attached/enclosed article in *Newsweek* magazine and thought it might interest you. It encouraged me to do a little research on your company. I am now convinced of two things: You are the kind of company I want to be associated with, and that I have the kind of qualifications you can use."

On a company's Web site, you will find lots of eye-opening information, including news and press clippings. You can use search engines to find interesting info about the company by typing in the company name as a keyword. Once you find a relevant article:

- With an e-mail, you paste the article and attach it.
- With a traditional letter, you enclose a copy of the article.

Of course, not every company you approach will have been mentioned in *Newsweek*, but if there is no mention in the press the chances are still good that their Web site can give you some insight that can be turned to advantage. Here are some real-life examples that you can adapt to your own needs:

"I have been following the performance of your fund in *Mutual Funds Newsletter*. The record over the last three years shows strong portfolio management. With my experience working for one of your competitors, I know I could make significant contributions . . ."

"Recently I have been researching the local _____ industry. My search has been for companies that are respected in the field and . . . which prize a commitment to professional development. I am such an individual and you are clearly such a company."

"Within the next few weeks I will be moving from New York to _____. Having researched the companies in _____, I know that you are the company I want to talk to . . ."

"The state of the art in _____ changes so rapidly that it is tough for most professionals to keep up. I am the exception, and I am eager to bring my experience to bear for your company."

Step Three

Now, having built a bridge between you and the reader, your the intent is to turn that INTEREST into a DESIRE to learn more. First, tie yourself to a specific job category or work area. Use phrases like:

"I am writing because . . ." or "My reason for contacting you . . ."

". . . should this be the case, you may be interested to know . . ."

"If you are seeking a _____, you will be interested to know . . ."

"I would like to talk to you about your staffing needs for _____ and how I might be able to contribute to your department's goals."

"If you have an opening for someone in this area, you will see that my resume demonstrates a person of unusual dedication, efficiency, and drive."

You might next call attention to your merits with a short paragraph that highlights one or two of your special contributions or achievements:

"I have an economics background from Columbia and a quantitative analysis approach to market fluctuations. This combination has enabled me consistently to pick the new technology flotations that are the backbone of a growth-oriented technology fund."

Similar statements applicable to your area of expertise will give your letter more personal punch. Include any qualifications, contributions, and attributes that prove you are someone with professional commitment and talent to offer. If an advertisement, or a telephone conversation with a potential employer, reveals an aspect of a particular job opening that is not addressed in your resume, you can use the cover letter to fill in the gaps. For example:

"I notice from your advertisement that A/V training experience would be a plus. In addition to the qualifications stated in my enclosed resume, I have over five years of experience writing and producing sales and management training materials in both these media."

It is through this third step that you want the reader to say, "Wow, this man/ woman really understands the job. I need to read on and learn more."

Step Four

Here's where your letter turns a DESIRE to know more into ACTION. The action you're shooting for is that the reader will dash straight on to your resume, and then call you in for an interview. You achieve this with brevity—always leave the reader wanting more. Offer too much information and you may be ruled out of consideration, so whet the reader's appetite but leave them asking questions.

Make it clear to the reader that you want to talk. Explain when, where, and how you can be contacted. You can also be *proactive* by telling the reader that you intend to follow up at a certain point in time if contact has not been established by then. Just as you worked to create a strong opening, make sure your closing carries the same conviction. It is the reader's last personal impression of you, so make it strong, make it tight, and make it obvious that you are serious about entering into meaningful conversation.

Useful phrases include:

"It would be a pleasure to give you more information about my qualifications and experience . . ."

"I look forward to discussing our mutual interests further . . ."

"While I prefer not to use my employer's time taking personal calls at work, with discretion I can be reached at _____."

"I will be in your area around the 20th, and will call you prior to that date. I would like to arrange . . ."

"I hope to speak with you further and will call the week of _____ to follow up."

"The chance to meet with you would be a privilege and a pleasure, so to this end I shall call you on _____."

"I look forward to speaking with you further and will call in the next few days to see when our schedules will permit a face-to-face meeting."

"May I suggest a personal meeting where you can have the opportunity to examine the person behind the resume?"

"My credentials and achievements are a matter of record that I hope you will examine in depth when we meet . . . you can reach me at _____."

"I look forward to examining any of the ways you feel my background and skills would benefit [name of organization]. I look forward to hearing from you."

"Resumes help you sort out the probables from the possibles, but they are no way to judge the caliber of an individual. I would like to meet you and demonstrate that I have the professional personality that makes for a successful _____."

"I expect to be in your area on Tuesday and Wednesday of next week and wonder which day would be best for you. I will call to determine. In the meantime, I would appreciate your treating my application as confidential, since I am currently employed."

"With my training and hands-on experience, I know I can contribute to _____, and want to talk to you about it in person. When may we meet?"

"After reading my resume, you will know something about my background. Yet, you will still need to determine whether I am the one to help you with current problems and challenges. I would like an interview to discuss my ability to contribute to your company."

"You can reach me at [home/alternate#] to arrange an interview. I know that your time investment in meeting with me will be repaid amply."

"Thank you for your time and consideration; I hope to hear from you shortly."

"May I call you for an interview in the next few days?"

"A brief phone call will establish whether or not we have mutual interest. Recognizing the demands of your schedule, I will make that call within the week."

Some people feel it is powerful in the closing to state a date—"I'll call you on Friday if we don't speak before"—or a date and time—"I'll call you on Friday morning at 10 A.M. if we don't speak before," when they will follow-up with a phone call. The logic is that you demonstrate that your intent is serious, that you are organized, and that you plan your time effectively (all desirable behavioral traits).

On the other hand, at least one "authority" has said that an employer would be offended by being "forced" to sit and await your call. Frankly, with thirty years of involvement in the hiring process, I have never met anyone who felt constrained to wait by the phone for such a call. What sometimes does get noticed, though, is the person who doesn't follow through on commitments as promised. Therefore, if you use this approach, keep your promise.

Writing the Cover Letter

Keep your sentences short—an average of twenty words per sentence is about right. Likewise, your paragraphs should be concise and to the point. In cover letters, paragraphs can often be a single sentence, and should never be longer than five lines. This makes the page more inviting for the harried reader, by providing adequate white space to ease eyestrain.

Short words work best, as they speak more clearly than those polysyllabic behemoths that say more about your self-image problems than your abilities. A good approach is to think in terms of sending a telegram, where every word must work its hardest.

While abiding by accepted grammatical rules, punctuate for readability rather than strictly following *The Elements of Style* or the *Chicago Manual of Style*. Get by on commas, dashes—and periods. And in between the punctuation marks, use the action verbs and phrases that breathe life into your work.

Cover Letter Examples

Here's an example that borrows and adapts phrases from the last few pages, you can write a dynamite cover letter with just such a "cut and paste" technique. Then make the adjustments necessary to customize your letter based on your professional and your knowledge of the target company. *Cover Letters That Knock 'em Dead* will give you hundreds of pages of powerful phrases to harvest for your own use.

James Sharpe
9 Central Avenue • Los Angeles, CA 93876
(516) 555-1212

November 16, 20–

Dear Mr. Bell,

Recently I have been researching the leading local companies in data communications. My search has been for companies that are respected in the field, and who provide ongoing training programs. DataLink Products keeps coming up as a top company.

I am an experienced voice and data communications specialist with a substantial background in IBM environments. *If you have an opening for someone in this area you will see that my resume demonstrates a person of unusual dedication, efficiency, and drive.*

My experience and achievements include:

• Complete redesign of a data communications network, projected to increase efficiency companywide some 12 percent;
• The installation and troubleshooting of a Defender IV callback security system for a dial-up network.

I have enclosed a copy of my resume, and look forward to examining any of the ways you feel my background and skills would benefit DataLink Products. While I prefer not to use my employer's time taking personal calls at work, with discretion I can be reached at (213) 555-5555 to initiate contact. Let's talk!

Yours truly,

James Sharpe

James Sharpe

In response to an advertisement, here is an example using a different selection of phrases:

JANE SWIFT
9 Central Avenue, Sunnyside, NY 11104

Dear Ms. Pena,

I have always followed the performance of your fund in *Mutual Funds Newsletter.*

Recently, your notice regarding a Market Analyst in Investor's Business Daily *caught my eye—and your company name caught my attention—because your record over the last three years shows exceptional portfolio management. With my experience with one of your competitors, I know I could make significant contributions.*

I would like to talk to you about your personnel needs and how I would be able to contribute to your department's goals.

An experienced market analyst, I have an economics background and a strong analytical approach to market fluctuations. This combination has enabled me to consistently pick the new technology flotations that are the backbone of the growth-oriented mutual fund.

For example, I first recommended Fidelity Magellan six years ago. More recently, my clients have been strongly invested in Pacific Horizon Growth (in the high-risk category), and Fidelity Growth and Income (for the cautious investor).

Those following my advice over the last six years have benefited from funds that consistently outperformed the market.

I know that resumes help you sort out the probables from the possibles, but they are no way to judge the personal caliber of an individual. I would like to meet with you and demonstrate that, along with the credentials, I have the personality that makes for a successful team player.

Yours faithfully,

Jane Swift

Jane Swift

Here is an example of a cover letter sent as a result of a prior telephone conversation:

James Sharpe
9 Central Avenue • Los Angeles, CA 93876
(516) 555-1212

Dear Ms. _____,

I am writing in response to our telephone conversation on Friday the 10th regarding a new- and used-car sales management position.

With a successful track record in both new- and used-car sales, and as a Sales Manager, I believe I am ideally suited for the position we discussed. My exposure to the different levels of the sales process (I started at the bottom and worked my way up) has enabled me to effectively meet the challenges and display the leadership you require.

I am a competitive person professionally. Having exercised the talents and skills required to exceed goals and set records as a Sales Manager, I believe in measuring performance by results.

I would appreciate a meeting where I could discuss in more detail my sales and management philosophy, and capabilities. Please call me at your earliest convenience to arrange a personal meeting.

Sincerely yours,

James Sharpe

James Sharpe

Here is an example of a cover letter to a headhunter:

James Sharpe
9 Central Avenue • Los Angeles, CA 93876
(516) 555-1212

Dear Mr. _____,

As you may be aware, the management structure at XYZ Inc. will be reorganized in the near future. While I am enthusiastic about the future of the company under its new leadership, I have elected to make this an opportunity for change and professional growth.

My experience lends itself to a management position in any medium-sized service firm, but I am open to other opportunities. Although I would prefer to remain in Los Angeles, I would be amenable to relocation if the opportunity warrants it. I am currently earning $65,000 a year.

I have taken the liberty of enclosing my resume for your review. Should you be conducting a search for someone with my background—at the present time or in the near future—I would greatly appreciate your consideration. I would be happy to discuss my background more fully with you on the phone or in a personal interview.

Very truly yours,

James Sharpe

James Sharpe

The Executive Briefing

The executive briefing is a different and dramatically effective form of cover letter, whenever you have some information about a job opening from a help-wanted ad, an online job posting, or a prior conversation. This kind of letter gets right to the point and makes life easy for the reader. Why send an executive briefing?

1. It quickly matches stated requirements against the skills you bring to the table, making analysis much easier for the reader

2. The initial resume screener in Human Resources might not have an in-depth understanding of the job or its requirements, so the executive briefing helps match an open requirement directly to your abilities. This can be a real help to someone working on fifty or more different openings at a time.

3. Your general resume invariably needs customizing for any specific job. (Overly broad resumes are like "one-size-fits-all" clothes—one size usually fits none.) The executive briefing allows you to fill in the gaps in a succinct and helpful manner.

4. Imagine for a moment that a great opportunity comes your way, but your resume is somewhat (or more than somewhat) out of date and you have to send something out immediately to take advantage of the opportunity of a lifetime. The executive briefing allows you to bring that work history right up to date.

An executive briefing can also help you through a screening and multiple interview cycle. Let me explain: you will be interviewed by a number of people, not all of whom can be expected to have a thorough understanding of the needs of the job—perhaps surprising but nevertheless true. When this happens, the problems begin.

A manager says, "Spend a few minutes with this candidate and tell me what you think." This means that sometimes other interviewers do not have any way to qualify you fairly and specifically for the needs of the job. While the manager will be looking for specific skills relating to projects at hand, the personnel department will be trying to match your skills to the vagaries of the job-description manual.

Also, by taking multiple copies of your resume and the briefing, carefully stapled together, you guarantee that everyone with whom you interview will have the job's specific requirements and your matching skills front and center when they sit down with you.

The executive briefing, which introduces you resume, as well as customizing and supplementing it, solves these problems with its layout. It looks like this:

From: top10acct@aol.com
Subject: **Re: Accounting Manager**
Date: February 18, 2006 10:05:44 PM EST
To: rlstein@McCoy.com

Dear Ms. Stein,

I have nine years of accounting experience and am responding to your recent posting for an Accounting Manager on Careerbuilder. Please allow me to highlight my skills as they relate to your stated requirements.

Your Requirements	My Experience
Accounting degree, 4 years exp	Obtained a C.A. degree in 2001 and have over four years' experience as an Accounting Manager
Excellent people skills and leadership	Effectively managed a staff of 24; ability to motivate staff including supervisors.
Strong administrative and analytical	Assisted in the development of a base reference skills-library with Microsoft Excel for 400 clients.
Good communication skills	Trained new supervisors and staff via daily coaching sessions, communication meetings, and technical skill sessions.

My resume, pasted below and attached in MSWord, will flesh out my general background. I hope this executive briefing helps you use your time effectively today. I am ready to make a move, hope we can talk soon.

Sincerely,

Joe Black
Joe Black

The executive briefing assures that each resume you send out addresses the job's specific needs and that every interviewer at that company will be interviewing you for the same job. It provides a comprehensive picture of a thorough professional, plus a personalized, fast, and easy-to-read synopsis that details exactly how you can help with an employer's needs.

The use of an executive briefing is naturally restricted to jobs you have discovered through your own efforts or seen advertised. It is obviously not appropriate when the requirements of a specific job are unavailable.

A BALANCED JOB SEARCH

IN A COMPETITIVE market, you need to make use of every tool that you can to land that ideal job; you cannot rely on just sending resumes to postings on Internet job sites.

Companies are always looking for employees. Even a company with no growth rate can still be expected (based on national averages) to experience a 12 percent turnover in staff over the course of a year. In other words, every company has openings.

A man who goes fishing and puts one hook in the water has only one chance of catching any one of the millions of fish in the sea; a man with two hooks in the water has double the chances of getting a bite, so the more hooks you have in the water, the better your chances of getting bites.

There are many, many ways to get interviews using the Internet, apart from responding to job postings; there are proven and effective techniques for networking, tools to research and approach employers directly, productive ways to use newspapers and magazines, techniques for tapping into the different headhunter communities, and many more, but no single channel of search is a guaranteed silver bullet. Any one of them could turn up the ideal opportunity for you and your future, so your plan of attack should embrace as many of these approaches as is practical to your situation.

I have touched on distribution of your resume as much as space will allow me in these pages, but without doubling the size of the book I need to refer you to *Knock 'em Dead: The Ultimate Job Seeker's Guide*, a book devoted to developing interviews by all practical means possible and then turning them into job offers. Your resume is an integral part of every single approach to the job search approach and continues its job throughout the interview and selection cycle.

It may surprise you that the role of your resume doesn't end with helping you get a foot in the door. If you followed my advice to focus your resume first on a specific target job, and then went about deconstructing the deliverables of that job from relevant recruitment advertising, you will have a resume that not only opens doors, but one that helps you prepare for the interview cycle.

After all, you created a job description based on those developed by employers and your resume reflects this focus. Consequently you already know the areas that employers are going to want to discuss and you know what you have to offer in these areas; with this blueprint you can set about preparing for the toughest of interviews with a degree of self-confidence. Because your resume has been built with the end user in mind, tailored to their needs and reflective of their language, there is a much greater likelihood that your resume will already have set a positive tone for your meetings and may well be used as a roadmap for the interviewers' questions.

Always take multiple copies of your resume with you to interviews. Often you can attach it to those annoying application forms and then just write on the form "See attached resume." You can have one on your lap during the interview to refer to, as the interviewer has one on his desk; it makes you look organized and helps to keep you from doing anything awkward or socially unacceptable with your hands. You can also offer copies to subsequent interviewers.

Your Knock 'em Dead resume will even work for you long after the last interview is finished. Right before the hiring decision is made, hiring managers usually sit down with the dossiers on leading candidates as a last refresher, so that a properly constructed resume can indeed not only open doors, prepare you for the interview and guide the course of the interview, it can also be your last and most powerful spokesperson. It is this agglomeration of reasons that makes the careful development of a properly focused resume such a valuable exercise for your future.

Your resume's impact goes far beyond opening doors and is well worth the investment of time it will take to get it right. Now take a little of that time to read through all the samples with your highlighter, flagging those phrases, words, and layouts that you feel might work for you, when adapted to your profession and particular work experience.

This probably won't be the last time you execute a job search, but invest yourself properly in understanding all the component parts of a successful plan of attack, and your future steps up the ladder of success will be the better for it.

THE RESUMES

THE RESUMES ON the following pages are based on the genuine articles, the ones that really did the trick for someone who had to translate his or her fantastic skills and background into a single, compelling document. Whether or not your background is represented in the following sample, use the resumes reproduced here as a starting point for composing your own.

Clinical Nurse Assistant

To emphasize Chantile's objective, a title was used in place of a statement along with a tag line to highlight the medical units where she has worked. Her jobs are grouped together to make it easier to read while allowing the resume to remain on one page.

Chantile Fausett

500 La Villa • Brentwood, New York 11717 • (631) 555-2233 • ERNurse@med.net

CLINICAL NURSE ASSISTANT

ER...Shock/Trauma...Immediate Care...Triage

- Two years experience as a Clinical Nurse Assistant in ER, Shock/Trauma, Immediate Care and Triage units.
- Hardworking and energetic; adapt easily to change, stressful environments, and flexible work schedules.
- Maintain strong observation, assessment, and intervention skills essential to providing competent patient care.
- Advocate for patients/family rights; effectively communicate a patient's needs and concerns to medical team.

Education

Western Community College, Brentwood, New York
Currently enrolled in Liberal Arts Program with a concentration in Nursing, 2005 – Present
Coursework: Anatomy and Physiology, Chemistry, Psychology, Sociology, Statistics

North Brentwood School of Nursing, Brentwood, New York
Clinical Assistant Skills Upgrade Program, 2007

Licenses & Certifications

New York State Certified Clinical Nurse Assistant, 2005
Basic EKG and Phlebotomy

Professional Experience

Clinical Nurse Assistant, North Brentwood Hospital, Brentwood, New York	4/04 – Present
—prior positions: Hospital Attendant; Pharmacist Assistant	Evening/Night Shifts
Pharmacist Assistant, One Way Pharmacy, West Islip, New York	6/02 – 10/03
Customer Service Representative, Safeway Transportation, Islip, New York	5/02 – 6/03

- Work with a team of nurses and physicians throughout Emergency Room, Shock/Trauma, Immediate Care, and Triage departments for Brentwood Hospital, one of the only Level I Trauma hospitals on Long Island.
- Care for up to 200 patients per shift within a 29-bed Emergency Room Unit, and for patients in a 7-bed Trauma Unit; assist with interbating of patients, life support systems, and general postmortem procedures.
- Provide direct patient care in areas of vital signs, phlebotomy, EKGs, treatment of surgical wounds, gynecological examinations, Activities of Daily Living, and patient transportation within the hospital.
- Prepare patients for transfer to all critical care units, demonstrating quick thinking skills and ability to multitask while remaining focused and calm under pressure.
- Under the direction of the staff nurse, perform initial assessments of patients upon admission within a fast-paced Triage unit, and establish a Plan-of-Care for all patients.
- Assist orthopedic physicians with splinting, casting, positioning, and set up of tractions.
- Closely monitor and report changes in patients' conditions and malfunctioning of medical equipment.

Registered Nurse

Cheryl used this resume to land her first RN position right out of college.

Cheryl Bloom, R.N.

89 Pine Road • Monrovia, NY 95777 • (555) 555-5555

Registered Nurse

✓ Strongly motivated graduate with experience in hospital, sub-acute and other health care settings.
✓ Clinical skills combine with dedication to excellent patient care, compassion, and professionalism to integrate patients' medical and emotional care.
✓ Able to relate to patients quickly and work effectively with physicians, peers and other health care professionals. Conscientious, team-oriented and eager to learn.

Education, Licensure and Certification

B.A. in Nursing, 2005
Chenneworth College, Croton, NY

Registered Nurse, New York State License, 2006

Basic Life Support with Automatic External Defibrillator, American Heart Association
CPR, American Heart Association
Certified Nursing Assistant, New York Nursing Assistant Registry, 2003

Additional: Math and Sciences courses, Flynn Community College, Monrovia, NY

Areas of Knowledge & Skills

- Physical Assessments	- Dispensing Medications/Intravenous Therapy
- Vital Signs/Blood Glucose	- Documentation/Care Maps
- Catheter Insertion	- Nasopharengeal & Oral Suctioning
- Finger Sticks	- Application of Dressings/Wound Care
- Patient & Family Education	- Cast Care/Pin Care/Traction Care/Tracheotomy Care

Clinical Training

Acquired hands-on clinical experience and knowledge in nursing procedures while completing several rotations at the following facilities. Experience with patients ranging from pediatric to geriatric.

Medical-Surgical	Rockport General Hospital
OB/GYN	Melville Memorial Hospital
Pediatric	Montessori School
Gerontology	Evergreen Health Care Center, Mediplex, Kimberly Hall, Meadowbrook

Employment in Healthcare

Patient Care Technician – Jackson Memorial Hospital, Croton, NY 2003–present
Provide post-operative care to patients on an 80-bed Medical-Surgical Unit. Diverse responsibilities include: monitoring vital signs, blood glucose and tube intake/output, collecting specimens, assisting with personal hygiene and feeding, and recording patient status. Transport patients to medical procedures and operate portable electrocardiogram. Educate patients and family members on home care.

Prior Employment

Wait Staff, Calinda's Restaurant, Monrovia, NY   1998–2005

Earned reputation for dependability, accuracy and delivering superior customer service by providing well-timed, professional service. Demonstrated skills in communication, organization and problem solving, as well as ability to work efficiently in a fast-paced environment. Gained computer skills.

Registered Nurse

Kate-Lynne went back to school for RN certification and needed a resume to highlight her new degree as well as her previous experience as an LPN and Certified Nurses Aide.

KATE-LYNNE KENNEDY, RN

102 Fulton Street
San Francisco, CA 94117

Tel: 415-984-8740
kate-lynne@msn.com

PROFILE

Recent RN graduate with over 10 years experience in healthcare and nursing profession. Comprehensive knowledge of nursing procedures and committed to delivering quality patient care. Successful in managing time and prioritizing tasks. Communicate well with staff, family, and patients. Punctual, reliable, and able to be counted on in a crisis.

~ Awarded scholarship from the <u>Long-Term Care Federation</u> for continued studies in nursing.

EDUCATION, LICENSURE, AND CERTIFICATIONS

Bachelor of Science in Nursing, May, 2006
University of California, San Francisco, School of Nursing, San Francisco, CA
License # 394-6568

Associates in Science, Nurse Education, 1997
Evergreen Valley College, San Jose, CA

Licensed Practical Nurse, California
License # 485-0710

CPR, The American Heart Association, 1997

PROFESSIONAL EXPERIENCE

MENDELSOHN HOUSE – San Francisco, CA   2001–2004
Charge Nurse
Provided quality patient care in a 200-bed residential nursing facility. Supervised Certified Nursing Assistants, Rehabilitation Aides, and assisted in training new licensed staff. Performed patient assessments, developed care plans, and coordinated with other disciplines including: physical therapy, occupational therapy, dietary, activities, and consult with psychologists, pharmacists, and social workers regularly. Distributed medications, as indicated by physicians; order and document labs by lab cards.

- Supervised night-shift as the one licensed nurse on duty.
- Provided patient care in Medicare Unit, observing patients' progress with medication, treatment and rehabilitation; reviewed shift documentation, ensuring accuracy and completeness of forms and monthly summaries.
- Resolved pharmacy problems relating to delays and reimbursement issues and ensured compliance with documentation requirements.
- Received rarely issued management recognition award for excellence in nursing, flexibility, and willingness to work varied shifts to accommodate scheduling needs.

EL CAMINO HEALTHCARE – Mountain View, CA 1999–2001
Nurse
Provided outsourced nursing care in various settings: Medsurg, Detox, Special Needs School, Long-term Care, Group Home, Adult Care.

VALLENCIA VILLA – San Jose, CA   1993–1999
Charge Nurse   (1997–1999); *Certified Nurses Aide*   (1993–1997)
Supervised staff of six CNAs, and one Rehabilitation Aide, in providing nursing care for two floors, 35 patients each. Monitored blood glucose, labs, therapeutic drug levels and equipment; performed assessments, treatments, and documentation. Organized staff/patient assignments and patient care.

Hospital Nurse

Stephanie recently completed a special program allowing LPNs to earn RN status by completing just two semesters of college. She is looking to make the leap to an RN position in a hospital.

STEPHANIE A. MONACO

862 Lafayette Parkway
Rochester, New York 14625
(585) 586-2389
sam862@yahoo.com

SUMMARY:

Graduate Nurse with over 12 years' healthcare experience, which includes patient care in long-term care facilities and private homes. Experience dealing with a broad range of medical conditions, including ventilator-dependent, dialysis, cardiac rehabilitation, post-operative orthopaedic, emphysema, heart failure, and Alzheimer patients. Outstanding interpersonal skills, including strong patient rapport, excellent ability to relate to patient families, and capacity to interact with nurses, physicians, and other providers. Demonstrated leadership skills, including directing activities of nursing aides and fulfilling other supervisory functions.

PROFESSIONAL EXPERIENCE:

LPN / Staff Nurse, Strong Memorial Hospital; Rochester, NY   **Jan. 2006 – Present**
- Provide direct patient care for two to five patients in a critical care step-down unit.
- Address patients' respiratory needs, including ventilator care.
- Implement treatment plans consistent with directions of physicians and RNs.

LPN / Team Leader, The Hemlock Hills Living Center; Mendon, NY   **2002 – 2005**
(An Affiliate of Highland Hospital & Strong Health)
- Accountable for day-to-day care of up to 50 residents in a long-term care setting.
- Supervised and delegated duties to six Certified Nursing Aides.
- Addressed treatment needs of Alzheimer, kidney dialysis, and cardiac/orthopaedic rehab. patients.
- Conferred with physicians, therapists, and other providers to develop and implement care plans.
- Assessed residents on a daily basis and reported changes to physicians and/or Nurse Practitioners.
- Interacted with families of residents to discuss care plans and otherwise address any concerns.
- Assisted Registered Nurse in fulfilling "Charge Nurse" duties on a recurring basis.

Nurse's Aide (Private Duty), The Collins Family / Willem R. Jeffords; Rochester, NY   **1997 – 2002**
- Addressed daily living needs of geriatric patients in their homes.
- Under direction of RNs and physicians, administered medications for heart failure and hypertension.
- Assisted clients with nutrition, ambulation, and daily exercise regimes.
- Conferred with nurses, physicians, and family members to discuss care plans and other issues.

Personal Care Assistant (Private Duty), Emerline VanderGelder; Rochester, NY   **1986 – 1987**
- Fulfilled the daily living needs of patient with emphysema and congestive heart failure.

EDUCATION:

Associate of Applied Science, Nursing   **May 2005**
Monroe Community College; Rochester, NY
GPA: 3.76 (through Fall 2007) / Enrolled in Advanced Standing Two Semester Option for LPNs
Eligible to sit for Registered Nurse certification examination.

Certificate – Licensed Practical Nurse   **2002**
Isabella Graham Hart School of Practical Nursing; Rochester, NY
Graduated in Top 20% of class / Clinical Rotations at The Genesee Hospital

CERTIFICATIONS:

Licensed Practical Nurse / CPR Certified / Basic Life Support (BLS) / Telemetry Certified

References Available Upon Request

Trauma Treatment

Richard is transitioning out of the Navy, where he gained a great deal
of experience in trauma treatment and crisis management.

RICHARD P. ISAACS, RN, BSN

529 SPRINGDALE ROAD
SPRINGWATER, NEW YORK 14560
585-624-6184
RICHI@CS.COM

DISASTER RESPONSE • ACUTE & CRITICAL PATIENT CARE • MEDICAL/SURGICAL CARE
Pediatrics / Geriatrics / Post-Surgical / Nuclear & Biological Hazards

Health care professional with over eight years' intensive experience in fast-paced military hospital
environments. Demonstrated capacity to provide direct patient care and effectively supervise support
staff in a variety of clinical settings. Specialized training in dealing with nuclear and biological exposure, as well as experience treating patients with infectious diseases including Typhoid, Meningitis,
AIDS, and other contagions. Proven capacity to function well in crisis situations, plus excellent ability
to relate to patients from diverse cultural backgrounds and various age groups.

PRIMARY CLINICAL EXPERIENCE:

LIEUTENANT, UNITED STATES NAVY (2003 – Present)
US Naval Hospital; Tokyo, Japan
*Patients encompass infants through geriatrics, with conditions including a broad range of
infectious diseases and physical injuries.*
Staff Nurse / Charge Nurse – Adult & Pediatric Care   **May 2007 – Present**

- Provide bedside care to patients; administer medications and implement physician orders.
- Confer with physicians and other care team members on treatment plans for various patients.
- Address the needs of patients in isolation with Typhoid, Meningitis, and other contagious diseases.
- Train and provide leadership for staff of seven RNs and LPNs in Charge Nurse role.
- Participate in field exercises to maintain readiness for combat deployment in support of
  Marine units.

Key Accomplishment:
*Restructured medical supplies inventory and wrote new Standard Operating Procedures
(SOPs) to improve departmental efficiencies.*

Staff Nurse / Division Officer – Post Anesthesia Care Unit   **May 2006 – May 2007**

- Served needs of post-operative patients, addressing special concerns of post anesthesia recovery.
- Otherwise supported surgical teams in treating patients with a broad range of medical conditions.

US Naval Hospital; Annapolis, Maryland
*Patient base included military dependents and retirees, as well as active military personnel,
including several "VIP" patients.*
Staff Nurse – Medical / Telemetry Acute Care Unit   **Apr. 2003 – Apr. 2006**

- Addressed acute care needs of medical patients, including oncology and infectious disease patients.
- Cared for patients in isolation wards with tuberculosis, AIDS, and other contagious diseases.
- Monitored cardiac activity of patients using state-of-the-art telemetry technology.

Accomplishment:
Selected to serve as part of Humanitarian Relief Response Team.

Richard P. Isaacs, RN
Resume – Page Two

PRIMARY CLINICAL EXPERIENCE *(continued)*:

LONG ISLAND GENERAL HOSPITAL; Riverhead, New York
Suburban/rural facility (eastern Long Island, New York) providing full range of medical services.
Staff Nurse / Charge Nurse – Medical / Surgical Unit   **2000 – 2003**

- Provided direct patient care including telemetry monitoring.
- Served needs of incarcerated individuals in conjunction with Suffolk County (NY) Sheriff's Office.

ADDITIONAL CLINICAL EXPERIENCE:

EXPOSERVE MEDICAL SERVICES; Annapolis, Maryland
Per Diem Registered Nurse – Maryland Children's Center   **2003 – 2006**
- Served the needs of pediatric patients in a clinical outpatient setting.

HEARTLAND NURSING SERVICES; Riverhead, New York
Per Diem Registered Nurse   **2002 – 2003**
- Cared for burn victims, cardiac patients, post-surgical patients, ICU patients, and the terminally ill.

EDUCATION:

MICHIGAN STATE UNIVERSITY; East Lansing, Michigan
Master of Science, Community Service   *Anticipated May, 2007*

STATE UNIVERSITY OF NEW YORK AT ALBANY; Albany, New York
Bachelor of Science, Nursing   **May 2001**
Sigma Theta Tau Honorary / Gold Key Award / Silver Key Award

JOHNSON & WALES UNIVERSITY; Providence, Rhode Island
Associate of Science, Hotel & Restaurant Management   **June 1986**

CERTIFICATIONS / SPECIALIZED TRAINING:

Registered Nurse
Advanced Cardiac Life Support (ACLS); Basic Life Support (BLS)
Pediatric Advanced Life Support (PALS I)
Intravenous Conscious Sedation (IVCS)

Nuclear & Biological Hazard Medical Training
Mass Casualty Training; Field Hospital Training; Shipboard Hospital Training
Suturing; Chest Tube Insertion

References Provided On Request

115

Nurse

Sarah Vincent

258 N. Caloon Avenue, Pensacola, FL 32548
Phone: (850) 555-8542 Email: svincent@yahoo.com

NURSING PROFESSIONAL
Legal Nurse Consultant ... Registered Nurse

EDUCATION

Legal Nurse Consultant Certification Program – Current
Kaplan College, West Palm Beach, Florida

Associate in Science in Nursing (R.N.) – 2000
St. Petersburg Community College, St. Petersburg, Florida

Associate in Science in EMS Management – 1995
EMT and Paramedic Certification Program
St. Petersburg Community College, St. Petersburg, Florida

CERTIFICATIONS / TRAINING

Advanced Cardiac Life Support (ACLS)
Pediatric Advanced Life Support (PALS)
EMT-Tactical, Counter-Narcotics Tactical Operations
Introduction to Chemical, Biological, & Radiological Defense

PROFESSIONAL EXPERIENCE

Registered Nurse, – Emergency Room, Radiology Specialist
MEASE HOSPITAL, Clearwater, Florida
Current
General nursing duties within a critical care setting.

Rescue Lieutenant – Firefighter – SWAT Paramedic
PINELLAS COUNTY FIRE RESCUE, Tampa, Florida
1993 to 2003
Directed field medical patient care and supervision.

Hospital Corpsman, 2nd Class, Fleet Marine Force
UNITED STATES NAVAL RESERVE, Jacksonville, Florida
1994 to 2002
Provided field medical patient care and coordinated urinalysis,
immunization, and annual medical/dental screening programs.

Emergency Medical Services Lab Supervisor
HILLSBOROUGH COMMUNITY COLLEGE, Tampa, Florida
1999 to 2002
Monitored and assessed student progress.

QUALIFICATIONS SUMMARY

Competent and knowledge-
able medical professional
with more than 10 years of
increasingly responsible
experience. Effective critical
thinking, problem solving, and
interpersonal skills.

EXPERTISE

Legal Nurse Consultant

- Direct initial client assessments to identify potential
  liability

- Organize and review medical charts and records

- Review surgeon and expert
  witness depositions

Nursing Expertise

- Direct patient care and
  advocacy

- Triage

- Intubation and airway
  management

- Medication administration

- Cardiac monitoring and
  EKG rhythm interpretation

- Conscious sedation

- Counseling and education

- Chart review quality
  assurance

Occupational Therapist

A great combination style resume for a recent master's degree graduate

EVELYN WILLIAMS

ewilliams@earthlink.com

VALUE TO YOUR ORGANIZATION

426 Lincolnshire Lane
Bowling Green, OH 43403
419.555.1234

➤ **Interpersonal skills** achieved by successfully communicating with physicians, patients, professors, co-workers, visitors, hospital personnel, and other agencies.
➤ **Leadership skills** displayed by developing and directing groups related to stress management, substance abuse awareness, assertiveness training, and self-awareness; volunteer assistant basketball coach.
➤ **Problem-solving skills** gleaned by determining and providing individualized care and rehab to patients with neurological, orthopedic, and generalized diagnoses in home and clinical settings, and by visualizing and preparing goals with functional outcomes to maximize patient independence level.
➤ **Organizational skills** as evidenced by the ability to manage and prioritize tasks in a fast-paced environment, co-organized EMU Reach Out "Run for the Homeless."

EDUCATION

EASTERN MICHIGAN UNIVERSITY, Ypsilanti, MI
Master of Occupational Therapy, 2006   GPA: 3.8

BOWLING GREEN STATE UNIVERSITY, Bowling Green, OH
Bachelor of Arts in Psychology, 2004   GPA: 3.33

WORK EXPERIENCE

1/04 – PRESENT   **PRIVATE RESIDENCE,** Ann Arbor, MI
Home Health Aide
8/04 – 12/05   **EVERGREEN CARE & REHABILITATION CENTER,** Medina, OH
Certified Nursing Assistant
9/03 – 8/04   **RAINBOW REHABILITATION CENTER,** Ypsilanti, MI
Rehab Assistant – Traumatic Brain Injury

CLINICAL/PRE-CLINICAL EXPERIENCE

3/04 – 6/04   **ST. VINCENT MERCY MEDICAL CENTER,** Toledo, OH
Physical Dysfunction, Inpatient Acute Care Setting
1/04 – 3/04   **HERITAGE HOSPITAL,** Taylor, MI
Psychosocial Dysfunction, Inpatient Psychiatric Hospital
9/03 – 12/03   **McPHERSON HOME SERVICES,** Howell, MI
Occupational Therapy In Home-Based Community Setting
1/03 – 4/03   **INTENSIVE PSYCHIATRIC COMMUNITY CARE,** Ann Arbor, MI
Intensive Clinical Case Management, Department of Veterans' Affairs

ACTIVITIES & AFFILIATIONS

American Occupational Therapy Association; EMU Stoic Honor Society Member;
Ohio Occupational Therapy Association

ADDITIONAL SKILLS

• First Aid • NeuroDevelopmental Techniques • CPR • MMT
• OSHA Bloodborne Pathogens • ADL • Adaptive Equipment
• Pre-fabricated Splinting • Spanish • Microsoft Office XP

Ophthalmic Doctor Assistant/Technician

Career transition: This former sales representative attained her ophthalmic
certification and then obtained successful employment in her new field.

THERESA R. KEEBLER
404-333-6822 • 3248 Derry Lane, Decatur, GA 30035

OPHTHALMIC DOCTOR ASSISTANT / TECHNICIAN
Building organizational value by assisting with diagnostic and treatment-oriented procedures

Technical Skills:
Precise Refracting/Work Up
Scribing
Goniometry
Sterile Techniques

Procedures & Treatments:
Chalazion Surgery
Glaucoma Treatments
Conjunctivitis
Diabetes Monitoring
Retinopathy of Prematurity
Macular Degeneration
Strabismus
Cataracts
Palsy
NLD Obstruction
Blepharplasty

Equipment:
A Scans
Lasers
Tonometry
Slit Lamp
Lensonetry
Keratometer
Visual Fields
Topography

QUALIFICATIONS SUMMARY

Personable and capable professional experienced in conducting diagnostic
tests; measuring and recording vision; testing eye muscle function; inserting, removing, and caring for contact lenses; and applying eye dressings.
Competently assist physicians during surgery, maintain optical and surgical instruments, and administer eye medications. Extensive knowledge in
ophthalmic medications dealing with glaucoma, cataract surgery, and a
wide variety of other diagnoses.

PROFESSIONAL EXPERIENCE

AUGUSTA EYE ASSOCIATES, Decatur, Georgia — since 2005
Hired as a **Technician/Assistant** for a cornea specialist in a large ophthalmic practice. Performed histories, vision screenings, pupil exams, and
precise manifest refractions. Assisted with a variety of surgical procedures.
Quickly build trust and rapport and streamline processes to ensure physician efficiency.

GUGGINO FAMILY EYE CENTER, Atlanta, Georgia — 2004 to 2005
Taught customer service techniques and promoted twice within two
months to an **Ophthalmic Doctor Assistant** for a pediatric neurology
ophthalmologist performing scribing, taking histories, preparing patients
for examination, and educating patients on treatment procedures.

DAVEL COMMUNICATIONS, Atlanta, Georgia — 2001 to 2003
Recruited as a **Regional Account Manager** and promoted within 3
months of hire to **National Account Manager**. Contributed to the company doubling in size within 10 months; maintained a 100% satisfied customer retention rate.

CHILI'S BAR & GRILL, Decatur, Georgia — 1995 to 2000
Hired as a **Hostess** and quickly promoted to **Server**.

EDUCATION

Bachelor of Science, Organizational Communication — 2001
University of Georgia, Athens, Georgia

CERTIFICATION

Certified Ophthalmic Assistant (COA) — expected July 2006

Dental Assistant

Burton wanted a position with a larger practice. The resume highlighted his extensive training and certifications as well as experience. It contains lots of information, in a great layout

Burton Roberts, CDA

DENTAL ASSISTANT
CDA, EFDA, CPR CERTIFIED

GENERAL OR SPECIALTY PRACTICE
ORAL SURGERY ▪ PERIODONTICS ▪ ENDODONTICS ▪ ORTHODONTICS

Highly skilled, energetic and flexible dental professional with experience in 4-handed dentistry, radiology, sterilization, laboratory, and office duties. Adept at earning patient's trust and confidence. Demonstrated initiative and commitment, and a proven asset to a growing practice.

DENTAL SKILLS SUMMARY

- 4-Handed Dentistry
- Preventative Care
- Instrument Sterilization
- Diagnostic X-Rays

- Infection Control
- Oral Surgery/Extractions
- Emergency Treatment
- Prosthetics/Restorations

- Teeth Whitening
- Casts/Impressions
- Root Canals
- Patient Education

CHAIRSIDE EXPERIENCE

- Prepare tray setups for dental procedures. Obtain dental records prior to appointment.
- Prepare patients for procedures – ensure comfort and develop trust; calm distressed patients; instruct patients on postoperative and general oral health care; take and record medical and dental histories.
- Oversee cleanliness of operatories and instruments; ensure safe/sanitary conditions using autoclave, ultrasound, and dry heat instrument sterilization.
- Assist dentist with extractions, fillings, and sealants. Take casts and impressions for prosthetics/restorations.

LABORATORY EXPERIENCE

- Prepare materials for impressions and restorations.
- Pour models and make casts.
- Expose radiographs and process X-ray film.

OFFICE EXPERIENCE

- Greet patients; arrange and confirm appointments; keep treatment records.
- Order dental supplies and materials; maintain stock in accordance with monthly budgets.
- Develop and document office policies and procedures. Share best practices with staff.

PROFESSIONAL HISTORY

Chairside Assistant, Dr. George Rose, Denver, CO, January 2005 – Present
Student Intern/Chairside Assistant, Dr. Victoria Mercer, Denver, CO, September 2004 – December 2004
Student Intern/Nitrous Oxide/Oxygen Administration, Dr. John Mann, Denver, CO, October 2004

EDUCATION AND PROFESSIONAL DEVELOPMENT

CPR Certification – Adult, Infant, and Child, American Red Cross, January 2005 – January 2007
Tooth Bleaching, Home Study Educators (ADA Continuing Education Recognition Program), 2006
Certified Dental Assistant, Front Range Community College, 2005
Expanded Function Dental Assistant (EFDA), University of Colorado School of Dentistry, 2005
Schuster Center for Professional Development, 2005
Colorado Radiology Certification, 2004
Nitrous Oxide/Oxygen Administration Certification, 2004
ADA Midwinter Dental Conventions, 2003 – 2006
Photocopier Technician Certification, 1996

B.B.A. University of Tacoma, Tacoma, WA, May 1993

123 W. Main Street ▪ Denver, CO 00000 ▪ 303.555.1234 ▪ burtrob@aol.net

Medical Assistant

LINDA BLACK

1234 WEST STREET
HOMETOWN, MI 01234
HOME PHONE (877) 555-5555

OBJECTIVE: To secure a position with a company that affords me the opportunity for advancement.

QUALIFICATIONS

Receiving a Certificate of Completion in Medical Assisting gave me knowledge of front office and back office skills. One of my strong points is working with numbers; I am also a fast learner. I also enjoy phlebotomy. I feel I would be able to perform any duty for which my education has prepared me.

EDUCATION

1997   Diploma, Highschool H.S., Anytown, PA

1998-1999   Medical Assistant Certificate of Completion, College of Medical Careers, San Diego, CA

EMPLOYMENT

2004-2006   *Self-Employed Child Care Provider*
Provided daily basic care for children.

4/03-6/03   *Bureau of Census, Assistant Team Leader*, Lansing, MI
This was a temporary job that included the duties of door-to-door interviews, distributing, collecting, and reviewing interviews from other enumerators. Reassigning those interviews or following up on them if necessary.

1999-2000   *Manpower, Accounts Receivable and Payable*, Indiana, PA
For a brief period, I gained employment through a temp agency that enabled me to perform various tasks in accounts receivable and accounts payable for two different medical affiliated facilities at separate times.

1/99-2/99   *Full-Time Externship, Internal medicine office*
Duties included basic front office skills, patient care and communication, assisting the doctor, and performing lab work.

Medical Assistant

Jennifer's actual paid experience was minimal and dated; her skills needed to be brought to the forefront. This new resume was presented at a job fair where she was hired on the spot.

Jennifer Martin
(555) 555-5555
email@address.com
1234 West Street
Hometown, NY 01234

MEDICAL ASSISTANT

Triage	Injections	Patient Scheduling
Medical Terminology	Phlebotomy	Chart Updating
Patient Intake	Vital Signs	ICD and CPT Coding
Dosage Calculations	Infection Control	Insurance Claims
Sterilization Procedures	Urinalysis	Accounts Payable/Receivable
Blood Smears and Blood Tests	Hematocrit	Collections
Lab Equipment Operation	EKG	Data Entry

EXPERIENCE

Patient Care
- Cared for in-home patients with complex, multi-symptom illnesses for three years
- Eased patient discomfort by conducting accurate assessment and drawing techniques
- Fostered healthy environment for diabetic patient through meal preparation, medication dispensing, and glucose level monitoring

Administrative
- Improved cash flow by recovering uncollectible accounts in excess of $1,000,000
- Increased accuracy of patient files by designing and implementing new patient update sheet
- Exceeded daily quotas and minimized overhead expenses with effective scheduling and management of part-time employees

Computer Skills
- Microsoft Windows, Word, Excel, and Works
- Corel Word Perfect
- Medical software including Medical Manager and Great Plains

EDUCATION

College of Medical Careers, San Diego, CA
Medical Assistant Certificate, 1999
Valedictorian

High School, Anytown, PA
Diploma – Science Emphasis, 1997

RELATED EMPLOYMENT HISTORY

Billing Specialist, Bookkeeper, Medical Assistant (various – Indiana and Somerset, PA)	1999–2000
Medical Assistant (Internal Medical Office – San Diego, CA)	1999
Long-term/Acute Care Provider (self-employed – Anytown, PA)	1995–1998

Occupational Health Services Manager

Susan was successful in finding an Occupational Health Services management position in another industry after being a casualty of airline downsizing.

SUSAN BROWN, RN, COHN-S/CM
Manchester, NH
Mobile: 603-450-9944
Pager: 800-726-3642 PIN#1937761
E-mail: susanbrown81@hotmail.com

OCCUPATIONAL HEALTH SERVICES MANAGER

Certified Occupational Health Nurse Specialist / Certified Case Manager / Certified Occupational Hearing Conservationist / Case Management / OSHA & DOT Compliance / Ergonomics / Worker's Compensation / Corporate Safety / Training / Customer Service / Problem Solving / Quality Assurance / Sales & Marketing

- 10 years direct experience developing innovative occupational health programs and establishing clinics.
- 14 years experience in trauma centers and critical care units.
- Success in driving revenue stream and cost-saving initiatives through strong combination of business management and clinical skills.
- Licensed Registered Nurse: New Hampshire and Massachusetts.
- Proficient in Sign Language, Microsoft Office, and Outlook.

PROFESSIONAL EXPERIENCE

Supervisor, Occupational Health Services, Southwest Air Lines, Manchester, NH   2001–Present

Recruited to implement and manage Southwest's first onsite employee health clinic in eight years. Accountable for care of work-related and non-occupational injuries and illnesses for 5000 airport employees (from baggage handlers to pilots). Coordinated care for another 1500 employees in New Hampshire and 1000 employees in Chicago. Hired and directly supervised 13 registered nurses. Managed $1,000,000 budget. Assisted with the launch of new Southwest clinics in four other airports. Standardized policies and procedures and created training programs.

Developed position to also encompass system-wide responsibilities, and established self as the resource for OSHA-related matters, insourcing opportunities, ergonomic issues, and post-job offer testing programs. Updated operational managers on daily events, occupational health program progression, new programs, ongoing testing, compliance achievement, drug testing program, etc.

Achievements

- Overcame resistance and established first-ever Manchester airport onsite clinic as an integral part of operations. Planned the department design, oversaw the architect and contractors, hired and trained staff, and developed an orientation manual from scratch.
- Conceived and implemented matrix to document value of occupational health services to Southwest. Demonstrated an average of 55% ROI each month.
- Generated annual revenue of $120,000 by spearheading a drive to insource business from other airport companies, promoting the utilization of the Southwest clinic instead of an offsite clinic.
- Initiated joint venture with Comair and opened a lucrative satellite clinic in Manchester for Comair employees.
- Innovated a post-job offer functional testing program to address the high percentage of injuries among new hires. Worked closely with Southwest Legal and Human Resources and researched vendors.
- Negotiated inpatient services volume discount with most utilized hospital system that will save $60,000+ per year.
- Developed an improved nurse orientation process and a charting quality assurance program.

- Coordinated availability of appropriate emergency care for passengers aboard flights that were diverted to Canada on 9/11. Arranged for medical providers to meet over 17 staggered flights and 1100 passengers that arrived over the course of the next 6 days following the event.

Trainer, Manchester, NH   1999–Present

Provided continuing education, with CEU's approved by New Hampshire Board of Nurses, on Workplace Violence Guidelines for Health Care Workers, Nuts and Bolts of Occupational Health Nursing, OSHA Compliance and the Occupational Health Nurse, and Worker's Compensation Fraud Prevention and Update.

Program Supervisor, Allied Health Corporation, Boston, MA   1998–2001

Accountable for providing a broad range of quality services in a convenient, efficient, and cost-effective manner for this 8,000-employee Hospital Based Occupational Health Services Program dedicated to "Business Health." Supervised staff of 50 at 35 different companies.

- Managed successful start-up of 8 freestanding occupational medicine walk-in clinics.
- Instrumental in winning $600,000 in new business through marketing the placement of clinics, doctors, and/or nurses at company sites.

Manager, Occupational Health Services, Cumberland Farms, Salem, NH   1995–1998

Managed department, worker's compensation benefits, OSHA compliance issues, and health and wellness initiative for this multi-million dollar division of Sara Lee Industries with 1,000 employees.

- Decreased compensation costs by 66% over three years.

Occupational Health Nurse, Granite Industrial Constructors, Boston, MA   1994
Provided occupational health and case management services to this large construction company.

Previous experience working at several medical centers and a trauma center providing direct emergency nurse care as a lead trauma nurse and charge nurse.

EDUCATION & TRAINING

Associate's Degree, Nursing, University of New Hampshire, Durham, NH   1983

Select Ongoing Professional Development (attended numerous occupational health and case management continuing education programs):

- 28 hours toward Bachelor of Science, Nursing, University of New Hampshire and Manchester Community College
- Certification Programs for Occupational Health Nurse Specialist, Certified Case Manger, and Occupational Hearing Conservationist
- 50 hours of OSHA Training

PROFESSIONAL MEMBERSHIPS

- Member, American Association of Occupation Health Nurses (AAOHN)—10 years
- International Airline Occupational Health Nurse Association
- American Board of Occupational Health Nurses (ABOHN)

COMMUNITY SERVICE
Manchester Association for the Hearing Impaired (1995–Present)

Pharmaceutical Sales and Service

Catherine was a bright sales and service specialist who was growing in her career responsibilities and accomplishments and wanted to move into more advanced management positions.

Catherine Atree

1441 Meadowbrook Road #A12 • Novi, Michigan 48375
248.380.6101 • catherineatree@yahoo.com

EXPERTISE:
PHARMACEUTICAL SALES & SERVICE

High energy sales professional with experience developing product awareness through building business relationships. A proven performer with a track record of outperforming sales goals, delivering high levels of customer service, and achieving successful sales results built on key strengths of:

- **Consultative Sales Skills** — experience and education involving custom pharmaceutical and consumer products
- **New Business Development / Territory Management** — prospecting and building a territory; identifying and capitalizing on opportunities, knowledge of sales cycles
- **Customer Retention / Relationship Building** — excellent communication (listening, speaking) and interpersonal skills
- **Goal Setting** — experience in setting and achieving both independent and team-driven targets

PROFESSIONAL EXPERIENCE

QUALIFIED HEALTHCARE INCORPORATED; Grand Rapids, Michigan
Largest domestic contractual sales and marketing partner providing solutions to pharmaceutical & healthcare industries
Pharmaceutical Sales Specialist, 2003-current
Manage team-driven pharmaceutical sales responsibilities in southeast Michigan territory. Interact with physicians, nurses, physician assistants, and medical professionals to represent a premier product line. Interact with other sales reps to do strategic planning, problem solving, and collaborative thinking. Manage 35-40 weekly calls on physicians to increase market share in territory.

- Coordinated product launch for new acid reflux drug (AstraZeneca).
- Petitioned physicians to contact their HMOs and recommend formulary status; received formulary standing in January 2005.
- Member of market-leading Prilosec sales team.
- Consistently over sales quota; won highest call activity contest. Regional sales leader for hypertensive drug.

OFFICE MAX [2000-2003]; Columbus, Ohio
Multibillion-dollar global retailer of office supplies, furniture, and technology
Business Development Specialist, 2001-2003
Promoted to develop new business while maintaining current business in competitive southeastern and central Michigan territories; focused on small to medium-size companies. Managed complete sales cycle from initial contact, through presentation and consultation, to close of sale. Acted as liaison between sales center rep team and corporate office in Boston.

- Consistently maintained above expected goal percentage in regional and corporate sales.
- Trained new reps in all areas of product presentation, solution selling, and customer service.

Sales Representative, 2000-98
Managed sales and account maintenance with companies. Independently maintained relationships with company personnel to increase visibility and credibility. Developed leads through cold calls; met with customers to identify needs.

- Developed new customers; maintained high goal percentages; recruited to higher position.

EDUCATION & TRAINING

UNIVERSITY OF MICHIGAN; Ann Arbor, Michigan
Bachelor of Science degree in Interdisciplinary Studies/Social Science with a focus in Health & Humanities; Minor: Psychology, 1998
Seminars: Leadership Sales, Presentations Skills

References available on request

Medical Sales Representative

Jennifer went out of her way to display her yearly achievements right up front.

Jennifer J. Rogers

116 N.E. 229th Street   555-555-5555
Vancouver, Washington 88888   jrogersmed@earthlink.com

Medical Sales Representative

Professional Profile

Impressive 17-year *Medical Sales Representative* career with proven track record in prospecting, consultative sales, new business development and account retention. Proficient in sales presentations, introducing and detailing products, conducting inservices with physicians and nursing staffs. Strong assessment abilities with outstanding perception of customer needs and ability to recommend effective solutions. Well-developed closing skills for large capital purchases. Experienced sales trainer providing training classes in a corporate classroom setting as well as field training. Highly motivated, enthusiastic, and committed to professional excellence.

Achievements – percentage of plan by year

2004 – 183%	2001 – 105%	1998 – 90%	1995 – 164%
2003 – 78%	2000 – 159%	1997 – 92%*	1994 – 110%
2002 – 100%	1999 – 138%	1996 – 111%	

*started new territory

Professional Experience

Experience includes the sales of medical supplies and capital equipment. As a Senior Monitoring Consultant, worked with sales representatives throughout the Western US to assist in the presentation and closing of large systems deals. Outstanding achievements include securing multiple orders for patient monitoring systems in excess of $1 million. Possess excellent product knowledge with quick learning abilities. Demonstrated a commitment to long-term customer relationships evidenced by strong repeat business.

Career Progression

WelchAllyn Monitoring • prior to 2003 known as Protocol Systems • Beaverton, Oregon
Senior Representative • *1999–Present*
Position achieved by recommendation of Sales Director and President
Sales Trainer/Sales Representative • Northwest – based in Portland, Oregon • *1997–Present*
Territory includes Oregon, Washington, Idaho, Hawaii, and Alaska
Medical Sales Representative • Southern California – based in Orange County • *1993–1997*
Co-Medical • Seattle, Washington – Territory based in Portland, Oregon
Medical Sales Representative • *1985–1993*
Providence Hospital Pharmacy Department • Portland, Oregon
Technician Coordinator • *1981–1985*

Honors & Awards

- Six Award Trips
- Multiple Sales Awards
- National Accounts Award Winner • *2001*
- Monitoring Consultant of the Year • *1999; 2001*

Education

Associate of Applied Science Degree • Medical Assistant Program
Mt. Hood Community College • *1976*

Medical Equipment Sales

Erik is seeking to transition from pharmaceutical sales to sales of medical equipment. The resume demonstrates a track record of accomplishments and outstanding sales and account development capabilities.

ERIK CLAYTON
erikclayton@email.com

5555 W. 55th St.
New York, NY 10024

Residence (212) 555-1234
Mobile (212) 555-4321

MEDICAL EQUIPMENT SALES

Top-producing sales professional with five years progressive experience, including three years in pharmaceutical sales. Natural communicator with expertise in forging solid working relationships with professionals at all levels. Proven ability to identify and capitalize on market opportunities to drive revenues and capture market share. Strong closer who consistently exceeds targets in a consultative sales environment.

—Core Competencies—

Sales & Marketing • Business Development • Account Development & Retention
Client Relations • Team Building & Leadership • Training & Educating
Prospecting & Closing Negotiations • Consensus Building
Problem Solving • Presentations • Public Speaking

PROFESSIONAL EXPERIENCE

Sales Representative • 2003 to Present
INDUSTRY-LEADING PHARMACEUTICAL CO., New York, NY
Represent leading pharmaceutical company in consultative sales of select medications to MDs, Pharmacists, Pharmacy Technicians and Pharmacy Managers throughout Metro New York area.

- Call on 250 accounts monthly; consistently exceed company targets.
- Increased product market share from 25%-46%.
- Educated clients on launch of product, achieving 35% market share within three months.
- Selected by District Manager, out of 12 representatives, to anchor and train new hires.
- Placed #2 in nation for sales of main product out of 2,500 reps.
- Achieved #1 in district two consecutive years, 2005, 2006.
- Nominated for *Representative of the Year* award (2005).
- Nominated for company's most prestigious award (2004).

Account Executive • 2001 to 2003
COMPUTER MASTER, New York, NY
Gained valuable sales and client relations experience with $5 million computer sales company.

- Serviced existing accounts and developed new business, including several major corporations.
- Increased territory gross sales by 20%.

EDUCATION

B.S. in Communications
NEW YORK UNIVERSITY, New York, NY; 2001

Professional Development
Company Sponsored Sales Training; 2005
Team Train the Trainer (Company home office, one week); 2005

Computer Skills: Windows, Microsoft Word, PowerPoint

Pharmacy Technician

OLIVIA S. KOSTER, CPhT.

5006 Mason Circle
Oradell, NJ 07649
201/555-0000

PROFILE

A focused and disciplined **Certified Pharmacy Technician** with more than eight years of retail experience, reflecting:

$ ability to read / understand / dispense prescriptions
$ knowledge of drugs and drug strengths
$ sound judgment, seeking professional assistance when needed
$ outstanding communication / customer service skills
$ awareness of legality issues
$ experience with inventory control and stocking
$ proficiency in computer operations / data entry

Well-developed communication skills, interacting effectively with people on all levels; speak English, French, Spanish and Hungarian.
Conscientious and detail-oriented with an earned reputation for dependability, integrity, efficiency and professionalism.

EXPERIENCE

| 1998 - | ARBUCKLE'S PHARMACY, 2/03-8/06 | Phoenix, Arizona |
| 2006 | WALGREEN'S PHARMACY, 5/98-12/02 | Phoenix, Arizona |

Senior Certified Pharmacy Technician

Provided assistance to registered pharmacist and pharmacy customers, managing up to 700 prescriptions daily:

$ Answered phones for orders and refills; answered questions on pricing.
$ Contacted physicians to verify prescriptions / refills and address third-party issues; communicated with warehouse and wholesalers for inventory information; followed up with customers.
$ Filled prescription under guidance of registered pharmacist; prepared labels using InterCom Plus system.
$ Worked with customers at Drop Off Window, ensuring optimum customer service to generate repeat and referral business.
$ Entered prescriptions into computer system's patient profiles and check for drug allergies.
$ Managed special orders; received and stocked inventory, maintaining appropriate documentation.
$ Received outstanding ratings from Safeway Secret Shopper Program.

EDUCATION

Rx School.com
$ Pharmacy Technician Liability Controlling Errors
$ Civil Liability and the Evolving Role of Pharmacy Technician

Walgreen's Drug Stores   Phoenix, Arizona
Pharmacy Technician Training – OJT

Scottsdale Community College   Scottsdale, Arizona
32 Credit Hours – Chemistry Emphasis

Medical Technology Sales

Jane Petroski

466 Alton Road
Fremont, CA 01177
(555) 555-5555

MEDICAL INDUSTRY PROFESSIONAL
Training Specialist / Pharmaceutical Sales / Medical Software Support

Radiologic Technology graduate integrating work and education to achieve career goal. Ability to communicate highly technical medical information to professionals, as well as to patients and their families. Persuasive public speaker delivering high-impact presentations to diverse audiences including board of instructors. Expert time manager with tenacity and perseverance to handle rejection without taking it personally. AART License. PC Proficient in MS Office, Lotus and industry-specific software.

EDUCATION

BS in Radiologic Technology with minor in Biology, Orange College, Santa Ana, California, 2005
Magna Cum Laude Candidate; Dean's List, 4 years
GPA 3.7 / 4.0; Multiple scholarship recipient
Selective Courses: Medical Terminology, Physics, Microbiology, Human Anatomy and Physiology

Radiologic Internship, Chapman General Hospital, Orange, California
Studied all Radiology modalities by rotating through areas of CV, Mammography, CAT Scan, Special Procedures, Ultrasound, Radiation Oncology, Diagnostic, Surgery, Nuclear Medicine and Patient Care. Observed procedures and participated in hands-on training; completed detailed patient histories.
Established network of physician contacts by demonstrating exemplary performance and proving competency / reliability in the operating room and at clinical sites.

Associate of Arts, Santa Ana Junior College, Santa Ana, California, 2000
GPA 3.2 / 4.0
Selective Courses: Sociology, Psychology, Microbiology

CONTINUING PROFESSIONAL DEVELOPMENT
Emergency and Triage Seminar, Chapman General Hospital, Orange, California, 10/01
Trauma Seminar, Chapman General Hospital, Orange, California, 7/01
Caring for Customer Service, A. D. Banker & Company (8-week course), Tustin, California, 8/90

PROFESSIONAL EXPERIENCE

CHAPMAN GENERAL HOSPITAL, Orange, California   2/01 to Present
CAT Scan Technician (Part time)
Administer quality CAT Scans for outpatients and inpatients, plus emergency and trauma patients, while pinpointing immediate problems to provide patient care. Trained on operation of G.E. and Phillips machines, acquiring knowledge of physics principles. Assess and triage patients according to procedural priorities. Facilitate communication between doctors and patients. Interact with patients' families in crisis situations. Delegate tasks, as necessary, to maintain homeostasis.
Dispense correct patient contrast and radiation dosage to prevent contraindications.
React quickly and accurately in trauma situations utilizing critical thinking and reasoning.

Continued on Page 2

ADDITIONAL EXPERIENCE

Accounting Clerk, LEWIS, RYAN & FESTER, Tustin, California   6/96 to 1/00
> Performed general accounting functions for tax and litigation law firm.

Office Manager / Secretary, AUTO SUPPLY OUTLET, Tustin, California 4/96 to 6/96
> Supported six outside account representatives, assisting with direct sales and customer service.

Accounting / Shipping / Line Manager, C&B EMBROIDERY, Tustin, California   11/94 to 4/96
> Supervised quality control and resolved problems as liaison between employees and owners.

Data Entry Clerk, BANK OF AMERICA, Santa Ana, California 2/94 to 11/94
> Rewarded several times for speed and accuracy with large dollar return items.

Office Manager, DELANEY CONSTRUCTION, Santa Ana, California   11/91 to 9/93
> Established business relationships with vendors, Labor Department and OSHA.

Accounting Clerk, CPA FIRM, INC., Anaheim, California   5/90 to 11/91
> Assisted Department Supervisor in this CPA firm; performed A/P, A/R and data entry.

Customer Service Manager, BANKS & COMPANY, INC., Orange, California   6/88 to 5/90
> Delivered train-the-trainer presentations on customer service techniques.

EARLY POSITIONS
Accounting Assistant / Secretary to Owner, 3/88 to 6/88
Reproduction Department Head / Relief Receptionist, 6/87 to 3/88
Rental Store Manager, 8/86 to 6/87
Dental Assistant, 6/85 to 8/86

PROFESSIONAL AFFILIATIONS / CERTIFICATIONS

AART License, 2005; American Registered Radiologic Technologists, Member, 2 years
CPR and Advanced Lifesaving Certifications, 2002
Radiologic Science Club, Charitable Volunteer Coordinator, Member, 2 years

COMMUNITY INVOLVEMENT

Ronald McDonald House: Prepared and served dinner to families through class project, 2004.
Hope House: Collected and delivered clothing and home products through class project, 2003.
Angel Tree: Collected gifts for children of incarcerated parents through church project, 2003.

Pharmaceutical Sales Representative

Melanie Moore

459 Birch Avenue * Austin, IL 60000
(555) 555-2809 * mmoore@yahoo.com

WHAT I CAN OFFER **CROSLEY** AS YOUR **NEWEST PHARMACEUTICAL SALES REPRESENTATIVE**

Meeting demanding customers' needs * "Selling" ideas to doctors * Communicating to get results under tough conditions * Using creative ideas to solve problems on my own

RECENT WORK HISTORY WITH EXAMPLES OF PROBLEMS SOLVED

Investigator *promoted from six eligibles to* **Hospital Liaison;** *promoted to* Training Supervisor and Hiring Manager, Illinois Department of Protective and Regulatory Service, Austin, IL 00 - Present

CAPABILITY: Well informed, senior, busy judges and **doctors usually approve my recommendations quickly because I've built their trust** without the benefit of formal training.

CAPABILITY: Regularly **win the day** with my ideas, even **after** penetrating **cross-examination** by some of the best attorneys in the business.

CAPABILITY: Persuaded senior decision makers to help us deliver better quality, reduce turnover, and make our employees more effective. Our **clients were served even better.**

CAPABILITY: My new training program lowers **costs, despite our diverse workforce. Team members** now **master training** that once intimidated them.

Child Specialist, State of Missouri, Division of Family Services, Kansas City, MO   99 - 00

CAPABILITY: Convinced a decision maker that **my plan would help his patient stay with a demanding treatment protocol.** Patient and her unborn child protected.

Account Manager, Dunhill Staffing, Austin, IL   98 - 99
Dunhill provided temporary clerical and light industrial workers to local employers.

CAPABILITY: Boosted our client's productivity and made us more productive at the same time. **Complaints fell to zero** and stayed there.

EDUCATION

B.S., University of Illinois, Austin,   97
Earned this degree while working up to 20 hours a week. GPA: 3.2.

COMPUTER SKILLS

Expert in Word and Excel; proficient in proprietary customer information software suite and Outlook; familiar with Internet search protocols

Preschool Teacher

A new mom moving back into the workforce as a preschool teacher.
She sent out one resume and received an offer.

PENNY R. HAYES

813-229-4578 • phayes@email.com
9888 Sunset Drive, Tampa, FL 33606

PRESCHOOL TEACHER

qualified by more than 10 years experience working with children. Possess ...

Solid *organizational skills* for planning and follow through and maintaining control of the classroom.

A *genuine love of children* and a desire to see each child succeed.

Superior *written and verbal communication skills*, with an ability to meet diverse personalities at their level.

Flexibility in dealing with the unpredictability of children in classroom situations.

A *willingness* to learn and improve skills and give whatever it takes to accomplish the goal.

"She tutors children who are in academic need and also works as an advocate for them with their teacher. I don't believe there is any task too big or too small for Penny to undertake as long as it will benefit students."

–Principal
Local Elementary School

RELATED EXPERIENCE

Homeroom Mom
Reading Tutor
School Volunteer
Assistant Cub Scout Leader
Sunday School Teacher
Substitute Teacher

SELECTED RELEVANT HIGHLIGHTS

Reading Tutor ... Selected by teachers and parents as a tutor for two first grade students failing in reading. Planned the agenda, selected age-appropriate reading and supplemental materials, liaised with teachers and parents, and supported and encouraged both students in their successful reading efforts.

Homeroom Mom ... Maintain a database of parent volunteers and ensure the appropriate items and volunteers necessary for special events and class parties. Act as the class representative for PTA functions.

Assistant Cub Scout Leader ... Stepped in to assist the Leader, preventing the dissolution of a 12-boy troop. Facilitate meetings and manage all the paperwork and records for the troop and each scout individually.

Sunday School Teacher ... Utilize the "Exploring Faith" early elementary curriculum to teach up to 10 children. Plan weekly lessons, arts and crafts projects, story time, and games with an emphasis on good classroom behavior.

School Volunteer ... Contributed 800+ volunteer hours over the past four years including reading to children, chaperoning field trips, assisting aides and teachers, tutoring, helping PTA with hospitality, leading fundraising events, and maintaining the Book Resource Room.

EDUCATION & TRAINING

Bachelor of Science – 1995
The Pennsylvania State University, University Park, PA

Leadership Training – 2005
Boy Scouts of America

Building Better Readers – 2004
Southeast Regional Vision of Education and the County Education Foundation

Volunteer Orientation – 2003 and 2004
Local Elementary School

Educational Program Manager

Teresa moved from working in daycare and preschool to working with special needs children. Her programs were later adopted throughout her district.

Teresa H. Long

1452 Stone Creek Way
Indianapolis, Indiana 46260

317-872-7607
E-mail: THLong@zero.net

Program Management / Administration / Leadership Development

My professional career reflects over 15 years of education, training, administration, and program management in the highly visible and uniquely challenging environment of Special Education. I possess a demonstrated record of success to customize learning programs for students in all grades and performance levels. Have built positive working relationships with support staff, administrators, parents, paraprofessionals and students. These skills and experiences provide the foundation for my service to West Central Joint Services as **Program Coordinator**.

Selected Accomplishments:

- Sought by Special Education Director to serve on team to create standards, protocols, and framework for assessing ED teachers and programs
- Administrated program needs for students and coordinated the interactions of support professionals, including but not limited to: Program Directors, Building Administrators, School Psychologists, Physical Therapists, Occupational Therapists, Speech/Language Pathologists, Autism Consultants, Orthopedic, Visual, Hearing and other health-impaired service coordinators
- Effective facilitator of case conferences, that fosters a productive partnership between parents and school personnel, and insures that the individual needs of each student are met
- Excellent oral and written communication skills with the ability to speak on a broad range of topics; reflecting depth and understanding of the resources and programs available to the special needs community
- Designed preschool program, with overall responsibility for recruiting, training, curriculum development and the establishment of "hands on" learning centers
- Created "behavior system" for Morgan County ED Classrooms, that was used as a "footprint" for other programs and buildings throughout the district
- Possess a solid working knowledge of the state and federal requirements that enable students to participate in programs and services for special needs
- Experienced with the implementation and evaluation of a wide range of assistive technology, programs have included but are not limited to: Boardmaker, PECS, Writing With Symbols, Kurzweil, and Alpha Smart
- Customized curriculum for LD, ED, and MiMH students and coordinated performance standards against Individual Education Plans
- Thoroughly communicate the change plans and service modifications following IEP Conferences, to ensure timely implementation of new and effective educational strategies
- Established thorough working knowledge and practical understanding of various academic assessment tools
- Functioned as department and building mentor to supervise new teachers and student teachers, helping them to increase competence and adapt quickly to school policies and procedures
- Participated in two building wide "Climate Audits"; as a staff member providing input and feedback to the review committee, and as an audit team member interviewing staff to develop a written review of results for school administration
- Recipient of the WRTV Channel 6 Shining Star Award, and two consecutive awards for Excellence in Education of Students with Autism, from MSD Wayne Township

Education

Academic Credentials:

Currently in pursuit of a **Master of Science** degree in **Education Administration**, as part of the **EPPSP (Experiential Program for Preparing School Principals)** at Butler University

Awarded a **Bachelor of Science** degree in Special Education from University of Michigan. Certified in Mildly Mentally Handicapped, Seriously Emotionally Handicapped, and Learning Disabled.

Professional Development:

Formal academic training and personal experience
has been enhanced with additional training from:

- The **Lindamood-Bell Institute**. Course of study included Lindamood Phoneme Sequencing Program, Visualizing & Verbalizing for Language Comprehension & Thinking, Seeing Stars – Symbol Imagery for Phonemic Awareness, Sight Words & Spelling, On Cloud Nine Math – Visualizing and Verbalizing for Math, and Drawing with Language. Certified LAC Test Administrator: Lindamood Auditory Conceptualization Test.
- **ADOS** – Autism Diagnostic Observation Schedule, Butler University (2006)
- **Differentiating Curriculum** – Indiana University – Purdue University at Indianapolis
- **Multi-Cultural Education, Cooperative Learning, Applied Behavior Analysis, and Effective Goal Writing** – Pike Township Schools.

Career History:

Primary/Intermediate ED Teacher
Hamilton County Elementary School 2002-present

Private Tutor and Assessor
Lindamood-Bell Process 2001-present

Executive Director/Teacher
The Child Connection Preschool 1998-2002

Middle School Special ED Teacher
Pike Middle School 1996-1998

High School Learning Disabled Teacher
Morgan County Schools 1993-1994

High School Learning Disabled Teacher
Shelby County Schools 1993

Secondary Teacher of Severely Emotionally Handicapped (Alternative School)
Boone County Office of Education 1990-1992

Direct Care Staff/Program Coordinator
Northern Hills Group Homes 1989-1990

Teacher (Entry-Level)

ALEKSANDER GRINKOV
3988 St. Paul Boulevard • Rochester, New York 14615   585-289-5188 • alek_g@rochester.rr.com

GOAL   To secure a Social Studies teaching position at the secondary education level, 7-12

CERTIFICATIONS   New York State Provisional Certification in Social Studies, 7-12, December 2004

EDUCATION   STATE UNIVERSITY OF NEW YORK AT FARMINGVILLE, Farmingville, NY
                        Currently pursuing Masters of Arts in Teaching Social Studies
                        Anticipated May 2005 – Overall GPA 3.8

                        Bachelor of Science, Business and Economics, concentration in History
                        Graduated May 2002 – Overall GPA 3.8

Honors   Graduated Magna Cum Laude   Phi Alpha Theta National Historical Society
                        Dean's List, 1998 – 2002, consecutively Sigma Beta National Honor Society
                        Golden Key National Honor Society   Phi Beta Kappa National Honor Society

Appointments   **Teaching Assistant,** State University of New York at Farmingville, 2/01 – 5/02
                        • Selected to teach Advanced Labor Theory and Microeconomics curriculums.
                        • Collaborated on the development/implementation of challenging
                          undergraduate lectures.

Internships   **Financial Analyst,** Strategic Systems, The Banker, New York, NY, 6/00 – 9/00

Activities Co-founder/Captain, Farmingville University's Men's Club Volleyball Team, 9/98 – 5/02
Planned and coordinated off-site tournaments, handled group transportation and lodging arrangements,
and resourcefully managed an annual budget of $10,000.

STUDENT   BRITTONWOODS SCHOOL DISTRICT, Brittonwoods, NY
TEACHING   Combined knowledge and experience in the following positions:
                        11/04 – 6/05   **Brittonwoods High School, Twelfth Grade**
                        9/04 – 10/04   **Brittonwoods Junior High School, Seventh Grade**
Twelfth Grade
   • Team teach and observe the instruction of Advanced Placement students, as well as class discus-
     sions on current events presented by community leaders Steve Israel and scheduled guest, Rick
     Lazio, centered on terrorism and related issues.
   • Foster a stimulating learning environment that integrates cooperative learning, role-playing, critical
     debates, graphic organizers, primary sources, and lesson review.
   • Promote higher-level thinking skills through development of reinforcement-based mastery learning
     techniques modeled for students' individual learning styles.
Seventh Grade
   • Held full responsibility for all aspects of instruction and classroom management activities for five
     daily Social Studies classes over a one-month period.
   • Taught comprehensive Social Studies units on Ancient Americans, Anthropology, Archeology,
     Economics, and Political Science, providing students with an understanding of past civilizations' tra-
     ditions, religions, agriculture, technology, military, government, and social structures.
   • Formulated, administered, and graded lesson-specific tests.
   • Participated in weekly Parent-Teacher conferences.

                        WESTFIELD SCHOOL DISTRICT, Westfield, NY
                        1/04 – 5/04   **Per-diem Substitute Teacher, Grades Seven – Twelve**
   • Effectively taught regular and special education while demonstrating an ability to manage class-
     room responsibilities and easily establish rapport with students.

WORK HISTORY   **Customer Relations Manager,** *Food & Country* Magazine, Mineola, NY, 6/99 – 5/03

Teacher (Experienced)

ROBERT A. DOWNEY
24 Autumn Drive • Mt. Kisco, New York 27146 • (914) 730-2187
rad24@aol.com

OBJECTIVE	To secure a position teaching English at the secondary education level, 7-12
EDUCATION	SAINT JOHN'S UNIVERSITY, Jamaica, NY **Bachelor of Arts in English, 2004** **Minor: Secondary Education**
	SELDEN COMMUNITY COLLEGE, Selden, NY **Associates in Applied Science, Liberal Arts, 2000**
CERTIFICATIONS	New York State Provisional Certification in English, 7-12 CPR / First Aid for Adults and Children
TEACHING EXPERIENCE	The following represents combined experience within the Calverton School District . . . CALVERTON MIDDLE SCHOOL, Brentwood, NY

4/04 – present   **Leave Replacement Computer Lab Teacher, Sixth Grade**
- Facilitate the interactive learning process in a virtual classroom setting, utilizing the School Vista program to teach lessons and basic Internet navigation/keyboarding skills
- Implemented an English/Social Studies interdisciplinary unit incorporating the use of the Internet, spreadsheets, Web diagrams, and creative writing exercises to research, organize, and depict their understanding of King Arthur and the Middle Ages

11/03 – 4/04   **Permanent Substitute Teacher, Sixth through Eighth Grades**
- Managed classroom responsibilities and maintained continuity of the learning process
- Incorporated cooperative education and role-playing activities to establish a relationship between course material and students' life experiences
- Devised a mock English Language Arts (ELA) test based on previous testing methodologies and content-specific rubrics; co-selected multiple choice questions for short stories; administered and proctored ELA standardized/mock tests
- Encouraged critical thinking skills through the use of challenging debate

9/03 – 11/03   **Leave Replacement English Teacher, Seventh Grade**
- Worked collaboratively with English, Science, Math and History teachers to implement an interdisciplinary unit on heritage, incorporating the use of essay writing, laboratory experiments, graphing, and historical research on family roots
- Taught students to formulate DBQs, enabling students to develop an understanding of diversity, individualism, and creativity through short story multicultural literature:
  - "Aida," authored by Leontyne Price (Egyptian and Ethiopian)
  - "The First Flute," authored by Dorothy Sharp Carter (Central American)
  - "L.A.F.F.," authored by Lense Nemioka (Asian-American)
- In participation with the cooperating Social Studies teacher, implemented an interdisciplinary poetry unit on Veteran's Day to develop students' creative/critical thinking skills, and an appreciation for the causes/effects of war through the use of personification, simile, and metaphors illustrated in war-related poetry
- Assisted in the planning and coordination of the 2003 Year Book, providing consultation on layout, and supervised the collection of student photographs, poetry, and song lyrics
- Interfaced with Guidance Counselors, Teachers and Parents at BPST and Parent/Teacher meetings to discuss and review curriculum development and student progress

4/03 – 6/03 **2/03 – 4/03**	WESTFIELD SCHOOL DISTRICT, Westfield, NY **Substitute Teacher, Grades K-12; Student Teacher, Tenth and Eleventh Grades**
CAMP DIRECTOR	SAINT JOHN'S SUMMER CAMP, Jamaica, NY, 1998 – present
SKILLS	Windows 95; MS Word/Excel 97; Word Perfect 6.0; School Vista; Claris Works; Internet

Teacher (Specialist)

Charlene Wilson
2158 Hampton Lane, Cincinnati, OH 45219
513.426.9568
cwilson@ci.cincinnati.oh.us

"Choose a job you love, and you will never have to work another day in your life."
—Confucius

PROFILE
A detail-oriented, high-energy ART TEACHER with the ability to motivate students to work at optimum levels while maintaining a comfortable, creative environment, and keeping a clear perspective of goals to be accomplished. Extensive experience in helping students broaden perspectives for personal expression through visual artistry. Qualified by:

Technical Skills	Self-Management Skills	Transferable Skills
Ceramics/Handbuilding	Resourcefulness	Perception & Enthusiasm
Collage	Creativity & Flexibility	Personal Expression
Paintings/Oils	Productive Competence	Artistic Impact

PROFESSIONAL EXPERIENCE
2003 – 2005   LIBERTY-BENTON ELEMENTARY SCHOOL, *Art Teacher*   Findlay, OH
Instructed grades K-4 at Liberty Benton Elementary in Art Studio and Art History; created weekly art lessons with a variety of subject matters and mediums in both two-dimensional and three-dimensional projects. Instructed a small group of students in a gifted art program; selected artwork throughout the year and facilitated the annual student art show.

2002 – 2003   DELAWARE CITY SCHOOLS, *Art Teacher*   Delaware, OH
Full-time substitute for grades K-12 in the Delaware City School district; part-time art teacher for grades 1-5 at Woodward Elementary.

COMMUNITY INVOLVEMENT
SUMMER 2002   ARTS FESTIVAL, *Table Leader*   Findlay, OH
Collaborated in meetings throughout the year to organize an art activity table.
Recruited community volunteers to assist children with art projects.

FALL 2003   ARTS PARTNERSHIP   Findlay, OH
Bank One Student Art Exhibit,
Entered 5 students' artwork: 4 students received honorable mentions and 1 student received third place.

SUMMER 2002   Summer Arts Camp, *Head Instructor*
Assisted in recruiting volunteers for art, dance and theatre for one-week camp.

2003 – 2005   RIGHT TO READ, *Committee Member*   Findlay, OH
Helped organize a week of activities to promote the importance of reading.
Designed theme T-shirts worn throughout Right-to-Read Week.

2005   MOTHER HUBBARD'S LEARNING CUPBOARD   Findlay, OH
Commissioned by local store to design logo "character" to be imprinted on bags, checks, bookmarks, and signs.

EDUCATION
BOWLING GREEN STATE UNIVERSITY, Bowling Green, OH
Bachelor of Science in Education Degree, 2000
Major: Art Education, K-12 with emphasis in Painting
Minor: Psychology GPA: 3.3

International Scholarship Recipient to SACI School of Art in Florence, Italy, 1999

Network Administrator/Programmer

Richard needed a resume that showcased his education
and certification in networking systems and programming.

Richard Hall, MCSE, CCNA
80 William Street ◆ Bronx, NY 10456 ◆ 718.123.4567 (h) 646.123.4567 (m) ◆ rhall@hotmail.com

NETWORK ADMINISTRATOR/PROGRAMMER

QUALIFICATIONS SUMMARY

Certified Network Systems Specialist with extensive technical experience in network administration and programming. Skilled in all areas of computer technologies including: installation, configuration, maintenance, troubleshooting, design and conversion. Successful in implementing $300,000+ cost reduction programs and improving operational efficiencies. Excellent organizational, team-building and communication skills.

TECHNICAL SKILLS

- MCSE+I
- Certified Linux Administrator
- Network Administrator
- LAN/WAN
- Network Firewalls
- Router Configuration
- Workstations

- CCNA
- C Programmer
- Windows NT/2003
- Software and Hardware Configuration
- System Integration
- Internet
- MS-SQL

PROFESSIONAL EXPERIENCE

Network Administrator/Programmer
CW Associates, New York, NY, January 2003 – present
- Researched and implemented $300,000+ cost-saving technology programs and operating systems; Oversaw and supervised network conversions from FileMaker Pro, Lasso and Webstar to MS-SQL, Php and Apache; Customized and monitored company search engines; Configured, installed and maintained Company VPN, Cisco Pix Firewalls and Routers; Updated company electronic mail system from QuickMail to CommuniGatePro.

Network Administrator
Networking Worldwide, New York, NY, February 2002 – October 2002
- Designed, installed and configured computers and peripherals; Maintained and repaired hardware, software and operating systems; Troubleshot and resolved application and electronic mail system issues; Managed four domain servers.

EDUCATION & TRAINING

Columbia University, New York, NY
Master of Science in Computer Science, 2005
Bachelor of Science in Computer Science, 2004

Microsoft Systems Certified Engineer, 2003
Cisco Certified Network Associate, 2003

Computer Support Technician

Joshua is a recent graduate of a computer help desk/computer support technician program, and his resume demonstrates commitment to excellence, team spirit, and customer focus—all qualities needed in his new line of work.

Joshua Michael Peterson

4 Borderland Court • Montclair, NJ 12345 • tel: 555-555-5555 • petersonjm22@aol.com

OBJECTIVE: HELP DESK / COMPUTER SUPPORT TECHNICIAN

PROFILE
- ✓ **Recent computer center graduate with proven technical abilities.**
- ✓ Demonstrated track record of achieving goals in a team environment.
- ✓ Highly motivated and dependable. Proven skills in problem solving, customer relationship management, and organization.

EDUCATION   The Computer Learning Center, **Skillman, NJ**   **2005 – 2006**

Computer Coursework completed in:
- ✓ **Networking Essentials**
- ✓ A+ Certification
- ✓ Intermediate Word 2003
- ✓ Beginning Word 2003
- ✓ Beginning Access 2003
- ✓ TCP/IP Protocol
- ✓ Beginning Windows NT
- ✓ Administering Windows NT
- ✓ Windows NT Core Technologies
- ✓ Windows NT Support by Enterprise
- ✓ Beginning Business on the Internet
- ✓ Beginning FrontPage 2003

Montclair University, **Montclair, NJ**   **2003 – 2004**

General first-year courses in Bachelor's Degree program (24 credits).

EMPLOYMENT   A Cut Above, **Montclair, NJ**   **2002 – 2006**

Receptionist / Cashier
- Successfully handled front desk and three incoming telephone lines for busy, upscale hair salon. Greeted and logged in steady stream of customers, coordinating appointments with hairdresser availability.
- Developed cooperative, team-oriented working relationships with owners and co-workers in this 12-station salon.
- Managed customer problems and complaints with tact and attention to prompt customer service. Received team and customer service awards.
- Experience gained in opening and closing procedures, cash register receipts, counter sales, light bookkeeping and telephone follow-up.

Pro Soccer Camp, **Princeton, NJ**   **Summers 1999 – 2002**

Trainer / Coach
- Assisted Women's Soccer Coach in 200-participant soccer camp. Asked to return as trainer for 3 seasons. Worked with individuals, as well as teams, to improve their attitude and resulting soccer performance.

ACTIVITIES   Jersey Waves **Soccer Semi-Pro Team**   **1999 – 2003**

- ✓ **Team consistently ranked in top 10 semi-pro teams in the nation.**

Washington Crossing High School Soccer Team   **1998 – 2001**

- ✓ Captain of team that won State Soccer Title in 2000
- ✓ Recognized as one of the top two mid-fielders in the state in 2001

Software Developer/Project Manager

Jackson A. Lewis

1532 W. 35th Terrace, Dallas, Texas 75032 Phone: 276-555-7225 Email: jacklew@sbc.global.net

SOFTWARE DEVELOPMENT / PROJECT MANAGEMENT

Expertise

Software Development Life Cycle, Process Automation, Vendor Management, Software Interfacing
Systems and Hardware Analysis, Maintenance, Upgrade, Customization, & Modification
Client & Vendor Presentations / Employee Recruiting / Employee Mentor and Trainer, Improved Efficiency

Operating Systems

UNIX, Solaris, IBM AIX, HP-UX, DOS, Windows 95/98/NT/2003/XP

Languages

Java (JSP, Servlets, Applets, EJB, J2EE), JavaScript,
Visual Basic, HTML, XML, C/C++, COBOL, PL/SQL

Databases

Oracle, SQL, JDBC, ODBC, Microsoft Access

Software/Programs

Weblogic Application Server, Websphere Studio Application Developer, Eclipse, Forte for Java
(Sun One), NetBeans, Visual Age for Java, MQ Series, TOPLink, CVS, RCS, Visual Source Safe,
Dreamweaver, Microsoft Project, Word, Excel, Outlook, PowerPoint, FrontPage

SUMMARY OF EXPERIENCE

SBC Corporation, Dallas, Texas
Software Engineer IV, April 2003 – Current
Software Engineer III, October 2001 – April 2003
Software Engineer II, July 2000 – October 2001

*Integrated communications provider serving 85 Million customers,
and employing a workforce of 90,000 worldwide.*

- **Lead Analyst** for **multiple projects** and **sub-projects** (with Regional, National, and International clients and vendors), performing supervisory functions, including task assignment, quality assessment, scheduling, and employee evaluation.
- Vendor development and management, including **Cingular Wireless, Telcordia,** and **RLG Systems.**
- Designed and developed Web-based production job scheduling system with multi-threaded server component, **automating scheduling process.**
- Managed Customer Records Database project, interfacing with vendor software, affecting **1 Million+** SBC customers and **700** internal personnel.
- **Improved** operational **efficiency** of Sierra Online Scheduling, **reducing personnel by 50%.**
- **2004 SBC Award of Distinction.**
- **Multiple Monthly SBC Awards of Distinction,** including May 2006, December 2005, March 2005, April 2004, August 2003, November 2002, July 2001, and September 2000.
- Developed **configuration management process** allowing multiple team members to access system without interference to other users.
- Created and presented seminar for EDP (Enterprise Development Project) process to client and software team. Implemented **customization or updating processes** to meet team needs.
- **Trained** over **40 employees** in use of systems and processes.
- **Mentored 20 employees** in technical and professional business aptitude, including associates in Sales and Marketing Systems, Operational Systems Support, and Resolution Support Services departments.

- Experienced in managing hardware-related projects.
- Maintain existing systems, upgrade existing hardware and operating systems, establish new hardware, and provide on-call support.

BPC, Ft. Worth, Texas
Programmer/Analyst, May 1998 – July 2000

*Medical-based applications company marketing software to
healthcare industry, including hospitals, laboratories, pharmacies, and doctors.*

- 24/7 **on-call crisis management** for all clients accessing Patient Management Systems.
- **Enhanced Patient Management software** with additional functionalities, utilizing COBOL, and Discern Explorer.
- **Modified** Patient Management software to correct flaws/errors.
- Planned and executed all phases of **project management,** including design, coding, testing, and implementation.
- Analyzed and resolved client software issues.
- Educated clients during **troubleshooting** process in **resolution of software issues,** while preparing them to independently repair similar issues in the future.
- Assisted management team in **selection of new associates,** including interview process.
- **Lead Developer** for Patient Management Team, guiding other developers and software specialists.

CIVIC CONTRIBUTIONS

Habitat for Humanity, May 2006

Grande Point Homeowners Association, Vice President 2004, Member 2002 – Present

EDUCATION & PROFESSIONAL DEVELOPMENT

Baylor University, Waco, Texas

B.S. Business Administration – Computer and Office Information Systems, May 1998

SBC Corporation, Dallas, Texas

"Advanced Project Management" April 2004
"Project Management Principles and Practices" May 2003
"Negotiations" August 2002
"Process Analysis and Maturity" January 2002
"Advanced C++" December 2001
"C++" November 2001
"Conflict Prevention and Resolution" October 2001
"Presentation Skills" March 2001
"Managing Basic Projects (Project Management)" February 2001
"Seven Habits of Highly Effective People" January 2001
"Java Workshop" December 2000
"Visual Basic" December 2000
"UNIX: Advanced Shell Programming" November 2000
"UNIX: Shell Programming" November 2000
"Oracle for Application Developers" September 2000

Network Administrator

David wants to transition his impressive and broad experience from technical consulting with the military to commercial endeavors in the corporate sector.

DAVID J. WAGNER, MCP

217 MAGNOLIA COURT, OAKLAND, NJ 07436
(201) 405-5555 HOME • (201) 405-8888 MOBILE • DJWAGNER@CSN.COM

Networks / Systems
Hardware Configuration:
Windows, UNIX, Cisco
Software Configuration
Systems Integration
Systems Configuration
Router Configuration
Intrusion Detection Systems
Frame Relay Networking
Network Planning
Network Firewalls
Peer-to-peer Networks
Ethernet Networks
Telephony & Fiber Optics
Internet Information Server
Switches & Hubs
ISDN / T1 Lines

Media & Peripherals
Voice & Data
TCP/IP

Project Management
Technology Consulting
Technology Management
Networking Infrastructures
Systems Implementation
Virtual Team Leadership
Relationship Management
Advanced Communications
Telecommunications
Security Analysis
Security Development
Applications Development
Evaluation & Testing
Troubleshooting
Resource Utilization
Inventory Management
Technology Training
End-User Training
Knowledge Transfer
Executive Presentations
Strategic Planning
Project Team Development
Team Building
Client Relations
Quality Assurance
Problem Solving

TEAM LEADER • PROJECT MANAGER • DEPARTMENT MANAGER
Network Administration • Systems Security Technology

✓ **Microsoft Certified Professional. A+ Certification.**
Accomplished technology consultant and project manager adept in desktop and network security / systems architecture planning, design, installation, configuration, maintenance and smooth project delivery.

✓ Accustomed to supporting multi-user networks, as well as leading high-performance technology and telecommunications solutions. Successfully employ technology to improve operations efficiency, reduce costs, and meet reliability and security goals and deadlines.

✓ Proven track record in team leadership and training, supplying a balanced mix of analytical, management, coaching and technical skills.

PROFESSIONAL EXPERIENCE

Senior Computer Scientist   2003 – present
S5 Systems Group (US Army technology consulting firm), Stockton, NJ

Technical Lead – Army Computer Systems Office (2004 – present)
Focus: Rollout of Army Partnership Tool Suite (APTS) system, implementing new functionality into live networks and systems.

- Lead Consultant and liaison (chosen by government project manager) in 7-member cross-functional team deploying integrated networks, systems, and technologies. Introduced real-time, peer-to-peer collaboration via new application, bringing far-flung team together and eliminating disconnects.
- Key player in development, testing, and implementation process, including custom tool suite development, to fit client needs. Integrate configuration, and supply installation support for pioneering technology collaboration.

Lead Network Engineer
Information Systems Engineering Office (2003 – 2004)
Focus: $24 million Communications Update & Planning System (CUPS). Evaluated, selected, and integrated advanced communications and networking products for the Communications Collaboration Team.

- Key role (network engineer / administrator / technician) leading 6-member team. Honed end-to-end project management and presentation skills.
- Pioneered first-ever use of security hardware/software, including intrusion detection systems (IDS), Cisco routers, and network management apps.
- Designed robust, mobile communications (and upgrades) to facilitate efficient network convergence and bandwidth utilization. Developed network management tools for real-time monitoring and troubleshooting.
- Field-tested flying local area network (FLAN), utilizing wireless Ethernet technology, which interconnected enroute aircraft to ground-based units.
- Proposed equipment purchasing savings of $2.5 – $6 million through services analysis, reducing duplication of physical space and equipment.
- Introduced new traffic routing method (tech) utilizing a defense satellite channel for communications, enabling netmetting in worldwide locations.

continued

141

HARDWARE:
Sun Microsystems
IBM PCs & compatibles
SCSI & IDE Hard Drives
Cisco Routers & Switches
3COM Switches & Hubs
Ascend Pipeline Series
Netgear Hubs
RAID Arrays (Sun)
Ethernet NICs
Printers, Scanners
CD-ROMs, Modems
CD-R & CD-RW Drives
Sound Cards, TV Cards
Tape Drives

Software (UNIX):
Solaris, Linux
HP UNIX, SCO UNIX
Cisco Works Essentials
BIND 4 & 9 (DNS)
X-Windows, Open Windows
SSH, Lynx, Pine, ELM
sh, csh, bash
ftp servers & clients
Eagle Raptor Firewall
Apache, Sendmail, IRC

Software (PC):
Windows, DOS
Novell Netware
MS Office, MS Outlook
WordPerfect, FrontPage
IRC, IE, Netscape
FTP Servers & Clients
Norton, Cisco
HyperTerminal, Kermit
HP Openview
Cisco Works Essentials
Carbon Copy
Seagate Backup Exec.
SCO Xvision

Software (Cisco IOS):
Internetworking OS
Network Address Trans.
Access Lists
Context Based Access
Intrusion Detection
Remote Syslog Logging
Routing Protocols

Signal Officer 1994 – present
113th Signal Battalion, NJ Army NG, Stockton, NJ

- Platoon Leader – Mobile Subscriber Equipment Company. Lead, develop and motivate 40 soldiers. Oversee inventory management of $4.8 million in vehicles, weaponry, security, and communications equipment.
- Mission – establish mobile subscriber equipment network (mobile phone network for combat soldiers in the field).

Computer Scientist 2001 – 2003
Computer Development Services, Inc., Oakland, NJ

- Lead technical consultant – Computer Services Security Branch (US Army) for setup, testing, and evaluation of networks/systems security technologies. Established configuration, installation procedures, and network topologies for all support tasks. Tech reports used as management measurement tool.
- Designed secure test bed network/domain on UNIX, Windows, and Cisco IOS providing e-mail, DNS, firewalls, routing, file serving, and accounting.
- Selected to serve as test bed manager for dry run and official testing, personally resolving testing challenges and intrusion issues.

Systems Administrator 2000 – 2001
Technical Solutions & Services Corporation, Oakland, NJ

- Installation, configuration, and troubleshooting software (UNIX, Linux, Windows, Solaris) on HP workstations, Toshiba laptops, and servers (Compaq, Diversified, HP, Sun). Prepared backups on multiple platforms and provided 24/7 technical support to data warehousing center.
- Oversaw corporate telecomm system, LAN physical extension, and technical purchasing (POs, quoting, authorizations, and receiving).

Technology Consultant 1999 – 2000
Campbell & Cohen (legal firm), Trenton, NJ

- Systems and network troubleshooting (Windows & Novell Netware) at multiple locations. Peer-to-peer training. Proposed LAN and equipment recommendations to stay ahead of the curve, which were implemented.

Systems Instructor / Client Support 1998 – 1999
Healthcare Information Group, Oakland, NJ

EDUCATION & CERTIFICATIONS

MS, Telecommunications Management, Rutgers University – in progress
BS, Accounting, The College of New Jersey, Ewing, NJ – 1998

Microsoft Certified Professional – Windows NT, Network Essentials
A+ Certification – Computer and Network Repair
Cisco Switching 2.0 & Routing 2.0 – towards CCNP in progress
Building Scalable Cisco Networks (BSCN) course – in-house training

PROFESSIONAL ASSOCIATION

Institute of Electrical & Electronics Engineers (IEEE)

Software Designer

Regina updated her resume after being off from work for quite some time due to surgeries after an accident. She wanted an updated resume just in case (after being away from work for over a year) the company decided to downsize her.

Regina Pierce

1974 Paramount Way
Toledo, OH 43623
Phone: 419.555.5555
Email: reginapierce@msn.com

* SOFTWARE DESIGN ENGINEER *
DELIVERING SOFTWARE TO REDUCE COSTS AND INCREASE EFFICIENCIES

Detail-oriented, highly motivated SYSTEMS SOFTWARE CONSULTANT with 8+ years of successful experience in designing, developing, and implementing software solutions to support strategic business objectives. Keen **problem-solving skills** evidenced by the implementation of innovative technologies across dissimilar architectures and multiple platforms to provide quality product functionality. An **effective communicator** who can easily interface with end-users, technical teams, and professionals on all levels.

Technology Expertise Includes:

- Astute strategic understanding of mainframe, client/server, and Internet environments.
- Experience in Object-Oriented design and development.
- Empirical knowledge of all system development life cycle phases and a structured approach to project management. Accurately develop end-user documentation.
- Proven ability to acquire knowledge rapidly and to apply new technologies for process improvement.
- Functional knowledge of the finance, billing, and operations areas of **Customer Information Systems.**

KEY PROJECT MANAGEMENT & LEADERSHIP

ERNST & YOUNG – * LEAD TECHNICAL ANALYST *
Customer Information System for Southeastern Utility Company

Challenge: To identify and resolve critical errors of newly developed software in the Primary Test region before migrating online and batch programs to Regression Testing region.

Action: Extensively used problem-solving skills while interacting with eight-member team, Software Engineers, Data Conversion, project manager, and end-users to understand client requirements. Executed and analyzed test suites resulting in quality assessments that verified product requirements and high quality code.

Result: Delivered high quality software that exceeded client expectations and was specifically requested to stay on as Technical Analyst of the Regression Test Team, supporting both test teams through first- site implementation.

ERNST & YOUNG – * CUSTOM DEVELOPMENT LEAD / SUPERVISOR*
Customization of Client / Server Customer Information System

Challenge: To resolve technical issues of the Open Client architecture that were slowing progress on the development of a $1.8M CIS system at a Canadian utility company. To develop a detailed design of Powerbuilder software modifications in the Operations area.

Action: (1) Supervised two developers in identifying the cause of the Open Client issues and in the completion of software modifications to resolve those issues.
(2) Developed detailed design of Powerbuilder software modifications to increase functionality and efficiency.

Result: My team successfully identified and resolved the Open Client issues ahead of schedule, streamlining the rest of the project back to schedule.

COMPUTER TECHNOLOGIES

Languages: SQL, SQL*Plus, PL/SQL, Transact SQL, C, Java, HTML, COBOL, Pascal, Scheme ▪ **Databases:** Oracle 8.x, DB2, Sybase, MS Access ▪ **Environments:** Microsoft Windows 95/98/NT/2003, DOS, UNIX, VMS, CICS ▪ CASE Tools: ADW 1.6, ADW 2.7 ▪ **Development Tools:** JDeveloper v.2.0, Oracle Designer v.6.0, Oracle Developer 2003 v.2.0, Oracle Forms v.5.0, Oracle Reports v.2.5, Dreamweaver 3.0 ▪ **Methodologies:** Oracle's Applications Implementation Methodology (AIM) & Custom Development Methodology (CDM); Ernst & Young's Application Implementation Methodology (SMM).

PROFESSIONAL EXPERIENCE

Corporate Affiliations: Oracle, Healthnet, Bell South, Eaton Corporation, Kellogg Company, Kelly Services Corporation, Price Waterhouse, Niagara Mohawk Power Co., Alabama Gas Co., Atmos Energy, Consumers Gas, Consolidated Natural Gas

ORACLE CORPORATION, **Senior Consultant / Technical Analyst**   2000 – 2006
Installed and configured Oracle Financial Applications at five large North American companies to enhance the accuracy, availability, and timeliness of financial data for strategic planning and reporting. Identified, designed, developed, and documented customizations and interfaces to Oracle applications. Delivered excellent results to each client. Consistently commended for ability to work independently or as a team member to complete assignments on time and under budget.

- Designed and developed on-line Help for a customized installation of Oracle's iBill – iPay system, a $1.2M Oracle initiative. Extensive use of Dreamweaver 3.0 to develop 16 HTML Web pages.
- Developed work plans for a $2.5 million implementation of the Oracle CPG/Oracle Financials solution using Project Workbench and Microsoft Project '98.
- Developed Configuration Management Standards for a $1.5 million global implementation of Oracle Applications at a large international temporary services agency. Developed initial template of the project's global work plan.

ERNST & YOUNG LLP, **Consultant / Programmer Analyst**   1996 – 2000
Demonstrated outstanding technical skills in design, development, and implementation of a large Customer Information System package at five North American companies.

- Conducted analysis of Finance System on the CIS project of a large utility holding company. Prepared and presented Joint Application Design sessions, creating modification control reports, and proposing and estimating solutions for complex system enhancements in the following areas of Finance: Credit and Collections, Accounts Receivable, and Payment Processing.
- Programmer/Analyst. Modified existing batch and on-line (CICS) programs and constructed new programs to support general ledger journaling and credit collection processes in the implementation of a COBOL/DB2 Customer Information System at a northeastern electric and gas company.

EDUCATION & TRAINING

BOWLING GREEN STATE UNIVERSITY, Bowling Green, OH
Bachelor of Science in Computer Information Systems

ORACLE PRODUCT TRAINING:

Oracle CRM eCommerce 3i (iStore)
Java Programming with JDeveloper v.2.0
Developer/2003 Release 2: Build Forms I and Report Builder v.3.0
Oracle Receivables Release II
Oracle Financials 10.7 SC Bootcamp: General Ledger, Purchasing, Payables, Receivables, &
Application Implementation Methodology (AIM) 2.0
Ernst & Young MCS Information Technology Individual Study (MITIS 1) & Study 2 (MITIS 2)

Technical Support Specialist

Gloria needed to present her technical, project management, and technical training/supervisory qualifications for an upcoming promotion possibility within her department.

Gloria Bartlett

6463 Apple Valley Road, Stevens Point, WI 54481
(715) 254-5555 Home ■ (715) 254-8888 Mobile ■ gloriabar@bol.com

Application Support Administrator / Technical Support Specialist / Desktop Support

Technologically sophisticated, bilingual (Spanish / English) IT Support & Training Specialist with hands-on experience in project lifecycle management for technical and intranet applications, Web site development and maintenance, and workgroup support. Proven desktop and network troubleshooting skills. Expertise in:

- ✓ Help Desk & Hardware Support
- ✓ System Upgrades / Conversions
- ✓ Peer-to-Peer User Groups
- ✓ First-Level PC Support
- ✓ LAN / WAN Architecture
- ✓ Web Content Upgrades
- ✓ Project Management
- ✓ Escalation Resolution
- ✓ Customer Service

TECHNOLOGY SUMMARY

Networking – LAN / WAN, Windows 2000 / NT 4.0 Server, TCP/IP, SQL Server

Operating Systems – Windows 95 / 98 / 2000 / XP, Windows 2003 / NT 4.0 Server, DOS 6.0

Applications – MS Office Suite 97/2000/2002 (Word, Access, Excel, PowerPoint), MS FrontPage 2003, Macromedia Dreamweaver 3.0, Adobe Acrobat 5 and PDF, Flash 4.0, Novell GroupWise 5.5, Adobe Pagemill 3, Lotus Suite 96, Corel Suite 96, Corel 9, Adobe PhotoShop, Kodak digital software, Symantec pcAnywhere 32, Internet Explorer, Netscape Communicator, and WinZip

Programming – HTML code, CGI, Java, JavaScript, C Programming, RPG 400, SQL, Visual Basic 5.0, Visual InterDev 6.0, AS/400, ASP code

PROFESSIONAL EXPERIENCE

WISCONSIN STATE TREASURY DEPT., DIV. OF TAXATION, Madison, WI   1998 – present
Senior Technician, MIS – Technical Support Activity (2004 – present)
Promoted to provide help desk support for 2003+ end-users (including remote users) in 9 locations throughout Wisconsin, as well as project management team leadership for special technical assignments. First-point-of-contact (Tier 1 Help Desk Technician) for support incidents, as well as end-user training.

- **Help Desk.** Ensure effective "one-stop" technical support for mainframe, WAN, LAN, and remote system. Install and update software, and setup, configure, and troubleshoot Reach Center equipment. Track and de-escalate technology and workflow problems, and assist Desktop Support Group and other IT groups.
- **Web site Development.** Project managed Division of Taxation's Web site redesign to text-only version, enabling fast and easy access for all users, including vision impaired. Supervised staff of 8.
- **Intranet Development.** Key player in creation, launch and maintenance of Division of Taxation intranet site, providing management with easily retrievable, up-to-date information for operations decisions. Initiated, created, and maintain Access users group intranet to facilitate information sharing and learning.
- **Project Management.** Led WIX CD-ROM project for 2 years, delivering interactive CD-ROMs with 1000+ tax-law-verified documents for simplified tax preparation (tax years 2004 & 2005) on schedule.
- **ASP Development.** Played pivotal role in beta-test programming and development of causal sales application (upgraded Alpha 4 database into back-end of Access 2000 and SQL Server, front-end into Internet Explorer via ASP programming).
- **End-User Training.** Expanded Reach Center offerings by designing, developing, and delivering advanced programs and manuals for MS Office, GroupWise, Novell Network, and Internet, making information easily understood and usable. Manage all Access courses, training and supervising 5 adjunct team instructors.

WISCONSIN STATE – continued
Technical Assistant, MIS – Technical Support Activity   (2002 – 2004)
First-level technical support for software installation, as well as setup and configuration of new equipment used in Division of Taxation (PCs, laptops, printers, scanners, projectors, digital & video).

- **IT Software Training.** Designed curriculum and materials, and delivered technical training, for introductory programs in Microsoft Office Suite (Word, Excel, Access), as well as Windows 95, keeping staff motivated and focused while improving job satisfaction and productivity.
- **Web site Support.** Functioned as Web Editor for Division of Taxation's Internet/intranet Web site, proofing and updating Web site information on a daily basis.
- **Database Maintenance.** Upgraded and maintained link-shared employee Access database with Chief of Staff's office, ensuring data integrity for training. Created database reports for management evaluation.
- **Technical Development Project.** Pioneered development and implementation of storage, archive, and retrieval system for electronic presentations used throughout Division of Taxation.

Principal Clerk – Technical Education   (2000 – 2002)
Promoted to provide installation, configuration, and troubleshooting support for new equipment and software in REACH Center, as well as evaluation and modification of skills assessment.

- **Training Center Database.** Initiated and implemented data gathering system in Access to compile, store, and retrieve statistics on computer training classes. Researched and wrote monthly reports used to evaluate training trends and staff training needs.
- **WI Saver Rebate Program.** Key team participant in initial, large-scale data compilation for WI Saver Rebate Program, including retrieval, distribution, quality control, and storage of data.

Senior Clerk Typist, Clerk Typist – Corporation Business Tax   (1998 – 2000)
Assisted auditors by researching taxpayer information on mainframe, ordered work files for Supervising Auditor using HLLAPI information system, and prepared report statistics using Excel spreadsheets.

WISCONSIN STATE DEPT. OF BANKING, Madison, WI (temp contract)   1997 – 1998
Data Entry Specialist / Legal Secretary
Front office support for attorneys and accountants: records management, legal document preparation, purchasing, and equipment maintenance. Used IS software for research and to process taxpayer complaints.

FIRST AMERICAN BANK, Stevens Point, WI   1993 – 1996
Customer Service Representative / Supervisor Teller
Instructed employees in use of computerized banking systems and procedures. Verified and audited financial reports and balance sheets. Cash management responsibility exceeded $100,000.

EDUCATION

Instructor Certification, **HRDI, Blue Bell, PA – 2003**
Courses: Curriculum Design, Performance Consulting, Training Presentations, Design Surveys and Questions, Determining Training Needs, and Active Techniques for Teaching.

Certificate in Computer Programming, The Computer Institute, Madison, WI – 2002
Courses: HTML, CGI, Java Programming, JavaScript Programming, RPG 400, C Programming, SQL, Visual Basic 5.0, AS/400 Subfiles & Common Language Queries, MS Office, Windows NT 4.0

Ongoing Professional and Technical Development in-house and at vendor locations (1998 – present)

Web Developer/Programmer

Here's an example of a young technologist creating a powerful one-two punch:

Kelly L. Hillman

225 Springdale Drive	Pittsboro, WA 12345	(888) 449-2200

Web Developer / Programmer or Database Programmer

Highlights of Qualifications

Accomplished and innovative Web Development / Programming Professional with a proven track-record of effective database / Web-page design for high-profile, technical companies and governmental organizations. Experienced in all aspects of architecture and accessibility techniques; hands-on working knowledge of Section 508 and W3C Standards. Skilled analytical problem-solver with the ability to quickly learn new technologies. Polished communication, presentation, training, and client relations skills; able to relate effectively to people at all levels and convey complex technical information in an understandable manner.

Technical Skills

<u>Programming / Scripting Languages:</u> HTML, XHTML, DHTML, CSS Stylesheets, ColdFusion, Fusebox, Perl, JavaScript, CGI Scripting, XSSI, Java, Java Servlets, JSP, JDBC, Swing
<u>Database Applications:</u> SQL, SQL / PL, Oracle, Access, Database Design and Architecture
<u>Software Applications / Programs:</u> Dreamweaver, Flash, Fireworks, Adobe PhotoShop
<u>Operating Systems / Platforms:</u> UNIX and Windows 95 / 98 / 2003 / NT

Professional Experience

Web Developer / IT Specialist, EXCEL SYSTEMS / EPA (Formerly LOCKHEED-MARTIN) – RESEARCH Triangle Park, WA (2005 to Present): Manage the maintenance, development, and enhancement of a Coldfusion application that interfaces with an Oracle database. Create, update, and maintain 11,000 Web pages / templates while ensuring compliance with section 508 and EPA Web guidelines. Perform Java Script and PDF conversions; resize, create, and maintain high quality graphics; compile a monthly report listing all Web pages, URLs, titles, and updates; produce content; integrate dynamic popup menus; and update employee Web-based information. Trained a temporary employee in all aspects of conversion operations and Dreamweaver applications.

- Managed the complete conversion of 20,000 EPA Web pages to meet section 508 Web site guidelines in both appearance and compatibility.
- Instrumental in successfully meeting all critical and stringent deadlines.
- Recognized by management for advanced skill level and efficiency.

Web Development / Maintenance – Pittsboro, WA (2004 to 2005): Oversaw all aspects of client Web site development. Performed a wide range of design and coding projects utilizing HTML, DHTML, XHTML, JavaScript, and Flash. Updated and maintained content and graphics for both new and previously existing sites.

- Spearheaded and managed all business, technical, and client relations functions.
- Developed and launched numerous high-impact Web sites in addition to successfully re-designing existing sites to create additional market exposure.

Junior Systems Programmer / Analyst, MCTC – Research Triangle Park, WA (2002 to 2004): Hired to develop and code Web-based applications and user interfaces in transmitting / integrating data with Oracle databases for a comprehensive governmental occupational network database. Served as a member of a technical team in developing multiple Web, database, data search, and retrieval applications.

- Recruited for a part-time position, promoted to full-time.
- Pioneered the research and development of guidelines for people with disabilities.

Marketing / Technical Support Assistant, URKG CORPORATION – Morton, WA (2000 to 2001)

Educational & Training

MS Computer Information Technology (Expected 5/03), REGIS UNIVERSITY – Colorado Springs, CO (GPA 3.96)
Bachelor of Arts in Sociology (2000), UNIVERSITY OF NORTH CAROLINA – Chapel Hill, NC (GPA 3.7)
Information Systems Programming (2002), DURHAM TECHNICAL COMMUNITY COLLEGE – Durham, NC (GPA 4.0)
HTML _ Advanced HTML _ Advanced Online Java Script Training _ Sun's sl285 Hands-on Java Workshop _ XML Certification Training _ Applied Systems Analysis and Design _ Object-Oriented Software

Network Architecture Specialist

John had just been laid off and needed to find another job. He is looking to stay in his field, and he wants a position that will utilize and compensate him for his Cisco Networks Certification and experience.

JOHN A. CHRISTOPHER

11 Barbara Lane • Simi Valley, California 80932 • (805) 816-3787 • fax (805) 792-9741 jacla@aol.com

Applications
Adaptec Easy CD Creator
Adaptec Direct CD
Carbon Copy
Cc Mail
Clarify
HP Colorado Backup
MS Active Sync
MS Office Professional
MS Outlook 98 and 2003
MS Internet Explorer
NetAccess Internet
Netscape
Norton Ghost
Partition Magic
PC Anywhere
Rainbow
Reflection 1
Reflection X
Remedy-ARS
Symantec Norton Antivirus
Visio
Windows CE

Operating Systems
Microsoft Windows 2000
Microsoft Windows NT 4.0
   Workstation and Server
Microsoft Windows ME
Microsoft Windows 95, 98
Cisco Router/Switch IOS
MS-DOS
UNIX

Hardware
Intel-based Desktops
Intel-based Mobile Computers
HP Colorado Tape Backup
Cisco 2500 Series Router
Hewlett Packard Pro Curve
Switches
CD Writer

Protocols & Services
TCP/IP
DHCP
DNS
NetBEUI
Remote Access Service
WINS

Networking
Ethernet
Token Ring
Microsoft Networking

Network Architecture Specialist
Cisco Certified Network Associate

Results-driven, self-motivated professional with solid experience supporting hundreds of users in multiple departments in the corporate environment. Recognized for outstanding support and services, process development, and project management. Able to manage multiple projects simultaneously and to move quickly among projects. Capable of leading or collaborating. Areas of expertise include:

- Network architectures and networking components
- Software and operating system deployment in corporate environments
- PC hardware installation/repair and disk imaging
- Troubleshoot complex operating system problems
- Call tracking, case management, solution integration

Accomplishments

- Reduced help desk calls by developing end-user training and knowledge database.
- Led migration for 3000+ client/server email accounts from HP Open Mail to MS Exchange.
- Developed data collection protocol for BLM Natural Resource Inventory.
- Mentored teammates on technical materials and procedures.
- Built relationships to quickly resolve business critical issues.

Certifications

Technical Certification for MS Network Support Program, 9/02
CCNA – Cisco Certified Network Associate, 8/02

Work History

Technical Support Engineer, ABC Technologies (Holt Services), 4/03 – Present
E-mail Migration Specialist, ABC Technologies (Holt Services), 11/02 – 4/03
PC Technician, RBM (The Cameo Group) 5/02 – 11/02
Customer Support Specialist, Center Partners, 9/01 – 5/02
Recycle Technician, RBM (WasteNot Recycling) 2/01 – 9/01
Soil Scientist, Bureau of Land Management, 5/00 – 10/00

Education

Pacific Institute Workshop – Goal Setting, Achievement, Motivation, 1/01
B.S., Soil Science: Environmental Mgt. – CA Polytechnic State University, 12/00
A.A., Mathematics, Mira Costa College, 7/97

Awards and Honors

ABC Shining Star Award for Outstanding Customer Service, October '04
Outstanding Services to Technical Services Division, January '03
High Quality Customer Service Award, RBM Technical Support March & April '02

LLOYD MORRIS

LLOYD@HOTMAIL.COM

790 GREENLAND PLACE
HELENA, MONTANA 59625
HOME PHONE: 406-555-5555

Summary

IS professional recognized for broad-based skills encompassing Web, hardware and software solutions. Move effortlessly through and adapt readily to ever-changing technologies. Areas of expertise encompass: project management, team leadership, staff supervision, coding, design, testing, user training/support, troubleshooting, customer relations.

Technical Skills

Software: MS Office Suite, Quattro Pro, DacEasy, Act!, Premier, Avid Cinema, Authorware, Director, PhotoShop, CorelDraw, VoicePad, Naturally Speaking, Impromptu, PowerPlay, Visio
Hardware: SCSI, RAID Systems, IDE, NICs, video/audio network hubs, switches, and routers
Web/Internet: Netscape Commerce Server, MS IIS, HTML, CGI, ISAPI
Databases & Technologies: dBase, Paradox, MS Access, MS SQL Server, Progress, DDE, OLE, OLE2, ActiveX, Automations Servers (in and out of process), Active Forms, DCOM, Memory Mapped Files, Compound Files, MS Transaction Server (version 1.0), NT Services, Named Pipes, Thunking, Multithreaded applications and libraries (Win32), WinSock, mail services, HTTP, FTP, NNTP, TCP, UDP, SMTP, POP3
Operating Systems/Services: MS DOS, MS Windows 3.11, 95, 98, NT Server/Workstation, UNIX, MS Exchange, MS SQL Server, WINS, RAS, DHCP, IIS
Programming Languages: Delphi, Pascal, Progress, C/C++, VB, Fortran, PowerBuilder, Perl, Assembly

Career Highlights

- Recruited to manage several major projects at Technical Services (TS):
- Reconfigured entire IS department. Developed specifications for new servers for file sharing, Web, and database. Redesigned network 100 Base T; installed T1; and enabled WINS, DHCP, Exchange Server, MS SQL Server and IIS.
- Revamped networks, servers, and Internet connections to resolve the weekly, sometimes daily, crashing of network.
- Project manager for medical/Internet project that was designed to provide continuing education courses online.
- Supervised two professionals in IS and Web development.
- Wrote several interfaces for authorware, I.E. 4.0 and Exchange, and created intranet as dynamic pages from MSQL database.
- Founded Holbrook Software, with sole responsibility for account development, project planning, staffing, and customer relations. Developed software solutions for several public agencies and private firms:
- Created an employee scheduling software, Illinois married filing status software with yearly upgrades and conversion program
- Developed a criminal history database, investigation and complaint software packages for City of Missoula, Montana Police Department.
- Developed a UCR (uniform criminal reporting) software package for state of Ohio. Program enables small cities, villages, and townships to participate in computerized national UCR.
- Created software to accommodate membership database, account histories, invoices, membership functions, bank deposits, reports, and rosters for the Joliet Brokers Association.

- Designed Vesex Computer Systems Web site, applying knowledge of HTML/CGI, security, and interactive pages, among other functions
- Developed user-defined help feature for online help
- Provided HTML/CGI and Winhelp training
- Created interfaces to third-party products
- Gained extensive expertise with large relational databases

Professional Experience

Holbrook Software   *2000 – Present*
Software Developer/Proprietor

Electronic Systems   *1997 – 1999*
Director of IS, Programming and Web Development

MIC   *1995 – 1996*
Software Developer

Vesex Computer Systems   *1993 – 1994*
Interface Developer/Web Programmer/Webmaster; Online Help Programmer

B. Hevers & Co.   *1988 – 1993*
Regional Computer Coordinator

CompuStat   *1987 – 1988*
Customer Service Representative

Professional Development

Coursework in Advanced Programming, Pascal, and Fortran

Systems and Network Manager

RONALD W. ROCEK
163 Lexington Road ◆ Syracuse, New York 12345 ◆ (315) 555-1212
rrocek@msn.com

Profile
- 15 years of management and hands-on background working in IT infrastructure.
- Experience with world-class banks and financial institutions in New York, London, Paris.
- Hold MBA in Banking and Finance.
- Chosen for the 2003 International Who's Who in Information Technology.

Areas of Expertise
network design • systems management • LAN administration • strategic planning • team formation and leadership • budget preparation • project planning and management • presentation • business writing • resource management • product and design research • vendor interface and negotiation • systems conversion • computer operations • systems implementation • branch start-ups and automation • disaster recovery • system migrations • data center overhauls and moves • applications support

Executive Development
A Fortune 100 Company, Syracuse, NY   2001 to present
Vice President and Manager of Network Operations
Control $1 million budget and oversee five technicians in the design, implementation, and support of company's WAN and LAN infrastructure. Handle heavy resource management and coordination with internal departments, vendors, and network integration companies to define scopes of work, technical designs, product selection, required resources, schedules, and price negotiation. Budget resources and prepare reports. Hire, schedule, and review technicians.

Projects
AT&T frame relay and Cisco router implementation, TCP/IP address conversion, Compuserve RAS implementation, Cisco switched Ethernet 100mb/1 gb Catalyst implementation, HP Open View and Cisco Works implementation, MS DHCP and proxy server implementation. Managed project teams at remote sites to implement NT servers, routers, PC hardware upgrades, and Windows 95/NT images. Co-managed 1,100-user move.

A Major Investment Bank, London   1998 to 2001
Network Manager
Managed WAN daily support, hardware installation/configurations, and network changes. Monitored/configured private frame relay voice and data network. Monitored ACC routers and NT servers. Performed Windows NT 3.51 server and workstation installations. Configured ACC routers, Adtran CSU's, and Newbridge 3612 and 3606 multiplexors for remote site installations.

A Large Multinational Bank, Paris   1995 to 1998
Network Operations Supervisor
Managed all network and computer operations for the international hub site, reporting directly to the Technology Manager and supervising a team of technicians and computer operators. Supervised three direct reports, supported traders, reviewed/upgraded operations, handled troubleshooting, researched products and interfaced/negotiated with vendors.

Computer and IT

- Completed full office start-up in Luxembourg in three months. Implemented LAN, voice, data, and video capabilities. Hired and trained computer operator to support local users. Implemented support procedures and documentation.
- Saved company over $50,000 annually: Migrated video conferencing from leased lines to ISDN, cleaned up multiplexor maintenance contracts, discovered overpayment on WAN lines. Set up a new process to review all invoices and pre-approved all purchases and communications costs before forwarding to Technology Manager.

Technology Expertise
Hardware: Cisco 7206/4700/25XX, Cisco PIX firewall, Cabletron MMAC+/Smart Switch 6000's/ MMAC8, Newbridge 46020/36XX, IDNX 20/12, CYLINK link encryptors, Paradyne CSUs, ACC routers, Northern Telecom Option 11, PictureTel 4000/M8000, VAX 4000/6310/8000, HSC50, RA60/80/82/90 disk drives, MTI disks in DSSI architecture, HP 9000 K100, Sun Ultra 10, HP Laserjet 3/4/5 and QMS laser printers, Dell/Digital/AST/IBM PC hardware, Intel/3Com NIC cards, Cabling knowledge includes category 3/5, IBM Type 1, fiber optic multimode, v.35, x.21, RS232.
Software: SWIFT Alliance v3.0, IBIS, ST400, Montran (CHIPS), Reuters, Telerate, ADP Executive Quotes, IFSL Green Bar Viewer, Euroclear, Tracs, Soar, MS Project 95, VISIO, MS Word/Excel/ PowerPoint, Lotus Notes v4.6, MS Mail, Ami-Pro, Lotus 1-2-3, DOS, Chameleon v4.6, Sybase v11, COBOL, Pascal, BASIC.
Protocols/Operating Systems: Cisco IOS version 11.x, TCP/IP, IPX, frame relay, EIGRP, OSPF, RIP, PPP, ISDN, SNMP, DHCP, WINS/DNS, Netbeui, NetBIOS, DECnet, LAT, VAX/VMS v5.5-2, Pathworks v4.1/5.0, Windows NT Server 3.51 and 4.0, Netware 3.12, HP-UX v10.2, Solaris v2.6.1, OS/400 v2.3.

Education and Professional Development
M.B.A. in Banking and Finance, Syracuse University, Syracuse, New York
B.S. in Interdisciplinary Studies, Rensselaer Polytechnical Institute, Rensselaer, New York
Computer Operations Diploma (500 hour program), Institute for Data Systems, Mahopac, New York.
Additional technology courses: Network Design and Performance, Advanced Cisco Router Configuration, Microsoft Project 95. SYBASE SQL Server Administration, SYBASE Fast Track to SQL Server, Fundamentals of the HP UNIX System, Pathworks V5 Migration Planning, RDB Database Administration, Pathworks Tuning and Troubleshooting, PC Architecture and Troubleshooting.

Computer and IT

Telecommunications/Information Systems Management

TED SMOTHERS

1234 Central Blvd.   San Francisco, California 94127
Home: (415) 555-1212   Cellular: (415) 555-5551   ted@smothers.com

**Voice & Data Communications, Information Technology,
Project/Budget Management, Strategic Planning**

Expert in the design, development, and delivery of cost-effective, high-performance technology and communication solutions to meet challenging business demands. Extensive qualifications in all facets of projects from initial feasibility analysis and conceptual design through implementation, training, and enhancement. Excellent organizational, budget management, leadership, team building, negotiation, and project management qualifications.

Professional Experience

Food Systems International, San Francisco, CA   *1998 – Present*
Achieved fast-track promotion through positions of increasing responsibility for multibillion dollar international company with 30,000 employees worldwide.

Telecommunications Manager   *2001 – Present*
Responsible for management of $15 million department budget. Fully accountable for overall strategy for telecommunications technology acquisition and integration, vendor selection and negotiation, usage forecasting, workload planning, project budgeting, and administration. Plan and direct implementation of emerging telecommunications solutions at all domestic locations consisting of 125 facilities. Provide direction regarding telecommunications technology to affiliates throughout U.S. Lead cross-functional project teams; supervise technical and administrative staff with 20 direct reports. Fully accountable for department's strategic vision and leadership. Representative achievements include:

- Directed $40 million annual MCI network conversion at 200 locations within six months, saving company $15 million over three years.
- Designed and managed implementation of network utilizing Lucent and Octel at more than 100 locations in 12 months, realizing annual cost savings of $1 million.
- Served as technical project director for $12 million consolidation of East Coast headquarters with West Coast location.
- Facilitated move of corporate headquarters involving 3,000 employees over a four-day weekend.
- Implemented video conferencing technology at more than 60 sites.
- Built a four-digit dialing network for Food Systems locations within a four-month period.

Assistant Manager of Telecommunications   *1999 – 2001*

Management Trainee   *1998*

Education

BS in Political Science, Northwestern University, Chicago, IL
Professional Development/Continuing Education: Various American Management Association workshops and courses; BCR technical/technical management courses.

Information Systems Audit and Control

Alan was seeking a new position and was offered a managerial role overseeing disaster recovery and business continuity planning.

ALAN R. GILLETTE

1209 East Lake Drive

Metairie, Louisiana 70006

(504) 555-5555

SUMMARY

Master Electrician (licensed in Louisiana A-15346). Experienced in all types of electrical work—residential, commercial, industrial, electrical construction, and estimating. Six years management experience as a Foreman.

EXPERIENCE

Cajun Electric-Metairie, Master Electrician   *1999 to present*

Responsible for all sales, estimating, work scheduling, billing, ordering of parts and equipment, maintenance of inventories, and customer service. Projects have included complete wiring of a manufacturing business after relocation, new home construction, repair of equipment, building additions. Have worked as a contractor and subcontractor.

Industrial Light-New Orleans. Journeyman Electrician   *1999*

Foreman on medium-sized projects, with crews of 2 to 10. Scheduled the work, checked quality and productivity, provided layouts and supervision.

Prudhomme & Sons-New Orleans. Journeyman Electrician   *1997*

Crew member on construction of the New Orleans Sheraton.

Bechtel-Saudi Arabia. Journeyman Electrician   *1996*

Worked on a nuclear power plant (heavy industrial project), where safety and reliability were extremely important.

Tujaques-New Orleans. Journeyman Electrician   *1994 to 1995*

A variety of commercial and industrial projects (hospital, high-rise condominiums, office-hotel complex).

TRAINING

Louisiana Technical College, New Orleans

Certificate in Completion of Apprenticeship program

PERSONAL

Willing to travel, relocate

References Available

Counselor

Angel needed emphasis placed on educational goals, as well as demonstrating career advancement. This was effectively done in the Expertise section and the Education section showing her direction toward her doctorate degree.

Angel Roswell

666265 SW Deviline Court • Beaverton, Oregon 77777
Email: angel200620@atbl.com • 333-333-3333

Professional Profile

Highly motivated, versatile, and resourceful **professional** with a **Bachelor of Science** degree in **Psychology** and currently in a **Master's** program specializing in **Marriage & Family Counseling**. Over five years experience with children ages 2-6 in a disciplined, learning atmosphere combined with performing human resource duties, training, and counseling for teachers, coworkers and parents. Strong support experience in an office atmosphere with expertise in research and writing. Eager to excel, learn quickly, personable, and appreciated among peers.

Expertise Includes:
- Highly effective writing skills.
- Strong research and reporting abilities.
- Experienced in budgeting, financial planning, fundraising, and donation solicitation.
- Naturally intuitive to children's needs with strong insight to unspoken needs.
- Strengths in listening, evaluation and counseling.
- Effective database management and marketing.
- Development of programs/projects with effective implementation.
- Strong presentation skills, both written and verbal.
- Proven negotiation abilities.
- Proficient in assuring compliance with city, county, state and federal governing agencies.
- Able to accept responsibility and delegate where needed.
- Well-developed organizational skills.
- Personable and work well with all types of personalities.
- Loyal, driven, honest, and committed to a job well done.

Professional Experience

Associate Director • Educational Services • Portland, Oregon • *2001-2006*
Head Preschool Teacher (promoted)
Head Jr. Preschool Teacher (promoted)
Assistant Jr. Preschool Teacher (promoted)
Rapid upward progression in job responsibility from initial assistant, performing work as needed, to assuming Associate Director responsibilities involving the entire school, i.e., curriculum, teaching, training, counseling, supervising, providing assessments, budget planning, negotiations, parent involvement, marketing and fundraising.

Receptionist/Office Assistant • In Basket Business Services, Portland, Oregon • *1996-2001*
Receptionist for 10 companies along with answering multi-phone lines. Data entry, including invoicing, posting payables and receivables, and verification of statements. Variety of office duties.

Marketing Coordinator • Automated Machine Tool, Portland, Oregon • *1999-2000*
Telemarketing for strong sales leads. Relief receptionist. Maintained database, literature files and price books. Letter composition.

Certifications
Certified • Parenting Classes through the philosophies of Jane Nelsen, Ed.D., M.F.C.C.

Education
On-going studies to qualify for **Doctorate Degree in Child Psychology** – *emphasis in* **Play Therapy**
Master's Degree – Marriage & Family Counseling • George Fox University • Portland, Oregon Campus
Degree expected 2007
Bachelor of Science • **Psychology** • Portland State University, Portland, Oregon • *2004*

Mental Health Counselor (Entry-Level)

Having acquired her bachelor's degree, as well as in-depth internship experience, Jessica is seeking a full-time entry-level position within the mental health career field.

Jessica Devlin
64 Walnut Creek Drive, Yardley, PA 19089
(215) 919-5555 Home • (215) 919-8888 Mobile • jessdev@home.com

OBJECTIVE: Entry-level Mental Health Counseling position, such as Residential Counselor, Mental Health Counselor, Mental Health Associate, Clinical Case Manager, or Partial Care Counselor.

EDUCATION
Bachelor of Science, Liberal Studies, double minor: Psychology / Professional Education   May 2006
Rutgers University, New Brunswick, NJ

Relevant Courses:

Introductory Psychology	Mental Illness	Developmental Psychology	Transcultural Health
Introductory Sociology	Psychodrama I	Educational Psychology	Theory of Personality
Physiological Psychology	Loss and Grieving	Sociology of the Family	Abnormal Psychology
Essential Helping Relations	Social Psychology	Field Experience I & II	Intro. Criminal Justice

MENTAL HEALTH INTERNSHIP
Mental Health & Guardianship Advocacy, Public Defender's Office, Trenton, NJ   2004 – 2005
- Interned for 3 programs in mental health field within Public Defender's Office: Mental Health Unit (Mercer County Field Office), Guardianship Advocacy Unit, and Special Hearings Unit (Megan's Law).
- Interviewed individuals at in-patient public and private facilities, such as Hagadom State Hospital (specializing in geriatric psychiatric care), Trenton Psychiatric Hospital (adolescents and adults), as well as the Carrier Foundation (children and adolescents) for Mental Health and Guardianship Advocacy programs.
- Assisted attorneys in Megan's Law legal cases by interviewing defendants for upcoming hearings, documenting and evaluating statements, and preparing materials for the court.
- Performed follow-up case management, interviewing clients to complete cases assigned, and submitted timely documentation and reports. Ensured confidentiality of all records and communications.

EMPLOYMENT
Substitute Teacher, Hamilton Regional School District, Hamilton, NJ   2006 – present
- Teach all subjects as substitute teacher for elementary and secondary schools, following lesson plans detailed by classroom teachers, as well as maintaining positive class atmosphere and discipline.

Hostess / Cocktail Waitress, Rusty Scupper, Princeton, NJ   2005 – present
- Coordinate seating, efficiently and promptly, for popular downtown restaurant with seating for 550 indoors and outdoors. Seat 200 customers per 8-hour shift, while serving 1000 bar customers per 5-hour shift.
- Efficiently seat and serve group parties and banquets, such as four 2005 Holiday parties (75 customers each) in one day. Received recognition for top-notch customer service and positive attitude under stress.
- Entrusted with $450 bankroll at beginning of each shift. Maintain 99+% "count out" (cash reconciliation) accuracy for monies collected and disbursed daily.
- Chosen by management to promote upcoming shows and events via on-site and off-site marketing pieces and public relations appearances.

Administrative Assistant, Claims Administration, Public Defender's Office, Trenton, NJ   Summer 2003
- Maintained orderly and productive environment in busy office with 6 attorneys. Effectively answered and transferred incoming phone calls on 8 lines, and scheduled 50 – 60 appointments daily for all attorneys.
- Word-processed, edited, and revised large volume of homeowners' claims and legal settlement documents weekly (20 – 25 documents, each 75 – 80 pages in length). Consistently completed assignments with short turnaround time (within 24 hours). Received live dictation, composed and sent correspondence and memos.

COMPUTER SKILLS
Windows 98, MS Office 2000 – Word, Excel, Access, PowerPoint, MS Outlook, PhotoShop, Internet Explorer

Clinical Psychologist/Social Services Professional

Veda's challenge was to present her wealth of qualifications in a neat, easy-to-read format.

Veda A. Merritt

3236 Sycamore Drive
View Park, CA 90043

Home: (323) 444-4444
Mobile: (323) 444-1234
vamerritt@netpro.com

CLINICAL PSYCHOLOGY & SOCIAL SERVICES ▪ COMMUNITY OUTREACH

PROFILE
Versatile, dedicated Social Services Professional with solid clinical and administrative acumen. Committed team player & resourceful leader with proven ability to motivate and generate results through hands-on management and a sound knowledge base. Proactive community services advocate, continually seeking out new resources to aid patients.

EXPERTISE
- ➢ Counseling & therapy for individuals, couples and groups
- ➢ Identifying & matching resources to fit client/patient needs
- ➢ Teaching and facilitating workshops to train peers, subordinates and clients
- ➢ Managing cases, including writing & reviewing case notes, and auditing case files
- ➢ Networking to develop & sustain services, then propagating community awareness
- ➢ Relationship-building with patients of all ages, socioeconomic & cultural backgrounds
- ➢ Formulating, launching & managing programs; developing new methods & procedures
- ➢ Directing Personnel operations, including payroll, grievance procedures, benefits administration & workers' compensation; enforcing EEO/Affirmative Action mandates

COMPUTER
Proficient in Mac & IBM Platforms _ Lotus Notes _ QuickBooks _ MS Office Professional

EDUCATION
Master's Degree in Clinical Psychology – 2005
Kildare University – Los Angeles, CA
Master's in Business Administration – 2001
University of Southern California – San Diego, CA
Bachelor of Arts in Management – 1996
University of Oak Hills – Lake Forest, CA
Class Representative – *Graduated with honors*

EXPERIENCE
Program Manager   **2004-Present**
Comprehensive Family Services – Culver City, CA. A social services agency.

- Provide counseling & therapy for individuals, couples, families and general groups.
- Team with social workers & other service providers to secure food, shelter, etc.
- Conduct Parenting Training classes _ Supervise monitored on-site visitations.
- Perform intake to assess mental history; refer to appropriate mental health agency. *To effectively deliver these services, I strive to gain clients' trust, assuage their fears, and get past the resentment & embarrassment that can ensue in these situations.*
- Facilitate multi-disciplinary case planning conferences _ Manage staff
- Conduct quarterly Community Networking meetings. *Built substantial network of service providers, which fortified our ability to provide resources & secure donations for clients' welfare.*

EXPERIENCE
Veda A. Merritt, Continued

Program Manager   **1997-2004**
Helping Hands, Inc. – Montrose, CA. Social Services facility funded by DCSS grant.

Managed 4 programs: *Family Preservation _ Juvenile Mentoring _ Healthy Start _ Supervised Visitations*
Provided in-home counseling & therapy / Assessed clients & patients / Conducted Parenting Training
classes / Hired, trained & supervised staff.

Benefits Specialist   **1997-2000**
Partners in Health – Norwalk, CA

- Managed company benefits of over $2 million annually.
- Managed five programs: Tuition Reimbursement / Employee Transportation / Service
  Contracts / Workers' Comp Early Return to Work / Retirement Plans.

Benefits Specialist/Workers' Compensation Case Manager   **1993-1997**
Community Medical Center – Downey, CA

- Increased employee benefits program from standard plan to flexible benefits plan.
- Launched early Return-to-Work program for employees out on workers' comp.
- Expedited profit realization by implementing special training for new recruits.
- Maintained up-to-date EEO/Affirmative Action Program for managers.

AFFILIATIONS
Supervised Visitation Network _ California Marriage & Family Therapists (CAFT)

PRESENTATIONS GIVEN
In-Services/Training: Child Abuse _ Mentoring _ Case Management _ How to Write Case Notes _
Suicide: When, Why & How to Report _ Working with Children's Social Workers

RECOGNITION

Awarded By:	In Appreciation For:
Los Angeles Home Connection….	Service and dedication to families
L. A. Children's Planning Council….	Extraordinary service & dedication to children
Dept of Children & Family Services….	Family preservation training
American Diabetes Association….	Diabetes Walk-a-Thon Leadership (Team Captain)

Willing to relocate • Available weekends

Guidance Counselor

Sharon wanted to get into another district closer to her home,
as she had a 1+ hour drive to work each day.

SHARON WISE

••

500 NOTTINGHAM STREET ~ PLYMOUTH, MI 48170
444.007.1111 ~ SHARON_WISE@HOTMAIL.COM

SCHOOL GUIDANCE COUNSELOR

Dedicated elementary, middle and high school guidance counselor, skilled at providing positive direction for students' academic, social, and emotional well-being. Work effectively with children with ADHD and with multicultural and diverse populations. Counseling Skills include:

Guidance Curriculum: Classroom Guidance Lessons; Career Awareness; Conflict Resolution/Social Skills; Developmental Awareness

Individual Planning: Student Assessments; Student Placement & Scheduling; New Student Transition; Academic & Career Advisement

Responsive Services: Mental Health; Family & Teacher Consulting; Crisis Intervention & Grief Management; Psycho-Educational Support Groups

Systems Support: Program Evaluation; Program Development & Coordination; Needs Assessment; Committee Participation

EDUCATION / CERTIFICATION

MA, *School Counseling,* UNIVERSITY OF DETROIT-MERCY, Detroit, MI
MA, *Teaching,* MARYGROVE COLLEGE, Detroit, MI
BA, *Teaching – Social Studies/French,* MICHIGAN STATE UNIVERSITY, East Lansing, MI

Certified – *Counseling* – K-12 – State of Michigan
Certified – *Social Studies & French* – grades 7-12 – State of Michigan
Certified – *LLPC* – expected completion 7/03

PROFESSIONAL EXPERIENCE

HARTLAND COMMUNITY SCHOOLS, Hartland, MI   2005 – 2006
SCHOOL COUNSELOR

Provide individual and small-group counseling sessions and large-group counseling presentations within classroom and guidance office environments for a school with 800 students. Participate in parent/teacher meetings to discuss and develop emotional and behavioral strategies for students with physical, mental, and emotional challenges.

- Developed 45-minute Bully-Proofing classes and presented them to each of 30 classes in the building.
- Wrote a monthly article for the school newsletter on a topic of relevance.
- Facilitated students participating in the Midwest talent search for the Gifted & Talented program.
- Held orientation for new students and their parents, providing them with a schedule of classes and showing them around the building.
- Created 30-minute Career Awareness/Exploration sessions so students would become exposed to various career options. Organized a Career Day, arranging for 40 speakers in various fields to talk with the students about their profession.
- Facilitated support groups dealing with social and coping skills, and conducted needs assessment and program evaluation with staff and students.
- Designed a survey for students and teachers to evaluate the guidance program.
- Hung a display of bully-proofing pledges in the shape of the American flag, with children earning hearts instead of stars for "acts of kindness."

- Participated as a team member for the School Improvement Team (SCIT).
- Performed Title I coordinator duties, planning and organizing initial structure mailings, assigning students to teachers, adhering to budgets, and scheduling classes.

NOVI COMMUNITY SCHOOLS, Novi, MI   2003 – 2005
GUEST TEACHER

Substituted in the middle school and high school, teaching most subjects, including special ed. Immediately tried to develop a rapport with students and engage in discussion of relevant topics. Facilitated the discussion to steer towards daily lesson plan. Discussion and debate kept students centered, entertained, and open to learning.

- Given long-term teaching assignment for students with disabilities. Taught math, science and social studies in grades 6 – 8 for a full semester. There were 5 – 10 students in each of four classes, ages 11 -13 – many students had ADHD. Wrote lesson plans, graded assignments and consulted with parents.

DETROIT PUBLIC SCHOOLS, Detroit, MI   1996 – 2003
FRENCH & SOCIAL STUDIES TEACHER

Taught five classes each day, with each class having between 30 – 35 students, engaging their curiosity and research abilities in structured classroom activities. Provided lectures, notes, study guides and projects for courses in American History, Government, Economics, World Geography, Global Issues, and French.

- Devised an effective structure for parent communication.
- Gathered resources as supplemental materials to be used in conjunction with assigned texts to give students a richer experience.
- Assigned different subjects each year, showed flexibility in providing first-rate learning experience for each subject.
- Developed a system to track work and assignments while moving to different rooms for each class period.
- Provided students with practical experience, such as making menus and calendars in French.
- Member of School Improvement team and on the committee to improve student self-esteem.

PROFESSIONAL MEMBERSHIPS

- American Counseling Association
- American School Counselor Association
- Michigan Counseling Association
- Michigan School Counselor Association

RECENT CONFERENCE PARTICIPATION

Launching Career Awareness – Oakland Education Service Agency
Legal Issues for School Counselors – Washtenaw County Counselors Association
Counseling Groups in Crisis – Michigan Association of Specialists in Group Work
A.D.H.D in the New Millennium – Oakland Schools
Bully-Proofing Your School – Oakland Schools
The Human Spirit & Technology – Michigan Counseling Association
Understanding Attachment Disorders – Medical Educational Service
Grief Counseling Skills – Cross Country University

Social Worker

Tanya decided to pursue a job search in a large metropolitan area when she realized that she was not reaching her potential while working in a rural setting.

Tanya S. Richards

246 Caretaker Lane
Paradise, LA 00000
555-111-2222

STRENGTHS

- Funded college education by working full-time throughout full-time enrollment.
- Interact well with diverse populations.
- Take responsibility and work well without supervision.
- Eager to relocate.

CAREER EXPERIENCE

January 2005–Present

Community Psychosocial Services, Ruston, LA 71270
Qualified Mental Health Professional

- Provide mental health services to individuals with mental illness diagnosis.
- Complete psychosocial evaluations to determine appropriateness.
- Work with the psychiatrist assisting in completion of the psychiatric assessment.
- Provide individual, family, and group therapy as well as psychosocial skills training.
- Prepare care plans, charting, and other reports necessary to provide ongoing tracking of client progress.

January 2003–December 2004

Louisiana Job Employment and Training, Rapides Parish Police Jury, Alexandria, LA 71301
Intake Officer

- Scheduled food stamp recipients for pre-employment programs.
- Interviewed applicants and recorded information to determine job skills and training, income information, and program eligibility.
- Reviewed all required documents from clients.
- Issued monthly stipend reimbursements to participants.
- Maintained records to provide a continuing history of pertinent action on each case.

January 1998–December 2002

G. B. Cooley Hospital, West Monroe, LA 71291
Resident Living Trainee

- Supervised mentally-retarded clients.
- Monitored progress on daily and monthly programs.
- Attended individual development training meetings to coordinate new programs to help clients function independently.

EDUCATION

Louisiana Tech University, Ruston, LA
B.A., Social Welfare, December 2002.

Substance Abuse Counselor

Roy is a recovering substance abuser who, after a life of carousing,
has found his true calling in helping others overcome addiction.

ROY NASH

4900 Boulevard, Carson City, NV 00000
(000) 000-0000

FOCUS

To acquire field experience necessary to become an alcohol and drug rehabilitation counselor

RELEVANT QUALIFICATIONS

➤ Former alcohol and drug abuser now in recovery, having completed a rigorous rehabilitation program without any recidivism for over 3 years.
➤ Avid supporter of others experiencing the nightmare of addiction; keenly sensitive to their feelings and needs to enable joining with clients in early stages of interaction.
➤ Confident facilitator; relate comfortably with diverse cultural and socio-economic populations in didactic sessions with groups of from 12 to over 40.
➤ Observant of clients' behaviors, with documentation of improvements or lack thereof, to assist authorities in planning appropriate actions upon their release from the 28-day program.

EDUCATION

St. Jude's College, Reno, NV

➤ Graduate of the Recovery Assistance Program Training (RAPT), 2005
➤ Completed 270 educational hours toward CADC certification. Curriculum included: Addiction and Its Effects; The Recovery Process; Family Counseling; Individual Counseling; and Group Counseling.
➤ Passed written exam given by the International Certification Reciprocating Consortium (ICRC), 2005

PROFESSIONAL EXPERIENCE

Counselor-in-Training at Straight and Narrow, a psycho-social 12-step rehabilitative agency in Carson City, NV (2005 to present).

➤ Conduct 1 1/2 hour didactic sessions to groups which include mentally ill chemical abusers (MICA), focusing on their recovery.
➤ Assist with the new client intake process, assessing and prioritizing service requirements.
➤ Orient prospective clients to the rehabilitative setting and the programs available to them.
➤ Facilitate the adjustment of introductory groups on a daily basis, providing them with support and encouragement to stay with the program.
➤ Schedule clients for art therapy and daily recreation, and coordinate their other activities.
➤ Ease clients' transition into didactic sessions by introducing deep breathing and relaxation techniques as a part of daily meditation preliminaries.

FORMER EMPLOYMENT

Bartender, Happy Days Lounge, Reno, NV (1994-2004)
Server, Bartolucci's Ristorante, Reno, NV (1992-1994)

VOLUNTEER ACTIVITIES

➤ Initiated support group in Carson City for parents of drug addicted/alcohol dependent children and adolescents, working closely with the police department and D.A.R.E. program.

Paralegal

Jody needed to highlight her formal training as well as transferable experience as she transitioned from law enforcement to paralegal work.

Jody Gilroy

4321 E. 129th #J8 ■ Denver, CO 00000
555.555.5555 ■ jgil@attol.com

PARALEGAL

Skilled office professional with exceptional interpersonal and communication skills. Highly organized and detail-oriented; efficiently manages time and projects with close attention to deadlines. Effective in stressful situations and able to successfully work with diverse populations. Persuasive and tenacious.

EXPERIENCE

- Drafting legal documents, affidavits, and preparing orders
- Conducting independent interviews and investigations without supervision
- Serving as liaison between attorneys, investigators, court clerks, and judges
- Researching case law using the library and Internet
- Proofreading for accuracy and consistency
- Opening and maintaining case files
- Proficient in Microsoft Office and scheduling applications

FORMAL TRAINING AND COURSEWORK IN CIVIL AND CRIMINAL LAW

Civil Litigation	Drafting of pleadings, preparation of motions, discovery and pretrial data certificates and trial notebooks
Ethics	Client confidences, conflicts of interest, unauthorized practice of law
Contracts	Offers, acceptance, consideration, illegal contracts, third-party contracts, contractual capacity, remedies, Uniform Commercial Code, discharge of obligations, provision
Research	Statutes, digest, case law, citators, encyclopedias, dictionaries, online databases
Torts	Negligence, intentional torts, strict liability, personal injury litigation, settlements
Criminal Law	Statutory and common law, criminal theory and interpretation of statutes
Public Law	Business and economic regulation and ethical considerations

EDUCATION

A.G.S. Pikes Peak Community College, Westminster, CO, May 2006

PROFESSIONAL DEVELOPMENT

- Leadership Training
- Administrative Plan, Policies, Procedures, and Programs
- Interviewing and Interrogation (Reid Technique)
- Conflict Management

WORK HISTORY

Peace Officer/Investigator, Boulder County, Boulder, CO 2003 – 2005
Communications/Correction Officer, Adams County, Denver, CO 2002 – 2003
Trainee, Southwestern Louisiana Criminal Justice Academy, 2000 – 2001
Intelligence Analyst, US Army, Fort Caron, LA 1998 – 2000
DUI Technician, New Orleans County Sheriff's Office, New Orleans, LA 1996 – 1997
Intelligence Analyst, US Marine Corps, Jacksonville, FL 1993 – 1996

Loss Prevention Management

Jerry's background in security for a large department store chain shows his fast-track progression to positions of increasing responsibility, which he used to transition into a corporate loss prevention environment.

Jerry Zeliff

■ 909 Omega Street ■ Peachtree, GA 00000 ■ Home (000) 000-0000 ■ Cell (000) 000-0000 ■ E-Mail jerry104@buzztalk.com ■

■ **Loss Prevention Management** ■ **Industrial Security** ■ **Fraud Investigation** ■

QUALIFICATIONS

- Expertise in investigation, analysis, and evaluation of internal and external theft cases gained through fast-track promotions over 8 years in retail security positions.
- Skilled trainer and motivator of loss prevention associates for a major retail organization.
- Experienced in collaborating with police and court authorities, as well as regional and corporate level investigators in matters leading to prosecution.
- Strength in timely and accurate tracking/preparation of investigative paperwork, which includes audits of shipping invoices, sales and inventory reports, and POS transactions involving underrings, check, credit card or refund fraud.

OPERATIONAL KNOWLEDGE

Equipment: Installation, testing and use of covert cameras, VCRs, two-way radios, alarm and fire systems, closed circuit TV, and Sensormatic devices.

Methods: Undercover investigation, observation towers, two-way mirrors, cash register monitoring, recognition of suspect shopper behavior.

Related Matters: Trained in CPR and first response techniques. Basic PC literacy for database search, inventory reporting and word processing.

CAREER PROGRESSION

<u>BLOOMINGTON'S DEPARTMENT STORES,</u> Chamblee, GA 1999 to Present
Shortage Control Auditor, corporate headquarters (since 2005)

- Implemented shortage awareness program through audits of all stores and distribution centers to assure compliance to company's policies and procedures. Followed up on matters of non-compliance.
- Through the audit process, identified areas where additional training was needed and instituted such.
- Resolved shortage related issues as they arose.
- Assisted in the development and monitoring of a high-tech security program, designed to reduce shortages in selected stores with high occurrences.
- Participated in financial audits.
- Wrote and edited company policies and procedures, particularly in the area of inventory.
- Increased electronic communications with stores via computer and POS system.

Loss Prevention Manager, multistore operations (2003-2005)

- Held charge position for all internal and external investigations at store level for two locations.
- Selected to fill position left vacant for 3 months. In less than 5 months, cleared up a paperwork backlog, reinforced procedures, then hired and trained new security staffs of 3 for each store.
- Instituted safety and security awareness program throughout sales floors, fitting rooms and checkouts.
- Implemented $1 million budget for the security function.

... Continued

<u>BLOOMINGTON'S DEPARTMENT STORES</u> (Continued)
Loss Prevention Manager, level "A" store, Atlanta, GA (2002-2003)
- Applied and expanded security techniques for one of largest stores in the chain, located in a busy mall.
- Communicated with other mall store security managers in efforts to apprehend shoplifters.
- Won "Manager of the Quarter" award, out of over 25 other managers employed in this store.
- Promoted to manage neglected multistore security situation.

Loss Prevention Manager, new store opening, Dalton, GA (2001)
- Assigned to management team to oversee the installation and testing of all security systems at new location.
- Screened, hired and trained new security personnel. Oriented all new hires for store opening. Implemented shoplifter detection incentive program.

Loss Prevention Manager, single store, Buford, GA (2000-2001)
- In first management assignment at strip mall store, trained staff of 3 in all store detective duties.

Manager Trainee, corporate headquarters (1999-2000)
- Intensive program covering cash office, distribution centers, receiving, service desk, internal investigations, theft detection and statistical work.

VOLUNTEER WORK

PEACHTREE AUXILIARY POLICE DEPARTMENT
Assist with patrol, traffic and related emergency police duties.

EDUCATION

JASPER COUNTY COLLEGE
A.A.S. in Criminal Justice with emphasis in private security, June 1999

Police Officer/Security Operations

Andrew has moved jobs a few times, so some short positions after his active-duty military time have been grouped together here. This is an interesting combination of law enforcement and medical background.

ANDREW LEXINGTON

555 Clear Water Path
Baltimore, MD 21045

555.555.5555 (h)
LEXINGTON@YAHOO.COM

Career Focus

Law Enforcement, Security, or Force Protection Operations

Personal & Professional Value

International Police Officer, Liaison Coordinator, and Police Instructor, with 6 years experience in law enforcement and military medical operations with specific expertise in the following:

- Excellent Interpersonal Skills
- Superior Oral and Written Communications
- Intelligence Analyst
- Brief High Level Delegations
- Instructor & Trainer
- Tactical Operations Analyst
- Counterterrorism Activities
- Service to Kosovo & Operation Desert Storm

- Troubleshooter & Problem Solver
- Self-motivated
- Surveillance
- Tradecraft
- Marksman
- Liaison & Intelligence Sources
- Solve Crimes
- Surgical Technician

PROFESSIONAL EXPERIENCE

International Police Officer, Contracted thru Brown & Root, Bosnia   *2002 to Present*

- Managed regular police duties from responding to murder and other crime scenes to handling neighborhood disturbances. Work with interpreters and train local national police officers in managing crime scenes including surveillance, tradecraft, report writing, investigations, interviewing witnesses, and suspects.
- Conduct frequent liaison with local nationals and law enforcement agencies. Conduct hands-on training for new personnel.
- Promoted to a Primary Field Training Officer and conducted classroom training teaching local nationals how to develop and establish a working police department. Moved on as a SWAT trainer, responsible for working with the top officers in the field. Played an instrumental role in the development and foundation building the Regional SWAT Team. Trained the special SWAT Team in lawful breaching of buildings, tactical entry methods, antiterrorism training, firearms instruction, team building, riot control, hostage extraction, vehicle extractions, explosives, etc.
- Utilized excellent mediation and interpersonal communication skills to bring the two groups together, solve problems, discuss issues, and form the multi-ethnic unit. Conducted constant liaison with local police and military forces to determine threat levels to ensure Force Protection.
- Further promoted to Liaison Officer. Gather intelligence information from various source operations and prepare and deliver briefings to high-level decision makers. Act as a bridge between NATO and the United Nations to determine when to use police forces to diffuse public or military uprisings or other threats.
- Monitor intelligence data gathering and collection activities in the tactical operations center. Gathered information culminating in the prosecution of seven bombings under terrorist activity.

Police Officer, Baltimore, MD   *1998 to 2002*

- Patrolman working within inner city neighborhoods. Responded to calls for service. Directed traffic at the scene of fires, investigated burglaries, or provided first aid as required to accident victims.
- Assisted other officers to secure crime or accident scenes, collect or protect evidence.
- Built relationships with local citizens mobilizing neighborhoods to help fight crime.

- Investigated suspected crimes including murder, burglaries, domestic violence/disturbances, gang problems, suspicious activities, and unpaid parking tickets.
- Communicated effectively both orally speaking with citizens and responding to emergencies or diffusing problems at crime scenes/accidents, and in writing reports of investigation. Interviewed witnesses and suspects at the scene.

One-Year Assignments:

Sales Representative, American General Insurance Company   1997 to 1998
- Certified and Licensed Insurance Sales Representative for health, fire and life insurance.

Law Firm Runner, Baltimore, Mason and Associates, Baltimore, MD   1996 to 1997
- Acted as a liaison between the law firm and the court system. Filed legal paperwork with all courts: Federal, State, Municipal, Appeals, etc.

Operating Room Technician, Columbia Infirmary Surgical Unit, MD   1995 to 1996
- Assisted doctors during surgery in the operating room as a sterile member of the surgical team.

Army Medic, U.S. Army National Guard, Fort Meade, MD 1989 to present

Called to Active Duty for Operation Desert Storm and Operation Iraqi Freedom
- Received hands-on surgical training on various procedures for over 500 documented surgeries. Familiar with medical terminology, prescription medications and doses.
- Tasked to operate a medical clinic during the Persian Gulf War. Performed surgeries in combat.

EDUCATION

- Bachelor of Arts, Interdisciplinary Studies, University of Maryland, 2002
  Emphasis on Psychology, Sociology, and Criminal Justice

PROFESSIONAL DEVELOPMENT

- International Police Programs—Police Assessment, Selection & Training Program (Conflict Analysis, Beretta M-9 pistol training, defensive tactics, baton and OC aerosol irritant and Officer Safety Defensive Mindset and Surveillance Detection)
- Problem Solving, Columbia Police Department
- Criminal Justice Seminar
- Emergency Vehicle Operator's Course
- Computerized Criminal Justice Training
- Police Academy, Elected Class Vice President (25 weeks)
- Operating Room Specialist & Certified Surgical Technician Course, U.S. Army Academy of Health Sciences, 1992 (4 months)

~ Received several awards for professionalism and exemplary performance in the military and police department ~
~ Supervised and organized the donation of over 7,000 hours of volunteer service to Children's organizations as President of college fraternity. Received a National Award for Service ~

Law Enforcement Officer

Because James is a recent graduate, his education section needed to come first; however, he also wanted to emphasize his experience as a trainer and team leader.

JAMES BURLINGTON

9803 Clinton Avenue
Lubbock, TX 79424

(806) 783-9900
jamesb@door.net

Career Profile

GRADUATING STUDENT
Career Targets: Law Enforcement ▪ Criminal Justice
Dependable, service-focused professional with strong background knowledge in Human Services and Criminal Justice, complemented by work experience reflecting promotion, excellent service delivery, and meticulous attention to detail. Able to manage multiple tasks and responsibilities in fast-paced, demanding environments; exercise calm approach in pressure situations.

Areas of Ability

- Customer Service
- Team Leadership
- Business Ethics
- Quality Standards

- Law & Rules Enforcement
- Public Service Delivery
- Public Speaking
- Team Collaboration

- Problem Solving/Resolution
- Workplace Organization
- Multi-Task Management
- Classroom Presentations

Education
Texas Tech University, Lubbock, TX
BSOE in Human Services, Emphasis in Criminal Justice
Completed August, 2006

Selected Upper-Level Coursework:

- Police Administration
- Minority Relations
- Criminal Investigations

- Vice & Narcotics
- Theories of Personality
- Introduction to Social Work

- Organized Crime
- Police-Community Relations
- Forensic Psychology

Work Experience

Certified Trainer / Bartender / Team Leader (2002 – Present)
Orlando's, Lubbock, TX
Promoted from original busser position to train staff of eight bussers in all duties; hand-selected by management to work bartending shifts in addition to training schedule. Provide hands-on instruction to new and established bussers; team with management to ensure fulfillment of all service and quality goals. As Bartender, interact directly with guests and team members, including servers, kitchen personnel, hosts, and managers; handle large amounts of cash on each shift.

Key Contributions/Accomplishments:
- Contribute comprehensive, quality training for diverse group of bussers; demonstrate patience with new employees and provide assistance during busy periods.
- Place uncompromising focus on guest service delivery; commended by management team for positive attitude and attention to guests' needs.

Garden Shop Associate (2001 – 2002)
Sutherland's, Lubbock, TX
Held responsibility for organizing garden shop, with emphasis on outside garden area; worked with team of five in arranging tables, displays, product placement, and inventory storage areas. Maintained area cleanliness and assisted customers as needed.

Key Contributions/Accomplishments:
- Earned consistently favorable performance evaluations and recommendation for promotion to Lead Associate position based on training and mentoring abilities.
- Maintained well-organized, attractive outside garden area to secure attention of customers and influence buyer decisions for key product offerings.

Volunteer – University Medical Center, Lubbock, TX. Worked in outpatient pharmacy for 18-month period; assisted with verifying inventory and filling prescriptions.

Airport Fire Chief

EDWARD JONES, II

813-422-8521 _ ejones@email.com
3079 Lands Crossing _ Lithia _ FL _ 33572

OBJECTIVE

To provide leadership and guidance as an Airport Fire Chief utilizing extensive training, distinguished service, and experience in the field.

PROFILE

Decorated military Fire Chief with 25+ years of experience in all aspects of fire-fighting operations. Consistent record of exceeding standards and expectations by choosing the most challenging assignments that were above and beyond the call of duty. Highly motivated and organized, with a documented ability to motivate and train units and subordinates. Areas of expertise include:

Fire, Rescue & Recovery	Politically Sensitive Operations
Emergency Medical Services	Safety Regulations/Standards & Inspections
Hazardous Materials	Curriculum Development & Instruction

CREDENTIALS

National Fire Academy Incident Command System Training	Fire Investigation
Fire Protection Internships at Skilled, Advanced, and Superintendent Levels	Fire Prevention Technician Course
Leadership for Mid-Level & Senior Managers	Ranger Propane Fire Safety School
Principles of Instructional Systems	Fire Protection Management Applications
	On-Scene Commander's Course Development

RECORD OF EXPERIENCE

UNITED STATES AIR FORCE 1970-Present

Randolph Air Force Base – Texas
Fire Chief, Hazardous Materials Program Manager, and Safety Design Review Authority
- Management of fire-fighting teams with a record of encountering numerous fires and medical incidents without injuries and minimal loss.
- Initiated and implemented changes within six fire fighting companies advancing a "satisfactory" inspection rating to an "outstanding" rating by headquarter experts.
- Secured initial accreditation for the Department of Defense from the International Fire Safety Accreditation Council.
- Directed childcare center staff toward flawless fire safety certification.
- Reduced construction costs by $2.5 million, utilizing lower cost materials and procedures.
- Increased OSHA compliance.
- Received an Air Force Achievement Medal for solving problems with the P-23 Fire Vehicle.

Ramstein Air Base – Germany
- Fire Chief, Hazardous Materials Program Manager, and Safety Design Review Authority
- Supervised a department of 95 personnel.
- Directed all operations as "On-Scene Commander" during major aircraft incidents, resulting in zero injuries and minimal damage.
- Presided as final review authority for fire safety designs and installations.

Andrews Air Force Base – Maryland
Fire Chief
- Served as main contact for fire, rescue, and emergency medical services for 234 Air Force families.
- Decreased base fires by 88%.
- Ensured highly visible fire protection for the President, visiting heads of state, and high-ranking dignitaries.
- Created a hazardous material program in a record six-month period.
- Passed OSHA inspection without a single discrepancy.

Eglin Air Force Base – Florida
Deputy Fire Chief
- Led and motivated unit of command from a "barely acceptable" inspection rating to an "excellent" rating by the Air Force Inspector General in only 100 days.
- Pioneered new standards for airfield barrier operations currently used in the United States and six other nations.
- Controlled politically sensitive operations in foreign territory.

Langley Air Force Base – Virginia
Shift Supervisor
- Acted as deputy fire chief in absence of fire chief; supervised 12 fire fighters.
- Participated in a cardiovascular study conducted by the Air Force, which set fitness standards for all active-duty members worldwide.

Los Angeles Air Force Station – California
Station Fire Chief
- Qualified as the youngest person to hold position within the previous 10-year period.
- Oversaw all fire fighting operations for Space Command Tracking Facility.
- Worked with Air Force civil engineers to ensure compliance of all buildings with OSHA safety regulations.

Robins Air Force Base – Georgia
Instructor
- Composed and facilitated curriculum to entry-level USAF fire fighters.
- Recognized as "Instructor of the Year."

Langley Air Force Base – Virginia
Fire Fighter
- Helped direct rescue and recovery missions at air crash sites.
- Awarded "Airman of the Quarter."

Edwards Air Force Base – California
Fire Fighter

Robins Air Force Base – Georgia
Student, United States Air Force Fire Fighting School

HONORS

- Air Force Commendation Medal with Two Oak Leaf Clusters (End of Tour Decoration)
- Meritorious Service Medal with One Oak Leaf Cluster (End of Tour Decoration)
- John P. Morely Memorial Award for Heroism in Lifesaving Operations

Security/Operations Management

Mark Barber

15711 Central Drive ◆ San Francisco, CA 94124

(415) 555-1212 ◆ barbermark@hotmail.com

Career Profile

- Over 14 years of management and leadership experience in security operations and related functions with prominent hotels, retailers, and security providers.
- Currently functions as Director of Security for a prestigious four star/four diamond hotel, earning the highest performance ranking in the company in 2001. Have directed up to 200 officers and developed/managed $500,000+ budgets. Possess an extensive knowledge of security industry standards.
- Develop and lead effective and united teams, transforming fragmented factions into a cohesive alliance of professionals producing exceptional results and adhering to strict codes of conduct. Employ a dedicated hands-on management style that has dramatically increased effectiveness and reduced turnover,
- Certified in Lodging Security Directorship, Hospitality Law, Hotel Security Management, Disaster Preparedness and Emergency Response, Threat Management, Workplace Violence, and OSHA Regulations. Member of the American Society for Industrial Security and the Northern California Security Chiefs Association.

Areas of Expertise

- Security industry standards
- Budget creation and management
- Human Resources management functions
- Recruiting, training, and development
- Coaching, counseling, and motivation
- Departmental turnarounds
- Program and procedures development
- Motivational team leadership
- Interviewing, selection, performance evaluations

Career Development

Director of Security Operations, Four Star Hotel, San Francisco, California   1997 to Present

- Manage all aspects of the security operation of this prestigious, top-rated, 600,00-square-foot luxury hotel with 300 rooms, a daily roster of 1,000 employees/guests, and 14 full-time security officers.
- Dramatically reversed poor performance history of key hotel departments, achieving ranking of first in the company in 2001
- Decreased number of security-related incidents by 30%, the lowest in hotel's history.
- Lowered workers' compensation injuries to 7 cases (of 300 workers), the smallest in the company's history.
- Raised quality/efficiency while reducing overtime by 65%, the lowest rate in the department's history.
- Instituted standards that did not allow a single successful safety or security litigation in five years.
- Earned top ranking as company's best managed department.
- Achieved lowest employee turnover rate in the entire company.

Produced these results by creating and implementing leading-edge programs including... Innovative training, evaluation, and TQM programs that produced employee motivation, attention, interest, cooperation, and desired response... Standard operating procedures for crisis management, disaster prevention and recovery, risk management, emergency response, incident investigation, and report writing... Detailed investigation standards for all security and safety incidents, including policy violations, and guest or employee injuries.

Chief of Security, DeLuxe Hotel, San Francisco, California   1996 to 1998

Directed security operations of this three star/four diamond national chain hotel with 200 guest rooms, 200 employees, and 6 security officers, devising effective security policies and procedures, and budgeting and monitoring department's expenditures.

- Produced a 20% decrease in security-related incidents.
- Reduced employee turnover by 50%.

Established new standard operating procedures. Developed and implemented emergency action plans. Contributed to creation of multiple departments' security and safety requirement training programs. Cooperated closely with the Human Resources department on OSHA, workers' compensation, and other industrial safety matters to ensure state and federal compliance.

Operations Manager, Redwood Security, San Francisco, California   1993 to 1995
Managed over 200 plainclothes and uniform contract security officers in multiple facilities, including defense contractors and film studios. Developed and promoted a proactive culture of risk management and prevention. Promoted through the ranks from Field Officer to Operations Manager, the highest rank within the division.
- Implemented new rewards and recognition programs that raised morale and provided continuous feedback.
- Frequently volunteered extended hours to meet clients' needs and critical project deadlines.

Acted as client liaison to develop partnerships and strategic loss prevention and asset protection programs. Oversaw Human Resources operations including officer selection, field deployment, training, scheduling, inspections, evaluations, and disciplinary actions. Established professional ties with local police authorities.

Loss Prevention Manager, Nordstrom's, Thousand Oaks, California   1990 to 1993
Oversaw security staff and operations at this upscale retailer.
- Protected assets and reduced legal liability by creating ongoing prioritized loss prevention initiatives.
- Developed effective loss countermeasure strategies and prevention awareness training programs.
- Conducted comprehensive internal audits and investigations for external/internal sources of loss and employee misconduct.
- Minimized accidents and injuries by managing effective safety programs.

Technology Skills
- Proficient in Microsoft Word, Excel, IRIMS, and PPM2000.
- PC proficient in Windows 98/95/3.1
- Extensive knowledge of computer-based, audio/visual, and access control systems.

Education and Certification
Bachelor of Science in Political Science, University of Southern California
Certifications:
- Lodging Security Director (CLSD), American Hotel & Motel Association
- Hospitality Law, AH&MA Educational Institute
- Hotel Security Management, AH&MA
- Disaster Preparedness and Emergency Response, City of San Francisco Fire Department
- Threat Management and Workplace Violence, City of San Francisco Fire Department
- OSHA Regulations and Workplace Violence, California Hotel & Motel Association
- Food Handler, San Jose County Department of Health

Security Services Sales

MARTHA SAYLES
333 Morrow Lane
Raleigh, NC 27612

(218) 555-5555
msayles@careerbrain.com

Professional Profile

Sales • Account Management • New Business Development Professional

Sales and Account Management Development professional with expert qualifications in identifying and capturing market opportunities to accelerate expansion, increase revenues, and improve profit contributions in highly competitive industries. Outstanding record of achievement in complex account and contract negotiations.

Key Strengths:

- Account development/management
- Customer service/satisfaction
- Bilingual English/Spanish
- Customer needs assessment
- PC proficient
- Consultative/solutions sales
- New market development
- Account retention
- Presentation and negotiations skills

Professional Experience

Key Account Executive, 1999 – Present

American Security Services, Largest privately held security company in the nation with annual sales over $400 million.
Recruited to start up and oversee the market development of contract security services in North Carolina. Conduct in-depth client need assessments and develop technology-based security strategies to ensure maximum efficiency.

- Achieve consistent annual sales production in excess of $2.5 million
- Built territory from ground zero capturing 55% of market share in region
- Expanded annual billable hours from 300 to more than 5,000, fostering a rapid growth in staffing from 30 to more than 300 employees in Raleigh branch
- Successfully negotiated and secured sales ranging from $300K to $1.2 million
- Earned several national and local awards for top sales performance, including the prestigious "Rookie of the Year" award

Account Executive/Loan Officer, 1998 – 1999

Equity Finance, Inc., Nation's oldest finance company, a division of a Fortune 500 company.
Generated and sold bill consolidation loans through telemarketing.

- Consistently exceeded monthly sales objectives
- Received national recognition as one of the Top 10 salespeople in the nation, and Number 1 salesperson in Raleigh branch.

Education

Bachelor of Arts, Business Administration/Finance (GPA 3.8) 1997
University of North Carolina, Chapel Hill

Catherine M. Sipowicz

36 Algonquin Drive • East Brunswick, NJ 08816 • 732.555.5555 • jcsipowicz2006@yahoo.com

INSIDE SALES MANAGER ~ OFFICE MANAGER

Professional Inside Sales Manager and Office Manager with over 10 years experience in all phases of the business cycle. Consistently exceed objectives and increase bottom-line profits for employers. A quick learner and an excellent communicator with an ability to perform well in a multi-tasking environment.

Extensive experience in the sales process from order entry through customer service. Thrive in manufacturing and production arenas; a detail-oriented individual, friendly and personable, a self-starter with a willingness to work well as a member of a team.

Creative and skilled analyst with strong problem-solving skills offering outstanding systems expertise (conversions, upgrades, and training), excellent computer and internet skills.

Areas of Expertise:

- Office Management
- Project Management
- Customer Service
- Customer Sales Profiles
- Inventory Control

- Credit and Collections
- Problem Identification/Solutions
- Sales Management Support
- Commission Reporting
- Inside Sales

Professional Experience

AMERICAN BOUQUET COMPANY, INC. – *Edison, New Jersey (1993 to 2006)*
Inside Sales Account Manager (2001–2007)
Responsible for maintaining $7 million of current business and coordinating all functions between the outside sales staff and the internal departments of the company.

- Directed and coordinated activities concerned with the sales organization including screening and evaluating new customers, performing credit authorizations, verifying client's sales history, and compiling monthly sales comparisons.
- Appointed as inside Sales Account Manager to handle a major supermarket chain buying $3 million of floral products, resulting in a 23% sales increase in the first year.
- Provided sales forecasts for holidays and special events which greatly increased the efficiency and accuracy of production schedules and purchasing requirements.
- Designed an innovative program to evaluate effectiveness of new marketing campaigns. Hired and supervised a merchandiser to track the program on a weekly basis.
- Developed an automated monthly sales comparison analysis with the IT department reducing the report generation time from 8 hours to 1 hour.

Office Manager (1996–2001)
Manage a multitude of tasks contributing to the daily operations of American Bouquet Company. Responsible for hiring, training, motivation and supervision of the telemarketing staff.

- Developed and implemented various systems for optimizing production resources and increasing efficiency. Designed Excel spreadsheets and standardized forms for use by all departments.
- Enhanced interdepartmental communications resulting in reduced production and billing errors.

Administrative Assistant (1993–1996)
Coordinated communications between sales and production. Performed credit checks, collections, and resolved price discrepancies. Responsible for inventory, price lists, and customer lists.

- Project Manager for developing, implementing, and maintaining an inventory control system that utilized coding to correlate new orders with production scheduling.

Education

BA in Political Science, **RUTGERS UNIVERSITY,** New Brunswick, New Jersey – 1993

Automotive Sales and Service

Jonathan brought attention to his specific expertise of being able to locate "hard-to-find parts" at the beginning of his resume and attractively displayed his skills balanced with well-placed graphic lines.

JONATHAN THOMPSON

1234 S.E. Milwaukie Avenue   Portland, Maine 22222   message: 555-555-5555

Sales / Service • Automotive-Truck Parts

Qualifications & Skills Summary

Over 20 years experience in the Automotive-Truck Parts industry specializing in locating the hard-to-find parts.

- Committed
- Dedicated
- Proficient under stress
- Effective in fast-paced environment
- Efficient problem solver
- Even-tempered
- Excellent customer service
- Honest
- Learn & adapt quickly
- Persistent

- Personable
- Reliable
- Resourceful
- Strong product knowledge
- Superb follow through
- TAMS Autolog & Triad Computer System
- Thorough
- Troubleshooter
- Trustworthy

History of Employment

Lead Counterman • GO Garage Parts, Inc. • Portland, Maine • *2003-2005*
Answered phones, received parts orders. Researched parts and supplied recommendations. Worked with shop equipment sales. Supplied customer service support often recommending specific tools for certain jobs. Looked up service bulletins on All Data and assisted technicians. Specialized in obtaining hard-to-find parts.

Parts Controller • Clark's Discount Honda Repair • Portland, Maine • *1999-2002*
Received orders and ordered parts. Maintained inventory control. Wrote service orders for customers. Test-drove vehicles. Company had 6 bays.

Counterman • Ed's Auto Parts • Portland, Maine • *1993-1998*
Looked up parts for walk-in and telephone customers. Received and processed orders from dealers and other shops. Troubleshoot and provide solutions for customers. Deliveries and some machine shop work.

Outside Sales • Roy Farnam Supply • LaGrande, Maine • *1983-1992*
progressively promoted from initial position of **Stock Clerk/Delivery**
Mixed paint for custom colors. Worked extensively in machine shop. Operated overhead Broach, performed valve jobs, installed valve guides and assembled two engines with excellent results.

Assistant Purchasing Agent • Union County Road Department • LaGrande, Maine • *1980-1982*
Purchased road repair supplies. Ordered parts for light to heavy trucks, caterpillars, graders, and rock crusher.

Advertising Sales (Entry-Level)

Melody J. Courtney

87211 Jennywood Lane • Glendale, OH 45246

555-555-5555 *cell*   home *777-777-7777*

Strengths: Enthusiastic, creative, and hard-working advertising major with demonstrated successful sales experience. Reputation for providing excellent customer service resulting in increased sales and improved customer retention. Eager to translate solid classroom and internship experience in advertising sales into bottom-line revenues in the radio/television industry.

Education: B.S. in Advertising, Case Western Reserve University, Cleveland, OH – May, 2003. Coursework included advertising research & strategy, design & graphics, media planning, ad sales & campaigns.

Senior Project
- *Challenge:* Create an advertising campaign for the Ohio Hospice Group.
- *Action:* As key member of a 6-person team, performed demographics survey, developed campaign strategies, created logo and slogan, authored and designed bilingual brochures, and created media kit within $250,000 budget.
- *Result:* After presenting project to 11-person panel, won first place out of 12 teams. The Ohio Hospice Group implemented the slogan and several campaign strategies.

Internships
Advertising Sales Representative, Great Lakes Advertising, Cleveland, OH, Sept. – Dec. 2002
- Sold print advertising to local businesses using cold calling techniques.

Production Assistant, TV5 (NBC affiliate), Akron, OH, Jan. – May 2002
- Assisted with production of 2 to 3 commercials a week. Accountable for delivering all technical equipment to the site and pre-production set up of lights, monitors, microphones, and cameras. Worked closely with sales department and producer, learning both the technical side of commercial production as well as sales and customer service issues.
- Handled pre-production and on-air tasks for the noon news, including studio set up, script delivery, running pre-taped segments during the news, operating on-air cameras and soundboards.

Sales/Customer Service Experience
Sales/Wait Staff, Great Lakes Brewpub, Cleveland, OH
- Consistently generate additional revenues utilizing thorough product knowledge and friendly sales technique to up-sell house specials and add-on items. Contender for the "$1,000 Night" sales award.

Host/Wait Staff, Jack's Seafood, Mentor, OH
- Developed repeat business by providing excellent customer service in fast-paced environment.

Awards/Memberships
- Won Silver Addy, an annual award for college students, 2002
- Served as Co-Director of Adwerks, developing ads for nonprofit organizations, 2001
- Member and committee chairperson of the Ad Society, a college professional organization, 2001 – 2003

International Sales/Marketing Manager

Meghan had worked her way through a fast-track entry-level program
and was ready to strike out on her own with another company.

MEGHAN M. ENGLAND

327 Bristol Circle • New Fort, NY 12345 • (888) 449-2200 • email@email.com

INTERNATIONAL SALES/MARKETING MANAGER
Strategic Planning/Staff Supervision & Training/Business Development

Highly accomplished and innovative marketing professional with key domestic and international experience in penetrating new markets, expanding existing accounts, and boosting profits. Fluent in English and Spanish. Results-oriented and visionary leader with proven success in new market identification, regional advertising, branding, and competitor analysis. Skilled in staff supervision and training, client relations, and strategic planning. Polished communication, presentation, negotiation, and problem-solving skills. Thrive in an intensely competitive, dynamic environment.

Core competencies include:

- Strategic Business Planning
- Budget Management
- Business Development/Planning
- Staff Training & Development
- Marketing Program Design

- Market Identification
- Team Building & Leadership
- Account Relationship Management
- International Client Relations
- Key Networking Skills

PROFESSIONAL EXPERIENCE

SAP AMERICA/SAP CHILE/LATIN AMERICA
Fast-track progression through the following key international marketing management positions:

Latin American Marketing Manager, **TAPP LATIN AMERICA – Newton Square, NY (2003 to Present)**
Direct and manage 360 degree company marketing programs throughout Argentina, Bolivia, Brazil, Chile, Colombia, Mexico, Paraguay, Peru, Puerto Rico, Venezuela, Uruguay, and the Caribbean Islands for the third largest software company worldwide. Oversee all aspects of Latin American regional marketing operations with broad responsibility for strategic planning and the indirect supervision of a staff of four marketing managers and various partner PR/advertising agencies.

Initiate, develop, and nurture new leads to generate additional sales revenues; collaborate with sales representatives to turnover leads and establish key relationships. Accomplish marketing goals by launching comprehensive marketing, advertising, and branding plans. Manage PR marketing functions through press releases, C-level executive interviews, press conferences, professional networking, and by creating an educational focus to allow greater company exposure. Ensure top-level customer satisfaction; collaborate with various outside agencies to administer and analyze customer surveys.

Develop and manage a $3 million marketing budget encompassing strategic industries such as banks, the public sector, and utility companies, as well as strategic solutions involving customer relationship management, enterprise resource planning, supply chain management, and small to mid-sized businesses. Design and implement regional advertising/branding strategies, and analyze progress through brand tracking studies and competitive reports. Pioneer and manage key relationships with high-profile industry analyst firms. Interact with an outside global advertising agency to effectively leverage internationally syndicated relationship marketing campaigns. Serve as a company representative, liaison, and central point-of-contact for providing vital information, managing market research, and resolving issues at all levels.

Key Accomplishments:

- Spearheaded and manage a highly effective electronic quarterly newsletter, resulting in increased communications among Latin American employees.

- Directed an extensive 8-month regional team project in successfully training and educating all Latin American marketing personnel on the newly implemented CRM system in the areas of budgeting/planning, campaign planning, preparation, execution/analysis, lead management, and reporting.
- Developed and initiated the first regional budget with the global marketing team.
- Pioneered the centralization of advertising, resulting in greater discounts and significant savings.
- Accomplished greater recognition for the company including the first, and many additional publications of the company president in regional magazine articles.

Marketing Manager, **TAPP CHILE – Santiago de Chile (2001 to 2003)**

Spearheaded, built, and launched the first marketing department for the company's Chilean subsidiary, with full responsibility for hiring, training, scheduling, supervising, mentoring, and evaluating marketing coordinator and marketing analyst staff members. Managed an $800,000 Enterprise Resource Planning marketing budget. Interacted directly with the sales team to implement marketing strategies and meet goals. Managed extensive market research and analysis functions by collaborating with a local agency to conduct focus group interviews in evaluating both company and competitor solutions. Involved in all aspects of production, public relations, sales, relationship building, and customer service.

Key Accomplishments:

- Created and implemented a lead generation program, resulting in an increased amount of qualified leads for Account Executives and improved revenues due to shorter sales cycle.
- Built solid PR operations by developing and managing high-impact press strategies; concurrently continued to initiate key media relationships, conduct press conferences and executive interviews.

Latin American Coordinator, **TAPP LATIN AMERICA – Wayne, NY (1998 to 2001)**

Managed the international roll-out and training for the company's Sales and Marketing Information System. Traveled extensively to various international locations to oversee all implementation and training functions. Concentrated on providing a full range of support to Finance and Marketing Directors.

Spanish Teacher, **CHASE CHEMICAL CORPORATION – Exton, NY (1998)**
Taught Spanish to top-level corporate executives.

Education & Credentials

BS in International Studies
EDUCATIONAL UNIVERSITY – Ross, NY (1997)

Language Studies
Seville/Segovia, Spain (1997)

Comprehensive Spanish Language Studies
Adelaide, Australia (1996)

Additional Professional Training in Business and Communications

Private Pilot License with instrument and commercial ratings

– Excellent Professional References Available on Request –

Database Administration

Jackie enjoys most the database administration portion of her current job and will be targeting employers that will give transition from database marketing to database administration.

Jacqueline Alois

188-17 Greenway, Salt Lake City, UT 00000
000-000-0000
jacqueline@alois.net

Database Management ◆ Marketing Communications ◆ E-mail Template Design

Profile

Sales and Marketing Support Professional with more than 14 years of experience in time-sensitive, fast-paced environments. Highly developed skills in oral and written communications, multitasking, attention to detail, and perseverance to completion. Keen insight into clients' perspectives, goals and target audiences. Proficient with various software programs including Word, Excel, Access and Goldmine.

Key strengths include:

◆ Database administration	Internal/external customer service
◆ Market research	Computer and procedural training
◆ Sales lead qualification	Project coordination
◆ Proactive problem solv ing	Relationship building
◆ Promotional copywriting	New account development

Professional Employment History

GRAYROCK COMMUNICATIONS INC., BEAR CREEK, UT   2002–PRESENT

Database Marketing Coordinator for trade-show design firm

- ◆ Assist the President, Creative Director and sales force of 7 in developing targeted messages to promote company's services (trade-show display design and client training seminars). Contribute ideas in brainstorming sessions and translate concepts into persuasive written materials (brochures, Web pages, and e-mail templates).
- ◆ Generate leads through extensive phone contact, which has facilitated the closing of numerous sales by determining clients' interests and addressing their specific needs or concerns.
- ◆ Enter and update all pertinent information for up to 500 clients and prospects on Goldmine system; create profiles and periodically send electronically distributed promotional pieces to keep company in the forefront for future business.
- ◆ Initially train new sales consultants on data mining to their best advantage as well as empower them for success in prospecting and cold calling. Organize sales assignments to avoid duplication of efforts.
- ◆ Coordinate all pre- and post-sale details with various departments.
- ◆ Demonstrated versatility and talent in several areas; was retained on staff despite 2 company downsizings.

QUIGLEY & VANCE, CARRINGTON, UT   2000–2002

Inside Sales Representative for graphic arts supply company

- ◆ Performed duties of sales liaison, assistant purchasing agent, and customer service representative.
- ◆ Streamlined department by automating the quote process and systematizing sales literature.

Education

Westview County College, Randolph, UT – A.A.S., Marketing Communications, 2000
Shelton Institute, Shelton, UT – Applied Writing and Database Administration courses, 2001

Sales and Marketing

179

Sales and Marketing Director

Kevin J. Borden

6 Helen Court
Monroe Township, New Jersey 08831
609-378-3456
E-mail: kevBorden@aol.com

Summary of Qualifications

Increasing responsibilities in the following areas:

- National Sales Management
- Corporate Advertising
- Supervision of Employees
- Training & Motivation
- New Account/Business Development
- Contract Management
- Marketing Programs
- Team & Relationship Building
- Performance Improvement
- Representative Liaison
- Purchasing/Inventory Control
- Vendor Relations

Profile

An accomplished sales and account management background, encompassing client relations and new business development....delivered presentations before Fortune 500 companies, manufacturers and distributors

Planned and conducted networking, canvassing, lead generation and direct marketing campaigns, as well as trade show presentations....recruited, trained and supervised employees....developed rapport with senior management, department heads, vendors, clients and sales personnel.

Professional Experience

SOLID TUBE CORPORATION, Clifton, NJ   2003-Present

Director of Sales & Marketing
Solid is the producer of welded pipe and welded tubing. Introduced a large customer base from the stainless steel industry to contract and continue as Solid's clients in the welded pipe and tubing area of the business.

- Hired eight sales representatives to sell Solid's products in different regions in the country.

- Developed new pricing strategies including rebates, freight considerations for inventory, business, and direct business to attract new accounts for long-term relationships.

- Personally covered local outside sales territories including New Jersey, New York, Pennsylvania, and Delaware.

- Ensured trust and service for new customers.

- Set up an inside sales group for sales training through New Jersey State Funding packages. The state-run program proved a significant savings for training expenses.

- Developed a new brochure and detailed chart for outside sales presentations to enhance our company's communications.

- Created programs for advertisements in various trade magazines and promotional vehicles that were successful in bringing in new inquiries regarding our products and ultimately new customers.

- Arranged outings for social events and served as liaison that designed new markets for growth opportunities.

- Defined markets and targeted the right customer populations for the sales force.

Professional Experience (continued)

SWIFT TUBE, INC., North Branch, NJ   **1988-2002**

Vice President of Sales   1996-2002
Sales Manager   1988-1996

Assumed full responsibility for all sales and marketing functions for this steel company. Played a key role in the organization's growth from $12 million to over $40 million in annual revenues, initiating and managing a series of business development strategies to increase activity from new and existing accounts.

Spearheaded programs to target previously untapped markets, which included a campaign geared toward the beverage industry that produced $8 million in annual sales.

- Secured lucrative agreements with such industry giants as Coca-Cola and Hess Oil, strengthening the company's overall competitive position.

- Built productive relationships with 10 independent representative agencies, instituting incentives, which heightened their efforts to promote the company's lines.

- Improved the performance of inside sales employees through effective training and motivation generating significant new business.

- Enhanced the company's image and visibility by launching aggressive advertising and marketing campaigns, which included ads in trade magazines, brochures and promotional items.

- Devised methods to facilitate more open communication between sales representatives and other departments in the company, including production, quality control and finance.

TUBE SALES, Cranbury, NJ   **1982-1988**

Purchasing & Inventory Control Coordinator

- Directed purchasing and inventory control activities for over $20 million of stainless steel tubing.

- Established a centralized purchasing system that generated substantial savings through more advantageous rates.

Education

Rider College, Lawrenceville, NJ
BS Degree in Business

Affiliations

Monroe Recreation Center, Coach
Forsgate Country Club, Member

Additional Keywords: stainless steel industry, welded pipe, welded tubing, steel industry, management, business development, sales, manufacturing sales, vendor negotiations, advertising, marketing, manufacturing account management, sales management.

Sales and Marketing

Sales Executive

Mary Ann was a recent college grad looking for a job
while she continued training as a performer in New York.

MARY ANN BURROWS

123 Randolph Street
Wilmington, Delaware 19801
(555) 555-5555

Outside Sales/Account Manager/Customer Service

Energetic and goal-focused sales professional with solid qualifications in large account management and customer relationship building/maintenance. Proven ability to develop new business and increase sales within established accounts and mature territories. Self-confident and poised in interactions across all business hierarchies; a persuasive communicator and assertive negotiator with strong deal-closing abilities. Excellent time management skills; computer literate. Areas of demonstrated value include:

- Sales Growth / Account Development
- Commercial Account Management
- Prospecting & Business Development
- Customer Liaison & Service
- Consultative Sales / Needs Assessment
- Territory Management & Growth

PROFESSIONAL EXPERIENCE

Morris Mtr. Co., Wilmington, DE   1998 – Present
SALES EXECUTIVE (2000 – Present)
Promoted and challenged to revitalize a large metropolitan territory plagued by poor performance. Manage, service, and build existing accounts; develop new business, establishing both regional and national accounts. Serve as key liaison for all customers and work as the only outside sales representative in the company. Produce monthly reports for major national accounts.

Selected Results
- Reversed a history of stagnant sales; delivered consistent growth and built territory sales 22%, to $4.75 million annually, in less than 2 years.
- Surpassed quota by a minimum of 20% for 14 consecutive months.
- Personally deliver 95% of all sales generated for the company's main site.
- Prospected aggressively and presented products to key decision-makers during cold calls; opened more than 60 new commercial accounts.
- Improved account service and applied consultative sales techniques; grew sales in every established account a minimum of 15%.

MANAGER, Harrisburg Store (1998 – 2000)

MANAGER TRAINEE, Wilmington Store (1998)
Initially recruited as a management trainee and rapidly advanced to management of a retail location generating $1 million annually. Supervised and scheduled 12 employees. Budgeted and produced advertising, oversaw bookkeeping, and set/managed sales projections and growth objectives.

EDUCATION AND CREDENTIALS

B.S., BUSINESS MANAGEMENT, 1998
Wilmington College, New Castle, DE

Additional Training

Building Sales Relationships, 2001
Problem Solving Skills, 2001

Professional & Community Associations

Member, Chamber of Commerce, 1999 – Present
Member, Country Club and Women's Golf Association, 1999 – Present
Youth Soccer Coach and FIFA Certified Referee, 2002 – Present

Senior Account Executive

STEPHANIE CARMODY

109 DRURY LANE, PRINCETON, NJ 08540
(609) 555-5555 HOME • STEPHCAR@HOME.COM

- **15+ years experience** building partnerships with leading corporations to develop consumer packaging, sales promotions, and collateral to strengthen brand identity and awareness. In-depth understanding of technology, household products, personal care, liquor, and food categories.
- Account management capabilities enhanced by professional design, production, printing, and technical background. Formal design education and commitment to ongoing professional development.
- Adept in Macintosh and Windows applications for graphic design, desktop publishing, word processing, spreadsheets, e-mail, database management, Web site development, and multimedia presentations.

Key Words

Consultative Sales	High-Impact Presentations
Customer Service	Problem Solving & Decision Making
Project Management	Sales Closing & Negotiating
Design Process	Team Building & Leadership

Achievements

- Generated nearly a million dollars in annual sales for packaging design firm by winning key accounts and cultivating relationships.
- Won four Package Design Council (PDC) Gold Awards for package design in personal care and household appliances categories.
- Won account with major multinational corporation and developed packaging, promotional displays, trade, and consumer collateral material. Facilitated the national redesign (60 SKUs) in order to establish products as the technologically superior brand within the category.
- Collaborated on the national implementation of a "company first" branding strategy. Key objective: to reinforce the brand name, weakened by a four-year trend of sub-branding. Brainstormed with marketing and creative executives to create a set of graphic standards to communicate the essence of the brand. Applied this branding system to the entire product line.
- Increased sales and distribution through development of innovative club-store packaging and promotions for a leading liquor supplier.
- Guided design and production of packaging and product launch materials for a 30 SKU line of household products. Product was picked up nationally by Wal-Mart and sales jumped 19% in an introductory period.
- Worked with a leading cereal maker to develop promotional back panel games, sweepstakes, and in-pack offers.
- Directed development of displays, brochures, and merchandising materials for Certs Candy and Ocean Spray Fruit Waves (created through licensing agreement).
- Introduced multimedia capability to firm's new business presentations. Created Web site content including a company tour, an interactive portfolio, and a creative access section—allowing clients online, confidential access to view work.

Career Chronology

Senior Account Executive   2001 – Present
Leading Package Design Firm, Princeton, NJ

- Hired as a junior account executive to assist in all aspects of client services. Within seven months, promoted to account executive to develop new business in the consumer electronics category. Established key contacts with industry leaders through cold calling, direct marketing and client presentations. Consulted with clients to determine marketing objectives, packaging requirements and budgetary limitations. Directed numerous packaging, promotion, trade and consumer collateral material projects. Managed staff of five to implement the electronic design and production process.

Computer Graphics Artist   1998 – 2001
Big Design Firm, New York, NY

- Worked with designers and art directors to take concepts through to highly refined computer-based production. Trained members of the design and production department in the use of Adobe Illustrator. Setup a high-speed remote viewing network enabling select clients to simultaneously view design concepts.

Account Executive 1994 – 1998
Freelance Placement Agency, New York, NY

- Instrumental in establishing a lucrative desktop publishing placement division. Identified and cultivated profitable markets. Managed and art-directed freelancers and worked with clients through all project stages.

Graphic Designer 1985 – 1993
ABC Marketing & Communications, New York, NY

- Accountable for all stages of the design and production of consumer packaging. Participated in beta testing of proprietary graphics software and various high-end peripherals, giving product reviews to manufacturers.

Education

BFA: Graphic Design, Industrial Design, Computer Graphics and Marketing – 1988
New York University

Ongoing Professional Development

- Earned Certificate in Sales Promotion – St. John's University
- Intensive seminars in Web site design, multimedia, and advertising – Brown University

Sales and Marketing

Telemarketing Professional

JONATHAN YOUNG

555 King Street Waterbury, Vermont 74106
Tel: (802) 555-1212 E-Mail: jon@jonyoung.com

Profile

Telemarketing Specialist/Sales Manager/Team Leader with proven ability to lead sales teams in fast-paced, high-volume environments. Able to coordinate multiple projects and meet deadlines under pressure. Outstanding record in training, motivating, and retaining employees. Knowledgeable in telemarketing business methods and applicable laws.

Telemarketing Experience

Telephone Sales Representative, United States Telemarketing, Waterbury, Vermont, 2002 – Present

Management Trainer, AT&T Net, Burlington, Vermont,   2001 – 2002
Directed performance, training, and recruiting for 13- to 15-person bay marketing long distance and wireless services by telephone to prospective customers across the country.

- Implemented creative sales contests and incentive programs that increased revenues, boosted morale, and minimized employee turnover.
- Trained top-performing sales teams on effective telephone sales and closing techniques.
- Supervised team performance through call splitting and statistical reporting. Maintained target levels for quality management.
- Exceeded corporate goals for team sales per hour and sales hours fulfillment. Consistently ranked in top three of 32 bays.

Team Leader, Domestic Features, Burlington, Vermont,   2000 – 2001
Managed 9-person telemarketing team marketing family-friendly videos for privately owned international film production company with $60 million in annual revenues.

- Led successful teams recognized for commitment to company cause of promoting nonviolent films with no sexual content or innuendo, and influencing the film industry to offer more films of this nature.

Sales Experience

Independent Sales Professional/Certified Flooring Inspector, Burlington, Vermont, 1999 – 2000

Store Manager, Stickly Carpets, Burlington, Vermont,   1997 – 1999
Managed sales and operations for retail flooring business. Directed sales teams, scheduling, goal setting, and motivational seminars. Purchased merchandise from mills, negotiated contracts, and administered promotions and product merchandising.

- Achieved annual retail sales averaging $0.5 million with a gross profit margin of 35%.
- Hired, trained, and managed goal-oriented sales teams with below-average turnover.
- Conducted in-service training seminars for sales representatives teaching detailed product information and sales techniques.

Training

B.A. in Human Services, University of Vermont, Burlington, Vermont, 1997
Ongoing Professional Development: sales training and motivational seminars with Anthony Robbins, Tommy Hopkins, Zig Ziglar, Stephen Covey

Sales and Marketing

Pharmaceutical Rep

Jenny needed to translate "sales" expertise gained in three years on a job most think of as far removed from selling. She was employed as a pharmaceutical rep in just 29 calendar days.

Jenny McClean

4040 East 50th Street
Silver Spring, MD, 20904
[301] 555-5555 (Office) – [301] 555-6666 (Home)
jamclean@hotmail.com

Summary of Qualifications
- Organized, efficient, and precise with strong communication and liaison skills
- Skilled in planning and execution of special projects during time-critical assignment
- Decisive and direct, yet flexible in responding to constantly changing assignments
- Able to coordinate multiple projects and meet deadlines under pressure
- Enthusiastic, creative and willing to assume increased responsibility
- Attention to details and strong follow-through

Special Skills
- Language – Fluent in Spanish
- Computer – UNIX, VMA, Lotus Notes, MS Office, Word Perfect, SPSS 8.0, ESRI
- Certified in radiation safety
- Experience with medical terminology
- Database development

Relevant Skills
Office Administration
- Collecting and recording statistical and confidential information
- Assembling and organizing bulk mailing and marketing materials
- Data entry, with exceptionally fast typing and related Office Administration activities
- Organization specialist, able to ensure smooth and efficient flow of functions
- Progressive experience in office management, scheduling, and support services, data analysis, and research collection

Customer Service
- Extremely sociable and able to put visitors at ease
- Excellent verbal and written communication skills
- Highly skilled at solving customer relations problems

Education
- Masters in Public Administration, George Washington University, Washington, DC
- BA, Sociology, Concentration in Spanish, University of Pennsylvania, Allentown, PA

Relevant Professional Experience
PUBLIC HEALTH DATA ANALYST/NHMA MEMBERSHIP COORDINATOR
The National Hispanic Medical Association Washington, DC

ADMINISTRATIVE PRACTICUM
The VA Healthcare System, West Haven, CT

GRADUATE ASSISTANT IN CONTINUING EDUCATION
The G.W. University, Washington, DC

POLO RL SPECIALIST
Hecht's Company Department Store, Pittsburgh, PA

LAW CLERK
Patton & Page Law Firm, Pittsburgh, PA

Real Estate Development

Michael had a background in law, and he desired to
transition into financial management/project management.

MICHAEL WILSON

94-332 East Main Street ◆ Overland Park, KS, IA 66210
Home: [913] 555-1298 ◆ Cellular: [913] 555-6598 ◆ E-mail: mwilson@oceannet.com

OBJECTIVE

A position in REAL ESTATE DEVELOPMENT that will utilize strong analytical skills, knowledge of market-place trends and practices, and benefit from my legal background.

OVERVIEW

- Organized, take-charge professional with exceptional follow-through abilities and detail orientation; able to plan and oversee a full range of events from concept to successful conclusion.
- Demonstrated ability to efficiently prioritize a broad range of responsibilities in order to consistently meet deadlines.
- Dynamic negotiator; effective in achieving positive results. Licensed Mediator in NJ.
- Demonstrated capability to anticipate and resolve problems swiftly and independently.
- Possess strong interpersonal skills; proven ability to develop and maintain sound business relationships with clients, anticipating their needs.
- Highly articulate, effective communicator, experienced presenter: possess excellent platform skills.
- Highly adept in utilizing state-of-the-art software packages for industry-related functions, from data and finance management to CADD. Hands-on experience with Argus and Project.
- Currently completing Master's Degree in Real Estate Development at NYU.

Demonstrated skills in:

- Research
- Urban Development
- Accounting
- Bankruptcy
- Small Business Planning

- Mediation
- Legal Writing
- Analytical Writing
- Financial Analysis
- Small Business Development

- Mergers & Acquisitions
- Real Estate Tax Issues
- Corporate Finance
- Administrative System Design
- Foreclosure

PROFESSIONAL EXPERIENCE

May 2002 – Present
SMITH & ASSOCIATES, Overland Park, KS
Special Projects Consultant for well-respected communications consulting firm. Firm's principal authored two critically acclaimed standards in the marketing/business field: *The New Positioning* and *The Power of Simplicity*.

- Perform directed Internet and other research in preparation for an upcoming book.
- Analyze research and draft description for inclusion in articles and future book.
- Specifically recruited for special projects on basis of past performance.

September 2001 – Present
RIVERVIEW ARTISANS INC., Overland Park, KS
Assistant Manager for firm affiliated with the Mapleridge Design Center.

- Collaborate with decorative artist on projects in the $75K range, custom building business furniture, conference rooms, mahogany libraries, etc.
- Perform multitude of skilled operations from rough milling to fine detail finishing and veneer application.
- Assist in project estimates and sales proposals.

PROFESSIONAL EXPERIENCE (continued)

June 2000 – December 2000
WALTERS, JUSTA & MILLSTEIN, Kansas City, KS
Law Clerk

- Gained valuable experience in bankruptcy proceedings.

January 2000 – May 2000
HONORABLE HENRY MARGOLIS, Kansas City, KS
Judicial Internship

- Legal research and writing on legalities relating to general equity matters.

September 1999 – December 1999
HONORABLE ROSE GIARDELA, Kansas City, KS
Judicial Internship

Summer 1999
STRATTON, BRIGGS & ROTHMAN, Overland Park, KS
Law Clerk

January 1997 – June 1997
UNITED STATES DEPARTMENT OF JUSTICE, Washington, DC
Intern

EDUCATION

UNIVERSITY OF MISSOURI, KANSAS CITY, Kansas City, MO
Master of Science: Real Estate Development   May 2003

UNIVERSITY OF KANSAS SCHOOL OF LAW, Lawrence, KS
Juris Doctor   June 2001
Admitted to Kansas Bar 2001
Honors and Activities:

- Seton Hall Constitutional Law Journal – NOTES & COMMENTS EDITOR (2000-98)
- Who's Who: American Law Students – 16th Edition (2000)
- Tax Law Society

KANSAS WESLYAN UNIVERSITY, Salinas, KS
Bachelor of Arts, Political Science   August 1998
Honors and Activities:

- Dean's List
- Pi Sigma Alpha Honor Society (for outstanding Political Science Majors)

REFERENCES

Excellent references will be furnished on request.

Bank Branch Management

SCOTT E. BOWMAN

19 Harrington Lane • Manalapan, NJ 07726 • 732.770.8956 • boman4765@hotmail.com

FINANCE ~ BANKING
Branch Management/Customer Service

Well-qualified and results-oriented **Finance and Banking** professional with experience and demonstrated accomplishments developing corporate growth, stability, and financial performance. Skilled analyst with strong organizational and communication abilities, and proven leadership qualities. Broad-based understanding of financial needs at all levels of business including evaluating, analyzing, and communicating financial data. Demonstrated broad-based strengths and accomplishments in:

Finance & Banking	Project Management	Teller Operations
Marketing Financial Services	Customer Service Relations	Loan/Account Origination
Team Management	Sales Management	Problem Solving
eBusiness Management	Communications	Continuing Education
Supervision/Leadership	Branch Management	Strategic Management

Recipient – Commerce Capital Markets Referral Award – July/August 2004

PROFESSIONAL EXPERIENCE

COMMERCE BANK, New Brunswick, NJ ~ 2004 to Present
CUSTOMER SERVICE REPRESENTATIVE (CSR)
Counsel clients in the selection of financial products in order to meet their financial planning and banking needs. Create and process client accounts providing excellent customer service. Sell and refer bank products based on specific sales focus (Commerce Capital Markets, Commerce National Insurance and Residential Mortgage). Identify prospective clients and develop and implement presentations for clients. Originate and process consumer and mortgage loan applications. Extensive knowledge of bank lending policies, practices, compliance, and underwriting criteria. Familiar with processing collateral loans, unsecured personal loans, asset-based loans, and mortgage-based loans. Process a myriad of loan documentation performing research activities when necessary.

Accomplishments:

- Consistently met and exceeded sales quotas and standards by cross-selling and up-selling bank products and services.
- Increased branch loan production volume.
- Sold a variety of loans by pulling CBA, creating loan worksheets, and making recommendations to lenders upon request.
- Ensured that loan policies and procedures were followed in accordance with audit guidelines.

STAR FIRE AUTOGRAPHS, Manalapan, NJ ~ 1999 to Present
BUSINESS MANAGER/PRINCIPAL
Established and currently manage Internet and mail order entertainment media business. Implemented strategic marketing programs successfully retaining clients and achieving market position. Instituted pricing structure after conducting extensive marketing research utilizing industry resources. Explored marketing and advertising opportunities adding value to new initiatives. Tracked data and improved business operations accordingly.

Accomplishments:

- Grew annual revenues to $30K.
- Authored inventory item descriptions and managed customer service relations.

EDUCATION/TRAINING

FAIRLEIGH DICKINSON UNIVERSITY, Madison, NJ
BA – History, Minor – Politics

COMMERCE UNIVERSITY BANK COURSES
Finance, Supervision, Business Management, Consumer Lending, Customer Service, Loan Products, Privacy Compliance, Loan Underwriting, BSA/AML, Foreign Assets Control, Bank Secrecy, etc.

COMPUTER SKILLS

Microsoft Office, Lotus Notes, dBase, Basic, HTML

Financial Services

Dara is seeking a promotion and will use this resume to post internally.

Dara E. Hanes
40 South Street
Aurora, CO 80018
(303) 555-58110
daraehanes_10@aol.com

Professional Profile
Results-oriented financial services professional exemplified by a steady increase of responsibility.
Customer-satisfaction focused: Utilize verbal communication skills and superior product knowledge to perform benefits analysis and proactively recommend and implement solutions. **Results-motivated:** Deliver highly effective and energetic service and sales presentations culminating in exemplary results. **Team-oriented:** Apply negotiation and team building skills to coordinate the activity between internal departments required to meet client needs.

Education and Licenses
MBA Regis University, Denver, CO   **May 2003**
BS Political Science (International Business concentration) Regis University, Denver, CO   **May 1997**

Series 6 & 63
Life, Accident and Health Insurance
Pursuing CFP Designation

Professional Experience
Big A Financial, Denver, CO   **August 1997 – Present**
Institutional Liaison   **September 2003 – Present**
- Create Time & Action plans geared toward the successful and timely implementation of all interdependent processes and compliance issues related to plan administration.
- Foster and maintain relationships with high priority institutions of $330,000,000 in assets and effectively retained 10 major institutional clients.
- Evaluate customer relationships and ensure that all recommendations and procedures are fully functional prior to their implementation.
- Monitor and proactively combat the administrative activities of competitors, resulting in the retention of 600 individual clients.
- Conduct sales and service meetings to determine best cost effective and efficient plan to implement.
- Assess and evaluate customer plan requirements by conducting needs assessments using service surveys.
- Advise institutions on changes or enhancements to administrative procedures and policies.
- Measure and manage internal procedures to identify and resolve service shortfalls.
- Coordinate communications between internal processing areas, ensuring proper plan implementation.
- Provide detailed financial information for the completion of Form 5500.
- Perform compliance testing and compute employer contributions.
- Develop strategies for implementing plan design changes.
- Interpret plan documents.

Service Plus Representative   **August 2000 – September 2003**
- Contributed to the development, implementation and control of specialized marketing campaigns targeted to individual customers.
- Monitored and combated the activities of competitors to influence individual customers.
- Conducted follow-up sales contacts resulting in increased annuity premium volume.
- Designed and implemented strategies to counter competitive tactics.
- Expanded new business from external rollovers and asset transfers.

Individual Telephone Consultant   **August 1997 – August 2000**
- Promoted Big A Financial's products, services and investment performance relative to those of competitors.
- Calculated and recommended optimal combination of products needed to achieve retirement goals.
- Counseled individuals on a broad range of financial planning issues using superior product knowledge.
- Guided individuals in establishing financial goals.
- Proactively corrected misinformation.

Accounting and Administrative Assistant

JEAN ENGLISH

●●

9 CENTRAL AVENUE, WINDSOR, ONTARIO N9V 1V2
HOME: (519) 555-1212
EMAIL: JENGLISH@CAREERBRAIN.COM

Accounting & Administrative Assistant
Accounts Payable & Receivable / Payroll / Computer Systems Expert

Organized and responsible Administrative & Accounting Assistant with more than 12 years of experience across diverse industries. Educated and energetic professional recognized as a quick learner with exceptional computer skills and the unique ability to manage several tasks in a stressful environment. Excellent communicator seeking a challenging position, utilizing current skills and abilities, with the opportunity for professional growth.

- Accounts Payable / Receivable
- Payroll / Payroll Systems
- Employee Scheduling
- Purchasing / Lease Agreements

- Microsoft Windows, Excel, Word
- Daily Ledger / Bookkeeping
- Customer Service
- Database Development

PROFESSIONAL EXPERIENCE

Manager of Casino Administration / Analyst 2001–present
Casino Royale, Windsor, Ontario
- Responsible for tracking, analysis and payment approval of all accounts payable for the department averaging $100,000 monthly.
- Created a computerized daily tracking system utilized by all managers and the casino President due to its flexibility and user friendliness.

Pit Manager 1999–2001
Casino Royale, Windsor, Ontario
- Accepted the challenge to learn the scheduling system for the staff of 1,000 during a crisis, allowing payroll to resume uninterrupted for the entire casino.

Floor Supervisor 1997–1999
Casino Royale, Windsor, Ontario
- After just one year as a dealer, was promoted to Floor Supervisor managing up to 300 dealers on a shift.

Agency Office Manager 1990–1997
Gulliver's Travel, Windsor, Ontario
- Managed all day-to-day operations including accounts receivable, accounts payable, bookkeeping, payroll, budgets, employee training and customer service.

Travel Agent 1985 – 1990
Gulliver's Travel, Windsor, Ontario

EDUCATION AND PROFESSIONAL CREDENTIALS

Computer Programmer Analyst, 3-year business program including accounting
St. Clair College of Applied Arts & Technology, 1986–1989

High School Diploma
Assumption College School, 1981–1983

Microsoft Excel Advanced, *2001* **Microsoft Access Advanced,** *2001*
Microsoft Excel Intermediate, *2000* **Microsoft Access Intermediate,** *2000*
Microsoft Excel, *1994* **Microsoft Word,** *1994*
St. Clair College of Applied Arts & Technology

Financial Consultant

Brian was laid off and seeking a broader executive level
finance role; he was offered a CFO position.

Brian Bachelor

16 Terryville Avenue, Bristol, CT 06010
Cell: 555-555-4321 Home: **555-555-1234**
E-mail: bbach@aoz.com

OBJECTIVE

Proprietary Trader / Hedge Fund Manager position continuing a successful record of profit generation.

PROFILE

- 12 years of high-performance in financial investment. Past 10 years as a Market Maker on the floor of the Pacific Stock Exchange with a consistent, verifiable record of achievement in competitive and volatile environments. Traded futures, options, equities, bonds and derivatives.
- Licensed Broker Dealer – American and Pacific Stock Exchanges.
- Demonstrated competencies in creative problem solving, decision making, negotiating and utilization of computer trading applications.
- Noted for options trading expertise, vision, initiative and ethics.

EXPERIENCE

Market Maker   1994-Present
JMS Trading, San Francisco, CA

- Earned over $10,000,000 in profits starting with $40,000 in equity. Reversed initial client investment within six months.
- Achieved strong and sustainable gains each year, regardless of market conditions, through a conservative trading approach.
- Acquired Lead Market Maker (one of three) designation for equity options traded on Microsoft and JDS Uniphase.
- Invested in and coached five novice traders—on Amex, PSE and CBOE—securing a $500,000 return within three years.

Financial Consultant   1992-1994
Morgan Stanley, Los Angeles, CA

- Cultivated and managed a base of 300+ clients (retail and institutions) with speculative investments, mutual funds, insurance, stocks, bonds, futures and options.
- Led the account development and service of a $24+ million portfolio in collaboration with management.
- Performed personal financial analysis including net worth, cash flow, income tax situation, investment portfolio analysis, insurance detail, retirement outlook and estate planning.

EDUCATION

B.A., Business Administration – Finance   1992
University of Southern California, Los Angeles, CA

- Co-created an options trading computer program that funded 1.5 years of education.

Credit Analyst

Sarah Jessica Ruth

27 Hightop Drive, Pennington, NJ 08534
(609) 466-5555 Home • Sarahjr@home.com

Branch Manager
Credit Analyst/Commercial Credit/Consumer Credit/Credit Administration/Credit Management/ Lending Office/Finance and Budgeting/Personnel Manager

Strong commitment to excellence. Dynamic presentation, communication, and marketing skills. Distinguished performance encompassing a steady advancement of increasing accomplishments resulting in fast-track promotion and progressively responsible banking duties. Motivated, results-oriented individual. Excellent planning, organizational, development and leadership qualifications. High-impact negotiator, spokesperson, and client service manager.

Professional Experience
ABC Financial, Regional Credit Manager: Manage 30 employees covering a tri-state region. Analyze competitor programs and develop marketing strategies for competitive market positioning to increase market share. Communicate effectively with dealers to initiate, develop, and maintain customer relationships and client satisfaction. Reporting, record keeping, and documentation of business deals, self audits, and budget control. Manage and track funding goals of credit analysts. Performance management of staff through effective training and evaluations. Conduct regular staff meeting and communicate company policy and procedures. Design, development, and implementation of effective succession plan to reduce staff turnover. (2001 – present)

Regional Branch Manager: Managed 16 employees covering the entire East Coast. Regulated and coordinated all aspects of branch operation to achieve volume and profit goals. Managed branch operation within established guidelines and budget parameters. Scope of responsibilities included lending, collections, marketing and sales, administration and personnel. Hired, organized, trained, and evaluated personnel in all phases of branch operations. Motivated production while organizing marketing activities and strategies in a changing market. Facilitated monthly market, projection, and production reports for Senior and Regional Vice Presidents. Generated quality customer service and ongoing customer loyalty. (2000 – 2001)

Assistant Manager: Evaluated and reviewed credit applications submitted by auto dealerships for credit line and contract purchase in accordance with company policy. Supervised office staff to ensure company policy and procedures. Performance management, training, and evaluation of personnel. (1997 – 2000)

Northeast Bank, Loan Officer/Credit Analyst: Conducted all aspects of consumer and commercial lending. Cultivated and maintained customer relationships through quality customer service. Promoted from entry-level trainee to Associate Loan Officer to Loan Officer/Credit Analyst within a 2-year period. Scope of responsibilities included cash flow, credit, financial statements, and budget spreadsheet analysis. (1995 – 1997)

Licenses and Education
Licensed Real Estate Agent (1998 – Present), Bachelor of Arts, Economics, University of Texas (1995)

Volunteer Work
Meals on Wheels, Big Sister

Credit and Collections

James is a bank executive who wanted to relocate to the Dallas/Fort Worth area. This particular format showcased his credentials in a straightforward, results-driven manner.

JAMES HOFFMAN

2212 Gate Drive _ Phoenix, AZ 85001 _ 928.444.0888

PROFESSIONAL OBJECTIVE

Opportunity with a Dallas-based financial services organization where expertise in commercial collections, credit administration, and financial analysis/structuring contributes to increased profits.

PROFILE

- Extensive general business experience in the financial services industry, with credentials in both line and staff positions. Areas of expertise:

  - credit/portfolio administration
  - asset structuring/restructuring
  - commercial collections
  - loan documentation
  - regulatory compliance

  - financial analysis
  - risk assessment/underwriting
  - problem asset resolution/loan work-outs
  - operations/information integration
  - lender liability issues

- Background in diverse environments ranging from major regional financial holding companies to large and small community banks.
- Driving force in the establishment of a newly chartered commercial bank in the Phoenix area.
- Customer-focused professional whose philosophy is to "do it right the first time."
- Viewed by clients as an individual who is worthy of their trust, and who holds their best interests paramount.
- Effective at building sound internal/external relationships to support client and organizational goals.
- Actively involved in leadership roles focused on community development.

EDUCATION

M.B.A. **Financial Administration**
Northwestern University, Evanston, Illinois, 1982

B.A. **Business-Economics**
Vanderbilt University, Nashville, Tennessee, 1980

Executive Professional Development Programs:

- Northwestern University – Management School for Corporate Bankers
- University of Texas – National Commercial Lending Schools
- Certified Commercial Lender – American Bankers Association
- Computer School for Executives – Bank Institute of America
- Leadership and Lending – National Credit Executives Association

EXPERIENCE

RIVCOM STATE BANK, Phoenix, Arizona   1998 – Present
- Founder/Charter Director/Executive Vice President and Senior Lending/Compliance Officer.
- Member of three-person team that founded and organized a new state-chartered FDIC insured commercial bank. Established nine-member Board of Directors.

Key Accomplishments:
- Led efforts in generating $17.2 million in start-up capital.
- Grew bank into a profitable organization with $120 million in assets, while maintaining strong loan quality.
- Personally managed 70% of the bank's borrowing client base and 60% of $72 million in total loans outstanding.

U.S. LEASING COMPANY, Fort Worth, Texas   1995 – 1998
- Senior Vice President, Leasing – Managed lease origination process for a national leasing company. Offerings included private label programs for five Fortune 500 companies. Trained, supervised and developed new team members.

Key Accomplishment:
- Introduced commercial bank quality underwriting procedures to correct prior portfolio deficiencies for leases averaging $75,000 per transaction.

STATE BANK AND TRUST, Springfield, Illinois   1989 – 1995
- Vice President and Senior Lending Officer – Responsible for bank's credit administration and management of commercial, consumer, and residential lending. Chaired loan and Community Reinvestment Act (CRA) committees.

Key Accomplishment:
- Developed and implemented new credit culture, achieving an all-time bank record of 1.12% ROA, from a negative .67%.

COMMERCIAL BANK, Chicago, Illinois   1983 – 1985
- Commercial Lending Officer – Special Loan Division – Established and managed new loan workout activity to support the bank's domestic commercial lending group.

Key Accomplishment:
- Directed reduction of internally classified credits and nonperforming assets by 70% each.

CIVIC AND PROFESSIONAL ACTIVITIES

- Board of Directors and Past President, Local Chamber of Commerce
- International Association of Bank Executives, Charter Member and Board of Directors
- Senior Board Member, National Banking Institute of Arizona

Insurance Claims Specialist

Laura D. Wenn

899 Lancona Road
Yonkers, NY 00000

(555) 555-5555
ldw56@yahoo.com

Career Profile

High-energy, cross-functional background as resourceful fast-track insurance claims specialist with an outstanding record of success in winning settlements and reducing claims payouts to acceptable and just amounts. Investigate, negotiate, and settle complex claims, from beginning stages up to trial, for Hartford and Aetna.

Areas of Expertise

Administration

- organized and effective performance in high-pressure environments
- presentation development and delivery
- word processing and spreadsheet development (type 60 words per minute)
- claims investigation with meticulous documentation
- heavy phones/switchboard
- skilled customer care
- Microsoft Office, Internet, and intranet proficiency

Insurance Claims

- commercial and personal lines liability
- property damage and bodily injury claims
- claimant, attorney, and litigation representation
- settlement and target value range setting
- medical and liability evaluation
- general liability, auto, homeowners, and products liability
- injury exposure values
- complex arbitration and mediation negotiation

Highlights

- Handle caseload of up to 230 pending commercial and personal lines claims. Establish contact within 24 hours, maintain impeccable documentation, and determine value of case based on liability/injury. Decide claim values up to $50,000. Negotiate/settle cases in mediation, arbitration, or litigation. Productive in judge's chambers, courtroom, or at mediation table.
- Delivered a $15,000 saving to Hartford by obtaining a defense verdict on a case that a judge suggested Hartford "buy out" for $15,000. Communicated with attorneys, evaluated liability/facts and determined feasibility for trial. Case went to trial and Hartford paid nothing but legal costs.
- Saved Aetna $40,000 on complex $100,000 second-degree burn claim by determining case's suitability for mediation, and meeting with judge and plaintiff's attorneys. Case was settled for a fair $60,000 without incurring major legal costs for Aetna.
- Promoted onto Aetna fast-track after only one year; became the youngest adjuster in company history. Track record of positive mediation, arbitration, and litigation outcomes is equal to or better than that of more senior professionals.
- Possess outstanding administrative/organizational skills, superior presentation and negotiation abilities, a passion for excellence, and a contagious enthusiasm. Work well in independent or team environments. Tenacious, with the stamina needed to function in high-pressure environments.

Employment

Hartford Insurance Corp., Claims Representative	2001 to Present
Aetna Claims Services	
Claims Specialist	2000 to 2001
Fast-track Representative	1998 to 2000
Claims Assistant	1997 to 1998

Education and Professional Development

A.A.S. in Business, Insurance, and Real Estate, Bronxville Community College
Pepperdine Law University: Two-day Negotiation Seminar

Industry Courses: Commercial General Liability, Claims Statements, Property Casualty Principles, Litigation Guidelines, Medical Terminology and Treatment, How to Handle Cases to Avoid Litigation, Accurate Reserving

MATTHEW A. SIMS

4545 OAKLAND • MEMPHIS, TN 38137 • (901) 555-3513 • MASIMS@AOL.COM

Career Profile

- Over ten years background in casualty insurance.
- Key player in the building of one of the nation's top ten insurers.
- Senior Vice President and Core Management Team member of Casualty Insurance. Recognized as an astute visionary, delivering fresh perspectives and keen assessments using intellect, judgment, and character. Known for making and upholding tough decisions.

Areas of Expertise

Management Skills and Insurance Experience:

- program creation/strategic planning
- resource development
- multimillion-dollar budget creation
- budget management/cost controls
- corporate restructuring
- relationship and team building
- boardroom-level presentations
- loss development and analysis
- high-level claims analysis and resolution
- high exposure claims
- severe injury and multiple policy management
- complex litigation management
- medical profession liability policies
- reserving and settlement authority

Executive Highlights

Accelerated Growth

- During senior management tenure, helped to grow company from 3,000 to 7,500 policyholders, adding a wide range of clients. Growth exploded business and caused expansion of department from 15 to 50 employees.

Financial Analysis and Cost Improvement

- Handled complex financial analysis and legal cost containment. Reduced litigation costs by 15% to 20%. Streamlined claims-handling process by enabling claims examiners to handle larger caseloads through realignment of custodial tasks to clerical staff. Collaborated with company actuaries to interpret and act upon loss trends and developments.

Profit and Loss

- Developed highly accurate, multimillion dollar budgets. In addition, effective personal handling of reserving and settlement authority, legal cost containment, favorable trial results, and efficiency measures directly affected corporate bottom line.

New Systems and Technology

- Significantly reduced legal costs through research, development, and implementation of innovative automated legal processing and auditing program.

Business Reorganization

- Following CI's recent acquisition, collaborated as key member of transition team to develop and implement efficient reorganization plan to achieve efficiency gains.

Career Advancement

- Fast-tracked from claims representative to vice president in four years. Was handpicked, recruited, and mentored by CEO during CI's initial period of accelerated growth.

Employment

Casualty Insurance (CI), Memphis, TN

- Senior Vice President   2002 to present
- Vice President   1996 to 2001
- Claims Manager   1995 to 1996
- Claims Supervisor   1994 to 1995
- Claims Representative   1993 to 1994

Management Summary

- Report directly to the CEO and Board of Directors. Oversee two direct reports administering activities over 60 headquarters and branch staff members. Direct and manage claims reserved in excess of $900 million, handling reserving and settlement of individual claims of up to $1 million.
- Daily functions include $4 million budget development and management, staffing, cost control, appointment of legal counsel, policy creation, determination of complex coverage issues, high-exposure claims monitoring, and interface with re-insurers/excess insurers.

Significant Achievements

- Track record of wide-ranging contributions in systems development, cost containment, and claims management. Maintained severity at flat levels for the past five years, reduced litigation costs, and improved beneficial trial results. Fast-tracked from claims representative to VP in four years.

Professional Development

- American Management Association continuing professional development courses include annual seminars on insurance issues, Accounting for Non-Financial Executives, Managing Conflict, Interpersonal Skills, Management of Reciprocals and Mutuals.

Education

Bachelor of Science in Biology, Memphis State University, Pre-Med Program

Communications

DEBRA JOY BISMARK

234 Mountain Road
Ringoes, New Jersey 08551
609 555-1561
E-MAIL: Bismark@ias.edu

SUMMARY OF QUALIFICATIONS

Communications and writing professional with expertise in areas including

- Research and Narrative Reports
- Academic Writing & Marketing
- Advertising & Promotional Writing
- Newsletters and Feature Stories
- Editorial Functions
- Community Relations
- Grant Writing
- Public Relations
- Proposals

WRITING

- Authored individualized newsletters for families of students with special needs (Warren Township Board of Education)
- Wrote detailed narrative reports citing student progress (Ocean Friends School, OFS)
- Wrote news stories, regular features for monthly newsletter with readership of 50,000 (American Institute of Chemical Engineers, AIChE)
- Wrote articles for student member magazine during six-year tenure as Communications Writer (AIChE)
- Poetry published in *Without Halos, US1 Worksheets, The Poet's Page*, and accepted into *Mediphors* and *Poet*
- Enjoy collaborating with colleagues to develop programs and implement projects. Articulate ideas clearly and concisely.

ACHIEVEMENTS

- Turned technical papers into crisp copy – Press releases received national recognition (AIChE)
- Created and ran building code research business in New York City (Architectural Support Services)
- Designed brochure educating parents on early literacy (Warren Township)
- Executive committee members wrote letters of appreciation for concept identifying a new engineering-in-schools campaign (Project VEGA, AIChE)
- Won a company-wide logo competition (AIChE)
- Created a proposal for a reading/writing clinic presented to the school board (Warren Township)
- Trained and advised colleagues in strategies for supporting early reading and writing (PFS)

TECHNICAL EXPERTISE

- Proofread and edited technical articles for a scientific journal (AIChE)
- Computer literate with working knowledge of Microsoft Word, Desktop Publishing (Ventura), Access database training
- Capable Internet researcher

EMPLOYMENT HISTORY

2005-present	Program Assistant (part-time)	THE INSTITUTE FOR ADVANCED STUDY, Somerset, NJ
2004-present	Reading Tutor	SELF-EMPLOYED
2003-2004	Teacher	OCEAN FRIENDS SCHOOL, Dover, NJ
1998-2003	Teacher	WARREN TOWNSHIP BOARD OF EDUCATION, NJ
1992-1998	Communications Writer	THE AMERICAN INSTITUTE OF CHEMICAL ENGINEERS, NY
1991-1992	Editorial Assistant	THE AMERICAN INSTITUTE OF CHEMICAL ENGINEERS, NY
1989-1991	Researcher	ARCHITECTURAL SUPPORT SERVICES, NY

EDUCATION

M.S., Social Work – Columbia University, New York, NY
Teacher training – Bank Street College of Education, The College of New Jersey, Rider University
B.A., Psychology – Montclair State College (University), Montclair, NJ

SUZANNE A. KENNEDY

2490 Ridge Overlook
Seacliff, NY 11579
516-555-1212

PROFESSIONAL *A New York Publisher of trade and scholarly books*
EXPERIENCE: **DIRECTOR OF ADVERTISING AND PROMOTION (March 2001-Present)**

Key responsibilities include: managing advertising/promotion department with staff of four; overseeing and actively engaging in all aspects of promotion, advertising, and publicity. I have established and am maintaining a 22-person national sales force and make seasonal visits to the nation's two largest bookstore chains.

Active in negotiating special sales and acquiring new titles, and as liaison with domestic and foreign rights agents. In 2001 I traveled to England, visited several publishers, bought and sold rights.

Frequently arrange author appearances on television and radio talk shows. As a company spokesperson, I have been interviewed numerous times by newspapers, magazines, syndicates, and radio stations.

ADVERTISING AND PROMOTION MANAGER (1999-2001)

Advertising and Direct Mail: Created, designed, and wrote copy for brochures, flyers, and display ads; created direct-mail campaigns; represented company at publisher's book exhibits.

Publicity: Wrote news releases, selected media, made follow-up calls, arranged author media appearances.

ASSISTANT EDITOR (1997-1999)

Responsibilities included reading authors' manuscripts, copyediting, proofreading; writing jacket copy, coordinating and writing copy for catalog. Some editing and proofreading was done on a freelance basis.

Compton Burnett (New York, NY) ADVERTISING COPYWRITER (1995-1997)

Responsible for designing and writing copy for bimonthly catalog and supplementary flyers. Created ads and brochures; wrote sales letters and edited and rewrote direct-mail pieces.

EDUCATION: State University of New York at Buffalo

Degree: B.A. in English, 1995
Minor: Social Sciences

SKILLS: Word processing, working knowledge of typography, research proficiency.

REFERENCES: Will be provided on request.

Event Planner

George wanted a job closer to home. Some of his past job titles did not fit with his career aspirations, and he wanted to focus on the specific skills needed for an Events Manager, so he used a functional style format.

George S. Easton
12 Lee Street, Middleburg, VA 20118
540-555-5470

PROFILE SUMMARY
Meeting Planning ▪ *Conferences* ▪ *International Events* ▪ *Fundraising* ▪ *Golf Tournaments*

Creative professional with expertise in all aspects of successful event/program planning, development, and management. Excel in managing multiple projects concurrently with strong detail, problem-solving and follow-through capabilities. Demonstrated ability to manage, motivate and build cohesive teams that achieve results. Sourced vendor, negotiated contracts and managed budgets. Superb written communications, interpersonal and organizational skills. First-class client relation and teaming skills. Proficient in Access, Excel, PowerPoint, Outlook, MS Project, Publisher, MeetingTrak and Corel WordPerfect.

PROFESSIONAL EXPERIENCE
Meeting Planning Management

Planned and coordinated government, association and private conferences, meetings, events and fundraisers. Coordinated all conference activities, workshops, meetings, tours, and special events. Trained, directed, and supervised teams to accomplish goals. **Saved $72,000 on most recent meeting.**

- As Team Leader, coordinated 10-26 annual workshops for Centers for Disease Control and Prevention.
- Coordinated 2004 National Conference on Smoking and Health. (2,000 participants)
- Organized 6,000-participant national annual conferences.
- Coordinated Global Scholarship Pre-Conference Training for 200 third-world participants.
- Developed and supervised education sessions at CSI's 2001 National Convention.
- Directed CSI's National Seminar Series.

Meeting Coordination

As Team Leader, coordinated production, distribution, and grading of exam materials. Supervised registration and tracking of continuing education units. Negotiated hotel and vendor contracts. Prepared and administered budgets. Arranged all on-site logistics, including transportation, accommodations, meals, guest speakers and audiovisual support. **Consistently come under budget for each meeting planned.**

- Developed and maintained 5,000-person database.
- Developed, promoted, and implemented CSI's National Certification Program.
- Managed logistics for a Regional Pacific Training in Guam.

Fundraising

Team player in the development, promotion and implementation of membership and retention programs for BUILD-PAC. Coordinated PAC fundraising events. Supervised high-donor club fulfillment benefits. Provided updated donor reports.

- Coordinated 2 PAC fundraising golf tournaments.

EVENTS MANAGEMENT EXPERIENCE
Conferences / Meetings / Program Coordinator   1997-Present

- Centers for Disease Control and Prevention/Office on Smoking & Health
- Tobacco Control Training & Technical Assistance Project
- Health & Human Services Department's Administration on Children, Youth and Families Grant Review Contract
- Food and Drug Administration
- Centers for Disease Control and Prevention/National Center for Health Statistics
- National Library of Medicine
- Housing & Urban Development Grant Review Contract
- CSI National Seminar Series
- CSI 1998 & 1999 National Conventions and Exhibits

PROFESSIONAL EMPLOYMENT
CORPORATE SCIENCES ■ Rockville, Maryland   2003-Present
Senior Conference Specialist

ROCKVILLE CONSULTING GROUP ■ Arlington, Virginia   2000-2003
Logistics Manager
Senior Conference Coordinator

CONSTRUCTION SPECIALISTS ASSOCIATION ■ Arlington, Virginia   1997-1999
Assistant Coordinator of Education Programs

NATIONAL ASSOCIATION OF PIPE WELDERS ■ Washington, D.C.   1997
Assistant Director, Fundraising

EDUCATION & CERTIFICATIONS
VIRGINIA POLYTECHNIC INSTITUTE & STATE UNIVERSITY ■ Blacksburg, VA
B.S. Exercise Physiology ■ 1996
Minor Psychology

Go Members Inc. MeetingTrak Certification ■ 2004

Certified Meeting Professional (CMP) – Pending Jan. 2005

PROFESSIONAL AFFILIATIONS
- Meeting Professionals International – Annandale Chapter (AMPI)
- Logistical Committee
- Educational Retreat Committee
- Member Services Committee
- Community Outreach Committee
- Connected International Meeting Professionals Association (CIMPA)
- DC Special Olympics – Volunteer
- Hands On DC – Volunteer
- SPCA of Northern Virginia – Volunteer

Human Resources Manager

Jane E. Barron

1234 Old Stone Mill Drive
Cranbury, New Jersey 08512
609-555-3927

Summary of Qualifications

Broad-based responsibilities in **Human Resource Management** including:

- Recruiting
- Training and Development
- Employee Relations Programs
- Office Management/Administration
- Counseling/Coaching
- Benefits Administration
- Compensation
- Systems/Computerization

Profile

Known as a dedicated, results-oriented manager with the ability to build rapport at all levels.....successful track record of motivating employees to obtain maximum performance and increase bottom-line profits for the company.....developed internal training programs that resulted in increased productivity and office innovation.....experienced supervisor, multi-tasker.....enjoy working in a fast-paced challenging environment.

Experience

AMERICAN LIST SERVICE, Princeton, NJ Headquarters   2000-Present
Human Resources Manager
Responsible for all aspects of human resources for this nationwide mailing list corporation. Initially recruited for start-up operations and increased Human Resources functions to include responsibilities in three other satellite locations: New Hampshire, New York, and California.

Director/Human Resources
- Direct all programs regarding employee relations, health, and welfare of the staff. Serve as a resource for new employees, counseling staff from executive levels to entry-level personnel. Travel to satellite locations to direct human resource functions.
- Serve as a coach and counselor for personal and career transitions within the company. Attend various human resources seminars. Keep abreast of the latest legal and professional advances in the field.
- Direct all recruiting operations; create job descriptions and internal job postings. Initiate job offers. Monitor costs of classified advertising and employment agency usage.
- Create, implement, and enforce the policies and procedures for formal disciplinary actions and dismissals.
- Execute exit interviews and assist hiring managers with human resource functions in their respective departments.
- Computerized human resources office systems to enhance productivity and on-line database administration.

Benefits Administration
- Develop on-going communication with all employees, keeping them informed of the full American List Counsel benefits package. Execute production of annual Employee Benefit Statement.
- Design, create, and implement all new benefits administration programs. Experienced in set up and maintenance of 401K plans. Responsible for researching and decisions regarding outside benefit packages.
- Perform cost analysis regarding various packages and set up appropriate benefit plans for satellite offices.
- Create and provide employees with disability letters and state disability paperwork. Serve as a liaison to benefit providers.

Training and Development
- Work with each department in developing specific training programs required for each position. Assist in preparing training materials to support departmental needs.
- Develop and implement training programs for general business functions including basic writing, stress management, and human relations.
- Prepare annual budgeting information regarding training programs and present policy recommendations to the Director.

MARKET RESEARCH CORPORATION, Cranbury, NJ   1998-1999
Office Manager/Administrative Director
- As Office Manager, responsibilities included preparing departmental budgets and hiring and training of 10+ employees. Performed complete office purchasing for the facility.
- Implemented a customized computer database that monitored travel expenses for sales representatives and executives. The system tracked pertinent account data and human resource information. Prepared reports; interfaced with management regarding suggestions for budgeted versus actual expenses.
- Instituted new policies and procedures to guide the entire sales force regarding purchasing and administrative procedures.
- Coordinated a departmental move to a larger facility; worked closely with interior space planners and designers.

HI-TECH SOLUTIONS, INC., Cranbury, NJ   1992-1998
Director of Human Resources
- Total responsibility for all activities relating to human resources including staff supervision, recruitment, benefits, insurance, training, personnel relations, goal setting, and MIS.
- Investigated and negotiated health insurance and other benefits coverage.
- Analyzed and procured appropriate insurance coverage for all areas of liability.
- Organized picnics, programs, parties, and other company-wide events to encourage "team" environment and a positive work atmosphere.

Business Administrator
- Initiated professional business practices and management to organize all aspects of office operations.
- Researched and recommended purchase of computers and appropriate software to meet financial and clerical needs.
- Trained other staff members in computer applications.
- Assumed responsibility for all accounting activities, including A/R, A/P, G/L, and P/R procedures.
- Analyzed cash flow for top management review.

Prior Employment

PRUDENTIAL MUTUAL FUND SERVICES, Edison, NJ   1990-1992
Group Leader
Adjustment Analyst

MERRILL LYNCH ASSET MANAGEMENT, Plainsboro, NJ   1989-1990
Assistant Supervisor

Education and Training

RIDER UNIVERSITY, Lawrenceville, NJ, 1985 Courses in finance and commerce
Completed numerous corporate seminars in Management and Human Resources encompassing legal issues, recruitment, compensation, and benefit administration. Member, Society of Human Resources Managers

Human Resources

Joseph is someone with a psychology education transitioning into Human Resources.

JOSEPH D. MORTEN

167 HELMAN LANE • BRIDGEWATER, NEW JERSEY 08807
908.555.5555 (H) • 908.444.4444 (FAX) • JMORTEN439@AOL.COM

HUMAN RESOURCES / CORPORATE TRAINING
Supervision ~ Business Management ~ Employee Relations ~ Coaching

Energetic, reliable and adaptable professional with a solid understanding of human resources, business operations and various corporate environments. Proven abilities in creatively identifying methods for improving staff productivity and organizational behavior. Recognized for ability to incorporate innovative management techniques to a multicultural workforce.

Results-oriented professional with excellent communication and interpersonal skills. Accurately perform challenging tasks with precision and attention to detail. Excel at organizing and setting up new procedures, troubleshooting and taking adverse situations and making them positive.

Competencies Include:
- Human Resources Management
- Operations Management
- Team building/Leadership
- Organizational & Project Management
- Training & Development
- Staffing Requirements
- Problem Resolution
- Employee Scheduling

Professional Experience

Waste Removal, *Plainfield, NJ (August 2000 – September 2005)*
CFA Administrator
Waste Removal is the nation's largest full-service waste removal/disposal company
- Maintained and monitored multiple databases for more than 120 pieces of equipment in the trucking company inventory.
- Generated accurate reports of budgets, repair costs, and personnel scheduling.
- Dramatically improved maintenance shop productivity through close budget monitoring.
- Served as a key link between management and mechanics, utilizing excellent interpersonal and communications skills. Acknowledged for improving the overall flow of information throughout the organization.
- Initiated, planned, and managed the implementation of high-turn inventory management systems and procedures. The new inventory system was credited with improving the operation of a very high volume parts operation.
- Assumed a leadership role in the company by completely reorganizing the physical inventory process to assure greater accuracy and system integrity.
- Managed the successful integration of two new parts operations, turning a possible negative situation into a very positive one.

Easy Video Entertainment, *Colonia, NJ (March 1997 – August 2000)*
Store Manager
Retail video rental and sales chain with over 600 outlets and 5,000 employees worldwide
- Managed all daily store operations including a staff of 5 employees. Responsible for recruitment, hiring, firing, training, and scheduling of all staff members.
- Ability to train and motivate staff to maximize productivity, and control costs with hands-on management and close monitoring of store budgets.
- Attained a 25% increase in sales over a 12-month period, leading all 45 stores in the district. The store ranked 40th in overall sales volume of the 600 stores in the company.
- Maintained a consistent Top 20 ranking for sales of high-profit coupon books.
- Used excellent leadership, team building and communication skills to develop subordinates and encourage cooperation and responsibility. Ensured compliance with corporate HR programs.
- Developed and implemented creative and aggressive promotional techniques that resulted in the store consistently exceeding its sales goals.

Education

BA ~ Psychology, FAIRLEIGH DICKINSON UNIVERSITY, Madison, NJ

MONICA JONES   724 Elm Drive   Transfer, PA 16154   724-555-2222

QUALIFICATIONS SUMMARY
Human Resource Management
Program Development, Recruitment, Training, Quality Process Management

EXPERIENCE
Philadelphia College of Textiles and Science, Philadelphia, Pennsylvania   1996 to Present

Director, Career Planning and Placement   2001 to Present
Liaison between college and industry, building international reputation through development of the following support and services:
- Direct professional staff of three, semi-professional staff of 10 and $175,000 operating budget in providing comprehensive placement service for 3,000 BS students, 250 MBA students, and alumni.
- Develop network of corporate and government employers within Business, High Tech, Creative, and Science areas.
- Annually achieve 90% placement of graduates, and hundreds of alumni at management level.
- Market on-campus recruiting program resulting in over 200 companies visiting each season.
- Host VIP campus visits and receptions.
- Extensive travel includes organizing and supervising trade shows, attending conferences, visiting industry.
- Provide input for academic program development through analysis of industry trends.
- Initiated seminar and workshop programs covering all aspects of career planning and search.
- Publish bi-monthly nationally circulated Job Opportunities Bulletin, Annual Placement and Salary Survey, Resume Book, and Student Handbook on Placement.
- Supervise internship and summer job programs for undergraduates.
- Directed software development and computerization of department, 1996.

Assistant Director, Placement Office   1996 to 2001

INVOLVEMENTS
- Selected for Task Force, Middle States evaluation for college accreditation, 2003.
- Visited/consulted with South African organizations on recruitment program development, 2002.
- Member, College Placement Council.
- Member, Middle Atlantic Placement Association.
- Past Chairman of Membership, Publicity and Office Training Committees.
- Published articles for trade journals, appear on media, conference speaker.
- Volunteer, Freedoms Foundation of America at Valley Forge.
- Member, Toastmasters International.
- Member, Colony Civic Organization, West Norriton, Pennsylvania.
- Accomplished photographer, enjoy painting.

EDUCATION
PHILADELPHIA COLLEGE OF TEXTILES AND SCIENCE
Evening Division, 1996 to 2001, Marketing/Management
Numerous Technical and Business Seminars
Executive Management Program
Werner Management Consultants, 2003

Trainer

Casandra lost her job and needed to move into a higher-level position for increased compensation. She did not have a college degree, so highlighting her skills helped employers get a quick overview of her many talents . . . and it worked!

CASANDRA B. JEELES

555 Riverside Drive • Houston, Texas 77027
713-555-1234 • casbjeeles@bxy.net

PROFESSIONAL OBJECTIVE

Training/Performance Development

PROFESSIONAL PROFILE

- Proven leadership and supervisory experience with ability to lead multiple projects/teams simultaneously.
- Outstanding project planning and project management skills, meeting tight time constraints/deadlines.
- Solutions-driven manager, mentor, and coach who relates well with all types of people at all levels.
- Strong organizational and analytical abilities applied to achieve desired goals, objectives and results.
- Unwavering commitment to excellence in building teams who are best of the best in serving others.
- Personal traits: professional; common sense; adaptability; focused; skilled trainer and team builder.

CORE COMPETENCIES

Passion for Customer Care Excellence:
- Instill a philosophy of immediate response to customer inquires – no such thing as "do it tomorrow."
- Value each individual customer, exceeding expectations and paying diligent attention to small details.
- Act and serve with integrity and trust, essential ingredients for successful, long-lasting customer relations.
- Create an environment where customers are ecstatic with service, creating action-oriented advocates.

Motivating and Training:
- Analyze company culture and structure to pinpoint obstacles and create new pathways or adopt existing model to build an environment of solutions and forward movement.
- Recognize hidden solutions, already existing or external, through research, active listening, observation.
- Help personalize company vision and goals by implementing strategies to create ownership/advocates.
- Analyze and monitor sales figures and statistics to establish firm foundation for future growth.
- Identify the extraordinary among the team, systems, and practices and build upon strengths.

Team Building:
- *"My job is to make the team successful"* – accomplished by coaching, nurturing, and stretching to reach beyond an individual's comfort zone to maximize personal/professional excellence.
- Discover talents/gifts of individual team members and build upon those to maximize results.
- Create an environment to link team members' strengths as the beginning of all endeavors.
- Capitalize on company structure, budgets, and timelines to build a *"let's do it"* framework.

Managing and Supervising:
- Orchestrate a team, discover core values of individual members, and build consensus of goals.
- Analyze budgets and expenditures to align with company vision, mission and direction.
- Automate and systematize rote and mundane functions to improve operating efficiencies.

Solutions Oriented – Analysis to Action:
- Thrive on converting obstacles into opportunities by recognizing root cause and developing solutions.
- Structure work environment where fear, failure and blame are not responses and/or defenses.
- Incorporate active listening to unravel challenges and rebuild – be it systems, technology, or people.

EXPERIENCE / EDUCATION

- Inside Sales/Assistant to Director – Strigle, Inc., Houston, Texas, 2002-2006
- Senior Executive Club/Top Sales – Halley Distribution, Inc., Midland, Texas, 1994-2002
- Various administrative roles, Houston, Texas, 1989-1994
- Numerous leadership, management, and customer relations courses – company sponsored, 1986-2006

Operations/Human Resources Manager

Jason needed to transition from seasonal work with national
fairs into a more traditional management career.

JASON CHAMBERS

1234 Main Street • Anaheim, California 55555
Home: (714) 555-5555 • Cellular: (714) 555-5551 • jchambers@chambers.com

---

Management Professional
Operations / Human Resources / Labor Relations / Staff Development

---

Dedicated organizational manager with track record of assuming positions of increased accountability. Background includes experience in industrial food service (world exposition food service management), restaurants, and catering. Proven leadership skills—able to recruit, retain, develop, and motivate employees to new levels of productivity. Communicate successfully and productively to any and all types of people. Excellent problem solver. Strong team orientation. Accomplished public speaker.

Core competencies include:

Verbal/Written Communications	Performance Evaluations	Prospective Employee Interviews
Relationship Building/Facilitation	Promotional Programs	Interpersonal Skills
Program Development	Policy Creation	Contract Negotiations

Particular Expertise in Boosting Profitability by Maximizing Sales and Reducing Costs

Employment History

XYZ EXPOSITION SERVICES-Costa Mesa, California   1989-2006
Leading provider of food service logistics and restaurant operations for world fairs and expositions.

Director of Personnel, Labor, and Human Resources / General Operations Manager
- 2005 French National Fair Exposition-Paris, France
- 2001 World Fair Exposition-Biel, Switzerland

Accountable for all phases of personnel management—hiring, staff development, evaluation, promotion, and separations. Created general employee contracts and work policy manuals. Controlled labor costs by optimizing staffing requirements according to customer visitations and by monitoring break times, clock-in/out accuracy, and on-the-clock productivity. Developed and monitored customer service systems. Created working relationships with government officials in European Union. Procured visas for core team members. Secured expo accreditation passes for all company employees.

Directed activities of all managers and assistant managers in supervision of multiple locations (8 in France, 10 in Switzerland) and up to 280 food service and facilities maintenance personnel. Also oversaw one beverage director to ensure full stocking and successful operating of all restaurants, bars, and food concessions. Reported directly to CEO.

Selected Contributions (French National Fair)
- Initiated full-scale recruitment of host-country hotel school interns. Secured a group of motivated general employees who were paid 20% less by law.
- Cut additional labor costs from 27% to 20%, significantly increasing net profit to investors. Company grossed $8.5 million in 6 months of operation.
- Streamlined staffing needs by reengineering food service stations, allowing employees to multi-task.
- Discovered thousands of overpaid dollars by auditing every paycheck for inaccuracies.
- Increased sales in Mexican food concession. Designed innovative ticket system to reduce line wait. Simultaneously eliminated loss of impatient customer sales and boosted service capacity.
- Successfully interpreted and complied with all host country labor laws and regulations. Faced comprehensive labor policy audit by host country's top labor official. Passed with flying colors.

Selected Contributions (World Fair, Switzerland)
- Streamlined staffing needs by designing employee multi-task and partnership system.
- Discovered and broke multiple-employee theft ring at two separate concessions.

- Played key role in company meeting exposition revenue goals (grossed $11.25 million in 6 months with only 9 concessions) by facilitating open and productive communication with management-level and general employees.
- Became conversant with Swiss labor laws, culture, and practices. Resulted in productive, lasting international business relationships.

Operations Consultant
- 2007 Canadian National Fair Exposition-Vancouver, B.C., Canada *preparation in progress
- 1995 World Exposition-Osaka, Japan
- 1989 World Exposition-Lisbon, Portugal

Participated in formulation of management structure, labor policies, employee handbook, management and employee training handbook, and operating guidelines in preparation for expo.

GOURMET FOODS, INC.-Costa Mesa, California   1998-1999,   2002-2004, 2006

General Manager
Monitor customer service levels, employee performance, and labor costs. Track and evaluate daily sales. Responsible for prospective employee interviewing and hiring. Teach and facilitate communication skills. Supervise up to 50, including concession managers, counter help, cooks, and cashiers for 4 locations.

Selected Accomplishments
- Launched innovative ongoing promotions.

  ✓ Costa Mesa police and fire department discount program.
  ✓ Home-meal and catering menu program.
  ✓ "Daily Special" program.

- Improved customer service levels by retraining employees in the following areas: quick/personal attention to customers, cleaning without turning backs to customers, and interpersonal communication skills.

WORLD GYM-Anaheim, California   1989-1992

Sales Representative/Personal Trainer
Performed membership sales. Helped customers achieve fitness goals.

ZAURUS PIZZA-Costa Mesa, California   1986-1988

Assistant Operations Manager
Promoted from positions as counter help/delivery to oversee operations of 4 stores. Supervised roughly 70, including store managers, counter help, cooks, delivery personnel, cashiers, and dishwashers. Ensured store cleanliness, product availability and timely delivery, and customer satisfaction.

Computer Skills/Foreign Languages

Internet (Netscape Navigator, Internet Explorer)
E-Mail (Outlook, Outlook Express)
MS Word, Excel

Beginning Conversational French

DAN DOLAN
104 Village Drive • Somerset, NJ 08873 • 732.555.1379 (H) • 908.555.1438 (C)

INVENTORY MANAGER / STORE MANAGER
Operations ~ Sales ~ Business Management
Delivered strong and sustainable revenue and profit gains in highly competitive markets

Empowering manager with multiple responsibilities and the ability to direct a large staff. Focus group efforts; counsel, mentor, and train employees. Experience in directing new store openings and store remodeling projects. Proven ability to perform multiple tasks at once with special attention to detail.

Consistently meet and/or exceed corporate goals and operational deadlines. Respond well in high-pressure managerial situations calling for excellent organizational skills and interpersonal communication skills.

A problem solver with strong leadership ability and an in-depth understanding of profitable business operations across many disciplines. Known for successful implementation strategies with a high commitment to excellence.

Professional strengths include:

- **Inventory Control**
- **Store Operations**
- **Customer Service**
- **New Store Startups**
- **Troubleshooting/Problem Solving**
- **Leadership/Mentoring**
- **Employee Staffing and Scheduling**
- **Shrinkage Control**
- **Productivity Improvements**
- **Payroll Forecasting**
- **Logistics**
- **Team Building and Training**

BUSINESS EXPERIENCE

SEARS CORPORATION   2001 – Present

SEARS CORPORATION, Linden, NJ   2003 – Present
Operations Executive
- Utilize a strong strategic planning management style to supervise a staff of 125.
- Responsible for the operations and flow of all merchandise from loading dock to sales floor. Annual sales of the store total $40 million.
- Direct the staffing and daily operations of 6 managers and their teams.
- Selected by Sears Corporate as one of 4 Senior Captains of the "New Store Team." Participated in startup of the Linden store in March 2003.
- The Linden store was in the top 10% of all Sears stores nationwide for operational excellence in 2005.
- Selected as Risk Assessment Captain for the district for last 2 years.
- Selected for the High Level Management team for the district.
- Completed the interview process and on the list to be Sears' next new store manager.
- Chosen as district Peer Trainer, Mentoring 5 additional Flow Executives at other stores.

Continued...

SEARS CORPORATION (Continued)

SEARS CORPORATION, Milltown, NJ   2001 – 2003
Hard Lines Executive/Flow Executive
- Hired as Flow Executive responsible for all freight into the store.
- Promoted from Flow Executive to Hard Lines Executive with responsibility for sales and sales floor management.

OFFICE DEPOT   1997 – 2001

OFFICE DEPOT, Lakewood, NJ   2000 – 2001
Store Manager
- Responsible for all facets of daily business functions and operations for the entire store. Store revenues grew to exceed $5 million.
- Responsible for staff of 40, including scheduling, sales quotas, performance reviews, daily staff duty assignments, and employee training.
- Implemented and maintained store policy and procedures as directed by company standards.
- Using a passionate execution style and strategic planning, the Lakewood store developed into a top performer in the region.

OFFICE DEPOT, Old Bridge, NJ   1999 – 2000
Sales Manager
- Increased sales by 20% in first year as Sales Manager.
- Increased gross margin by 32% through an increase in extended warranty sales of 17%.
- The Old Bridge store was the winner in a company-wide contest for having the highest warranty sales to overall sales ratio.

OFFICE DEPOT, Princeton, NJ   1997 – 1998
Operations Manager
- In charge of all incoming freight, staff scheduling, and inventory rotation.
- During first year as Operations Manager, shrinkage decreased from 3.2% to .32%.

EDUCATION

Cook College, **_New Brunswick, NJ_**
B.S. Environmental Economics – 1997

Purchasing Director

Peter's resume was shortened from a four-page resume which listed 30+ bullets outlining responsibilities for each job, and no impact/achievements/value-add.

PETER M. RABBIT

333 Court Hill ▪ Underhill, NY 11111
(H) 111.111.1111 ▪ (C) 111.111.1111
ptrrbt@aol.com

PURCHASING DIRECTOR
SENIOR PROJECT MANAGER
SENIOR OPERATIONS MANAGER

Professional Summary

Driven operations leader offers extensive hands-on experience and a consistent track record in **exceeding goals** for large-scale domestic and international capital projects, **fostering growth** and **delivering strong and sustainable gains**. A self-starter with a proven ability to conceptualize and implement **innovative solutions**. **Technologically competent,** past achievements demonstrate a clear ability to utilize new, **cutting edge technologies** as a means of updating processes/systems. **Highly effective leadership and motivating skills** support the development of cohesive teams (union and non-union) in the collaborative achievement of strategic goals. **Extensive experience** partnering with influential business leaders within successful organizations.

▪ CORE COMPETENCIES ▪

Business Planning	Financial Analysis	Quality Assurance
Business Process Reengineering	Influencing Skills	ERP/MRP
Contracts Administration	Negotiation Skills	Supplier/Vendor Management
Cost Containment	Logistics Management	Systems Implementation
Efficiency Improvement	Project Management	Warehouse Management

Selected achievements

- Initiated the development of a **first-ever computerized purchasing/inventory system** for the Newspaper Company resulting in substantial reductions on labor and materials costs; these improvements resulted in a request for support in the implementation of the system from the USA-based Newspaper. Subsequently consulted on the second successful implementation.
- **Reduced operating costs by $500,000 per year** by outsourcing an "in-house" printing department.
- Provided comprehensive capital procurement services for the **$300 million construction and start up of two large daily newspaper printing press facilities.**
- **Significantly increased waste recycling revenues by $545,000 per year** through successful negotiations with individual recycling firms.
- Directed an **operating budget of over $180 million** during construction and operations of the **Famous World Exhibition.**
- Initiated the development and implementation of a **first-ever budget tracking and reporting system in support of a $90 million capital project**; this system accelerated the project's successful completion—**90 days ahead of schedule and $1 million under budget.**
- Shortly after assuming responsibility for Security operations, **reduced in-house theft, drug and alcohol abuse by 99%, while reducing costs $100,000 per year.**

Relevant Experience

Independent Consulting   2005 to Present
- **Sourced and introduced a comprehensive, cutting-edge finance management software solution,** which enabled a $5 Million business to more effectively manage sales, inventory and distribution.
- Established warehouse management procedures, facilitating highly effective **inventory planning and control** practices; **trained and coached warehouse crew.**
- Established the foundation for a **fully integrated logistics management function** consolidating inventory, warehousing and distribution.

NEWSPAPER COMPANY, Manager, Procurement & Security   1991 to 2005
*Hired as Assistant Manager of Purchasing. Quickly demonstrated **aggressive turnaround management capability,** resulting in **significant increases in responsibility**—Fleet, Security, Facilities, and $40 million in newsprint inventories.*
- Established clear processes and procedures, and **centralized purchasing and inventory management** via first-ever electronic system in the southern newspaper system, **reducing costs by $500,000/year.**

- Introduced new technologies resulting in **increased efficiencies and cost-savings**; technologies included fax services and color scanning, which increased turnaround in ad presentation and makeup and **saved $125,000/year**.
- **Reduced annual operating costs by $500,000/year through offshore purchasing and vendor partnerships.**
- Successfully **sourced national and international vendors, negotiated and administered contracts** and executed **procurement strategies** on several large-scale capital projects: Development of a new $60 million facility; $97 million development project for implementation of new printing processes.
- **Directed international sourcing and managed logistics,** which included customs documentation and inspections.
- Served as **Project Manager in the design of a waste management system,** providing detailed specifications and managing project activities; **generated a significant increase in revenue.**
- **Overhauled the Security function**—outsourcing, modernizing equipment, establishing and training contract staff on new procedures and roles; significantly reduced costs, and nearly eliminated all incidences of theft.
- **Initiated and implemented the "pay in advance" system**—now used internationally among all newspapers—which contributed to a significant increase in revenue.
- **Revamped First Aid and Safety program,** and **implemented Assassination Protection Program.**
- Managed sale of assets from old facilities, building deconstruction, and **seamless relocation of 900 employees.**

WORLD EXHIBITION, Manager, Site Operations Procurement   1987 to 1991
World Exhibition's 6-month World Fair exhibition is orchestrated and attended by over 70 countries, each with its own on-site pavilion. Managed comprehensive procurement services for construction and start up of operations. Held signatory responsibility for all purchases, and spearheaded profitable vendor partnerships.
- **Hired and established a procurement team and introduced new technology,** which facilitated shared communications and increased procurement and materials handling efficiencies; Successfully managed procurement activities throughout liquidation and site deconstruction.
- **Orchestrated first-ever buyback contracts** for heavy equipment and machinery utilized by the Exhibition, regaining a full 50% of the initial purchase price; negotiated and received free maintenance, providing additional cost savings; **Negotiated service contracts** for site equipment and operations.
- **Demonstrated creative problem-solving skills,** which enhanced operations ability to provide ongoing entertainment, while significantly reducing operating costs.

PAPER COMPANY, Project Budget Controller/Buyer   1984 to 1987
Provided project support for a $90 Million operations implementation.
- **Led the development of an innovative financial tracking and control system.**
- **Controlled spending and ensured consistent use of the system, enabling a perfectly balanced budget.**
- Identified an opportunity to apply for a tax break, **saving an additional $600,000** at project's end.

Previous Experience

BIGWIG COMPANY, Project Expeditor, 1982-1984
CHEMICAL COMPANY A, Project Buyer, 1981-1982
CHEMICAL COMPANY B, Project Buyer/Expeditor, 1979-1981
BIG DOG COMPANY, Materials Supervisor, 1978-1979

Technologies

Accpac, Crystal Report Builder, Dun & Bradstreet, EDI, Microsoft Office, Purchase Soft, RAL, Visio

Professional Development

North American Newspaper Purchasing Association
American Society for Industrial Security
School Institute: Business/Marketing Management Diploma

Peter M. Rabbit, page 2.

Purchasing Manager

MARC M. KELLEY

714 GLENVIEW ROAD   (888) 888-8888
HAMBONE, WA 88000   EMAIL@EMAIL.COM

Results-oriented **FINANCE PROFESSIONAL**. Consistently successful in controlling costs and improving net profitability while continuing to support critical operations. Background includes procurement responsibility up to $5 million annually. Excellent communicator with a good attitude and sense of humor. Tenacious negotiator with keen vendor management skills. Strong research and analysis, organization, and decision-making abilities. PC proficient with Word, Excel, and MainSaver.

CAREER SUMMARY

Purchasing / Maintenance Assistant, NAES Energy Services, Hambone, WA, 1997-present
Progressed from Purchasing Assistant to Maintenance Assistant. Selected by upper management to train as Assistant Plant Operator.

- Conducted and oversaw all procurement operations—requisitions, purchase orders, price negotiation, receiving, delivery verification. Commodities consisted of chemicals, hardware, consumables, office supplies, and maintenance equipment.
- Prepared weekly and monthly reports of dollars committed and delivery status. Ensured inventory was current and needs were met. Performed preventive maintenance and assisted mechanic with machinery repairs.

Subcontract Administrator, Huge Aircraft Company, Second, CA, 1987-1996

- Administered yearly government subcontract purchases of $1+ million. Solicited bids, negotiated prices, awarded jobs. Interfaced with representatives of many different organizations. Coordinated with Engineering, Program, Quality, Price, and Cost Analysis staff through completion.

Received High Achiever Award for saving over $100,000 annually.

Purchasing Manager, Electro-Line, Mainstream, OH, 1984-1986

- Procured electronic components of purchases in excess of $5 million annually, including price negotiation, and delivery. Ensured compliance with applicable Government Procurement Regulations.

Buyer, Huge Aircraft Company, Second, CA, 1980-1984

- Placed purchase orders for computer and test equipment, electronic hardware, optics, and other commodities.

*Received Corporate Superior Performance Award for
outstanding attitude and work performance.*

EDUCATION / ADDITIONAL TRAINING

B.S., General Business Administration, University of Arizona
CPR / First Aid Certification – Licensed Forklift Driver
Continuing Education includes Teaming Techniques, Negotiation Skills, and other relevant classes.

Management Consultant

TODD JAMES
444 Winding Road Avenue
Alexandria, Virginia 22302
202-234-5212
toddjames@rix.net

Professional Profile

A seasoned, highly motivated senior executive with a successful track record in international operations and project management. Recognized for exceptional problem solving and motivational skills as well as the ability to **negotiate, deal, and close successfully across cultural barriers**. Extensive experience in management consulting in diverse industries, ranging from unit construction and mining/drilling operations to industrial equipment procurement, sales and distribution. **Bilingual with extensive international experience,** including Africa, the Middle East, South Asia, and Western Europe.

Areas of Impact

International Conflict Resolution • Worldwide Corporate Security • Risk Assessment
Operation and Project Management • New Business Development • International Law
Global Emergency Planning • International Public Relations • Recruitment/Training

Career Highlights

- Successfully provided diplomatic, risk management, and crisis resolution services to a broad range of Fortune 100 companies, Ambassadors, Heads of State, cabinet ministers, and senior government officials, U.S. and foreign.
- Successfully negotiated, on behalf of Pete's Oil, with an east African government to resolve a cross-cultural crisis and avoid closure of a $1 billion distribution facility.
- Developed and implemented logistics and training programs involving several thousand U.S. and foreign personnel and a $40 million annual budget. Effectively achieved all objectives with a budget savings of 12%.
- Directed Jones & Jones, Big Truck Co., and Movers International in the successful negotiation of more than $15 million of capital equipment sales to a west African government.
- Conducted numerous feasibility studies and risk assessments, both political and economic forecasts, for a variety of projects including gold, platinum and diamond mining, nuclear energy development, port, railroad and packaging facilities.

Employment History

International Affairs Consultant
Professional Services Provided to: Whitman International, Virginia Properties International, Pete's Oil, Tall Trees, Inc., Rothstein's Petroleum, Movers International, Jones & Jones, Big Truck Company, Top Flight Airlines, Technology USA, PTR International, Ltd., National Telecommunications Foundation, Master Technologies.

National Security Agency
Near East and Africa Referent...Chief of Station...Chief of Operations...Chief of Branch, Counterterrorism...Deputy/Chief of Station.

Education

Juris Doctorate, *International Law,* University of Denver, Denver, CO
Master of Arts, *History,* University of Denver, Denver, CO
Bachelor of Arts, *History,* New College, Sarasota, FL

Traffic Control (Shipping and Receiving)

DAPHNE TREEMONT

1235 Corbin Drive   dtreemont@email.com
Greenwich, CT WY 06830   Residence (203) 555-1234
                                                                                          Mobile (203) 555-5678

SUMMARY OF QUALIFICATIONS

- Extensive, large volume *Traffic Control, Shipping & Receiving* knowledge; strong leadership abilities.
- Solid record of promotions based on performance. Insightful commitment to positive communication.
- Willing to take on new challenges within demanding deadlines utilizing progressive, results-oriented performance style.
- Strong time management and interpersonal skills. Extremely organized.
- Self-motivated, adaptable, loyal team player. Impeccable work ethic.
- Competent blueprint reading capabilities. Computer literate—proficient with spreadsheets.

EXPERIENCE

ABC EXTRUSION, Division of General Corporation, Greenwich, CT   1995 to 2003
Manufacturer of machinery for the rubber & plastic industry. Company name changed several times due to new ownership. Retained as a valuable employee through each transfer.

- **Traffic Control Manager**—Facilitated all shipments of large machinery and spare parts. Coordinated all paperwork and documentation including Bill of Lading, Certificate of Origin and Customs documents. Entered applicable data into computer system.
- **Receiving Manager**—Handled all receiving and stockroom department responsibilities. Identified, tagged and located parts in stock area. Retrieved components and piece parts for assembly floor personnel. Skilled using Federal Express Powership & Pitney Bowes shipping equipment.
- **Receiving**—Supported all receiving department functions. Identified, verified and received parts optimizing the computerized database.
- **Stockroom**—Stocked parts; recorded and cataloged items in database. Assisted in retrieving parts for assembly floor work orders.
- **Shipping**—Prepared and arranged UPS shipments and packing of parts. Operated UPS equipment documenting size, weight and type of cargo. Typed Bills of Lading and Customs forms. Recorded all shipping data.
- **Data Entry**—Logged all new parts and stockroom locations into database.
- **Expediter**—Identified, traced and accelerated parts in process to the next manufacturing operation. Directed finished parts to appropriate assembly areas. Tracked and updated shortage lists.
- **Licensed**—to operate overhead crane, forklift and overhead lifts.

HOMETOWN MARKET, Greenwich, CT   1978 to 1995
Produce Market

- **Owner/Manager**—Directed and oversaw daily store operations. Supervised up to ten employees. Facilitated operational performance of store, implemented all phases of management functions inclusive of inventory, presentations, display, advertising, customer and employee relations, all accounting/bookkeeping, payroll and receivables. Generated and maintained reports, spreadsheets and mailing lists of over 10,000 people.

CONTINUING EDUCATION

- Blueprint Reading Certification, ABC
- Forklift Operation, ABC
- Crane Operation, ABC
- Accounting I, II, Connecticut State University

References Available Upon Request

Operations Management and Human Resources

Vice President of Operations

Melissa Cahill

21 Fairview Place   **Houston, TX 77002**   **713-555-1212**   **mcahill210@aol.com**

SUMMARY OF QUALIFICATIONS

Vice President of Operations, Manufacturing. 20+ years experience in the creative leadership of multisite manufacturing operations to improve productivity, quality, and efficiency. Facilitated significant cost savings through expertise in:

- Operations Systems
- Strategic Planning
- Cost Management
- Facilities Design
- Offshore Production

- Manufacturing Process
- Quality Control
- Supplier Partnership
- Human Resources/Labor Relations
- Compliance

PROFESSIONAL EXPERIENCE

Acme Automotive Products, Houston, Texas   *1992 – 2002*
A national leader in the manufacturing of automotive water pumps with annual sales of $380 million and 1,500 employees.
Vice President of Operations

- Managed the company's two plants in Texas and Mexico. Directly supervised two plant managers, a materials manager, advanced manufacturing systems manager, distribution manager, manager for special projects, and training and a Quality Control Division.
- Initiated and secured ISO9002 certification in two plants on the first application.
- Reorganized preventative maintenance schedules that decreased scrap rates by 50% and virtually eliminated rework rates.
- Orchestrated teamwork and communication between marketing and production to ensure customers received precise delivery dates and improved quality.
- Guided efforts with a major supplier to turn around its sub-quality standards. Avoided a change to the competition's vendors that could have been costly. Result: vendor achieved ISO9000 certification and is now rated top in field.

A1 Heating Corporation   *1982 – 1992*
A residential and industrial water heater manufacturing company.
Vice President of Mexican Operations, Bordertown, Texas   1988 – 1992
Plant Manager/Director of Operations, Portland, Oregon   1984 – 1988
Manager of Manufacturing, Milwaukee, WI   1982 – 1984

- Instituted a quality control system in Mexican operation that resulted in highest product quality in industry. Responded to suspicions from customers and suppliers about quality of Mexican-produced goods by arranging for decision-makers to see plant in operation.
- Reduced accident rate 200% and turnover rate (from 12% to 3% per month in four years) in Mexican operations by implementing unilateral training programs (e.g., skills, teamwork, supervisory).
- Negotiated commitments from vendors to ensure JIT system.
- Established a 50,000-square-foot distribution center to improve service to mid-continent customers.
- Prevented theft of valuable copper shipments by working with Mexican police.
- Selected by senior management to solve problems in Canadian plant, which resulted in opening on schedule. Efforts led to promotion to Vice President of Mexican Operations.

- Improved Portland plant operations efficiencies as a result of executing a comprehensive study. In four years increased output significantly and profits by 200% by optimizing space, decreasing product damage during production, and consolidating shipments.
- Oversaw Milwaukee plant closing and transfer to modern facilities. Responsibilities included identification of most economical way to equip new plant, comprehensive study on disposal of buildings, and employee transition management. Production levels remained stable and efforts led to promotion to Director of Operations.

Hillcrest Water Products, Inc., Dayton, Ohio   *1977 – 1982*
Manufacturing Engineer

EDUCATION
MBA, Apex School of Management, University of Dayton, Dayton, Ohio
Bachelor of Science (Mechanical Engineering), University of Wisconsin, Madison, Wisconsin

ONGOING PROFESSIONAL DEVELOPMENT
- Strategic Planning Seminar, Columbia University Executive Program
- Leadership at the Peak, Center for Creative Leadership
- World Class Manufacturing & Process Capability Studies, K. W. Farn & Associates
- Human Resources Seminar, American Manufacturing Association
- The Employee Team Concept, The Center for Productivity
- MRP II, Oliver Wight
- Understanding Border Culture, Maquiladora Associates

Operations Management and Human Resources

218

Louis Edwards

1234 Ocean Road • Wilmington, NC 97979 • (999) 999-9999 • louis@email.com

Emerging Technologies Globalization Executive
Deal Maker / Market & Product Strategist / Business Developer / Negotiator

Results-driven and innovative Telecommunications Industry Executive with a 20+ year successful track record driving revenue growth and winning market share primarily in turnaround, start-up and high growth situations. Consistently deliver strong and sustainable revenue gains through combined expertise in Strategic Business Planning, Product Management, Market Strategy, Contract Negotiations, and Customer Relationship Management. Recognized for exceptional ability to assess business unit capabilities, identify and implement appropriate business and product re-engineering measures thus assuring bottom line growth. Rare ability to establish the organization's vision, develop "C" level relationships and negotiate the deals that guarantee success.

<u>Key Accomplishments</u>

- "C" level relationship builder with a track record personally negotiating contracts with companies such as Xerox, Lockheed Martin, Bank of America, Morgan Stanley, EDS, Visa, Oracle, Microsoft, Nortel, Boeing, Nordstrom and The Gap.
- Consistent track record developing contracts and terms that utilized company capabilities and met customer needs, including the first pre-paid international contract. This allowed the company to accelerate into the international market achieving $1+ billion in revenue. This approach became the industry standard.
- Turned around an under-performing business unit lacking leadership by redesigning and motivating the sales and services teams, successfully recovering 60% of the lost accounts and adding new business to increase revenues to $5+ million annually in the first 12 months.
- Conceived and coordinated the global account management process; identified customer needs and product capabilities, spearheaded product and service level agreement changes to win the first global contract. Not only did this grow market share from 7% to 100% and revenue from $330,000 to $6 million per month, it set new industry standards in global business practices.
- Revitalized a product offering by identifying and implementing an International Reseller Channel, re-engineering the existing product through the addition of a conversion process adding packaging enhancements and aligning a service/support structure extending the product life by 2 years and capturing a potential revenue of $10 million annually.
- Within 45 days, conceived and implemented a National Accounts Program, establishing pricing model, sales organization structure and customer service delivery format, successfully increasing revenue from $12 million to $27 million per month. This program became the standard for the entire company.
- Led the company's new technologies market development (VPN, Web Hosting, co-locating Internet) securing sales in excess of $15 million within 6 months.

<u>Employment Summary</u>

Software Company, Inc.   **2004 – Present**
Vice President, Business Development and Alliances, Philadelphia, PA
Recruited to drive the product development process and expand market reach through the implementation of an international reseller channel and strategic business alliances.

- Negotiated contracts with Fuji Xerox, Xerox, Accenture and Lockheed Martin capturing $10 million in potential revenue.
- Managed the re-negotiation of two existing alliances that will net the company at least $2 million over the next 12 months.
- Established a new technology relationship with Open Text extending the company's reach in the Life Sciences market.

International Telecom, Inc.   1997 – 2004
Regional Vice President National Accounts, Nashville, TN
Recruited to develop a major account program and subsequently developed a national account program.
Responsibilities included full P&L, $20 million operational budget and more than 250 personnel.
  • During a 15-company acquisition period, including the ITI acquisition, (the largest in Telecomm history),
    consistently exceeded all business objectives.
  • Managed the best corporate A/R and bad debt levels, achieved outstanding customer retention level of 94%
    and managed corporation's lowest employee turnover rate of 10%.
  • Developed and implemented a National Account Program expanding revenues within the first year from $180
    million to $260 million and achieved Top Regional Vice President award for outstanding revenue increase.
  • Averaged a 21% annual internal revenue growth and was selected to the President's Club from 1998 through
    2003 by continually identifying new business opportunities and establishing the right teams, resources and
    support to grow the organization and meet the customer's expectations.

ABC Telecom, Inc.   1995 – 1997
Executive Director – Global Accounts, California
Promoted to manage the Western US team of 139 sales and support staff, 5 direct reports and to oversee 35 national
accounts.
  • Managed and negotiated $750 million in contracts with "C" level players including BOA, Visa, Microsoft, The
    Gap, Sun, Apple, Oracle, AMD and Nordstrom. Grew market share from less than 15% to 48% in two years.
  • Averaged 122% of revenue target every year.

ABC Telecom, Inc.   1992 – 1995
Branch Manager, California
Recruited to grow and manage the Bank of America account, successfully leading a team of 39 cross-functional
members.
  • Grew annual sales and revenue from $3.6 million to $80 million within two years, attaining 100% market
    share.
  • Spearheaded largest commercial sale in ABC history, valued at $400 million, successfully converting the entire
    Bank of America network to ABC in less than 6 months while maintaining 100% customer satisfaction.

BS&S   1986 – 1992
Field District Manager, San Francisco, CA
  • Consistently exceeded quota, averaging 112% and made President's Club every year while in sales/sales
    management positions.
  • As staff member for the President of BS&S Information Systems, was responsible for revenue and issues for all
    national accounts west of the Mississippi, approximately 200 accounts, achieving 109% of the revenue quota.

BS&S   1983 – 1986
National Account Management, BS&S Headquarters, New York, NY
  • Negotiated and implemented the largest state government equipment contract, valued at $20 million.
  • Named to Management Development Program (top 2% of all management personnel), recognized for
    superior executive and leadership potential.

Education

Bachelor of Arts, New York University

Career Development: Intensive 18-week BS&S account management and product training seminar

Senior International Marketing
and Business Development Executive

CAMILLE TORRE
9 Zentral Strasse
Dusseldorf, Germany

ctorre@hotmail.com

Expertise in Product Development • Commercialization & Global Market Expansion
Telecoms • Consumer Electronics • Sports & Leisure Industries

Dynamic management career leading turnaround and high-growth organizations through unprecedented profitability and explosive market growth worldwide. Combine extensive strategic planning, competitive positioning, life cycle management, channel management and product development/ management qualifications with strong general management, P&L management, organizational development, workforce management, and multicultural communication skills. MBA; multilingual – fluent German, English, Italian, intermediate Japanese.

PROFESSIONAL EXPERIENCE

MAJOR ELECTRONICS COMPANY, Dusseldorf, Germany   1995 to 2003
The second largest electronics company worldwide ranking #15 in the Global Fortune 500 ratings.
Senior Vice President Marketing

- Executive Board Member recruited to design marketing strategies and implement systems/ processes to lead a worldwide marketing function as part of the business group's aggressive turnaround program.
- Accountable for a $250 million marketing budget. Oversee worldwide marketing operations including business strategy and benchmarking, technology strategy, market research, consumer marketing, regional marketing (EMEA, Asia, U.S.), marketing communications, new media including Internet, intranet, and extranet, and business-to-consumer e-commerce. Manage a staff of 77 through 10 direct reports.
- Led the marketing initiatives for the successful launch of two mobile phone product lines transitioning losses of $200 million in 97/98 to profits of $30 million in 98/99 and doubling world market share to approximately 8%.
- Delivered a 5-point improvement in brand awareness, and 50% relevant set improvement for mobile and cordless phones throughout China and Europe.
- Introduced a worldwide marketing communications spending performance initiative slashing communication costs by $10 million.
- Identified and initiated business development strategies and technology vehicles instrumental in developing international marketing partnerships and equity investments.
- Established a price/value-based market analysis instrument together with the market research and consumer marketing groups to develop pricing accuracy generating revenue increases exceeding $20 million.
- Directed e-commerce marketing initiatives leading to the development of 7 operational online stores in 5 European countries generating 4 million contacts with CAGR of 20% per week, followed by development of a virtual Customer Care Center.
- Conceived and initiated PR strategies for a new product launch generating over 130 million contracts within a few months.
- Led improvements in competitive market intelligence through enhancements to statistical reports and customer satisfaction surveys.

ELECTRONICS COMPANY, Bonn, Germany   1990 to 1995
A leading European high-end TV, audio and consumer electronics company.
Marketing Director

- Joined this privately held company to improve product life cycle management and channel marketing initiatives. Oversaw budget administration, strategic planning and market research, international communications, training and product management. Directed a staff of 21.
- Instituted a series of channel management and segmentation improvements to correct market planning and positioning initiatives and reduce price erosion throughout retail distribution channels.
- Led development of product definition, life cycle management, and market launch strategies positioning company as the value-based market leader of high-end TV sets in Germany with market share exceeding 14%.

ABC BICYCLE COMPANY, Berlin, Germany   1986 to 1990
A global leading automotive, motorcycle and bicycle component equipment manufacturer.
Director of Marketing International

- Led transition from an engineering-driven traditional gear hub manufacturer to a market-oriented competitor in the sport and leisure industry. Reported to Division President.
- Established a marketing department, devised strategies for over 1,000 SKUs within 6 product lines, delivered a profit for the first time in 8 years, and boosted new product sales ratios from 10% to 40%.
- Headed up a special internal R&D audit and restructuring project leading to the creation of marketing-driven product development teams. Replaced 15% of R&D personnel, established R&D controls, reduced R&D costs by $500,000, and earned a $30,000 project completion bonus.

ABC AUTOMOTIVE, Wolfsburg, Germany   1983 to 1986
Leading automotive and home appliance manufacturer.
Product Group Manager

- Oversaw European product management and marketing initiatives for the $500 million Electronic Division. Successfully introduced brands in France, Italy, and England.

EDUCATION

M.B.A., University of California, Berkeley

Diplome d'enseignement Supérieur Europeen de Management, Centre d'Etudes Européennes Supérieures de Management (CESEM), France

Diplom-Betriebswirt (FH), Business Administration, Europäisches Studienprogramm für Betriebswirtschaft (ESB)

INTERNSHIPS

Country Chamber of Commerce, Osaka, Japan, Oskar Duisberg Society Scholarship

Counseled German and Japanese firms in all aspects of business for their respective countries.

Kornwestheim Club Vertrieb GmbH, Kornwestheim, Germany, Marketing concepts in direct sales.

Senior Management

222

Senior Management Executive

JANE B. URATA
●●●

3131 CARMEL ROAD • SAN DIEGO, CALIFORNIA 92109
HOME: (858) 555-0234 • CELLULAR: (858) 555-0235 • E-MAIL: JU_ARBORIST@PLANTNET.COM

New Business Development • Strategic Partnerships • Product Marketing

Accomplished Senior Executive with a strong affinity for technology and a keen business sense for the application of emerging products to add value and expand markets. Proven talent for identifying core business needs and translating into technical deliverables. Launched and managed cutting-edge Internet programs and services to win new customers, generate revenue gains, and increase brand value.

Unique combination of technical and business/sales experience. Articulate and persuasive in explaining the benefits of e-commerce technologies and how they add value, differentiate offerings, and increase customer retention. Highly self-motivated, enthusiastic, and profit oriented.

Expertise in Internet services, emerging payment products, secure electronic commerce, smart card technology, and Java.

AREAS OF QUALIFICATION

Business
- Sales & Marketing • Business Development • Strategic Initiatives
- Business Planning • Project Management • Strategic Partnerships
- Business & Technical Requirements • Revenue Generation
- Contract Negotiations • Relationship Management

Technical
- Electronic Commerce • Encryption Technology • Key Management
- Public Key Infrastructure • Firewalls • Smart Cards • Stored Value
- Digital Certificates • Internet & Network Security • Complex Financial Systems
- Authorization, Clearing, Settlement • Dual and Single Message

PROFESSIONAL EXPERIENCE

ABC Credit Card Corp., San Diego, CA   *2002 to Present*
E-COMMERCE AND SMART CARD CONSULTANT

- Developed strategic e-commerce marketing plans for large and small merchants involving Web purchases and retail transactions using a multifunctional, microcontroller smart card for both secure Internet online commerce and point-of-sale offline commerce.
- Combined multiple software products for Internet and non-Internet applications: home banking, stored value, digital certificates, key management, rewards & loyalty program, PCS/GSM cell phone, and contactless microcontroller with RF communications without direct POS contact.
- Consulted on business and technical requirements to define new e-commerce products and essential deliverables for ABC Credit Card, valued at $2.5 M, supporting and enhancing Internet transactions.
- Analyzed systems relating to the point of sale environment in the physical world and at the merchant server via the Internet for real-time authorization, clearing, and settlement.
- Managed projects including the requirements management system for electronic commerce products affecting core systems: authorization, clearing, and settlement. Provided expertise about business and technical issues regarding SET and the Credit Card Payment Gateway Service.

Communications Technology Corporation, Miami, FL   *1997 to 2002*
MANAGER OF WESTERN REGION CHANNEL PARTNER PROGRAM

- Developed and maintained business relationships with large Fortune 500 customers and partners that use or resell client-server software for applications and contracts involving e-commerce and smart card technology for a variety of Internet/intranet products: home banking, EDI, stored value, digital certificates, key management, perimeter defense with proxy firewalls, secure remote access.
- Negotiated an exclusive contract with one of the largest government and commercial contractors in the industry, projected to generate $2-4 million over a 24-36 month period. Contract includes secure remote access, telecommuting, secure health care applications.

Avanta Corp., Miami, FL   *1993 to 1997*
SENIOR SOFTWARE ENGINEER / SOFTWARE INSTRUCTOR

- Designed new programs and trained software engineers in object-oriented analysis and design using UML. Solutions were implemented in C++ in a UNIX environment.
- Managed a software engineering group of 53 individuals. Developed in-house program that saved over $150,000 in training costs for state-of-the-art communications system software development.
- Received Peer Award for outstanding performance; earned a performance evaluation rating of 4.2/5.0.
- Developed and maintained C and C++ communication software in a UNIX environment.
- Created curriculum and course materials that reduced overall training costs by more than $150,000. Coordinated and presented software training programs.

EDUCATION AND CREDENTIALS

- B.S., Electrical Engineering, University of Miami, Emphasis: software engineering, Minor: Psychology, President of the Sigma Sigma Fraternity
- Top Secret Security Clearance with Polygraph

Senior Sales and Marketing Manager

JAMES P. DELOREAN
529 Caledonia Road | Atlantic City, NJ 08404 | (609) 555-1212
delorean30@msn.com

Top-producing sales and marketing professional with nine years of management experience in world-class organizations. Consistently successful in developing new markets, penetrating new territories, identifying and capturing new business, and managing large-scale events for Fortune 500 companies worldwide. Goal-driven manager committed to developing outcomes mutually benefiting the company and the client. Excellent qualifications in building corporate relationships with industry leaders.

Areas of expertise include:
- New Account Development
- Key Account Management
- Client Needs Assessment
- Contract Negotiations
- Competitive / Strategic Planning

- Large-Scale Meeting / Event Planning
- Catering Planning / Management
- Co-Marketing Partnerships
- Relationship Management
- Customer Service / Satisfaction

PROFESSIONAL EXPERIENCE

EXQUISITE RESORT SUITES, Atlantic City, NJ   1999 to 2003
Senior Sales Manager
Joined company to lead market entry/penetration initiatives throughout the Northeast Region of the U.S. for this privately-held exclusive resort with 800 suites, a 60,000 sq. ft. conference center, and a full range of guest amenities. Managed business growth among Fortune 500 corporate accounts and national association accounts.
- Developed and maintained relationships with corporate meeting planners of major accounts including IBM, AT&T, Ralston Purina, Bell South, AT&T, Siemens, Medtronic, and others to develop custom-tailored business meeting packages.
- Worked closely with corporate planners throughout all phases of strategic and tactical planning, coordination, and execution of major events to ensure superior service and guest relations.
- Captured national association accounts including American Cancer Society, American Heart Association, New York Bar Association, and New Jersey Institute of CPAs.
- Sold and orchestrated multi-year bookings to numerous associations and corporate accounts.

Achievements
- Built territory and increased revenues from $1 million to over $7 million within first year.
- Achieved 157% of annual booking goals (2,500 room nights per month).

BUSCH GARDENS, Tampa, Florida   1996 to 1999
Catering Sales Manager
Challenged to develop new markets and products for multicultural groups visiting Walt Disney World.
- Identified target market, initiated contact with prospects, developed proposals, and forged major account relationships.
- Worked closely with corporate planners at Exxon, Compaq, IBM, Frito Lay, McDonald's, and others to create unique and extravagant parties and events ranging up to $2 million per event.
- Sold, planned, and coordinated catered group events for corporate accounts and private parties ranging from 2 to 19,000 guests.
- Developed comprehensive strategic and tactical plans for every phase of event including logistics, transportation, food and beverage, entertainment, and gifts to create a memorable occasion.

- Oversaw scheduled events and served as troubleshooter and liaison between park operators, managers, and corporate clients to resolve issues and ensure guest satisfaction and loyalty.
- Compiled planning, tracking, and forecasting reports using proprietary computer system.

Achievements
- Achieved 130% of Catering Sales & Service Team Goals, 1999.
- Consistently exceeded individual annual sales goals.

INTERNATIONAL HOTEL, Tampa, Florida   1988 to 1996
Fast-track promotions through a series of increasingly responsible positions based on business growth and improved sales revenues for this high-volume airport property.

Sales Manager-Midwest   (1995 to 1996)
Sales Manager-Orlando   (1992 to 1995)
Associate Director of Catering   (1988 to 1991)
Catering Manager   (1988)

- Created innovative guest packages for corporate accounts locally and nationally for this first-rate property with 300 rooms, a 12,000 sq. ft. conference center, and several guest services facilities.
- Developed corporate and professional relationships throughout the industry and coordinated with other properties to accommodate extremely large groups.
- Identified target accounts and consistently developed new business driving increased revenues.
- Promoted property through trade show and convention participation, including public speaking engagements for large groups.
- Planned and coordinated exclusive large-scale intimate client events for the affluent.

Achievement
- Achieved 131% of sales goals throughout the Midwest Region,   1996

CHINESE COURT RESTAURANT, Orlando, Florida   1986 to 1988
Catering/Sales Manager
Successfully sold Chinese-themed parties to international wholesale and corporate convention groups.

EDUCATION

B.S., Marketing – University of Nevada at Las Vegas,   1985
B.S., Multinational Business Operations – University of Nevada at Las Vegas,   1985
Diploma, Certificat de Langue Francaise, Institut Catholique De Paris,   1986
(Study Abroad Program)

PROFESSIONAL DEVELOPMENT

Sales Training:
International Hotel, BEST Programs (Building Effective Sales Techniques), Top Achiever Sales, Travel Management Companies, Best Practices
Designation
Certified Meeting Professional (CMP)
Affiliations
Meeting Planners International, Member
American Society of Association Executives, Member

Senior Technology Executive

MITCHELL T. NORDSTROM

621 Sawmill Road
Charleston, West Virginia 25301
(304) 555-1298 (days) / (304) 555-4520 (evenings)
mtanord@cs.com

Accomplished Management Executive with 15+ years of experience and a verifiable record of delivering enhanced productivity, streamlined operations, and improved financial performance. Natural leader with strong entrepreneurial spirit and a special talent for transitioning strategy into action and achievement. Highly effective team building and motivational skills.

Multifunctional expertise includes:

- Corporate Information Technology
- Staffing & Management Development
- Quality & Productivity Improvement
- Marketing Strategy & Management
- Strategic & Business Planning
- Customer Service & Satisfaction
- Operations Management
- Team Building & Leadership

PROFESSIONAL EXPERIENCE

Roberts Company   1995 – Present
CHIEF INFORMATION OFFICER, Roberts Co., Charleston, WV (2000 – Present)
PRESIDENT, Martins Systems (Roberts Co. subsidiary), Elmview, WV (2000 – Present)

Appointed to these dual senior-level positions and challenged to create and execute technology strategy for Roberts Co. and subsidiaries of the $700 million Roberts Information Services Corporation. Concurrently provide executive oversight for the development and deployment of software products/services and MIS solutions for Martins Systems, affiliate offices, and 3,900 independent agents.

Provide leadership for a team of 200 management and support personnel. Administer a $16 million annual budget. Scope of accountabilities is expansive and includes planning and strategy, operations management, human resource affairs, customer service, marketing, management reporting, and communications.

Key Management Achievements

- Built the complete corporate technology infrastructure from the ground up. Developed technology strategies and tactical plans mapped to align with corporate goals.
- Serve as a member of the corporate Leadership Council. Define corporate vision; develop business plans, create strategies, and establish tactical goals for all business units.
- Established a high-performance management staff and created a team-based work atmosphere that promotes cooperation to achieve common corporate objectives. Instituted a series of initiatives that substantially improved communications between staff and management.
- Developed and integrated programs to maximize productive and efficient use of technology throughout the corporation. Instituted "user champions" to serve as technical experts within each business unit, launched executive "boot camps" to train management in aggressive computer use, and built responsive help centers for technical support.
- Spearheaded creation and implementation of a customer information and marketing team responsible for developing an award-winning marketing program, promotions, direct-mail campaigns, and demonstrations and tours.
- Created innovative processes utilizing product specialists for management of sales leads and distributor networks, resolution of customer escalated issues, and provision of workflow and engineering consulting for company offices and agents.

Senior Management

Key Technical Achievements
- Led implementation of client/server software suite that won the industry's 1999 and 2001 Title Tech Discovery Award for best and most innovative title industry software.
- Spearheaded development of numerous technical infrastructure projects including the corporate Internet presence, corporate intranet, Web hosting solutions for independent agents, and electronic commerce solutions for offices, agents, and service providers in the real estate industry.
- Orchestrated development of an award-winning marketing program, Power Tools for the Modern World, that won the local and district GOLD ADDY awards for best overall marketing program.
- Guided development and implementation of a title industry software suite installed in 400 systems throughout the distributor network. Designed and deployed training programs to ensure high quality service levels.
- Managed creation of an Electronic Underwriting Manual that was selected as best policies and procedures implementation in the National Folio Awards competition, 1999.
- Led design and implementation of a 1,200-user corporate WAN, a centralized help desk, a 2003-user corporate e-mail system, and a comprehensive training center for desktop applications.

PRESIDENT, Roberts Gilday, Gilday, FL (1991 – 1995)
Promoted to manage all operations for this Roberts Company subsidiary. Took over leadership for a staff of 25 and recruited/built to 90+ personnel. Oversaw all management reporting, finances, marketing, product delivery, and closing services.

Key Management Achievements
- Delivered profits throughout a severe recession that crashed the local real estate market.
- Maintained a consistent 15% market share despite a tripling in the local competition.
- Achieved standing in the top 15% in profitability and revenues across all company offices nationwide.
- Created and deployed a realtor marketing program including a series of 20 seminars; built strong industry relationships and established a reputation as the area's premier experts.
- Pioneered innovative marketing strategies to reach new markets and build a network of industry professionals.

COMMERCIAL CLOSER, Roberts Gilday, Gilday, FL (1988 – 1991)
Hired to develop and manage a commercial closing division. Achieved the highest market share of commercial closings in the local market.

EDUCATION
Juris Doctor, West Virginia University (1988)
Bachelor of Arts, Business, West Virginia University (1985)

PROFESSIONAL ACTIVITIES
Frequent Lecturer, Title Tech Technology Conferences, 1998 – Present
Member, Systems Committee, American Land Title Association, 1997 – Present
Member, "Technology 2003" Planning Committee, American Land Title Association, 1997 – Present

Senior Technology Executive

BRENDA FRANKS

95 Lane Road   Los Angeles, CA 900071   (888) 888-9888   Bfran@yahoo.com

---

SENIOR TECHNOLOGY EXECUTIVE
Project Management ◆ *Multimedia Communications & Production* ◆ *MIS Management*

Exceptionally creative management executive uniquely qualified for a digital media technical production position by a distinctive blend of hands-on technical, project management, and advertising/communications experience. Offer a background that spans broadcast, radio, and print media; fully fluent and proficient in interactive and Internet technologies and tools.

Proven leader with a strength for identifying talent, building and motivating creative teams that work cooperatively to achieve goals. Highly articulate with excellent interpersonal skills and a sincere passion for blending communications with technology. Capabilities include:

- ◆ Project Planning & Management
- ◆ Account Management & Client Relations
- ◆ Multimedia Communications & Production
- ◆ Information Systems & Networking
- ◆ Conceptual & Creative Design
- ◆ Work Plans, Budgets & Resource Planning
- ◆ Department Management
- ◆ Interactive / Internet Technologies
- ◆ Technology Needs Assessment & Solutions
- ◆ Team Building & Leadership

PROFESSIONAL EXPERIENCE

LaRoche Investments, Inc., Los Angeles, CA   *1989 – Present*
VICE PRESIDENT OF MIS (2000 – Present)
ASSISTANT VICE PRESIDENT OF IT/CORPORATE COMMUNICATIONS   (1995 – 2000)
CORPORATE COMMUNICATIONS OFFICER   (1991 – 1995)
ASSOCIATE   (1989 – 1991)

Advanced rapidly through a series of increasingly responsible positions with this U.S.-based, European investment group. Initially hired to manage market research projects, advanced to plan and execute corporate communications projects, and in 1995, assumed responsibility for spearheading the introduction of emerging technologies to automate the entire company.

Current scope of responsibility is expansive and focuses on strategic planning, implementation, and administration of all information systems and technology. Lead technical staff members, manage budgets, select and oversee vendors, define business requirements, and produce deliverables through formal project plans. Manage systems configuration and maintenance, troubleshoot problems, plan and direct upgrades, and test operations to ensure optimum systems functionality and availability.

Technical Contributions
- Pioneered the company's computerization from the ground floor; led the installation and integration of a state-of the-art and highly secure network involving 50+ workstations running on 6 LANs interconnected by V-LAN switching technology.
- Defined requirements; planned and accelerated the implementation of advanced technology solutions, deployed on a calculated timeframe, to meet the short- and long-term needs of the organization.
- Orchestrated the introduction of sophisticated applications and multimedia technology to streamline workflow processes, expand presentation capabilities, and keep pace with the competition.
- Administered the life cycle of multiple projects from initial systems/network planning and technology acquisition through installation, training, and operation. Saved hundreds of thousands in consulting fees by managing IS and telecommunication issues in-house.

Business Contributions
- Created and produced high-impact multimedia presentations to communicate the value and benefits of individual investment projects to top-level company executives. Tailored presentations to appeal to highly sophisticated, multicultural audiences.
- Assembled and directed exceptionally well-qualified project teams from diverse creative disciplines; collaborated with and guided photographers, videographers, copywriters, script writers, graphic designers, and artists to produce innovative presentations and special events.
- Performed market research and analyses to determine risks and feasibility of multiple investment projects valued at up to $150 million. Developed and recommended tactical plans to transform vision into achievement.

Broadcast, Print, and Radio Advertising & Production   *1974 – 1988*
DIRECTOR OF ADVERTISING, Schwarzer Advertising Associates, New York, NY (1986 – 1988)
ADVERTISING ACCOUNT EXECUTIVE, Schoppe, New York, NY (1987) / Rainbow Advertising, Brooklyn, NY (1984 – 1986) / Marcus Advertising, Phoenix, AZ (1983 – 1984) / WCHN, WTYR, AND WSCZ, Boston, MA (1982 – 1983) / WFDX-TV, WFDX-FM, WKLU, WERS, WQRT, Lehigh Valley, PA (1974 – 1981)
WRITER/PRODUCER, RADIO PROGRAMMING, WPTR, Detroit, MI (1974)

Early career involved a series of progressive creative and account management positions spanning all advertising mediums: multimedia, television, radio, and print. Worked directly with clients to assess complex and often obscure needs; conceptualized and developed advertising campaigns to communicate the desired message in an influential manner.

Achievement Highlights
- Designed, wrote, produced, and launched advertising campaigns that consistently positioned clients with a competitive distinction. Developed a reputation for ability to accurately intuit and interpret clients' desires and produce deliverables that achieved results.
- Hand-selected and led creative teams consisting of graphic designers, artists, musicians, talent, cartoonists, animators, videographers, photographers, and other freelancers and third-party creative services to develop and produce multimillion dollar advertising campaigns.
- Won accolades for the creation, production, and launch of a 4-color fractional-page advertisement that generated the greatest response in the history of the publication. Honored with a featured personal profile recognizing achievements.
- Developed and applied a unique style and advertising philosophy that accounted for the nuances of human psychology and utilized innovative, brainy, and sometimes startling techniques to capture attention and influence the target market.

EDUCATION & TRAINING

A.A.S, Broadcast Production, Russ Junior College, Boston, MA, 1974
Continuing education in Marketing Research and Broadcast Production, 1984 – 1986
The School of Visual Arts, New York, NY

TECHNICAL QUALIFICATIONS

Innate technical abilities and interest in emerging technologies and digital communications. Trained and fully versed in all aspects of network design, implementation, installation, and maintenance. Advanced skill in the installation, configuration, customization, and troubleshooting of software suites and applications, hardware, and peripherals within the Windows environment (3.x, 95, 98, NT 3.5, NT 3.51, NT 4). Proficient with most Web development, multimedia, word processing, spreadsheet, graphic/presentation, and database tools and applications.

Senior Management

230

Administrative Assistant

Intent on working for a conglomerate, Lillian needed to communicate
her skills in a way that would stand out from the competition.

Lillian V. DiFrancesa
123 WENDELL AVENUE ◆ RUTHERFORD, NJ 07070
201.555.0000 ◆ LILLIEVEE@MYDOMAIN.COM

Career Profile
Administrative assistant with strong organizational and interpersonal skills, able to multitask a variety of responsibilities and challenges.

Related Skills
- Types 65 wpm
- Transcription
- MS Excel
- Purchasing

- Planning & Scheduling
- MS Word
- Written Communication
- Customer Service

- Internet Research
- Filing
- Telephone Reception
- Interdepartmental Coordination

Selected Achievements
- Handled 30-50 daily incoming calls on a six-line telephone system, offered a customer-friendly greeting, and promptly routed calls to proper party among 65 employees.
- Scheduled weekly meetings for all employee levels and their clients, greeted and escorted visitors to staff members' offices, and provided hospitality service (food and beverage) as requested by staff.
- Composed and distributed interoffice memorandums via electronic, voice and traditional paper means, increasing delivery and receipt of important information, and preserving the confidentiality of sensitive data.
- Assembled media kits for marketing and public relations departments, saving approximately $35,000 in additional labor costs.
- Scheduled 15-20 monthly client and internal meetings for both on-site and off-site locations, ensuring housing, catering and materials.
- Coordinated domestic and international travel arrangements for ten senior-level executives on a weekly basis using Internet travel sites that saved company an average of $100 – $200 per round-trip airfare ticket.
- Established confidential electronic file system for all correspondence and incoming faxes, creating a history for staff and eliminating excess paper and chance of exposing sensitive data to unauthorized personnel.
- Dispatched three messengers on bank runs and special assignments as requested by management, coordinating trips to ensure that multiple stops were made each time. This saved the company approximately $25.00 per messenger per day in excess travel expenses.
- Sorted and distributed mail for 65 employees.
- Ordered office supplies through the Internet, taking advantage of online savings and using electronic means to ensure accuracy and distribution of supplies to employees. This logging process helped improve the accuracy of inter-department charge backs.

Employment History
Administrative Assistant Birnbaum, Hirschfield and Associates, East Orange, NJ 1993-2007
Secretary/Receptionist Logic Systems and Solutions, New York, NY 1984-1993

Education
Associate Degree in Liberal Arts from Union County College, Elizabeth, NJ

Receptionist

With this resume, Keisha had no trouble finding another
job after her last employer moved out of state.

Keisha A. Jackson

1305 Lakeshore Drive ♦ Apartment 10-B ♦ Chicago, IL 00000 ♦ (555) 555-5555 ♦ kaj200@netmail.com

PROFILE

Responsible and dedicated office professional with 15 years of experience in heavy-volume, fast-paced environments. Cooperative team player who enjoys working with people and utilizing direct telephone contact. Detail-oriented, thorough and accurate in taking and relaying information. Well-organized to handle a variety of assignments and follow through from start to finish. Strong work ethic, with eagerness to learn and willingness to contribute toward meeting a company's goals.

- Visitor reception and routing
- Multi-line phone system operations
- Data entry and retrieval (Word and Excel)
- Customer relations
- Sales department support

- Account maintenance/reconciliation
- Order processing and billing
- Research and resolution of problems
- Regular and express mail distribution
- Office supplies and forms inventory

WORK HISTORY

CONCORD GROUP, INC., CHICAGO, IL   1998-2007
Personal and commercial insurance company
Receptionist
- Represented the prestigious image of this company in a high profile position requiring public contact with important clients in the sports and entertainment field as well as various other industries.
- Entrusted with opening the office daily and handling confidential material.
- Operated 24-line Premiere 6000 phone system, routing calls/faxes appropriately, and relaying messages accurately. Saved managers' time by screening unwanted calls.
- Reorganized shipping room to run more efficiently and operated automated labeling/tracking system (Powership), processing 5 to 50 outgoing packages daily.
- Ensured prompt delivery of express packages.
- Took initiative to update insurance certificates on computer.
- Participated in hiring a new assistant and trained her in company procedures.

PAPERCRAFT USA, CHICAGO   1994-1997
Nation's largest distributor of specialty paper
Telephone Account Coordinator (Customer Service Representative)
- As one of 80 employees in a busy call center averaging 200 incoming calls per hour, handled the ordering process, billing, and issuing credits or rebills to ensure accurate account records.
- Consistently achieved excellent scores in the mid-90s on monitored activities.
- Provided support to sales representatives all over the country.
- For four months in 1996, assisted the product director, creative director, and vice president of sales, providing them with daily sales activity reports and analyses, pricing updates, and sales strategy presentations for company's two divisions.
- Processed invoices and deliveries for international shipments.

HJR VENDING COMPANY, CHICAGO, IL   1992-1994
Distributor of confectionery items sold in vending machines
Customer Service Representative
- Worked in a team of six, processing telephone orders from individuals and retailers, including four house accounts. Resolved billing discrepancies.
- Offered information on promotions and discounts, which encouraged larger orders.

THE PLAYHOUSE, CHICAGO, IL   1987-1997
Director of day care center
- While raising a family, owned and operated a full-service day care center for preschool children.
- Administered all aspects of the business (billing, accounts payable, accounts receivable, and maintaining client files).

Office Support Professional

Janet is a longtime (15 years) worker within the veterinarian field who successfully moved into an administrative assistant's job in a medical office. She sent out one resume and got the job.

JANET COOPER

813-248-9988 • JCOOPER@EMAIL.COM
2833 NEWSOME ROAD, VALRICO, FL 33594

OFFICE SUPPORT PROFESSIONAL
Receptionist ... Clerk ... Administrative Assistant

EXPERTISE

Records Management

Customer Liaison

Front Office Operations

Workflow Planning / Scheduling

Troubleshooting / Problem Solving

Inventory Control

COMPUTER SKILLS

- Microsoft Word
- Cornerstone Proprietary Contact Management Software

TRAINING

Eastern States Conference in Orlando – Annual training for receptionists and managers

---

Top-performing office assistant with a reputation for professionalism, integrity, creativity, resourcefulness, and competence. Superior communication and listening skills. Strong client focus, with attention to detail and excellent follow through.

SELECTED CONTRIBUTIONS

- Redesigned administrative processes to streamline functions, eliminate redundancy, and expedite workflow. Initiated the conversion from manual processes to a fully computerized office. Implemented the automated Gevity HR Payroll Program.
- Improved customer service by developing a new client survey, soliciting feedback to quickly resolve client complaints and ensure top-quality service and satisfaction.
- Launched an employee-of-the-month incentive program to build unity and promote outstanding customer service.

PROFESSIONAL EXPERIENCE

Practice Manager – 1993 to 2006
Receptionist – 1992 to 1993
COMPLETE ANIMAL HOSPITAL, Tampa, Florida
(Veterinary clinic comprised of 6 doctors, 10 technicians, and 7 receptionists with annual revenues of $1.4 million)
Oversaw scheduling, managed inventory, and trained receptionists. Accountable for financial reports including daily deposits, monthly billings, and collections.

Receptionist – 1990 to 1992
WILLIAM SMITH, DVM, Fayetteville, North Carolina
(One-doctor veterinary clinic, 2 technicians, 2 receptionists)
Professional and cheerful first point of contact. Broad-based experience in answering multiple telephone lines, scheduling appointments, and filling prescriptions.

RELATED EXPERIENCE

Administrative Assistant
CENTEL BUSINESS SYSTEMS, Fayetteville, North Carolina

Clerking Assistant
OSTEOPATHIC SCHOOL OF MEDICINE
Ohio University, Athens, Ohio

Office Assistant (Initial Resume)

After interviewing Barbara, it became clear that she did more than her resume reflected. Aside from her initial resume being poorly formatted, it lacked focus, an interesting summary, and a content-rich presentation of her experience.

BARBARA WINSTON

190-12 Arthur Avenue, Brentwood, NY 11717

• • • 631 555-5555 • • •

OBJECTIVE

TO OBTAIN AN OFFICE ASSISTANT POSITION, ENABLING ME TO UTILIZE MY SKILLS AND DEVELOP CAREER PROGRESSION.

SKILLS

WORD PERFECT 5.0 AND 6.0
LOTUS 123
MICROSOFT WINDOWS 98
KEYBOARDING
DICTAPHONE, OFFICE PROCEDURES
KNOWLEDGE OF BUSINESS AND ORAL COMMUNICATIONS
MEDICAL FORMATS
WORK HISTORY

12/01 to Present

SIX AREAS UNIVERSITY, BRENTWOOD, NY
LIBRARY CLERK

ORGANIZING CIRCULATION DESK. ATTENTION TO DETAIL, EDITING, DATA ENTRY, XEROXING, FAXING, FILING, ASSISTING STUDENTS WITH RESEARCH, ADMINISTERING TESTS.

3/99 to 6/00

BRENTWOOD SCHOOL DISTRICT, BRENTWOOD, N.Y.
TEACHER'S AIDE / CLERICAL

ASSISTED TEACHERS WITH SPECIAL EDUCATION STUDENTS, COMPUTER LAB, LUNCH ROOM MONITOR, PERFORMED DUTIES IN PUBLICATIONS DEPARTMENT, CLERICAL DUTIES SUCH AS COLLATING, HAND INSERTING AND PROOF READING.

EDUCATION

10/97

SECRETARIAL SCHOOL OF AMERICA
MORRISTOWN, N.Y.
Certificate In Information Processing
CUMULATIVE GPA – 3.6

1/85

JOHN WILSON TRAINING SCHOOL
BRENTWOOD, NY
Certificate In Medical Assisting

EXCELLENT REFERENCES AVAILABLE UPON REQUEST

Office Assistant (Revised Resume)

The result of this before and after resume is dramatic in many ways. It has gone from a confusing document to a personal marketing tool that clearly expresses Barbara's objective. Most importantly, the experience section is very detailed and interesting to read compared to before.

BARBARA WINSTON

190-12 Arthur Avenue, Brentwood, NY 11717 ◆ 631 555-5555 ◆ BWinston@aol.com

Seeking a position in the capacity of **OFFICE SUPPORT ASSISTANT** within a general business or medical office environment, bringing the following experience, skills, and attributes:

◆ ◆ ◆

Extensive experience working in general public, educational, and medical office settings.
Interface well with others at all levels including patrons, patients, professionals, children, and students.
Caring and hardworking with excellent interpersonal communication, customer service, and office support skills.
Windows 98/DOS, MS Word, Dictaphone, CRT data entry, basic Internet skills, and medical terminology.

Work Experience

Circulation Desk Associate, Six Areas University, Brentwood, NY   **12/00 – Present**
Provided diversified information services and research assistance to the general public and student populations

- ◆ Assisted patrons in obtaining a broad selection of books, periodicals, audio-visuals, and other materials.
- ◆ Catalogued library materials, prepared bibliographies, indexes, guides, and search aids.
- ◆ Performed multifaceted general office support, and administered academic placement tests.

Teacher's Aide / Office Assistant, Brentwood School District, Brentwood, NY   **3/96 – 6/00**
Assigned to the Publications Department, Computer Lab, Special Education Resource Room, and Lunch Hall

- ◆ Assisted grade-level teachers with diversified clerical support in areas of document proofreading, duplication, collating and distribution, classroom management, student monitoring, and miscellaneous assignments.
- ◆ Easily established rapport with students, and interfaced well with parents and school-wide faculty members.

Nursing Assistant, Our Lady of Consolation, West Islip, NY   **6/90 – 1/96**
Physical Therapy Aide, Mother Cabrini Nursing Home, Dobbs Ferry, NY   **3/85 – 6/90**

Held the following combined responsibilities at Our Lady of Consolation and Mother Cabrini Nursing Home:

- ◆ Obtained vital signs and followed up with timely and accurate medical records-keeping procedures.
- ◆ Interfaced extensively with patients, staff personnel, orthopedic surgeons, and neurologists.
- ◆ Observed and reported changes in patients' conditions and other matters of concern.
- ◆ Performed ambulatory therapeutic treatments such as range of motion, gait training, and whirlpool baths.
- ◆ Transported patients to and from the hospital for emergency care and scheduled tests.
- ◆ Ensured the proper use of equipment and medical devices such as wheelchairs, braces, and splinters.
- ◆ Assisted patients with personal hygiene, grooming, meals, and other needs requiring immediate attention.
- ◆ Maintained sanitary, neatness and safety conditions of rooms in compliance with mandatory regulations.

Education

Certificate, Information Processing, 1997
SECRETARIAL SCHOOL OF AMERICA, Morristown, NY

Certificate, Medical Assisting, 1985
JOHN WILSON TRAINING SCHOOL, Brentwood, NY

BRENDA FORMAN

45 Duquesne Street
Parlin, New Jersey 08859

Residence: 732-251-4681

CUSTOMER SERVICE PROFESSIONAL

SENIOR CUSTOMER SPECIALIST • BILLING • CREDIT

Shipping and Dispatching • Inventory Control

Top-performing customer service specialist with more than 20 years experience in diverse environments. Outstanding reputation for keeping and maintaining excellent customer service standards. Experienced in working with high volume calls and answering intricate inquiries.

Train and observe other customer service staff. Take pride in order processing accuracy and efficiency; receive excellent customer feedback. Punctual in meeting deadlines. Interact with the President of my present company on a daily basis. Known to go the "extra mile" for customers and colleagues. Dedicated, efficient, task-oriented employee.

Perform the functions of Order Processing Specialist, Diversified Account Specialist, and Crediting/Billing Specialist. Skilled planner with the ability to analyze client needs and achieve objectives. *Professional strengths include:*

- Customer Service
- Shipping Receiving
- Manufacturing Processes
- Troubleshooting Accounts
- Leadership/Supervision
- Sales Force Support
- Accounts Receivable
- Inventory Control Functions

- Pricing/Quoting Customers
- Processing Orders
- Expediting Deliveries
- Tracking
- Special Attention Order Entry
- Customer Service Observations
- Billing
- Written Reports

BUSINESS EXPERIENCE

EDWARD SMITH, Cranbury, NJ **2000 – Present**

Senior Customer Service Representative and Trainer
Team Leader

- Currently serve as a Team Leader for this fine art and supplies manufacturer. Responsible for training and observation of other customer service employees. Lead customer service meetings and prepare written reports of findings.
- Replace supervisor in her absence.
- Ensure that discounts are applied correctly, and credits are entered in a timely fashion.
- Work with orders from start to completion. Interact daily with Daler-Rowney sales force and district manager.
- Handle customer requests. Take orders via fax, place on our system, send to purchasing, then send to warehouse, edit order, bill, print, and send to customers.
- Process all orders from Wal-Mart, our largest customer, through an EDI system.
- Work with Internet order processing systems including Microsoft Orbit program, Navision Financial Program, Trading Partners, Retail Link, Microsoft Word, and Excel.

- Attend trade shows and handle special orders in the field. Work with export customers.
- Print back order reports on a weekly basis. Work with potential new clients and their sales representatives regarding administrative work.
- Process numerous order per day including 500-1,000 keyed lines. Write reports in Microsoft Excel and Word.
- Responsible for the issuance of all return authorization numbers and UPS call tags. Research credits and input information into our system.

ROLL INDUSTRIES, Cranbury, NJ   **1991-2000**

Shipping/Receiving Coordinator
Customer Service Representative

- Responsible for a wide range of shipping/receiving and customer service functions for this Fortune 500 carpet manufacturer. Handled an extremely high call volume. Processed orders, answered customer inquires, tracking inbound/outbound shipments; expedited deliveries and set up delivery schedules. Prepared UPS shipments and participated in cycle counting and quarterly inventories.
- Attended trade shows and expedited special attention orders.
- Coordinated with and supported sales representatives in the field. Performed cash receipt reconciliations and resolved customer complaints, disputes or discrepancies.
- Received Employee of the Month Award out of 300 people.

CONTINENTAL LIFE INSURANCE, Plainfield, NJ   **1989 – 1991**

Customer Service Representative

- Responsible for pricing/quoting customers, answering phone inquiries, processing orders, and expediting deliveries along with troubleshooting accounts.

CHILDCRAFT, Plainfield, NJ   **1988 – 1989**

Customer Service Representative

- Duties similar to above. Position required ability to work in a high-pressure/fast-paced environment.

ACTION TUNGSTROM, East Brunswick, NJ   **1985-1988**

Shipping/Receiving Coordinator/Accounts Receivable Clerk

~ LETTERS OF RECOMMENDATION AND REFERENCES UPON REQUEST ~

Customer Service Professional

Anne's resume states several benefits she would bring to a position in an insurance office.

Anne Granger

1234 Pinewood Street
Charleston, SC 00000

(000) 000-0000
agranger@fastmail.com

PROFILE

Customer service professional, skilled in problem solving and responsive to needs of clients, coworkers and management. Poised, resourceful and adaptable to any office environment. Organizational ability to handle multiple priorities and meet deadline schedules. Attentive to detail, with sharp awareness of omissions/inaccuracies, and prompt to take corrective action. A self-starter and quick study, eager to assume increasing levels of responsibility.

OFFICE SKILLS

Professional phone manner; data entry and word processing; updating/maintenance of files and records; composition of routine correspondence.

EMPLOYMENT HISTORY

CUSTOMER SERVICE REPRESENTATIVE

Liberty Insurance Corporation, Charleston, SC (2002-2007)
Hired as data entry operator and advanced to customer service position in less than a year. Took over problem desk, which had been inadequately handled by 2 previous employees. Worked closely with underwriters, answering client inquiries by phone or mail. Analyzed complex situations affecting insurance coverage. Recognized opportunities to increase sales and advised clients when coverage was lacking in specific policy areas.

Key Accomplishments: During major restructuring of company resulting in 70% staff reduction, assumed more than triple the normal account responsibility, from 450 to over 1,500, while still in training. Simultaneously studied for insurance licensing course; passed exam on first try, with score of 95.

APPLICATIONS SCREENER

Marshall & Reiner Insurance Agency, Charlotte, SC (2000-2002)
(Applications processing center for Mutual Surety Corporation)
Screened homeowners' new lines of business applications, verifying coverage against individual state regulations. Filled in whenever needed for switchboard, typing, and clerical assignments.

HOMEMAKER/CHILD CARE RESPONSIBILITIES (1993-2000)

CENSUS TAKER

U.S. Census Bureau, Charleston, SC (1993)
Visited individuals who had not filled out census forms properly. Worked in a multi-ethnic territory, overcoming language barriers and mistrust. Clarified discrepancies and ensured accuracy and completeness of reported information.

SUBROGATION CLERK

Royal Guard Insurance Company, Middleton, SC (1991-1993)
Started as receptionist and promoted shortly thereafter to handle various clerical assignments in Subrogation Department. Prepared paperwork for file with arbitration board. Kept subrogation ledgers up to date for auditors' review.

EDUCATION

Carolina State University – 65 credits in Business Administration (1989-1991)
American Insurance Academy – Completed 12-week basic course in Property and Casualty, Insurance Law, and Health Insurance (2003)

Retail Manager

Scott needed a resume that would highlight his strong retail
and store management experience.

SCOTT KELLY

761 Stoneham Avenue
Woburn, MA 01801

(781) 932-6093
ScottKelly3@hotmail.com

RETAIL ~ SALES & MANAGEMENT

Successful retail manager with over 14 years of experience in Sales, Purchasing/Buying, Customer Service, Inventory Management, Merchandising, Staff Recruitment and Supervision. Proven ability to increase sales revenue and improve profitability through effective sales consultation, merchandising, purchasing, and inventory management. Demonstrate a high level of motivation and enthusiasm in all aspects of work.

- **Record of improving sales, successfully introducing new products, and growing customer-base.** Expanded business for large volume – wine specialty – liquor establishment.
- **Excellent leadership skills**—can communicate effectively with employees and motivate them to perform at their best. Can set direction for the team. Hands-on approach to training.
- **Established record of dependability and company loyalty.**
- **Experience in both general merchandising and specialty retail sales.** Extensive knowledge of the wine industry including suppliers, distributors, and consumers; extensive product knowledge.

PROFESSIONAL EXPERIENCE

Manager (General Operations), *O'Leary's Discount Market,* Woburn, MA   **1996-present**

Direct the daily operation of a high-volume liquor/wine specialty store, servicing over 1,000 customers per week. Manage staff of 15 in the areas of sales and customer service, cash management, budgeting, sales forecasting, employee relations, merchandising, promotions, and security.

- Steadily increased revenues through strong focus on customer service, excellent merchandising, and teamwork.
- Attracted new clientele to store through the development of a full-service wine department. Expanded product line, increased sales and special-order purchasing by implementing specialized sales methods, such as promotional wine-tasting events.
- Established strong reputation on the South Shore as leader for extensive wine inventories at competitive pricing, including regularly stocked hard-to-find selections.
- Trained staff in selling through increased product knowledge and food and wine pairing.
- Participated regularly in trade tastings, shows, and vintner dinners, including Westport Rivers Vineyard, Nashoba Valley Vineyard, Prudential Center and World Trade Center events.

Manager (Stock and Display), *Ames Department Stores,* Boston, MA   **1994-1995**

Managed a staff of 12 in a large, national general merchandise store. Marketed and sold products; developed merchandise and promotional displays; maintained stock levels.

- Increased profits through effective displays and merchandising.
- Improved operations through effectively supervising daily staff assignments.

Stock/Inventory Manager, *Beantown Gift,* Boston, MA   **1992-1994**

Managed purchasing and supervised sales staff for a high-traffic specialty gifts store.

- Expanded customer base by offering a wide range of attractive product displays and creating a welcoming atmosphere that increased the comfort level of patrons.
- Supervised staff of three, ensuring quality of store display and product inventory levels.

Additional experience includes entry-level inventory/shipping-receiving position at Boston University (1990-1982).

Store Manager

RUSSELL CHAMBERLAIN

RUSSCHAMB@COMCAST.NET
68 PARK DRIVE • OLDSMAR, FLORIDA 33357 • 813-555-1212

WORK EXPERIENCE

Manager, A National Kitchen Utensil Retailer.   2000-present
Manage daily operations of a $2-million annual business. Staff of 12 people.
Responsible for increasing sales and profitability and decreasing expenses.

Increased gross margin by 25% and net contribution by 105% on a 3%
sales increase.

Senior Assistant Buyer, Stern's, Oldsmar, FL.   1996-2000
Controlled open-to-buy purchase journal, profitability reports, weekly three-
month estimate of sales, stocks, and markdown dollars. Planned and negotiated
sales promotions, advertising, and special purchases.

Coordinated training and teamwork with managers and merchants in the
22 stores.

Increased department sales 18% more than the Division's increase.

Assistant Buyer. Assisted selection and distribution of merchandise. Managed
all buying office functions while learning to plan sales, control stocks, and markdown dollars. Created weekly, monthly, and seasonal financial plans.

Developed all systems to support the growth of the branch from a $1-million vol-
ume to a $4-million annual volume.

Buyer/Manager, Gulf Gifts, FL.   1993-1996
Bought merchandise for two different gift stores. Directed daily store operations
and sales. Directed merchandise presentation, inventory control, and customer
service. Scheduled and supervised a 7-person staff.

Increased sales volume 22% more than corporate projection.

Manager, Willis & Geiger, New York, NY.   1990-1993
Direct daily store operations. Analyzed trends in fashion, merchandise, and consumer needs. Planned effective marketing strategy, displays, advertising, and an
employee sales program.

Increased annual net sales volume by 33%.

EDUCATION   Fashion Institute of Technology, New York, NY. B.A. Merchandising, 1989

Visual Merchandising Specialist

Vera Lighthouse

605 Independent Street   Home: (516) 555-1212
Manhassat, NY 11575   veral2345@earthlink.net

With fifteen years experience in Visual Merchandising Management, I have successfully:

- Coordinated all Visual Merchandising in Macy's third-most-profitable store.
- Supervised visual aspects of a successful $3 million store renovation with responsibility for new fixturing and merchandising.
- Conducted seminar in Visual Merchandising for all new department managers in Macy's eastern region.
- Utilized innovative image control techniques that contributed to a new high-fashion store's becoming the volume leader for its entire chain in one year.

RECENT ACCOMPLISHMENTS

Visual Merchandising Manager of a Macy's store with a $40 million sales volume, I coordinated fixturing, merchandising, and seasonal changes for all twelve departments, along with responsibility for overall store image.

- Analyzed stock levels to determine new fixture needs, prepared requirement reports, and coordinated on-time deliveries of all fixtures.
- Reporting directly to the Vice President for Corporate Visual Merchandising, I supervised five Visual Merchandising Managers brought in from other stores to assist in the project.
- Interfaced with both union and non-union construction personnel while directing movement of departments under construction.
- Guiding all Department Managers through renovation and construction, I familiarized them with new fixturing and applicable merchandising techniques.

EARLIER ACCOMPLISHMENTS

As District Display Director for Laura Ashley Inc., a 100-store specialty women's ready-to-wear chain, I developed fashion awareness, coordinated displays, and trained staff, including new District Display Directors throughout the country. Reporting directly to the Corporate Display Director, I was:

- Given responsibility for image control at the company's new flagship store on 57th St, where fashion image was crucial. My innovative merchandising and display techniques contributed to this store's becoming the number-one-volume store for the entire company by its first anniversary.
- Recognized for my planning, organizing, and coordinating abilities, I was involved in several new store openings throughout the U.S. and Canada.

As Display Coordinator/Visual Merchandising Manager with ESPRIT, Inc., I progressed to having a five-store responsibility. Developing my functional skills, I was promoted to Visual Display troubleshooter for a multi-state region.

EMPLOYMENT

MACY'S, 1990 – Present
LAURA ASHLEY, 1986 – 1990
ESPRIT DE CORPS, 1982 – 1986

EDUCATION

A graduate of Harper College, Palatine, Illinois, with a specialty in Fashion Design, I have also completed intensive course work in Architectural Technology which has significantly contributed to my expertise in store renovation and floor plan know-how. Course work in photography has rounded out my background.

PERSONAL

Interests include apparel design and construction, sketching, and freehand drawing.

Merchandise Buyer

The use of a title and keywords list allows the reader to see exactly what Mary's objective is and the scope of her skills in relation to the position of interest. Notice the keywords are very specific rather than general attributes.

Mary J. Sanders

111 East End Avenue • Elmhurst, New York 55555 • (555) 8888-0000 • shop2drop@retailworld.net

Assistant Buyer

Skilled in areas of:

- Wholesale / Retail Buying
- Product Merchandising
- Inventory Replenishment
- Product Distribution and Tracking
- Sales Analysis & Reporting
- Regional Marketing Campaigns
- Information Systems
- Vendor Relations
- Order Management

Professional Experience

Merchandise Buying / Coordination

- Report directly to London-American's Director of Sales, providing support in areas of commodities buying and merchandising activities that reach annual sales volumes of $3 million for the division.
- Collaborate with multiple buyers to facilitate the marketing efforts of new products, and development of promotional calendars, product launches, and employee incentive programs.
- Maintain open lines of communication between manufacturers, sales teams, vendors, and warehousing personnel to expedite product orders, distribution, and problem resolutions.
- Reported directly to the Senior Buyer of Steinway Bedding in charge of day-to-day retail merchandise buying and merchandising activities impacting bedding sales across 37 Northeast locations.
- Successfully trained 45+ Steinway employees on a complex LAN database management system.

Sales Tracking, Analysis & Reporting

- Perform LAC's weekly sales analysis activities on regional/local transactions, achieving a recovery of $1,800,000 from 2001 to 2007 resulting from identification and resolution of accounting discrepancies.
- Develop sales books reflecting product lines, monthly promotions, discontinued items, order forms and transparencies utilized by sales teams and personnel throughout 26 store locations.
- Formulate price breakdowns and track sales levels to determine product volume adjustments, replenishments and allocations with a demonstrated proficiency in internal networking systems.
- Researched, compiled, and recorded Steinway's historical data to develop innovative sales strategies through close examination of inventory and product availability, pricing, and store promotions.

Work History

Assistant Buyer / Sales Analyst   7/00 – Present
LONDON-AMERICAN COMMODITIES, LTD. (LAC), Valley Stream, New York

Assistant Buyer / Merchandise Coordinator   4/96 – 7/00
STEINWAY BEDDING, Woodbury, New York

Education

Associates in Science, Business Management, 1996
STATE UNIVERSITY of NEW YORK at COBLESKILL

Sommelier

Angelica's resume was tricked out to look like a menu.

Angelica Merceau
242 W. 103rd Street, Olathe, Kansas 66206
Phone: 913-555-2323 Email: wineangel@yahoo.com

Sommelier Extraordinaire

Piedmonts by the Bay, San Francisco, CA
Master Sommelier, September 2001 – Present

➢ Expertise in all aspects of wine, including regions of the world and their products, grape varietals, fortified wines, methods of distillation, international wine law, cigar production, and proper storage and handling.
➢ Manage wine inventory averaging over 12,000 bottles, worth $2,550,000.
➢ Supervise and personally train staff of 25 sommeliers and wine stewards in pairing wines with cuisine, presentation of wine, brandies, liqueurs and cigars, and selection, preparation, and placement of glassware.
➢ Coordinate all wine-tasting events, and varietal seminars.
➢ Handle all client inquiries and complaints.

Bordeaux Steak House, New York, NY
Sommelier, May 1999 – January 2001
Lead Wine Steward, December 1997 – May 1999

➢ Supervise and train staff of wine stewards in all aspects of wine presentation, pairing with cuisine, and glassware selection and placement.
➢ Choose appropriate cuisine and wine pairings, assist clients in selection of wines, brandies, liqueurs, cigars, properly present and decant wines, and select and place stemware.

Education, Certifications and Professional Development:

➢ Columbia University, New York, NY
B.A. Food History, May 1997
➢ Court of Master Sommeliers, Napa, CA
Master Sommelier, 2001
➢ International Sommelier Guild, Grand Island, NY
*Sommelier Diploma Program, 1999
*Wine Fundamentals Certificate, Level II, 1999
*Wine Fundamentals Certificate, Level I, 1998
➢ Sommelier Society of America, New York, NY

Varietal Courses:
*Cabernet Sauvignon, 1999
*Sauvignon Blanc, 1999
*Chardonnay, 1999
*Merlot, 1999
*Sangiovese, 1999
*Syrah, 1998
*Pinot Noir, 1998
*Riesling, 1998

Professional Memberships

➢ *Association de la Sommellerie Internationale (ASI)*
Member, 2001 – Present
➢ *The Sommelier Society of America*
Member, 1999 – Present

Restaurant Server

Valerie uses an "Outstanding Achievements & Recommendations" section to bring attention to her strengths, and she has done a nice job in identifying the type of restaurants in which she has gained experience.

Valerie W. Butler

333 S.E. Riveredge Drive • Vancouver, Washington 33333
222-222-2222 cell • home 555-555-5555

Server

Professional Profile

Energetic and highly motivated ***Food Server*** with extensive experience in the food service industry. Expertise lies in working with the fine dining restaurant, providing top-quality service, and maintaining a professional demeanor. Solid knowledge of the restaurant business with strengths in excellent customer service, food and wine recommendations.

Get along well with management, coworkers and customers. Well-developed communication skills, known as a caring and intuitive "people person," with an upbeat and positive attitude. Highly flexible, honest, and punctual, with the ability to stay calm and focused in stressful situations. Committed to a job well done and a long-term career.

Outstanding Achievements & Recommendations

- Served notable VIP clientele including clients associated with Murdock Charitable Trust.
- History of repeat and new customers requesting my service as their waitress.
- Known for creating an atmosphere of enjoyment and pleasure for the customer.

"...Valerie was warm, friendly, kind and very efficient.
We didn't feel rushed – she handled our requests and
we appreciated her genuine 'May I please you' attitude...."

Related Work History

Waitress • Banquets • Heathman Lodge • Vancouver, Washington • *2005–present*
Northwest seasonal cuisine.

Banquets • Dolce *Skamania Lodge* • Stevenson, Washington • *2004–2005*
Casual to fine dining restaurant.

Waitress • Hidden House • Vancouver, Washington • *1996–2004*
Exclusive fine dining restaurant.

Waitress • Multnomah Falls Lodge Restaurant • Corbett, Oregon • *1995–1996*
Historic Columbia Gorge Falls restaurant serving authentic Northwestern cuisine.

Waitress • The Ahwahnee at Yosemite National Park • California • *1 year*
World renowned award-winning fine dining restaurant – sister lodge to Timberline Lodge.

Steamfitter

Fred had experience in highly specialized jobs. His expertise and training were attractively emphasized with graphic lines.

Fred G. Jamisen

9999 Abernethy Road • Oregon City, Oregon 9999
555-555-5555

Steamfitter

Professional Profile

Highly skilled, conscientious, and precise **Steamfitter** with over 6 years experience and 10,000+ hours of training in all aspects of Steamfitting. Familiar with all required codes, appropriate use of equipment, steamfitting techniques, safety standards, and proper procedures to prevent injuries. Proficient in reviewing plans, blueprints and specifications for steamfitting projects with proven ability to provide expert recommendations. Well-developed troubleshooting skills with accurate and precise repairs. Experienced EMT willing to volunteer EMT services on the job. Excellent communication skills, personable, trustworthy, adaptable, and committed to a long-term career.

Expertise and Training Includes:

- Air Conditioning and Refrigeration Systems and Equipment
- Boilers
- Commercial and Industrial
- Conduit Flex, Duct and Controls
- Electrical and Electronic Contracting
- HVAC, Air Conditioning and Refrigeration
- Instrumentation
- Outdoor Installations
- Overhead and Underground
- Process Systems and Equipment
- Steam and Heating Systems and Equipment
- Troubleshooting and Maintenance
- Welding Processes including Orbital Welder Arc 207
- Wire Pulling, Wiring Devices, Removal and Finish

Licenses

Pressure Vessel and Boiler License Class V • *State of Oregon*
United Association of Steamfitters • *Local 290*

Employment History

Steamfitter • United Association of Steamfitters • Portland, Oregon • *6 years*
Assignment to various companies and projects as needed.

Paper Machine Operator • Crown Zellerbach Corp. • West Linn, Oregon • *11 years*
previously owned by James River and Simpson Paper Company
EMT *(Emergency Medical Technician)* • Served as volunteer EMT for the paper mill.

Sales Representative • Pepsi Bottling Company • Portland, Oregon • *8 years*
Beverage sales.

Military

U.S. Army • **Specialist E-4 – Nuclear Missile Technician** • *Honorable Discharge* • *1979*

Education

Associates of Applied Arts • **Humanities**
Carroll College • Helena, Montana *and* Clackamas Community College • Oregon City, Oregon

TOM PARSONS

52 DUNE DRIVE
MATAWAN, NJ 07747

732.610.3896
E-MAIL: DTJNPAR@AOL.COM

AUTOMOTIVE SERVICE MANAGER

Twenty-three years successful customer service management experience within the automotive industry; proven track record meeting challenges and creatively solving a myriad of problems. Extensive knowledge of automotive warranty policies and procedures. Decisive hands-on manager with an interactive management style able to lead several service teams and administrative staff. Ability to motivate employees' performance levels and develop rapport with diverse audiences; excellent employee relations. Developed excellent product and service knowledge throughout career. Computer literate with experience of Microsoft Office. Broad-based responsibilities and knowledge include:

- Customer Service
- Problem Solving
- Leadership, Supervision & Training
- Service Repair Analysis
- Safety & Quality Control
- Warranty Expertise
- Product Knowledge
- Conflict Resolution
- Team Building
- Service Accounting (Expenses/Revenues)
- Technical Knowledge/Efficiency
- Operational Policies & Procedures

PROFESSIONAL EXPERIENCE

KEASBY NISSAN & SUBARU, Keasby, NJ ~ 1992 to Present
Service Manager

- Direct reports include 35 staff (Service Advisors, Service Teams, Cashiers, Receptionists, Lot Attendants, & Detailers)
- Manage Nissan and Subaru Service Departments while supervising service advisors and administrating client issues; ensure customer satisfaction.
- Solve product issues for both departments while working with company representatives and senior management.
- Improve department productivity and solve warranty issues when necessary.
- Monitor departmental budget taking correct actions when required.
- Oversee the development and implementation of new Subaru franchise, and obtain required certification for service department.
- Achieve 2.2 hours per service order ratio for each customer.
- Eliminate expense and waste while reducing employee time-schedule loss.
- Perform repair order analysis, and monitor team efficiency improving shop utilization and work in process ratios.
- Analyze monthly owner first reports for Nissan, and communicate findings with staff.

ESSEX COUNTY NISSAN, Stanhope, NJ ~ 1987 to 1992
Service Manager

- Direct reports included 13 staff (Service Advisors, Service Teams, Cashiers, Lot Attendants, & Detailers)
- Oversaw entire Service Department ensuring complete customer satisfaction.
- Communicated with Nissan Service Representatives regarding product issues and warranty concerns.
- Improved departmental productivity implementing several new programs.
- Conducted repair order and service department analysis.
- Substantially increased service revenues and volume by 60% during first fiscal year.
- Maintained warranty expenses within manufacturers' guidelines.
- Transferred to another location to manage larger department.

HAYNES NISSAN, Bloomfield, NJ ~ 1982 to 1987
Service Consultant

- Handled and wrote over 20+ customer service orders per day.
- Sold service and maintenance plans to clients.
- Coordinated service orders with technical staff ensuring quality control through entire service process.
- Prepared final accounting of orders.
- Implemented first statewide service team model for dealerships.
- Transitioned to new organization after company purchase.

Heavy Equipment Driver

Treavor was interested in driving heavy equipment in the Middle East.

TREAVOR BLACK
9999 CR7555 + Rolling Hills, Texas 79000
(999) 999-9999 + (806) 777-7777 (C)

+ DRIVER / HEAVY EQUIPMENT +

PROFILE

- Skilled driver with Class A Commercial Driver's License (CDL), Expires 1/29/08
- Over two million miles driving commercial vehicles loaded with general or refrigerated freight.
- Superior driving / safety / inspection record and on-time delivery.
- Excellent health and physical condition.
- Mechanically inclined and maintenance minded.
- Customer-service oriented; personable with instructional communication skills.

VEHICLE EXPERTISE

Several tractor / trailer rigs including refrigerated vans	32 years
National 2003 Flatbed Trailer	3 years
2006 2T Ford F550 with Jerr-Dan Bed, Hydraulic Wench, Diesel	1 years
2004 35T Pete Wrecker with Nomar Bed, Hydraulic Wench, Diesel	3 years
Racetrack road graders and water trucks	13 years

TRUCKING EXPERIENCE

Truck Driver, ROLLING HILLS WRECKER, Rolling Hills, Texas   2003 – present

Clean up heavy equipment wreck sites and transport vehicle remains to Rolling Hills Wrecker storage facility. In addition to using wrecker with hydraulic wench, utilize refrigerated vans, cow trailers, flatbed trailers, and Jaws of Life, as situation requires. Interface with customers and insurance providers. Maintain daily log and State / Federal paperwork. Worked dispatch and accepted management responsibilities as needed.

- Receive consistent raises due to outstanding performance.
- Underwent police background check to secure driver's position.

Truck Driver, GORGE TRANSPORT, Rolling Hills, Texas   2000 – 2001

Leased refrigerated truck to haul produce and meat products throughout California, Washington, Oregon, and Texas. Worked 12-14 hour days; maintained daily logs and trip sheets; and hired own loaders (lumpers) at docks.

Owner / Driver, BLACK TRUCKING, Rolling Hills, Texas   1993 – 2000

Leased out transport truck during summers to clients that included Blackcrest Transportation, WWW Trucking, and Gorge Transport. Drove during winters.

OTHER EMPLOYMENT

Promoter, SUN CITY SPEEDWAY, Sun City, Texas (summers)	2002 – 2003
Manager / Promoter, PLAINS SPEEDWAY, Rolling Hills, Texas (summers)	1990 – 2002
Auctioneer, Panhandle Texas Area	1996 – 2002

EDUCATION

High Plains College, Rolling Hills, Texas, Real Estate License	1998
Buddy Lee Auctioneer School, Freeze, Montana, Auctioneer	1996

248

Material Handler

Glenda used her "Outstanding Accomplishments & Achievements"
section to bring strong focus to her capabilities.

Glenda Pension

356 N.E. Musical #303 • Portland, Oregon 88888
Email: pen333333@attbi.com • 555-555-5555

Material Handler

Professional Profile

Energetic, highly motivated, and organized Material Handler with extensive experience in purchasing, inventory control, and shipping / receiving. Strong liaison and negotiator for improving product delivery and lowering expenses. Well developed tracking and research abilities. Outstanding communication skills. Personable, independent, and committed to producing top-quality work. Positive and upbeat attitude; get along well with co-workers and management. Thoroughly enjoy a challenge and committed to a long-term career.

Experience Includes

• Accuracy	• Import	• Order Pulling	• Quality Assurance
• Customer Service	• Inventory Control	• Ordering	• Receiving
• Dedication	• Liaison	• Organization	• Shipping
• Export	• Negotiator	• Purchasing	• Tracking

Outstanding Accomplishments and Achievements

- Advocated to get certification through Quality Control to achieve FAA approval on specific products.
- Secured credit, due to my personal reputation, for a company in Chapter 11 bankruptcy.
- Negotiated effective contracts to obtain product shipment with little or no shipping charges.
- Recaptured thousands of dollars in warranty monies for company.
- Developed and implemented inventory tracking system.
- Reorganized and set up efficient stock room.

Professional Experience

Enlargement Printer • Qualex, Inc. • Portland, Oregon • *2003-2007*
Temporary Associate • Manpower • Portland, Oregon • *2002-2003*
Inbound Auditor / Quality Control • Columbia Sportswear • Portland, Oregon • *2001-2002*
Warehouse Tech / Quality Control • Dr. Martins Airwair • Portland, Oregon • *1999-2001*
Records Clerk • America West Airlines • Phoenix, Arizona • *1998*
Purchasing Agent • MarkAir Express, Inc. • Anchorage, Alaska • *1996-1998*
Japan Airlines Liaison for Inventory Management by Alaska Airlines
    Alaska Airlines • Anchorage, Alaska • *1994-1996*
Purchasing Manager / Warranty Administrator / Inventory Control
    Stateswest Airlines – USAIR Express • Phoenix, Arizona • *1991-1994*

Education and Training

    Beechcraft Warranty Training • Indianapolis, Indiana • *2001*
Various classes offered by OSHA and Japan Airlines
    Hazardous Materials Training • San Francisco, California • *1995*
    Business *emphasis* • University of Alaska – Anchorage • Anchorage, Alaska • *1995*

Personal Driver

John needed to refocus his background as a driver to effectively target a position as a personal driver/chauffeur at a large, local corporate headquarters facility.

John Collins

526 Farmer Road • Corring, WI 12345
myemail@myemail.com • (888) 449-2200

PERSONAL DRIVER / CHAUFFEUR
TRANSPORTATION • DOT REGULATIONS • MAINTENANCE • CLIENT RELATIONS

ACCOMPLISHED AND DEDICATED DRIVER / TRANSPORTATION SPECIALIST WITH A PROVEN TRACK-RECORD OF INCREASING EFFICIENCY, QUALITY, AND CUSTOMER SATISFACTION. SKILLED IN ALL ASPECTS OF VEHICLE MAINTENANCE, DOT REGULATORY COMPLIANCE, DRIVING OPERATIONS, EXPENSE MANAGEMENT, CLIENT RELATIONS, AND CUSTOMER SERVICE WITHIN STARTUP AND HIGH GROWTH ORGANIZATIONS. RESULTS-ORIENTED AND DRIVEN PROFESSIONAL WITH A SOLID WORK ETHIC AND DEDICATION TO EXCELLENCE. PROFESSIONAL COMMUNICATION, NEGOTIATION, CONFLICT RESOLUTION, PROBLEM-SOLVING, AND TECHNICAL / TROUBLESHOOTING SKILLS.

Core Competencies

- Professional Driver
- Expense Management
- Client Relations

- Chauffeur
- DOT Regulatory Compliance
- Customer Satisfaction

- Transportation Specialist
- Customer Service
- Vehicle Maintenance

Professional Experience

JOHNSON DELTA CORPORATION – Farmington, WI   2001 to Present

Full Service Driver
Manage a wide range of full-service transportation and customer service functions including collecting payments and delivering products.
Oversee routine vehicle maintenance and process all Department of Transportation (DOT) regulations paperwork. Serve as an account manager with full responsibility for tracking and maintaining customer / order records and facilitating communications between owner / manager clients, sales, and company management. Collaborate with technical and maintenance personnel to arrange machine repairs, replacements, and new placements for services. Service machines and troubleshoot technical onboard computer problems. Operate forklifts to load and unload equipment. Train new employees in onboard computer operations and correct procedures / techniques.

Key Achievements:
- ➤ Recognized by the company for achieving a four-year safe driving record; received a letter of commendation.
- ➤ Played a key role in the suggestion and implementation of having off calls regulated instead of automated to significantly increase quality and customer satisfaction.
- ➤ Promoted to account management responsibilities due to dedication and professionalism.

ROECKER JONES – Mission City, WI 1999 to 2001

Driver
Ensured correct products were delivered to the proper business locations and managed all aspects of vehicle safety and maintenance.
Recruited to manage daily transportation, warehousing, order-taking, and customer service / client relations functions to ensure top-level service. Effectively learned warehouse layout to increase efficiency and operated forklifts to load and unload trucks. Assisted in unloading products at each stop and provided direct customer service to resolve issues at all levels. Managed petty cash receipts / reports and compiled / delivered all required paperwork.

Key Achievements:
- ➤ Recipient of a letter of commendation for "Excellence in Customer Service."

EDUCATION

Studies in Business • PHCC COLLEGE – Jones, WI

Apartment Management (Joint Resume)

Pamela and Katherine needed a combined resume for use in
applying as Team Managers. This format was highly effective.

Pamela Heshe ❧ Katherine Heshe

1234 S.E. 23rd Avenue   Rhododendron, Oregon   555-555-5555

Apartment Managers

PROFESSIONAL PROFILE

- Highly motivated, dynamic and energetic with over 30 combined years experience successfully working with diverse personalities.
- Experienced management and maintenance of various houses and plexes.
- Possess strong organizational skills and effective paper processing techniques.
- Expert bookkeeping abilities.
- Skills include: Minor repairs, simple plumbing, light electrical, painting, pool maintenance, landscaping, strong maintenance and clean-up experience.
- Effective in pre-qualifying new lease applicants and collecting rents in a timely fashion.
- Personable, loyal, honest, committed, creative, able to maintain property impeccably, and get along well with tenants and management.
- Able to be bonded, if necessary.
- Computer literate.

Pamela Heshe

EMPLOYMENT HISTORY

Medical Assistant • Portland, Oregon • *1993-2007*
- OHSU Sellwood/Moreland Clinic • *2002-2007*
- Medical Temporaries • *1993, 1994, 1998, 2000, 2002*
- Mount Tabor Medical Group • *1999-2000*
- Dr. Samuel Miller • *1994-1998*

EDUCATION

Medical *Emphasis* • *1988*
- Clackamas Community College
  Oregon City, Oregon

Graduate
- Portland Community College
  Portland, Oregon

Graduate
- Oregon X-Ray Institute
  Portland, Oregon

Katherine Heshe

EMPLOYMENT HISTORY

Accounting Manager / Administrative Assistant
- National Metal Distributors, Inc. • *2003-2004*
  Vancouver, Washington

Bookkeeper • *2001-2003*
- Aerospace & Corrosion International
  Vancouver, Washington

Letter Carrier • *1979-2000*
- United States Postal Service
  Portland, Oregon

MILITARY

United States Air Force • *1974-1978*
- Disbursement Accountant

EDUCATION

Elliott Bookkeeping School • *2001*
Accounting • *1979*
- Portland Community College
  Portland, Oregon

Fitness Trainer

Anna has a great start in her career as a fitness trainer with super client results that are detailed in the resume for an action-packed, results-oriented document.

Anna Mead
5235 N Halsey Drive, Richmond, Texas 77853 • 256-555-7772 • fitness77@sbcglobal.net

Physical Fitness Specialist

BACHELOR of SCIENCE KINESIOLOGY
December 2004
Texas A&M University   *College Station, Texas*

PROGRAMS DEVELOPED

- Volleyball League
for health club members

- Women's Self Defense

- "Silver Hearts"
group exercise class for mature members over sixty years of age.

- "HealthPlex Holiday Challenge"

- "Suit Up for Summer"

- Personalized exercise programs for clients

- "Tiny Mites"
gymnastics for preschool

- "Gymnastic All-Stars Cheerleading Program"

GROUP EXERCISE CLASSES

- Yoga for Fitness

- Muscle Pump

- Rock Bottoms

- Aquafit

Proficient in the use of PC and Macintosh computers.

Motivated and driven

FITNESS SPECIALIST

brings eighteen months of ENERGETIC professional training experience to health and wellness programs yielding enthusiasm, commitment and results.

SELECTED ACHIEVEMENTS

- Develop strong and strategic weightlifting program for male clients.

- Implement customized fitness programs for group and individual clients.

- Manage personal training programs, results and profiles for 13 clients.

PROFESSIONAL CERTIFICATIONS

- IDEA Personal Trainer • YogaFit Certified Instructor
- CPR & First Aid • NSCA & ASCM Professional Member

PROFESSIONAL PHYSICAL FITNESS EXPERIENCE

EXERCISE PHYSIOLOGIST

- **Develop, produce and implement** internal and external marketing plans.
- **Instruct and create** programs for Cardiac Rehabilitation Phase III members.
- **Organize** Fitness Team and Health Assessment Testing schedules
- **Exceed expectations** and **deliver excellent customer service.**

PERSONAL TRAINER

- **Develop** personalized exercise programs for each client.
- **Monitor** the transition and progressions of each client into new, more effective exercises.
- **Prepare** exercise prescriptions.

FITNESS INSTRUCTOR

- **Instruct** various Group Fitness and Yoga classes.
- **Conduct research** on the latest trends and newest exercises.

GYMNASTICS COACH
Head Level Five Compulsory Coach

CLIENT PROFILES

Profile: Female, age 33 – Stay-at-home mom
Goal: Lose weight and get in shape after birth of baby.
Results: Within 4 months, weight: 147 to 128 lbs; body fat: 30.8% to 18.9%

Profile: Senior male, age 57 – Retired
Goal: Exercise to maintain and get the benefits for his heart.
Results: Developed regulated fitness program to reach target heart rate.

Profile: Female, age 40 – Professional
Goal: Lose weight (100 lbs.) and get in shape.
Results: Lost 12 lbs. and 14 inches in a six-week period.

PROFESSIONAL EXPERIENCE

ABM HEALTHPLEX – Richmond, Texas   **January 2005 – Present**
UNITED GYMNASTICS – Richmond, Texas   **2001 – 2004**
SPELLING GYMNASTICS – Richmond, Texas   **1999 – 2001**

Everyday Jobs

Aesthetician

Anita is an aesthetician moving up in her chosen profession.

ANITA KELLER

9001 E. ASPEN DRIVE, FOUNTAIN HILLS, AZ 85233
480/555-0000 • AKELLER@123.NET

PROFILE

An experienced state-licensed **Aesthetician** seeking a rewarding career opportunity in a service-driven, team-centered spa / resort setting.
Consistently exceed client expectations; recognized for a gentle, soothing touch with a pleasant attitude, while demonstrating capability in areas of:

- skin care / facials • body treatments / wraps • waxing • lymphatic drainage • chemical peels • masks
- aroma therapy • multivitamin treatments • make-up • acupressure and Oriental massage treatments

Familiar with a wide product range including:

- Dermalogica • Murad • Obagi • Trucco • Jan Marini • Epicuren • Bio Elements
- Biomedics • Skinceuticals • MD Forte • Neo Clean • Magica

Licensure:

- State of Arizona Aesthetician License
- State of California Aesthetician License

AESTHETICIAN EXPERIENCE

HUDSON WILLIAMS DAY SPA, 3/03 – 7/06   Palm Springs, California
NITA FOSHEE, 4/03 – 7/06   Costa Mesa, California
Aesthetician
Working by appointment, provided comprehensive aesthetology services, from oxygen facials and anti-aging skin treatments, to waxing, body wraps and aroma therapy for these upscale spas.

- Noted for customer service excellence to build a loyal customer base.

OTHER

PARSONS AGENCY, 7/06 – Present   Fountain Hills, Arizona
Personal Assistant
Provide production support for advertising agency, monitoring media placement, preparing and analyzing invoices and coordinating / scheduling talent for ads.

- Additionally serve as **make-up artist / stylist** on location / photo shoots to maximize visual impact.

EDUCATION

International Dermal Institute   Los Angeles, California
Continuing Education in Aesthetology 2005
Classroom and hands-on training in:

- European Skin Care Techniques • Vitamin Therapy for Skin Health • Aroma Therapy • Body Therapy
- Wellness Therapies for Body, Mind and Spirit • Results-oriented Tips for Maximum Prescriptive Retailing

Walters International School of Beauty   Costa Mesa, California
Aesthetology Certificate Program (600 hours) 2003
Course work encompassed:

- Microdermabrasion • Salt Glow Body Scrub
- Advanced Skin Care • Make-up Techniques
- Color Theory • Contouring and Corrections
- European Skin Care Techniques • Vitamin Therapy for Skin Health
- Aroma Therapy • Body Therapy
- Wellness Therapies for Body, Mind and Spirit
- Results-oriented Tips for Maximum Prescriptive Retailing

Property Management

GINA L. NELSON, CDA
33 Mahoney Road • Omaha, NE 68106 • (000) 123-0123

OBJECTIVE

Position in Property Management.

QUALIFICATION HIGHLIGHTS

- More than six years of experience assisting in the management of multiple rental properties.s
- Thoroughly familiar with both tenant and landlord laws and guidelines; experienced in collections and municipal court procedures.
- Extensive business background in general management, customer service and support, and subcontractor supervision.
- Advanced computer skills and demonstrated proficiency in streamlining administrative tasks through the application of technology.
- Resourceful and innovative in problem solving; adapt quickly to a challenge. Strong prioritization, delegation, and planning skills.
- Relate warmly to diverse individuals at all levels; respectful yet assertive communication style.

KEY SKILLS & ABILITIES

- Perform background, reference, and credit checks; select quality tenants and maintain high occupancy rates.
- Show available properties to prospective tenants; negotiate lease and rental agreements.
- Handle tenant communications; respond to requests for maintenance and answer questions.
- Troubleshoot and resolve disputes, including evictions and cleaning/damage deposits.
- Research legal issues utilizing Nolo Press publications, file court documents, and represent property owner in court.
- Schedule and supervise subcontractors; oversee upgrades, maintenance, and renovations.
- Plan and manage budgets; execute general accounting functions.
- Set up and maintain computerized property management systems.
- Coordinate and track rent collection, maintenance, and repairs. Proactively address security issues.

CAREER HISTORY

Assistant Property Manager (2001 – Present)
Smith's Realty, Omaha, NE
Assist in the management and oversight of multiple residential rental properties. Set up efficient administrative systems, coordinate rent collection, handle tenant disputes, and resolve legal issues.

Owner-Manager (1989 – 2001)
Computer Works, Omaha, NE
Founded and managed this micro/mini-computer sales and systems integration company. Achieved status as a Southwestern Bell Master Vendor.

EDUCATION

Metropolitan Technical Community College (1988 – 1989)
Emphasis in Business Administration

The New Executive Resume

Traditional thinking has it that as resumes only get a cursory first-time reading (about 45 seconds, and 90 percent of that time spent on the first page), rarely get thoroughly examined, and that consequently all resumes must be as brief as possible. The standard chant for professionals who think constantly about these matters says this: "One page for every ten years experience and never more than two pages." This still holds true for the majority of professionals, but not for all.

In certain quarters I may be regarded as a resume heretic, because I believe that for some professionals in some situations such as senior technologists, scientists, and certain medical professionals—as well as many Director level, most VPs, and just about all C-suite executives—this rule no longer holds true; in fact, adhering to it can be a detriment to a successful job search.

The practical issues creating the need for this change are really quite simple: the increasingly complex requirements for more senior jobs creates the need for adequate reflection of these multifaceted competencies in a written document.

Such competency must be shown through ever deepening experience supported by steadily increasing responsibility and illustrated by achievement. Management expertise and its achievements separate from professional and market sector skills also need clear illustration; additionally there are the necessities of professional visibility through publishing, speaking, and other leadership roles that are relevant in many senior level jobs. For example, I recently advised a big Pharma COO with a half-page history of board appointments, all of which had utmost relevance given his target job. Science is one of the "publish or perish" professions, and you'll see a resume example in the next few pages that contains almost a full page addressing publications, presentations, and professional affiliations; in such instances, mass adds weight.

Let's take a moment to recall the roles your resume plays in a successful job search: it gives you an achievable focus (without which you cannot be successful); it opens doors; it acts as a road map for interviewers; and it is your spokesperson long after the last interview is over. In short, the thinking that goes into the focus and execution of your resume has a significant impact on every facet of your successful job search. Not surprisingly for professionals in the higher ranks of some professions, an adequate story sometimes cannot be told in two pages, and cramming it in with 9- and 10-point fonts is certainly not the answer—the people in a position to hire such candidates are simply not going to struggle with the fine print.

At the same time the Internet has changed the face of recruitment advertising in at least two dramatic ways:

1. Space is no longer an issue, so recruitment advertising has changed from a few terse lines to hundreds and sometimes thousands of words.
2. The descriptors used in the recruitment advertising and job descriptions increase the need for a data-dense resume—one that is going to be retrieved from the resume databases because it uses the right keywords in adequate frequency to catch the attention of the database spiders.

Putting these considerations together: the complexity of some professional and most executive work, along with the need to communicate effectively by using the traditional device of the resume in the new electronic media, has birthed knowledge-era executive resumes of considerable length and density.

My thinking has changed to such a degree on this issue that in my private coaching practice, where I work with senior professionals on the national and international stage, I am suggesting, encouraging, supporting, and approving data-dense resumes in the three-to-eight-page range, because these resumes are clearly necessary to hit home runs for players in the major leagues.

Executive resumes will still get a cursory first-time review, whether they come directly to human eyes or are dragged up by keywords from a database. This means that, just as much as ever, a resume needs to be clearly focused on a specific job with that first page screaming understanding, capability, and achievement in the target area of expertise.

When the first resume page communicates clearly and contains a compelling message, the subsequent pages will get read with serious attention. The established standards of clarity and brevity (wherever possible) still hold; it's just the complexity of work at the higher levels that has increased and requires explanation. So resume length for today's executive becomes a clear-cut issue of form following function.

The examples you'll see in the next few pages are courtesy of my colleagues at the Phoenix Career Group *(www.phoenixcareergroup.com)*, where we work with executives like this everyday. If you are in need of powerful executive documents, Phoenix or martinyate.com is the place to go.

Executive Resumes

DONALD T. THOMAS

2009 Churchill Drive
Aliso Viejo, CA 92656
donaldthomas@gmail.com

Home: 949-254-9396   Mobile: 949-339-2709

SENIOR-LEVEL EXECUTIVE
FINANCE, CORPORATE STRATEGY & DEVELOPMENT
Expert in Leading & Partnering Corporate Finance with Enterprise Strategies, Initiatives, Transactions & Goals

PROFILE & VALUE

Strategic Finance Expert—Dynamic CFO with extensive experience and exceptional success in conceiving, planning, developing and executing strategic and tactical finance initiatives that drive top-line performance and bottom-line results. Technically proficient in all aspects of the finance and accounting functions, and expert in partnering corporate finance with enterprise strategies, initiatives and objectives.

Corporate Strategy & Development Specialist—Characterized as a rare visionary, strategist and tactician. Consistent originator of bold, innovative business strategies that have extraordinary results on growth, revenue, operational performance, profitability and shareholder value. Heavy transactions background including startup financing, industry rollup, merger of equals, acquisition and sale.

Consummate Management Executive—Top-performer and valuable contributor to corporate executive teams. Extremely versatile with high-caliber cross functional management qualifications, experience-backed judgment and excellent timing. Outstanding role model. Talented team builder, mentor and leader.

Diverse Industry & Situational Experience—public and private; small and Fortune 500; startup, rapid growth, turnaround, post-IPO, post, acquisition integration, bankruptcy—consulting services, real estate, hospitality, resort/vacation property, travel companies doing business in highly regulated industries in US, European and global arenas.

Extraordinary Personal Characteristics—Articulate, intelligent, ambitious, self-driven and creative. Outstanding corporate ambassador to customers, industry groups, regulatory bodies, private investors, Wall Street analysts, board members, and other internal and external stakeholders. Speak conversational French and German.

QUALIFICATIONS & EXPERTISE

Vision, Strategy, Execution & Leadership

Strategic Corporate Finance

P/L & Performance Improvement

Financial Forecasting, Analysis & Reporting

Cost Analysis, Reduction & Control

Treasury, Tax, Internal Audit

GAAP, SEC & Statutory Reporting

Corporate Development & Strategic Alternatives

Due Diligence, Deal Structuring & Negotiation

Financial & Legal Transactions

Growth Management & Business Development

Organizational Design & Transformation

Turnaround & Restructure

Cris is & Change Management

Internet Strategies & IT Projects

Team Building & Leadership

Investor, Analyst, & Board Relations

Executive Advisory & Decision Support

PROFESSIONAL EXPERIENCE

DTT Management Consulting, San Diego, CA   2000 to Present
Successful Management Consulting Firm—Significant Repeat Business and Value-Added Partner to Leading Consulting Firms (e.g., Alix Partners, PKF Consulting)—Retained by Startup, Small-Cap and Fortune 500 in US, UK, and ASIA

PRINCIPAL

Operate an independent firm specializing in the delivery of a full-range of consulting services—strategic business planning; strategic finance; corporate strategy, development and financing; organizational design; operational and financial turnaround; marketing; and market research and strategy. Identify and acquire new business, and manage all aspects of the project lifecycle—from scope of work through provision of deliverables, follow-up and relationship management—for large-scale, long-term projects. Engaged by corporate clients representing a broad-range of industry sectors—travel and tourism; hospitality; real estate development; marketing services; and technology and Internet.

Management Successes
- Leveraged professional reputation contacts worldwide to build and grow a successful management consulting firm.
- Acquired significant repeat business and positioned the firm as a value-added partner to high-profile management consulting firms in the US and UK (e.g., ABC Partners, DEF Consulting).

Key Engagements

- **Turnaround & Change Management**—Retained (by principal consultancy group) to evaluate a key strategic business unit of a $500 million resort/vacation sales company in Chapter 11. Performed in-depth analyses of operations, identified deficiencies and risks, and presented recommendations for restructure and turnaround of call center operations, program management, inventory control and member services functions. Engagement contract was extended to serve as Chief Business Architect during execution and post-C11 transition/recovery phases.
- **Operational Startup & Financing**—Retained by UK-based client of a $10 million marketing services business to advise and participate in creating a business plan, raising capital, and executing a startup in the global event management and incentives sector.
- **Corporate Strategy & Finance**—Retained by independent US resort developer to determine the viability and ROI of expanding into international markets. Analyzed business, financial, marketing, competitive intelligence, and geopolitical issues impacting the world tourism and hospitality sectors. Pinpointed key target markets, and authored business strategy and financial plan for launch of a luxury boutique hospitality brand.
- **Corporate Strategy**—Engaged in joint consultancy project with ABC Consulting in developing a full-scale corporate strategy plan for $500 million public hospitality company. Researched and analyzed internal and external organizations, market opportunities, competitive differentiators, business models and challenges.

CDE Group, Ltd., London, England   1999 to 2000
Venture Capital-Backed Dot-Com Startup Operating in a Niche Sector—Fine Arts and Antiques Online Sales/Auction

MANAGING DIRECTOR

Held full P&L accountability—recruited by and reported to the investor group and Chairman of the Board—for an early-stage Internet company. Developed and executed strategy, managed finance and operations, directed sales and marketing, steered technology development, and managed relationships with internal and external stakeholders. Led a core team of three executives—Director of Sales, Director of Operations, Manager of Finance & Administration—and provided indirect oversight to team of 18 in sales, operations, IT, finance and administrative roles.

Strategy & Leadership Successes

- Revised corporate strategy to leverage core competencies—a well-established network of dealerships and virtually unlimited source of product—and position the firm as inventory and distribution solution to another company.
- Conceived and executed viable exit strategy—vs. minimum requirement of additional 2+ years' investment to achieve breakeven—by identifying a buyer and negotiating sale of the company to a US-based business. Provided investors with ROI on their original investment/commitment of 660%+.

STUV Corporation, Inc., Orlando, FL   1997 to 1999
$500 Million Company—One of Largest Resort and Vacation Development/Sales Companies in US—in Rapid Growth Through International Expansion, Strategic M&A, Industry Rollup and IPO

VICE PRESIDENT—BUSINESS DEVELOPMENT

Key member of the executive committee—retained in company's buyout of UK-based LSI Group—in charge of the strategic and tactical business development activities during period of dynamic growth and change. Crossed-over functional lines to address product development, marketing, branding, sales, corporate communications, legal and regulatory matters. Administered $10 million business development budget. Reported directly to the CEO/COO, led a team of five Director-level executives, and interfaced with Board of Directors, Wall Street analysts and strategic alliance partners.

Strategy & Leadership Successes

- Led the company's single most significant post-IPO strategic initiative—conceptualization, development and execution of transformation of the company's infrastructure, business model, product offering and marketing strategy—without negative impact on sales, operational performance or customer service during execution.
- Shifted the business model and organizational structure—from a disconnected collection of resort properties—to a membership-based vacation sales company with an exclusive, points-based vacation product, and strong value proposition with single marketing message.

Business Development Results

- Credited with personal contributions to explosive growth—from $330 million in 1997 to $500 million in 1999—by spearheading the development and rollout of an innovative vacation ownership product and complementary offerings.
- Expanded market reach and brand recognition by initiating and leveraging relationships with high-profile strategic business partners—American Airlines, Time Warner, HSN, MemberWorks and others in the travel, hospitality and marketing services industries.

XYZ, Ltd., Lancaster, England   1994 to 1997
$65 Million, Privately Held Enterprise—One of Largest Vertically Integrated Vacation Ownership Companies in Europe—Specializing in Development and Management of Resorts, and Marketing and Sales of Timeshares and Travel Services

DIRECTOR—BUSINESS DEVELOPMENT (1995 to 1997)
CHIEF FINANCIAL OFFICER (1994 to 1995)

Held two key executive positions on the management team—both reporting to CEO (one of two principal shareholders)—following a major debt restructure, physical relocation and preparation for sale. As CFO, managed all aspects of the corporate finance and administration functions (including treasury, tax, statutory reporting and internal audit) for headquarters and 10+ overseas branches. Directed the preparation and analysis of financial statements, budgets, forecasts, desktop "dashboards" and other essential management reports. Hired, trained, mentored and managed a team of 28 including three senior financial and accounting professionals.

As Director of Business Development, identified, created and capitalized upon both innovative and traditional business opportunities. Conceived, developed and managed strategic and tactical messaging, branding, marketing, sales, and relationship building initiatives. Directed product development, positioning and go-to-market strategies, and launched a series of breakthrough concepts and techniques—trial membership, incentive-driven referral program, customer/prospect profiling, direct-to-consumer sales, interactive multimedia presentations.

Strategy & Business Development Successes
- Key contributor to providing deep due diligence to ABC in its purchase of LMN Group—activities and relationships that led to recruitment to executive position with the acquiring company.
- Credited with personal contributions (strategy, finance, operations, business development)—to growth—from $40 million to $65 million—profitability—from 5% pre-tax margin in 1994 to 11% in 1997—and shareholder value—from $15 million to $55 million at sale of the company in mid-1997.

Finance & Operations Results
- Built and managed a best-in-class finance and accounting function. Managed the complete turnaround of the corporate finance organization to include new systems, technologies, processes and personnel.
- Provided the executive team and stakeholders with comprehensive, meaningful decision support by restructuring virtually all financial reporting systems.

WXY Group, London, England   1987 to 1994
One of London's Largest Public Accounting and Business Consulting Practices—Professional Services for Entrepreneurial Public and Private Companies in Real Estate, VC Funding, Hospitality and Leisure Travel Sectors

Rapidly Advancing Levels of Seniority to:
MANAGER—CORPORATE FINANCE & INVESTIGATIONS DEPARTMENT (1992 to 1994)

Managed client engagements involving deep due diligence for numerous acquisition and funding transactions. Provided a full range of advisory services and functions including creating/opining on corporate development strategies, authoring business plans, preparing projection models, and performing operational and financial assessments. Developed expertise in fraud and litigation support, debt workout and internal audit. Interfaced with firm's Partners, investment bankers, private investors, senior-level corporate executives, board members, industry specialists, and regulatory officials.

Key Engagements
- **Debt Restructure**—Contributed to restructure of £100+ million debt with complex asset security position.
- **Fraud Investigation & Litigation**—Provided support on several high-profile engagements including collapse of a private financial services firm (represented WXY as the client) and a Formula One motor racing team.
- **Corporate Recovery**—Contributed to financial and operational turnaround of several hospitality and leisure firms.

EDUCATION & CREDENTIALS

British Chartered Accountant—ACA—(CPA equivalent), Institute of Chartered Accountants in England and Wales
G Mus (Hons)—Four year degree in Music (with honors), Royal Northern College of Music, Manchester, England
Training in Corporate Finance and Treasury, Association of Corporate Treasurers

PROFESSIONAL AFFILIATIONS

Institute of Chartered Accountants in England and Wales (ICAEW); American Resort Development Association (regular speaker and panelist at conventions) (ARDA); American Marketing Association (AMA); San Diego Chamber of Commerce; Association of Chartered Accountants in the US (ACAUS); American Real Estate Society (ARES); and Financial Management Association (FMA)

DONALD T. THOMAS
donaldthomas@gmail.com

HIGHLIGHTS OF A CAREER IN EXCELLENCE
Addendum to Resume

EXCELLENCE IN CORPORATE STRATEGY & TURNAROUND
Managing Director—early-stage Internet startup

Challenge   Revise corporate strategy and turnaround operational and financial performance of a venture capital-backed, early-stage startup—fine arts and antiques dot-com.

Actions   Evaluated the original business plan against actual conditions and projected outcomes based on multiple scenarios. Created and executed a decisive strategy for "repackaging" the company's value proposition as an inventory and distribution solution to larger companies. Halted overspending, implemented strict financial controls, restructured operations and reengineered business processes.

Results   Provided investors with viable business strategies and alternatives, and at their direction, executed an exit strategy through the successful sale of the company for $10 million in stock. Provided investors with 660% ROI on their original investment/commitment.

Strengths   I am a turnaround specialist—I can rapidly assess a complex business situation, formulate a solution that meets overall commercial objectives (even if the solutions are a radical departure from initial direction), and inspiring and gaining buy-in for dynamic change.

EXCELLENCE IN STRATEGY & BUSINESS DEVELOPMENT
VP—Business Development, large resort development and sales company

Challenge   Lead high-profile, mission-critical strategic business initiative—characterized by COO as "betting the ranch"—to restructure and transform a $500 million resort and vacation development and sales company.

Actions   Developed and executed strategies, and planned and managed on virtually all cross-functional aspects of the business. Steered development of an appealing customer value proposition in an innovative product offering—"Club Main Attraction" a points-based vacation club—communicated through a clear, strong brand and marketing message. Partnered with legal counsel in structuring products that met state/federal regulatory guidelines. Built and led a team of top-performing strategic marketing professionals to execute rollout to 1,000+ person sales force.

Results   Exceeded expectations of founders/executive management and Wall Street analysts—rewarded in 1999 for exceptional corporate contributions by receipt of a specially created Award for Vision—in conceiving and driving innovation in corporate strategy, infrastructure and product marketing.

Strengths   I am a true visionary and talented business leader who is always originating new concepts, innovating bold strategies, creating opportunities, and applying highly developed finance, marketing, business management and people skills to take on huge challenges and overcome daunting challenges.

EXCELLENCE IN COST REDUCTION & PERFORMANCE IMPROVEMENT
CFO—large European, vertically integrated vacation ownership company

Challenge   Resolve serious financial and operational performance issues—increasingly high costs and productivity bottlenecks in the travel and reservations division.

Actions   Streamlined divisional operating processes, realigned key personnel, and updated and improved the payment processing and banking functions by establishing a relationship with a high-tech banking institution.

Results   Improved customer service while slashing invoicing and collection costs—from 10% to <5% and $5 million; and as volume grew to $25+ million, reduced the ratio even further—and created seamless connectivity in processes, communications and culture between the division and the rest of the organization.

Strengths   I am an expert in leveraging best practices, technologies and relationships to enable and maintain inter-organizational cohesiveness, and operational performance excellence.

EXCELLENCE IN DECISION SUPPORT

CFO—leading European resort developer

Challenge   Provide comprehensive, meaningful and accurate decision support to the Principals of a privately held, multi-site resort development and sales enterprise.

Actions   Led complete restructure of the corporate finance and accounting organization, and all related systems, controls, processes and technologies. Introduced sophisticated forecasting, analysis and reporting tools, restructured the financial reports, refined the budgeting/variance analysis process, and implemented open-architecture accounting IT solutions/applications. Rebuilt, retrained and mentored the 28-person finance and accounting team, and advised senior-level management in optimal utilization of new financial information.

Results   Created and led a top-notch finance and accounting organization that produced timely, precise, meaningful financial and operational data—executive decision support and departmental financial accountability credited with the company's realization of 65% improvement in profitability (despite zero revenue growth) within one year of implementing new corporate finance regime, and delivery of significant ROI in successful sale of the company two years later.

Strengths   I am valuable to any corporate executive team through my ability to provide mission-critical decision support, and I am proficient in building and leading best-in-class finance and accounting organizations.

EXCELLENCE IN STRATEGIC & TACTICAL BUSINESS DEVELOPMENT

Director of Business Development—European vacation ownership company

Challenge   Continue to grow revenue and market share despite dramatic changes in the European vacation ownership sector—new legislation impacting multiple areas of the business model (ban on down-payment at point of sale, expanded disclosure requirements, statutory cancellation period).

Actions   Went to senior sales executives with a new sales model—multimedia technology, new sales showroom environment, upgraded sales presentation and collaterals—and gained approval from shareholders for investing in the strategic and tactical innovations.

Results   Distinguished the company as an industry leader—first vacation ownership company (in both US and UK) to utilize new technology-enabled sales/communication tools—a significant feature in sale of company. Maintained corporate revenue performance while reducing cancellation rates by 5%+.

Strengths   I am continuously devising ways to drive growth, operational performance and profitability—despite any internal or external challenge. With acute understanding of the marketplace, I am able create and execute business development strategies and tactics that put my company in front of the competition.

EXCELLENCE IN TURNAROUND & CHANGE

Consultant—international resort and vacation timeshare company

Challenge   Restore financial and operational health to a key strategic business unit—an SBU critical to the survival of the company—for an enterprise in post-Chapter 11 transition.

Actions   Contributed industry and business unit expertise (personally created, developed and exceeded performance objectives during period of 1997 through 1999) to a joint venture consulting engagement with ABC Partners (turnaround specialists). Evaluated existing operations and mapped-out a new strategy, organizational structure, business model (personal property vs. deeded real estate) and culture.

Results   Delivered the plan for putting in placing a robust organizational structure with best-practices for risk management, inventory utilization, call center operations, program management, financial reporting and member communications/satisfaction. Retained on extended contract to serve as Chief Architect (reporting to Interim CEO) to contribute cross-functional leadership to on-going project phases. Received second extension (reported to permanent executive committee) to manage post-C11 integration of the US and European programs. Combined annual cost savings of turnaround initiatives exceeded $5 million annually.

Strengths   In addition to industry expertise—resort and vacation timeshare—I bring the full complement of business and finance management qualifications. I am quick to identify and create solutions to complex business issues, and am proficient in managing large-scale, long-term, mission-critical projects.

SAMUEL HARRINGTON, Ph.D.

VA Dept. of Health & Human Services
Public Health Laboratories
6 Hazen Drive, Fairfax, VA 22033
Office: 800-555-5555
harringtons@dhhs.state.va.us

1012 South Street
Fairfax, VA 22033
Home: 571-555-5555
Cell: 571-555-5555
harringtonsam@aol.com

SENIOR EXECUTIVE—SCIENTIST
Chief Science Officer—Executive Director—Program Manager—Senior Scientist/Researcher
Biotechnology Enterprises—Molecular Research & Diagnostics Organizations

CAREER PROFILE & DISTINCTIONS

- Dynamic, entrepreneurial business professional with high-caliber general management qualifications ... strong orientations in finance and technology ... proven leadership talents. Led the startup of three biotechnology R&D organizations and turned-around an existing test / surveillance laboratory.

- Accomplished senior-level scientist and recognized innovator in modern technical and managerial strategies, principles, methodologies and processes for the biotech industry. Designed and developed numerous scientifically / commercially significant diagnostic reagents and assays.

- Professional experience spanning diverse clinical and technical settings; private biotech firms ... large R&D operations ... public health organizations ... hospitals ... academic facilities ... federally-funded homeland security projects.

- Accustomed to, and effective in high-profile scientist executive roles ... managing large organizations ... overcoming complex business/technical challenges ... gaining respect from competitors and peers ... communicating complex concepts to technical and non-technical audiences ... maintaining impartiality in politically charged environments ... fostering consensus and generating cooperation from multicultural, multidisciplinary teams.

- Confident, assertive, diplomatic and outgoing with exceptional communication, public speaking and interpersonal relations skills. Multicultural, bilingual professional—speak fluent Arabic and English.

MANAGEMENT QUALIFICATIONS

Entrepreneurial Vision, Strategy & Leadership	P&L and Operations Management
Financial Planning & Management	Budget Planning, Analysis & Control
Program & Project Management	Process Design / Improvement—Business & Technical
Staff Training, Development & Supervision	Technology Investments & Solutions
Team Building, Mentoring & Leadership	Marketing, Communications & Public Relations

AREAS OF EXPERTISE

Molecular Diagnostics R&D	Molecular-Based Surveillance
Disease Investigation & Management—Infectious & Genetic	DNA Fingerprinting & Gene Banking
Laboratory Management Quality Improvement & Assurance	Regulatory Affairs & Compliance—CLIA, CAP
Advanced Laboratory Procedures & Technologies	GLP, CQA, CQI
Homeland Security Strategies, Policies & Programs	Crisis / Emergency Preparedness & Response

PROFESSIONAL EXPERIENCE

State of Virginia, Fairfax, VA   1999 to Present

STATE MOLECULAR BIOLOGIST
Department of Health & Human Services, Public Health Laboratories (PHL)

Hold full P&L accountability for Virginia's only public health reference laboratory—infectious disease testing and surveillance services, bio-terrorism detection, prevention and response—serving the state's 1.2 million citizens. Manage all aspects of business operations (e.g., strategic planning, budgeting, financial reporting, staffing, workflow, administrative affairs, internal/external customer service, quality, regulatory reporting / affairs). Provide technical and managerial oversight to six primary areas of laboratory operations: test development, disease surveillance, disease outbreak investigations (including emerging infections, air-water-food-borne infections), and testing for bio-threat organisms / bio-terrorism. Manage $600K capital budget and $250K annual budget for operations. Lead a three-person management team and provide indirect supervision to seven technical and non-technical support employees.

DIRECTOR OF MOLECULAR DIAGNOSTICS—State of Virginia—*Continued:*

Management & Leadership Successes:

- Put the State of Virginia "on the map" in the U.S. biotech industry. Distinguished the facility as one of the best labs in the nation, and one of the first public health organizations to receive federal funding for bio-terrorism testing and preparedness.

- Evolved a very basic laboratory operation into a dynamic scientific organization staffed with talented, highly trained professionals utilizing state-of-the-art technologies and contemporary methodologies to perform sophisticated testing / surveillance of emerging infections.

- Led an ambitious campaign to secure $600K+ investment in technology (state and federal sources). Achieved financial accountability and discipline throughout the organization in order to maximize ROI.

- Equipped the organization and prepared the staff to handle both routine and emerging infections (including potential bio-terrorism organisms) despite the challenges of operating under serious financial and staff constraints.

- Converted the test development strategy from a successive to concurrent approach. Reengineered laboratory processes and workflows enabling completion of 80,000+ tests in FY 2001/2002.

- Designed and led intensive training and career development programs—trained / qualified four professionals in advanced molecular testing—and provided team coaching and one-on-one mentoring.

- Served as an effective representative / spokesperson for the organization to internal and external parties—scientific community, state / federal agencies (CDC, FDA, USDA, other public health laboratories), regulatory officials, media, and the public—and continue to advocate on behalf of the MDX / PHL and its activities, budgets, personnel and projects.

Clinical Projects & Achievements:

- Distinguished as the state's top-ranking science officer providing consulting, advisory and leadership services on matters related to molecular diagnostics.

- Led the entire development cycle—design, validation, application, training, troubleshooting—of molecular diagnostics-based assays for rapid investigation, diagnosis and surveillance of emerging / reemerging infectious diseases including E. coli, Salmonella, West Nile Virus and Noro Virus.

- Participated in validation of new rapid tests developed by CDC for BT organisms including anthrax, smallpox and the emerging virus responsible for SARS.

Columbia University Medical Center (CUMC)—Mailman School of Public Health, New York, NY　　　1992 to 1998

PROGRAM COORDINATOR—DEVELOPMENT
Division of Molecular Diagnostics

Key member of a seven-person management team for a key division within this large, diverse healthcare conglomerate—2nd largest medical center in New York and largest in northeastern area—comprised of several regional hospitals and specialty institutions (including Columbia Cancer Institute and Starzl Transplant Institute). Managed the business, clinical and technology aspects of test development. Led a team of 13 full-time technologists.

Management Achievements:

- Established the MDX developmental laboratories from the ground up—lab was a model followed by other laboratories throughout the U.S.—and provided the vision and operational framework for accommodating emerging technologies and future expansion

- Contributed to planning, development and control of annual budgets of nearly $1 million for operations—including $200K for capital equipment.

- Developed/presented formal training programs—one-month courses in lecture and wet lab formats—to physicians on topics related to emerging/advanced molecular diagnostics methodologies, technologies and applications.

Clinical Projects & Achievements:

- Developed DNA fingerprinting method to distinguish between closely related isolates of Legionella pneumophila—causative pathogen for Legionnaire Disease. Existence of this technique thwarted potential litigation (six-figure damage claim) by a former patient against the hospital.

- Developed test for identifying four most common gene mutations of Gaucher Disease among Ashkenazi Jewish populations. Delivered $110K+ per year in revenue from laboratory test fees.

The Methodist Dallas Transplant Institute (MDTI), Dallas, TX 1995 to 1998

SCIENTIST/CONSULTANT

Contributed expertise in molecular diagnostics to a multidisciplinary team of professionals—immunology, molecular biology, genetics, cell biology, other disciplines—working clinical R&D activities for the oldest/largest comprehensive international organ transplant programs in the world (a division of the University of Texas Medical Center). Developed customized, specialty reagents utilized in research at the Institute.

Clinical Projects & Key Accomplishments:

- Developed 2-hour assay—vs. existing test requiring 24+ hours—for detecting presence of low-level HCV in donated livers to be used in transplantation.

- Established custom oligonucleotide design and synthesis service. Generated $150K+ in annual revenue (commercial value exceeded $300K).

Applied Genetics Laboratories, Inc. (AGL), Melbourne, FL 1991 to 1992

PROJECT LEAD/STAFF SCIENTIST

Managed a five-year, $2.5 million project funded by the National Institute of Environmental Health Sciences (NIEHS) for R&D of early cancer detection/treatment methods. Provided technical and managerial oversight to all aspects of the project lifecycle. Tracked and controlled project budgets. Supervised four laboratory technologists.

Clinical Projects & Key Accomplishments:

- Designed and executed protocols for searching for TSGs in mice genome and detecting mutations enabling early diagnosis of cancer in humans.

- Participated in presenting annual project report to National Institute of Environmental Health Sciences in North Carolina.

Kuwait Institute for Scientific Research, Shwaikh, Kuwait 1985 to 1987

RESEARCH SPECIALIST
Department of Biotechnology

Established and managed Kuwait's first molecular genetics laboratory. Developed research strategies and managed projects. Provided consulting/advisory services on business and scientific issues. Built and led a team of 10 scientists, and hired/managed administrative support staff.

Research Projects & Key Accomplishments:

- Distinguished as the only molecular biologist in Kuwait, and independently started and managed mission statement, business/clinical strategy, business/laboratory operations, policy/procedure formation, budget, staff, equipment for this, the first molecular genetics laboratory in the country.

- Co-Principal Investigator on three-year, $480K+ project involving establishment of basic tools and methodologies for subsequent production of high-value compounds—single cell proteins—for use as animal feed supplements.

TEACHING EXPERIENCE

University of Virginia, Hampton, VA 2000 to Present

ADJUNCT ASSOCIATE PROFESSOR
Department of Microbiology

Served in a consulting role as a biotechnology subject-matter expert. Led presentations to faculty and graduate students on topics related to molecular diagnostics, public health and bio-terrorism. Provided advice on technical issues and made recommendations for academic/scientific programming.

Florida State University, Tallahassee, FL 1987 to 1991

RESEARCH ASSOCIATE

Supervised graduate students and taught undergraduate coursework in chemistry. Worked with senior scientists on projects.

TEACHING EXPERIENCE—*Continued:*

Kuwait University Faculty of Medicine, Jabriya, Kuwait   1985 to 1987
LECTURER
Provided classroom and laboratory instruction in biochemistry and molecular biology to undergraduate students. Led/participated in scientific research with focus on rheumatic fever.

EDUCATION
Ph.D.—Medical Biochemistry, West Virginia University, Morgantown, WV, 1983
MS—Biochemistry, Duquesne University, Pittsburgh, PA, 1979
B.Sc.—Biochemistry, Kuwait University, Khaldiya, Kuwait, 1977

PUBLICATIONS—*a partial list*

Samuel Harrington. Molecular Diagnostics of Infectious Diseases: State of the Technology. Biotechnology Annual Review, Elsevier Publishing Company (2000).

Samuel Harrington, Robert Lanning, David Cooper. Rapid detection of hepatitis C virus in plasma & liver biopsies by capillary electrophoresis. Nucleic Acid Electrophoresis Springer Lab Manual, Dietmar Tietz (ed), Springer-Verlag, Heidelberg (1998).

Samuel Harrington, William Pasculle, Robert Lanning, David McDevitt, David Cooper. Typing of Legionella pneumophila isolates by degenerate (D-RAPD) fingerprinting. Molecular and Cellular Probes, 9 405-414 (1995).

John A. Barranger, Erin Rice, **Samuel Harrington,** Carol Sansieri, Theodore Mifflin, and David Cooper. Enzymatic and Molecular Diagnosis of Gaucher Disease. Clinics in Laboratory Medicine, 15 (4) 899-913 (1995).

Samuel Harrington, Robert W. Lanning and David L. Cooper. DNA Fingerprinting of Crude Bacterial Lysates using Degenerate RAPD Primers (D-RAPD). PCR Methods and Applications. 4 265-268 (1995).

Samuel Harrington, Carol A. Sansieri, David W. Kopp, David L. Cooper and John A. Barranger. A new diagnostic test for Gaucher Disease suitable for mass screening. PCR Methods and Applications, 4 (1) 1-5 (1994).

David L. Cooper, **Samuel Harrington.** Molecular Diagnosis: a primer and specific application to Gaucher disease. Gaucher Clinical Perspectives, 1 (3) 1-6 (1993).

PRESENTATIONS—*a partial list*

Samuel Harrington and Krista Marschner. "A new, two-hour test for Bordetella pertussis using the SmartCycler," 103rd General Meeting of the American Society for Microbiology (ASM), Washington, DC, May 2003.

Samuel Harrington. "Methods & Applications of DNA Fingerprinting Techniques," Five 1- and/or 2-week-long workshops presented at the University of Puerto Rico, 1997 through 2003.

Samuel Harrington and Denise Bolton. "Development of a duplex real time RT-PCR test for surveillance of West Nile and Eastern Equine Encephalitis viruses using the SmartCycler," 102nd General Meeting of the American Society for Microbiology (ASM), Salt Lake City, UT, May 2002.

D.K. Voloshin, A.W. Pasculle, S.P. Krystofiak, **S. Harrington** and E.J. Wing. "Nosocomial Legionnaire's disease: an explosive outbreak following interruption of hyperchlorination," Interscience Conference on Antimicrobial Agents and Chemotherapy, San Francisco, CA, October 1995.

S. Harrington. "Genetic identification technologies: PCR and DNA fingerprinting," Second UN-sponsored Conference on the Perspectives of Biotechnology in Arab Countries, Amman, Jordan, March 1993.

S. Harrington, G. L. Rosner, D. L. Cooper and J. A. Barranger. "A new PCR-based diagnostic test for Gaucher Disease (GD)," Amer. J. Hum. Genet. 53 (supplement) 1755, 1993.

Bahr, G., **Harrington, S.,** Yousof, A., Jarrar, I., Rotta, J., Majeed, H. and Behbehani, K. "Depressed lymphoprolypherative responses in vitro to different streptococcal epitopes in patients with chronic rheumatoid heart disease," Conference on Infectious Diseases in Developing Countries, Kuwait City, Kuwait, March 1987.

PROFESSIONAL AFFILIATIONS

Member, American Society for Microbiology—ASM   Member, Association for Molecular Pathology—AMP
Consultant, INTOTA Corporation   Member, Council of Healthcare Advisors, Gerson Lehrman Group

Senior Executive–Scientist (addendum)

SAMUEL HARRINGTON, Ph.D.

VA Dept. of Health & Human Services
Public Health Laboratories
6 Hazen Drive, Fairfax, VA 22033
Office: 800-555-5555
harringtons@dhhs.state.va.us

1012 South Street
Fairfax, VA 22033
Home: 571-555-5555
Cell: 571-555-5555
harringtonsam@aol.com

Leadership Addendum—Science & Management

Dr. Samuel Harrington brings exceptional value through the combination of his core management qualifications, leadership talents and scientific knowledge, proficiency and experience. He continues to develop his cross-functional general management skills and remains on the cutting-edge of scientific advancements and contemporary topics in biotechnology.

BUSINESS MANAGEMENT & ORGANIZATIONAL LEADERSHIP
—Strategies, Initiatives, Contributions & Successes—

Much more than a scientist, Dr. Harrington is a management professional who is experienced and successful in directing organizations, programs, projects and teams. He brings strategic perspective, business acumen, sound judgment and financial discipline to private and public organizations involved in the life sciences/biotechnology fields.

> *"His work ethic is exemplary and his professional demeanor a model for others to emulate."*
> David L. Cooper, Director, Division of Molecular Diagnostics, University of Virginia Medical Center

> *"The quality of Samuel's work is exceptional ... and he excels this area [communications]"*
> Chief, VA Public Health Laboratories

Organizational Development & Leadership

Dr. Harrington has provided both technical and managerial leadership to scientific organizations, and over the course of this 20+-year career, he has:

- Established the Virginia Public Health Laboratory as an important participant/contributor to the national biotech industry.
- Led the complete organizational startup of the MDX developmental laboratory for the Division of Molecular Diagnostics at the University of Virginia Medical Center.
- Contributed the vision, technical expertise and business management capabilities to create and direct Kuwait's first molecular genetics laboratory.

Business & Finance Management

Dr. Harrington's ability to achieve operational and financial performance objectives within the departments he leads has made significant contributions to the ROI, profitability and value of the larger organizations. As demonstrated by his track record, Dr. Harrington takes personal responsibility for all general business, daily operations and budgeting/cost control initiatives. For example, he has:

- Authored and executed the business plan for the MDX molecular development laboratory for the University of Virginia Medical Center (UVMC), and integrated it into the main organizational structure.
- Participated in planning, administering and controlling $1 million operating budget for the Division of Molecular Diagnostics at UVMC.
- Achieved all budgetary performance objectives and gained financial discipline within the Virginia PHL.

Laboratory Operations Management

With more than 20 years' of academic, research and management work in science, Dr. Harrington is well-qualified in establishing, staffing, managing and improving the performance of laboratory operations/organizations. For example:

- Manage all aspects of operations—including disease surveillance, disease outbreak investigations, test development and testing for bio-threat (BT) organisms—in a "best in class" public health laboratory.
- Established Virginia's first Microbial Gene (DNA) Bank.
- Modernized and improved performance in key operational areas—productivity, efficiency, personnel qualifications, quality, compliance—for the State of Virginia's PHL.

BIOTECHNOLOGY / BIOMEDICAL RESEARCH, DEVELOPMENT & DIAGNOSTICS
—Projects, Activities, Contributions & Achievements—

"[Samuel Harrington's] strengths [include]... scientific knowledge and technical expertise, quality of work, initiative, sense of humor and ability to get along with people."

"[Dr. Harrington] set up an RT-PCR procedure for West Nile Virus which brought much praise to the PHL for its ability to quickly deal with a developing public health problem."

"[Dr. Harrington] has shown a great deal of initiative in learning about Virginia's infectious disease needs and developing molecular procedures for their detection and identification."

Chief, VA Public Health Laboratories

Dr. Harrington's career is focused on Infectious Disease, Molecular Diagnostics and Genetic Disorders.

Molecular Diagnostics of Infectious Diseases

Dr. Harrington's work in molecular diagnostics of infectious diseases has involved extensive research, surveillance, testing, assay development and publication. He is proficient in the utilization of sophisticated laboratory methodologies, techniques and technologies including, but not limited to: DNA fingerprinting (PFGE, Ribo Printing, PCR-based fingerprinting – RAPD/AFLP); DNA/RNA sequencing; PCR (including Real Time, RT-PCR, multiplex); oligonucleotide primer/probe design and synthesis; Southern hybridization; molecular cloning; and recombinant DNA technologies.

- Developed a two-hour RT-PCR test for the detection of B. pertussis directly from crude clinical specimens, thereby eliminating the need for traditional labor-intensive, time-consuming specimen processing (DNA extraction) step. Laboratories across the U.S. (e.g. SC, OK, FL., others) and Europe (Germany and Spain) have requested permission to use this test in their laboratories, and a Canadian diagnostics company has expressed interest in participating with validation studies. Presented this work at the 103rd General Meeting of the American Society for Microbiology in Washington, D.C., May 2003.

- Developed and presented (at the 102nd General Meeting of the American Society for Microbiology in Salt Lake City, UT, May 2002) a duplex RT-PCR test for surveillance of West Nile and Eastern Equine Encephalitis viruses using SmartCycler®.

- Developed and managed the design, validation, application, test and troubleshooting of molecular diagnostics-based assays for rapid identification and surveillance of emerging infectious diseases for the State of New Virginia PHL.

- Distinguished the NH PHL as one of the first labs in the U.S. to participate in proficiency testing (RT-PCR) for SARS utilizing a RT-PCR test developed by the CDC - validated test is being performed routinely at VA PHL.

- Developed a RT-PCR test for the rapid detection of the food-borne pathogen Noro (Norwalk) virus from human stools using melt-curve analysis of the amplified product—several PHLs have requested permission to use this test in their facilities.

- RNA isolated from mosquito pools inhibits West Nile virus real-time RT-PCR. Presented findings at the 3rd International Conference on Emerging Infectious Diseases in Atlanta, Georgia in March 2002.

- Investigation of simultaneous outbreaks of S. pneumoniae and H. influenzae in major medical center. Presented abstract at the 6th Annual PulseNet Update Meeting in Ann Arbor, Michigan in April 2002.

- Molecular Diagnostics of Infectious Diseases: State of the Technology. Invited article summarizing emerging technologies and applications in the rapid diagnosis of disease. Published in Biotechnology Annual Review, Elsevier Publishing Company, 2000.

- Rapid detection of hepatitis C virus in plasma and liver biopsies by capillary electrophoresis. In: Nucleic Acid Electrophoresis Springer Lab Manual, 1998.

- Developed and co-presented an abstract entitled "Nosocomial Legionnaire's disease: An explosive outbreak following interruption of hyperchlorination," presented at the Interscience Conference on Antimicrobial Agents and Chemotherapy in San Francisco in October 1995.

- Co-developed "Depressed Lymphoprolypherative Responses *in vitro* to Different Streptococcal Epitopes in Patients With Chronic Rheumatoid Heart Disease," presented at the Conference on Infectious Diseases in Developing Countries held in Kuwait in March 1987.

Molecular Diagnostics of Genetic Diseases

Either independently or as a member of a team of multidisciplinary professionals, Dr. Harrington has conducted a wide-range of scientific research/experimentation, developed mutation screening assays, written/published numerous articles and delivered presentations covering a vast spectrum of areas related to genetic diseases.

- Developed mutation screening and detection assays for a number of genetic diseases such as breast cancer (BRCA-1 mutation screening), Fanconi's anemia, Canavan's disease, Factor V Leiden, Fragile X syndrome and Huntington's disease.
- Molecular Diagnosis: a primer and specific application to Gaucher disease. Gaucher Clinical Perspectives 1 (3) 1-6, 1993
- Phenotype, Genotype, and the treatment of Gaucher Disease. Clinical Genetics. 49 111-118, 1996.
- Enzymatic and Molecular Diagnosis of Gaucher Disease. Clinics in Laboratory Medicine. 15 (4) 899-913, 1995.
- A review of the molecular biology of glucocerebrosidase and the treatment of Gaucher disease," published in Cytokines and Molecular Therapy, 1995.1 149-163, 1995.
- A new diagnostic test for Gaucher Disease suitable for mass screening. PCR Methods and Applications 4 (1) 1-5, 1994.

BioSecurity

Dr. Harrington champions interest and involvement in the conduct of scientific research and development, especially diagnostic test development and validation, of organisms and pathogens potentially used in biological terrorism/warfare. His work makes him of significant value to organizations and programs involved in related medical practice and public health programs, actions, projects and policies—to ultimately bridge the gap between public health specialists/organizations, the public, government agencies/intelligence community and primary care providers.

In April 2003, the U.S. House of Representatives overwhelmingly approved President Bush's "Project Bioshield," solidifying national interest and commitment to preparedness against potential bioterrorism attack.

- Distinguished the Virginia Public Health Laboratory (VA PHL) as one of the first in the U.S. to be awarded funding for bio-terrorism testing and preparedness.
- Established the MDX laboratory as the first PHL in the U.S. to use SmartCycler® for the development and routine testing of emerging infections including BT organisms - enabling the laboratory to participate in validation studies with CDC and Lawrence Livermore National Laboratory in developing assays for BT organisms.
- Implemented and supervised internal proficiency testing—within CDC protocols—and personnel cross-training programs at the VA PHL.
- Initiated VA PHL's participation in PulseNet (National Molecular Sub-Typing Network for Food-Borne Disease Surveillance), a network of laboratories (including CDC, FDA, USDA, state and local PHLs) adhering to standardized microbial surveillance procedures using Pulsed Field Gel Electrophoresis (PFGE) in performing gene sub-typing—a membership of particular importance to being equipped to respond to potential bio-terrorism threats/incidents.
- Adopted CDC-based Anthrax testing procedures, facilitating VA PHL's selection as a testing beta site by the Lawrence Livermore National Laboratory.
- Led Virginia's participation in President Bush/CDC's strategy for immunizing public health workers and first responders against Smallpox—including ensuring the capacity for testing for the vaccine strain of Smallpox and other related viruses.

DNA Fingerprinting & Gene Banking

- Established Virginia's first microbial DNA bank with 1,000+ DNA and RNA samples from various pathogens—food-borne pathogens, West Nile virus, Hepatitis C virus, Noro virus isolates—each containing nucleic acids in one or more formats: highly purified genomic DNA or RNA, immobilized (aerosol-resistant) purified DNA, agorose DNA plugs (ready for PFGE analysis) and viable organism (whenever possible).
- Developed and presented several one- to two-week long workshops on methods and applications of DNA fingerprinting techniques at the University of Puerto Rico during the years of 1997 through 2003.

Executive Resumes

269

<u>DNA Fingerprinting & Gene Banking</u>—*Continued:*

- Developed a DNA fingerprinting method to distinguish between closely related isolates of Legionella pneumophila, the causative pathogen for Legionnaire Disease—providing the only way to track the transmission of this pathogen from patients to hospital rooms/hospital rooms to patients. A six-figure liable suit against the University of Virginia Medical Center (University Hospital) was thwarted as a result of the availability of this technique.

- Co-authored an abstract to on tDNA-PCR amplification of species-specific polymorphic bands in plasmodium faciparum, plasmodium berghei and plasmodium yoelii at the University of Puerto Rico in San Juan, 2001.

- Authored "Typing of Legionella pneumophila isolates by degenerate (D)-RAPD fingerprinting," published in Molecular and Cellular Probes, 1995.

- Co-authored and presented "Microsatellite Analysis (MSA) Using the Polymerase Chain Reaction (PCR) of Paraffin Embedded Material for Distinction of Tissues From Different Individuals," at the United States and Canadian Academy of Pathology (USCAP) Specialty Conference in Toronto, Canada in March 1995.

- Authored "DNA Fingerprinting of Crude Bacterial Lysates using Degenerate RAPD Primers (D-RAPD)," published in PCR Methods and Applications, 1995.

- Authored and presented "Genetic identification technologies: PCR and DNA fingerprinting" at 2nd UN-sponsored Conference on the Perspectives of Biotechnology in Arab Countries, held in Amman, Jordan in March 1993.

<u>Other Biomedical Research</u>

- Authored, "Prediction of biologic aggressiveness in colorectal cancer by p53/K-ras-2 topographic genotyping," published in Molecular Diagnosis, 1996.

- Authored, "Distribution and evolution of CTG repeats at the myotonin protein kinase gene in human populations," published in Genome Research, 1996.

- Authored "Loss of heterozygosity in spontaneous and chemically induced tumors of the B6C3F1 mouse," published in Carcinogenesis, 1994.

- Authored "Identification of allelic loss in liver tumors from the B6C3HF1 mouse," published in Cell Biology Supplement, 1992.

- Authored, "Antibody levels and in vitro lymphoproliferative responses to streptococcus pyogenes erythrogenic toxin A mitogen of patients with rheumatic fever," published in Clinical Microbiology, 1991.

- Authored, "Isolation and characterization of developmentally regulated sea urchin U2 snRNA genes," published in Developmental Biology, 1991.

- Authored, "The U1 snRNA gene repeat from the sea urchin (Strongylocentrotus purpuratus): The 70 kilobase tandem repeat ends directly 3' to the U1 gene," published in Nuclear Acids Research, 1991.

- Authored "A developmental switch in the sea urchin U1 RNA," published in Developmental Biology, 1989, and presented at the American Society for Biochemistry and Molecular Biology meeting held in San Francisco in January 1989.

- Authored, "Isolation and characterization of tandem repeated U6 genes from the sea urchin Strongylocentrotus purpuratus," published in Biochemistry Biophysics, 1994, and presented at the Developmental Biology of the Sea Urchin meeting in Woods Hole, MA (August 1988) and at the Annual Meeting of Florida Biochemists in Miami in February 1988.

- Authored, "Modified nucleosides and the chromatographic and aminoacylation behavior of tRNA[ile] from Escherichia coli C6," published in Biochemistry Biophysics Acta, 1988.

Special Reports

Once in a very long while a new idea comes along in the world of job-hunting. The Special Report is one of those ideas. It presents you as an expert in your field without overtly saying you are job-hunting, and as such gets the reader to create an initial impression of you that is very different from that of a typical job seeker. A special report is not for everyone, but if you really know your business and you like to write, this can be a very helpful tool to add to your job-hunting arsenal.

A Special Report has the appearance of a newspaper, newsletter, or trade magazine article that focuses on a commonly recognized challenge in your profession; but rather than mass publication it is created by you to send directly to end users. You create it by using your professional knowledge and packaging it in a written document. Just about anyone in your field who receives one will read a well-written and properly edited special report, and at the end they'll get to read the resume of the person who created it. While a resume gets very little initial time investment, your report can have the reader building a respectful relationship with you even before they know you are available and looking. Special reports have titles like:

Computer Conversion: Plan it, Move on it, and Roll it out!

Three simple things you can do that double the effectiveness of your school resource center

Research reveals little used sales technique that dramatically improves product sales in financial investment market

Ten simple actions any FCM, BD, Bank, Prop Trading, and/or Treasury Director can take to head off trouble at the pass

Seven Secrets of the Successful Waitperson

Special reports all aim to help the reader solve problems, make money, save money, or save time. Think of them as departmental reports, position papers, or articles (whichever works best for you), where the goal is to give the reader some useful information they can actually use. This is why a special report is not for everyone. You have to know your stuff and enjoy the writing process, but as I always say, anyone can write so long as they don't have a so-called life! If this is you (at least the part about having an affinity for writing) read on, you will not only learn a new job hunting technique you'll be contributing to your professional credibility and visibility in ways that reach well beyond this job hunt.

In the space available here, I can't show you how to write short, job-hunting-oriented, nonfiction articles—a.k.a. Special Reports. Instead, I'll explain the basic structure and packaging and then refer you to a couple of additional resources.

What Goes into a Special Report?

- A benefit-oriented title
- An introduction
- The body copy usually in the form of "tips" or "mistakes to avoid"
- Author info (usually, your resume)
- A binding

The key to this Trojan horse approach is to include your resume with contact information in the author information section. If your resume isn't right for the job, you can use a biography that highlights information you feel is more relevant to the reader; in this instance you'll be able to cut and paste one of your broadcast letters without the salutation.

The proper length is up to you, and opinions differ. Some will tell you that special reports can be as long as you like, and I have seen some that run to 6,000 words (about ten pages). Personally, I think you should keep your report to between 600 and 1,000 words—in other words, about the length of a regular newspaper column (or the length of this section on what goes into special reports, which runs about 1,000 words). I say this for two reasons:

- Writing takes time away from the main thrust of your job-hunting activities, and you cannot allow this great secondary approach to affect your focus.
- You don't want to share everything you know about a particular subject on paper; you want to be able to continue the conversation in person with yet more information to share.

There is another benefit to this approach. Job offers usually go to the person who turns a one-sided examination of skills into a two-way conversation between professional colleagues. The nature of the special report goes a long way toward defining you as someone quite different to almost every other candidate.

If you look at the examples below and think that this might be a useful approach for your needs, but you feel you need more help, go to *www.salarynegotiations.com*, the Web site of longtime career consultant Jack Chapman, who developed the whole Special Report idea.

If you do try this as an additional approach for your job hunt, you will be able to re-use the fruits of your efforts. You can submit your article for publication to professional newsletters and magazines, and you can turn it into a presentation. In fact, your notes for the special report simultaneously form the outline of a business presentation. So even outside of the context of your job hunt, this approach of putting your professional expertise into a different delivery medium can have a significant impact on your professional visibility and credibility.

Now look at these samples.

SPECIAL REPORT EXAMPLE #1: WAITRESS

BACKGROUND:

With NO experience directly as a waitress, Christine, a college freshman, got hired. She had only been a hostess at "23"—Michael Jordan's Restaurant near the University of North Carolina. She had observed waiters and waitresses, and she had definite ideas about what differentiated the satisfactory from the excellent. She wanted to "jump over" the menial waitress positions and get hired by an upscale, four-star restaurant (read: big tips!). This way, she positioned herself as an exceptional waitress who had the boss's viewpoint of the job.

TITLE: Christine's Four Keys to an Excellent Waitperson

EXCERPT FROM INTRODUCTION:

Excellent waiter, waitress? It's not all that complicated to be just a satisfactory wait-person. Practically anyone can write down an order and bring food to the table. Surprisingly, it's not all that hard to be an outstanding waitperson, either—but not everyone does it. I've put down my thoughts, here, on the 4 keys to excellence on the job as I see it. It will help you get an idea of my philosophy.

EXCERPT FROM RULES SECTION:

Key #3 *There's always a way to get people what they want.*

When you know that customers want more than just food, that they want a pleasant time as well, possibilities arise. As hostess at 23, waitstaff would often complain to me about customers ordering things not on the menu, or prepared a certain way. When, out of curiosity, I checked it out with the cooks, and they almost always said, "No problem." So it was the waitperson creating a problem for a customer—that problem didn't exist! I find that if you put your mind to it, there's always a way to keep the customer satisfied.

OUTLINE OF THE REST OF THE REPORT:

Key #1): Remember that your job is not "things to do," but people to take care of.

Key #2) The friendlier you are, the friendlier the customers will be.

Key #3) There's always a way to get people what they want.

Key #4) It's a job for you, but it's a business for your boss.

Summary

RESULTS: Christine leapfrogged into a fine-dining (and fine tipping) job.

SPECIAL REPORT EXAMPLE #2: SALESMAN

BACKGROUND:

Mike's success at sales came from meticulous attention to detail (read: boring!), but he turns that dull skill into a reason to be hired! His report shows how astoundingly elementary your report "rules" can be and still make an indelible impression. (His first rule is, "Answer the Phone.") He focused on software sales to financial investors, but this type of report could be applied to almost any type of sales. Mike also got the Hiring Decision Makers' attention in the cover letter by mentioning that theirs was one of the firms he called in his "secret shopper" research.

TITLE: Research Reveals Little Used Sales Technique That Can Dramatically Improve Sales [to the Financial Investment Market.]

EXCERPT FROM INTRODUCTION:

Recently I undertook a research project to determine how companies might improve their sales. I called several companies and said, "I would like to buy your software."

It was astonishing to me that from over twenty companies, I only reached someone knowledgeable about the product 14% of the time. Equally surprising was that only 28% of the organizations had someone return my call. Almost 40% didn't bother to send me any information. And even when they did, only 4% followed up with a phone call.

This confirmed my hunch. Just by applying a sales principle I've used for 18 years, namely follow-up consistency, any one of these firms could experience a dramatic increase in sales. Here is how consistent follow-up can be easily applied in five areas to increase sales. I'm embarrassed at how basic these actions are, but remember—only 14% of my calls reached a salesperson!

EXCERPT FROM RULES SECTION:
Follow-up Consistency Rule #1: ANSWER THE PHONE.

Having a dedicated line that is answered by a knowledgeable, helpful, friendly, live human being is essential in sales. No voice mail allowed! Not every line needs to be answered this way (although that's nice if you can afford it), but each and every call from potential customers must receive this follow-up consistency.

On one of my calls an operator informed me she could not take my name and address for information—that would have to be handled by a salesperson. She then informed me that she could not transfer me to a salesperson because they were all gone for the rest of the day. It was 11 a.m.!

QUESTION: Have you called your own sales line recently? What happened next?

OUTLINE OF THE REST OF THE REPORT:
Rule #2) Return messages;
Rule #3) Send the materials;
Rule #4) Don't just call the prospect, get through;
Rule #5) Never discard the names of prospects.
Summary

RESULTS: Mike got interviews with EVERY ONE of the 20 firms he had called as a "secret shopper." He got job offers from two of them.

SPECIAL REPORT EXAMPLE #3: FINANCIAL INVESTMENT SERVICES CFO

BACKGROUND:
Scott was seeking a high six-figure CFO job in the investment field. Billion dollar scandals at Enron, MCI WorldCom, and Tyco had just occurred so his report caught people's attention. His simple techniques to prevent these catastrophes were powerfully linked up with the war-stories attached to each rule.

TITLE: How to Uncover Financial and Operational Trouble Before Your P&L Blows Up . . . Ten Simple Actions any FCM, BD, Bank, Prop Trading and/or Treasury Manager or Director Can Take to Head Off Trouble at the Pass

EXCERPT FROM INTRODUCTION:

When a company is in, or about to be in trouble, there are <u>always</u> flashing yellow warning lights. The good news is that <u>problems rarely travel alone</u>. Usually they create a pattern of circumstances that aren't individually recognized as problems, but when the puzzle pieces are assembled—wham! It's an open invitation to red ink. It may be up to you to recognize enough of those pieces in time to stop the entire puzzle from being completed.

For the past 20 years, as a troubleshooter CFO or COO at financial services firms, I've learned to read the signs. And what are some of those signs?

EXCERPT FROM RULES SECTION:

Rule #2: *Pay attention to your checks after they're cashed and cleared.*
How are they endorsed?

Your employees? The ones who can't trade because you won't let them, why is one or more of their checks endorsed over to a third party or brokerage firm—hidden trading account in their own name?

Your customer? Why are multiple checks for identical amounts drawn on a single customer's account and endorsed over to multiple third parties? Unregistered pool? What if one of those third parties is your employee in a position to allocate trades or initiate commission rate or brokerage rate changes in your computer system?

Your vendor? Why are checks always endorsed to the name of a company you don't recognize? Is it an innocent d/b/a or are you dealing with a middleman who is marking up goods or services you could get for less by going direct?

OUTLINE OF THE REST OF THE REPORT [FOUR SAMPLES OF THE TEN RULES):

Rule #1) Periodically, sort your name and address file. Look for dual-identity payments.

Rule #3) Review a month of original trade tickets, blotters, out-trade sheets. Slowly. It's worth it.

Rule #6) Use simple line graphs to compare periods. It's easy to be caught up in the day-to-day.

Rule #9) Regularly review IB/RR/AP/Broker/Trader Payouts. Without exception, the most consistent source of hidden losses is linked in some way to Payouts.

RESULTS: Scott's report opened doors to networking interviews with "heavy hitters" in his field, which led to his new job.

SPECIAL REPORT EXAMPLE #4: SHIPPING TERMINAL MANAGER

BACKGROUND:

Keith worked for Yellow Freight. Besides getting all the trucks loaded, unloaded, and on the road on time, he also loved to catch cheaters—people collecting disability who weren't really disabled. His title is very intriguing and benefit oriented.

TITLE: A Simple Way to Put a Couple Hundred Thousand Dollars Right to the Bottom Line: Watch People Who Aren't There, Make Sure Nothing Happens

EXCERPT FROM INTRODUCTION:

This report's title says how "watching people who aren't there" and "making sure nothing happens" can save you money. I have found that few simple techniques to watch people who are out because of injuries, and a few principles of safety to make sure that nothing (bad) happens, will put $200,000 or more to the bottom line each year.

EXCERPT FROM RULES SECTION:

Rule #1: *Call at Odd Times*

When I have a man out, I'll put in calls every once in awhile ostensibly to get some information. "Where is that bill of lading?" "Truck #3 seems to be acting up, how did it run for you?" At 2:30 in the afternoon, or home at night. I'll remind them their doctor's appointment is tomorrow. They soon learn they will be caught if they aren't home.

This cuts costs because besides clipping the wings of the ones who are playing hooky, saving time off, or receiving disability payments, it also alerts the 80% with real injuries that if they ever want to fake it, that they'll have a hard time.

OUTLINE OF THE REST OF THE REPORT [FOUR SAMPLES OF THE RULES]:

Rule #2) [Watch people...] Make them come in to the facility.
Rule #3) [Watch people...] Call the Bluff of "Regular Offenders."
Rule #4) [Nothing happens...] Have safety meetings lead by peers, not supervisors.
Rule #7) [Nothing happens...] Reward safety in teams to create peer pressure for safety.

RESULTS: The report was the focus of several telephone networking conversations, which led to interviews and a great job.

CAREER CONSULTANTS AND RESUME WRITING SERVICES

As part of your job search, you might feel the need to look into getting extra help from a professional resume writer and/or a career counselor. A professional in the field might be able to help you develop a more polished layout or present a particularly complex background more effectively.

As in any other profession, there are practitioners at both ends of the performance scale. I am a strong believer in using the services of resume writers and career consultants who belong to their field's professional associations. They tend to be more committed, have more field experience, and have an all-around higher standard of performance, partly because their membership demonstrates their commitment to the field and partly from the ongo-

ing educational programs that these associations offer to their members.

The three major associations in the resume-writing field are: the Professional Association of Resume Writers (PARW, *parw.com*), the National Resume Writers Association (NRWA, *nrwa.com*), and Career Masters Institute (CMI, *www .cminstitute.com*). All three associations have hundreds of members and provide ongoing opportunities for members to gain mentoring experience and additional training. They all offer resume-writing certification and operate e-mail list servers for members with access to e-mail.

Two important smaller organizations are CertifiedResumeWriters .com and CertifiedCareerCoaches. com. These two Web sites are designed to connect job seekers with certified career professionals who meet specific resume writing and career coaching needs. All of the resume writers on these two sites are active members of one or more of the above associations and have taken the time to achieve accreditation in different aspects of the resume writing and career coaching process.

Finally there is the Phoenix Career Group *(www.phoenixcareergroup.com)*, a small group of highly qualified and exceptionally credentialed career manage-ment consultants and resume writers spread all over North America. This is a by-invitation-only marketing consortium of independents who all know each other through membership in other groups. Although I do not offer these one-on-one services myself, I am a member of Phoenix solely for the camaraderie and value I receive from rubbing shoulders with a select group of mature and committed professionals.

The following is a list of career consultants and professional resume writers. All of these have contributed to the *Knock 'em Dead* books and are members of one or more of the above groups.

Martin Yate, Executive Career Strategist

E-mail: *martin@knockemdead.com*

Martin Yate, CPC

Typically works with C-level and C-level-bound professionals facing challenges in the areas of Job Search, Interviewing, and Career Strategy.

Phoenix Career Group

www.phoenixcareergroup.com

Debbie Ellis, CPRW, CRW

Serving career-minded professionals to senior executives, the Phoenix Career Group is a one-of-a-kind consortium of 15 industry-leading professionals specializing in personal branding, resume writing, career management coaching, research, and distribution.

A First Impression Resume Service

www.resumewriter.com

Debra O'Reilly CPRW, CEIP, JCTC, FRWC

Debra provides job-search and career-management tools for professionals, from entry level to executive. Areas of specialty include career transition and the unique challenges of military-to-civilian conversion.

A Resume For Today

www.aresumefortoday.com

Jean Cummings M.A.T., CPRW, CEIP, CPBS

Distills complex high-tech careers into potent, memorable, and valuable personal brands. Provides resume writing and job search services to executives and managers seeking to advance their careers in high tech.

A Word's Worth Resume and Writing Service

www.keytosuccessresumes.com

Nina K. Ebert CPRW/CC

Serving clients since 1989, A Word's Worth is a full-service resume and cover letter development/career coaching company with a proven track record in opening doors to interviews.

A+ Career & Resume, LLC

www.careerandresume.com

Karen M. Silins CMRS, CCMC, CRW, CECC, CEIP, CTAC, CCA

Expertise includes career document development, career exploration and transition, assessments, job search methods, networking, interviewing, motivation, dressing for success, and career management strategies.

Abilities Enhanced

www.abilitiesenhanced.com

Meg Montford MCCC, CMF, CCM

Helps enable radical career change, as from IT trainer to pharmaceutical sales rep and technical writer to personal trainer. Career coaching and resumes by a careers professional since 1986.

Advanced Resume Services

www.resumeservices.com

Michele Haffner CPRW, JCTC

Resumes, cover letters, target mailings, interview coaching, and search strategy/action plan development. Specialty is mid- to senior-level professionals earning $75K+. Complimentary critique. Over 10 years of experience. Guaranteed satisfaction.

Advantage Resume & Career Services

www.CuttingEdgeResumes.com

Vivian VanLier CPRW, JCTC, CCMC, CEIP, CPRC

Full-service resume writing and career coaching serving clients throughout the U.S. and internationally at all levels. Special expertise in Entertainment, Management, Senior Executives, and Creative and Financial Careers.

Arnold-Smith Associates

www.ResumeSOS.com

Arnold G. Boldt CPRW, JCTC

Offers comprehensive job search consulting services, including writing résumés and cover letters; interview simulations; career assessments and coaching; and both electronic and direct mail job search campaigns.

Brandego LLC

www.brandego.com

Kirsten Dixson CPBS, JCTC

Creates Web Portfolios for executives, careerists, authors, consultants, and speakers. Includes experts in branding, career management, multimedia, copywriting, blogging, and SEO to express your unique value.

Career Directions, LLC

www.careeredgecoach.com

Louise Garver JCTC, CPRW, MCDP, CEIP, CMP

Career Directions, LLC, is a full-service practice specializing in resume development, job-search strategies and career-coaching services for sales and marketing executives and managers worldwide.

Career Ink

www.careerink.com

Roberta Gamza JCTC, JST, CEIP

Offering career marketing and communication strategy services that advance careers. Services include precisely crafted resumes and customized interview training sessions that persuade and motivate potential employers to action.

Career Marketing Techniques

www.polishedresumes.com

Diane Burns CPRW, CCMC, CPCC, CFJST, IJCTC, CEIP, CCM

A career coach and resume strategist who specializes in executive-level military conversion resumes and federal government applications. She is a careers industry international speaker and national author.

Career Solutions, LLC

www.WritingResumes.com

Maria E. Hebda CCMC, CPRW

A certified career professional, she helps people effectively market themselves to employers and position them as qualified candidates. Provides writing and coaching services in resume and cover letter development.

Career Trend

www.careertrend.net

Jacqui Barrett MRW, CPRW, CEIP

Collaborates with professionals and executives aspiring to ignite their careers or manage transition. The owner is among an elite group holding the Master Resume Writer designation via Career Masters Institute.

Cheek & Cristantello Career Connections, LLC

www.cheekandcristantello.com

Freddie Cheek M.S. Ed., CCM, CPRW, CRW, CWDP

Resource for resume writing and interview coaching with 25 years' experience satisfying customers and getting results. Creates accomplishment-based resumes that help you achieve your career goals.

Create Your Career

www.careerist.com

Joyce Fortier CCM, CCMC

Company collaborates with clients as a catalyst for optimum career success. Services include resume and cover letter services, and coaching services, including job search techniques, interview preparation, networking, and salary negotiation.

ekm Inspirations

www.ekminspirations.com

Norine T. Dagliano FJST, Certified DISC Administrator

More than 18 years of comprehensive and individualized career transition services, working with professionals at all levels of experience. Specializes in federal job search assistance, assisting dislocated workers, and career changers.

Executive Essentials

www.career-management-coach.com

Cindy Kraft CCMC, CCM, CPRW, JCTC

Prepares professionals and executives to outperform the competition. Top-notch marketing documents, a focused branding strategy, and job search coaching result in a multi-faceted, effective, and executable search plan.

Executive Power Coach

www.ExecutivePowerCoach.com

Deborah Wile Dib CPBS, CCM, CCMC, NCRW, CPRW, CEIP, JCTC

Careers-industry leader helps very senior executives stand out, get to the top, and stay at the top. Executive brand development, power resumes, and executive power coaching services since 1989.

Guarneri Associates

www.Resume-Magic.com

Susan Guarneri NCC, NCCC, LPC, MCC, CPRW, CCMC, CEIP, JCTC, CWPP

Comprehensive career services—from career counseling and assessments to resumes and cover letters—by full-service career professional with top-notch credentials, 20 years of experience, and satisfied customers.

JobWhiz

www.JobWhiz.com

Debra Feldman B.S., M.P.H.

Personally arranges confidential networking appointments delivering decision makers inside target employers. Engineers campaign strategy, innovates positioning, and defines focus. Banishes barriers accelerating job search progress. Relentless follow-up guarantees results.

The Loriel Group - CoachingROI : ResumeROI

www.ResumeROI.com

Lorie Lebert CPRW, IJCTC, CCMC

A full-service career management provider, offering personalized, confidential support and guidance; moving client careers forward with focused customer service.

The McLean Group

yourcareercoach@aol.com

Don Orlando MBA, CPRW, JCTC, CCM, CCMC

Puts executives in control of the career they've always deserved. Personal, on-demand support that helps busy managers get paid what they are worth.

Mil-Roy Consultants

www.milroyconsultants.com

Nicole Miller CCM, CRW, IJCTC, CECC

Creates the extra edge needed for success through the innovative design of dynamic resumes and marketing tools that achieve results.

Partnering For Success, LLC

www.resumes4results.com

Cory Edwards CRW, CECC, CCMC

Resume writer and career coach currently achieving 98% success rate getting clients interviews. Specializing in all resumes, including federal, SES, postal, and private sector from entry-level to executive.

Resume Suite

www.resumesuite.com

Bonnie Kurka CPRW, JCTC, FJST

Career coach, resume writer, speaker, and trainer with more than 11 years' experience in the careers industry. Specializes in mid- to upper-level management, IT, military, and federal career fields.

The Resume Writer

www.theresumewriter.com

Patricia Traina-Duckers CPRW, CRW, CEIP, CFRWC, CWPP

Fully certified career service practice offering complete career search services, including personalized civilian/federal resume development, business correspondence, web portfolios, bios, CVs, job search strategies, interview coaching, salary research, and more.

Resume Writers

100PercentResumes

www.100percentresumes.com

Daniel J. Dorotik, Jr. NCRW

Global career development service specializing in the preparation of resumes, cover letters, and other associated career documents. In addition to traditional formats, prepares online-compatible documents for Internet-driven job searches.

ResumeRighter

www.ResumeRighter.com

Denise Larkin CPRW, CEIP

A mount-a-campaign, market-yourself, total-job-search support system. They promise to: Present your qualifications for best advantage. Write an attention-grabbing cover letter. Coach you to ace your interview.

Write Away Résumé and Career Coaching

www.writeawayresume.com

Edie Rische NCRW, JCTC, ACCC

Creates targeted resumes and job search correspondence for clients in every vocation, and specializes in helping others discover their "Authentic VocationTM," shift careers, and resolve issues using "QuantumShiftTM" coaching.

INTERNET RESOURCES

APPENDIX · APPENDIX · APPENDIX · APPENDIX · APPENDIX · APPENDIX

B

These are really Knock 'em Dead Internet resources, with links to Web sites in twenty-two job search and career-management categories.

You'll find the big job banks, profession specific sites for eighteen major industries, association, entry level, executive, minority sites and more. You'll discover tools that help you find companies, executives and lost colleagues, plus sites that help you choose new career directions or find a super qualified professional resume writer, job or career coach.

To save time, you can come to the *knockemdead.com* Web site, where you can click on each of these resources and be connected directly—no more typing in endless URLs!

Association Sites

www.ipl.org
The Internet Public Library. Lots of great research services of potential use to your job search. This link takes you directly to an online directory of professional associations.

www.weddles.com
Peter Weddle's employment services site also offers a comprehensive online professional association directory.

Career and Job Coaches

www.knockemdead.com
Martin Yate CPC Executive Career Strategist
E-mail: *martin@knockemdead.com*

Martin typically works with C-level and C-level bound professionals facing challenges in the areas of Job Search, Interviewing and Career Strategy.

www.phoenixcareergroup.com

A private, by invitation only, association of seasoned and credentialed coaches, of which I am a member. I know all the Phoenix consultants professionally, and I'm proud to know most of them personally; they're the finest you'll find.

www.certifiedcareercoaches.com

A Web site that features only certified career coaches.

www.certifiedresumewriters.com

A Web site that features only certified resume writers.

Career Assessments

www.assessment.com

A career choice test which matches your motivations against career directions. I've been using it for a number of years.

www.crgleader.com

Links to career planning and choice tools. The first free career choice test listed wasn't very helpful, but the site has other good resources.

www.analyzemycareer.com

A well-organized and comprehensive career choice online testing site.

www.careerplanner.com

Affordable RIASEC oriented career choice testing by an established online presence.

www.careertest.us

Allows you to take online career tests and get reports in minutes.

www.college911.com

Helps you find colleges based on your interests. No career choice tests; rather a site you might want to visit after you have a general sense of direction.

www.livecareer.com

Home page says it's free, and the free report is okay as far as it goes, which is not very far. To get a full report you will pay $25 and there are also premium options, but you don't know this until you have spent 30 minutes taking the test! Despite this slight of hand, a good career choice test with comprehensive reports.

www.princetonreview.com

A $40 online test; this is a good solid test and the site is easy to navigate.

www.rockportinstitute.com

Excellent career choice tests for all ages. Although priced on a sliding scale dependent on income, they start at $1,500 for someone earning 40K a year or less.

www.self-directed-search.com

This is the famous SDS test developed by John Holland. An extremely well-regarded test, and at just $9.95 it's a great deal.

Career Choice and Management Sites

www.acinet.org

A site that offers career choice and advancement advice via testing for job seekers at all levels. Has good info on enhancing your professional credentials.

www.phoenixcareergroup.com

A premier site featuring deeply experienced and credentialed career counselors available for consultation on an hourly basis.

www.quintcareers.com
Career and job-search advice.

www.rileyguide.com
Excellent site for job search and career management advice. It's been around for years and is run by people who really care.

Career Transition
Military Transition

www.destinygroup.com
A great site for anyone transitioning out of the military. The #1 post-military careers site.

www.corporategray.com

www.taonline.com
Military transition assistance.

Other Transition

www.careertransition.org
For dancers once their joints go.

College and Entry Level Job Sites

www.a1education.com
Directories and links for colleges and graduate schools, test prep, financial aid, and job search advice.

www.aboutjobs.com
Links and leads for student jobs, internships, recent grads, expats, and adventure seekers.

www.aftercollege.com
Internships and co-ops, part-time and entry level, Ph.D.s and post-docs, teaching jobs, plus alumni links.

www.backdoorjobs.com
Short-term and part-time adventure and dream jobs.

www.blackcollegian.com
Premier site for black college students and recent graduates; help and sensible advice in areas of concern for the young professional.

www.campuscareercenter.com
Job search, career guidance, and advice on networking for transition into the professional world.

www.careerfair.com
Career fair directory.

www.collegecentral.com
A networking site for graduates of small- and medium-size community colleges.

www.collegegrad.com
A comprehensive and well-thought-out site full of good information for the entry-level job seeker; probably the best in the entry-level field.

www.collegejobboard.com
A top job site for entry-level jobs; includes jobs in all fields.

www.collegejournal.com
Run by the *Wall Street Journal*, it's a savvy site for entry-level professionals, with lots of resources.

www.collegerecruiter.com
One of the highest traffic sites for students and recent grads with up to three years' experience. Well-established and comprehensive job site.

www.ednet.com
Reports on college aid, college selection, career guidance, and college strategy.

www.entryleveljobs.net
It's been around since 1999, and it does have jobs posted, though much is out of date.

www.graduatingengineer.com
A site for graduating engineers and computer careers.

www.internshipprograms.com
A good site if you are looking for an internship.

www.jobpostings.net
The online presence of one of the biggest college recruitment magazine publishers in North America; includes jobs across U.S. and Canada.

www.jobtrak.com
Now owned by Monster, it's their presence in the entry level job market.

www.jobweb.com
Owned and sponsored by the Association of Colleges and Employers. It's a great way to tap into the employers who consistently have entry level hiring needs.

www.snagajob.com
For part time and hourly jobs.

College Placement and Alumni Networks

www.mcli.dist.maricopa.edu
Resource for community college URLs.

www.utexas.edu
Resource for locating college alumni groups.

Diversity Sites

janweb.icdi.wvu.edu
Job Accommodation Network: a portal site for people with disabilities.

www.bilingual-jobs.com
Like the name says: a site for bilingual jobs, in America and around the globe.

www.blackcollegian.com
Premier site for black college students and recent graduates; help and sensible advice in areas of concern for the young professional.

www.business-disability.com
Run by the National Business and Disability Council, job search through listings of member organizations, post resumes, career events, and internships.

www.bwni.com
Business women's network.

www.christianjobs.com
Full-featured employment Web site focusing on employment within the Christian community.

www.diversitylink.com
Job site serving women, minorities, and other diversity talent.

www.eop.com
The online presence of the oldest diversity recruitment publisher in America. For women, members of minority groups, and people with disabilities.

www.experienceworks.org
Training and employment services for mature workers, 55 and older.

www.gaywork.com
A job site featuring a resume bank and job postings for gay men and women.

www.hirediversity.com
Links multicultural and bilingual professionals with both national and international industry sectors. Clients primarily consist of Fortune 1000 companies and government agencies.

www.imdiversity.com
Communities for African-American, Asian-American, Hispanic-American, Native-American and women. No jobs or overt career advice, but lots of links for members of minority communities on issues that affect our lives.

www.latpro.com
The number-one employment source for Spanish- and Portuguese-speaking professionals in North and South America. The site can be viewed in English, Spanish, or Portuguese. Features both resume and job banks.

Executive Job Sites

www.netshare.com
Been around since before the Internet with tenured management; really understands and cares about the executive in transition. Job banks, resources, etc.

www.6figurejobs.com
Solid and well-respected site; includes job banks, resources, etc. A warning: some of their career advice seems very nonspecific and geared to selling services.

www.careerjournal.com
Run by the *Wall Street Journal* with all the bells and whistles, this is an excellent executive transition site.

www.chiefmonster.com
Monster's site aimed at the executive area, though it's difficult to differentiate from the rest of the brand. Comprehensive job postings.

www.execunet.com
One of the top executive sites (along with Netshare, 6 Figure, and the WSJ site). Job banks and resources. Founder Dave Opton has been around a long time and runs a blog with interesting insights.

www.futurestep.com
Korn Ferry is the search firm behind the site. You can put your resume in their database, which is not a bad idea.

www.spencerstuart.com
Executive site for eminent search firm Spencer Stuart. You can put your resume in their database.

www.theladders.com
Like pretty much all the executive sites, you pay for access. Good job board and aggressive marketing means this site has become a player in the space very quickly.

Finding Companies

flipdog.monster.com

www.corporateinformation.com
In addition to having an alphabetical listing of over 20,000 companies, you can also research a country's industry or research a U.S. state. Also, if you register with the site, it will allow you to load the company profile. Within the address section, you will find a link to the company's home page.

www.eliyon.com

www.goleads.com

www.google.com

www.infospace.com

www.searchbug.com

www.superpages.com

www.wetfeet.com

General Job Sites

flipdog.monster.com

hotjobs.yahoo.com

www.4jobs.com

www.americasjobbank.com

www.bestjobsusa.com

www.career.com

www.careerboard.com

www.careerbuilder.com

www.careerhunters.com

www.careermag.com

www.careers.org
Good one-stop site for job search resources.

www.careershop.com

www.careersite.com

www.directemployers.com

www.employment911.com

www.employmentguide.com

www.employmentspot.com

www.job-hunt.org
Excellent site with sensible in-depth advice on job search and career management issues.

www.job.com

www.jobbankusa.com

www.jobfind.com

www.jobwarehouse.com

www.jobweb.com

www.localcareers.com

www.mbajungle.com
Site for current entry level-ish and future MBAs.

www.monster.com

www.nationjob.com

www.net-temps.com

www.quintcareers.com

Diversity Job-Seeker Career, Employment, Job Resources

www.snagajob.com

www.sologig.com

www.summerjobs.com

www.topusajobs.com

www.truecareers.com

www.vault.com

www.wetfeet.com

www.worklife.com

Job Posting Spiders

www.indeed.com

www.jobbankusa.com

www.jobs.just-posted.com

www.jobsearchengine.com

www.jobsniper.com

www.worktree.com

International Sites

www.ukjobsnet.co.uk
UK Jobs Network: the easiest way to find vacancies throughout the UK.

www.4icj.com

www.careerone.com.au

www.eurojobs.com

www.gojobsite.co.uk

www.jobpilot.com

www.jobsbazaar.com

www.jobserve.com

www.jobstreet.com
Asia-Pacific's #1 job site.

www.monster.ca
Monster Canada

www.monster.co.uk
Monster UK: England's #1 job site.

www.overseasjobs.com

www.reed.co.uk

www.seek.com.au
Australia's #1 job site.

www.stepstone.com

www.topjobs.co.uk

www.totaljobs.com

www.workopolis.com
Canada's #1 job site.

Job Fairs

www.careerfairs.com
CareerFairs.com is the fastest one-stop internet site for locating upcoming job fairs and employers. In some cases you can even find the specific positions you desire and the specific positions you are trying to fill.

www.cfg-inc.com
Career Fairs for all levels: Professional and General, Health Care, Technical, Salary, Hourly, and Entry to Senior Level.

www.preferredjobs.com

www.psijobfair.com

www.skidmore.edu

Networking Sites

network.monster.com

socialsoftware.weblogsinc.com
This blog maintains a comprehensive listing of hundreds of networking sites. If you want to check out all your networking options, this is the place to start.

www.40plus.org
Chapter contact information.

www.alumni.net

www.distinctiveweb.com

www.eliyon.com
Helps you find people and companies.

www.execunet.com
An extensive network of professionals with whom you can interact for advice, support, and even career enhancement through local networking meetings. To locate meetings near you (U.S. and the world), check under 'Networking' on their Web site.

www.fiveoclockclub.com
National career counseling network.

www.fiveoclockclub.com
Network with members and alumni
database.

www.rileyguide.com

www.ryze.com
Helps people make connections and expand
their networks. You can network to grow
your business, build your career, and find
a job. You can also join networks related to
your industry for free.

www.tribe.net

www.womans-net.com

www.linkedin.com

Newspaper Sites

newsdirectory.com
Links to newspapers (global).

Profession Specific Sites

Advertising, Public Relations, and Graphic Arts

www.adage.com

www.adweek.com
Adweek Online

www.amic.com
Advertising Media Internet Center

www.creativehotlist.com

Communication Arts

www.prweek.net
PR Week

Aerospace and Aviation

www.aerojobs.com

www.avcrew.com

www.avjobs.com

www.spacejobs.com

Agriculture and Horticulture

www.agricareers.com

www.fishingjobs.com

www.hortjobs.com

Broadcast, Communications, and Journalism

www.b-roll.net

www.cpb.org
Corporation for Public Broadcasting

www.crew-net.com

www.journalismjobs.com

www.telecomcareers.net

www.womcom.org
AWC Online

Business, Finance, and Accounting

www.accounting.com

www.bankjobs.com

www.brokerhunter.com

www.businessfinancemag.com

www.careerbank.com

www.careerjournal.com

www.cfo.com

www.efinancialjobs.com

www.fei.org

www.financialjobs.com

www.jobsinthemoney.com

Education

www.aacc.nche.edu
American Association of Community
Colleges

www.academic360.com

www.academiccareers.com

www.chronicle.com

www.higheredjobs.com

www.petersons.com

www.phds.org

www.teacherjobs.com

www.ujobbank.com

www.wihe.com
Women in Higher Education

Engineering

www.asme.org

www.chemindustry.com

www.engineeringcentral.com

www.engineeringjobs.com

www.engineerjobs.com

www.enr.com
Engineering News Record Magazine

www.graduatingengineer.com

www.ieee.org

www.mepatwork.com

www.nsbe.org
National Society of Black Engineers

www.nspe.org
National Society of Professional Engineers

www.swe.org
Society of Women Engineers

Entertainment, TV, and Radio

www.castingnet.com

www.eej.com
Entertainment Employment Journal

www.entertainmentcareers.net

www.showbizjobs.com

www.themeparkjobs.com

www.tvandradiojobs.com

www.tvjobs.com

Healthcare

www.accessnurses.com
Travel nursing jobs

www.allnurses.com

www.dentsearch.com

www.healthcaresource.com

www.healthjobusa.com

www.hirehealth.com

www.jobscience.com

www.mdjobsite.com

www.medcareers.com

www.nurses123.com
Nurses can use this site to find nursing jobs
across the U.S.

www.nursetown.com

www.nursing-jobs.us
Nursing jobs in the U.S.

www.nursingcenter.com

www.nursingspectrum.com

www.physemp.com

Human Resources

www.hrjobnet.com

www.hrworld.com

www.jobs4hr.com

www.shrm.org

www.tcm.com

IT and MIS

www.computerjobs.com

www.computerjobsbank.com

www.dice.com

www.gjc.org

www.mactalent.com

www.tech-engine.com

www.techemployment.com

www.techies.com

Legal

www.emplawyernet.com

www.ihirelegal.com

www.law.com

www.legalstaff.com

www.theblueline.com

Nonprofit

www.execsearches.com

www.idealist.org

www.naswdc.org

www.nonprofitcareer.com

www.opportunityknocks.org

Real Estate

www.realtor.org

Retail, Hospitality, and Customer Service

www.allretailjobs.com

www.chef2chef.net

www.chefjobsnetwork.com

www.coolworks.com

www.hcareers.com

www.leisurejobs.com

www.resortjobs.com

www.restaurantrecruit.com

www.supermarketnews.com

Sales and Marketing

www.careermarketplace.com

www.jobs4sales.com

www.marketingjobs.com

www.marketingmanager.com

www.marketingpower.com

www.salesheads.com

www.salesjobs.com

Science, Chemistry, Physics, and Biology

www.biocareer.com

www.biospace.com

www.bioview.com

www.bmn.com

www.eco.org

www.hirebio.com

www.medzilla.com

www.microbiologistjobs.com

www.pharmacyweek.com

Recruiter Sites

www.kellyservices.com

www.kornferry.com

www.manpower.com

www.napsweb.org
A job seeker can search the online directory by state, specialty, or by individual. Be sure to check out the headhunters who are designated C.P.C.s—the few but the best.

www.randstad.com

www.recruitersonline.com

www.rileyguide.com

www.snelling.com

www.spherion.com

www.staffingtoday.net
Search the database by state, skills, and type of services you need (temporary/permanent/profession) and it will tell you about staffing services companies in your area.

www.therecruiternetwork.com

Reference Checking

www.allisontaylor.com

Researching Companies

bls.gov

iws.ohiolink.edu
A place for getting started with company research.

iws.ohiolink.edu
Helpful in understanding industry research.

newsdirectory.com

www.competia.com

www.fuld.com

www.industrylink.com

www.learnwebskills.com
A business research tutorial that presents a step-by-step process for finding free company and industry information on the Web. This online course will enable you to learn about an industry, and locate company home pages.

www.quintcareers.com
The quintessential directory of company career centers.

www.quintcareers.com
Guide to researching companies, industries, and countries.

www.thomasregister.com

www.vault.com
Company research.

www.vault.com
Industry list.

www.virtualpet.com
Teaches you how to learn about an industry or a specific company.

Resume Creation

Knockemdead.com
E-mail: *martin@knockemdead.com*

www.phoenixcareergroup.com

certifiedresumewriters.com

parw.com

Resume Distribution

www.resumemachine.com

Salary Research

www.jobstar.org

www.salary.com

www.salaryexpert.com

Telecommuting

www.homeworkers.org

www.jobs-telecommuting.com

www.tdigest.com

www.tjobs.com

Web Resumes/Portfolios

www.brandego.com

www.qfolio.com

RESUME KEYWORDS

The keyword verbs on pages 55–56 describe your working actions, while the keyword nouns that follow showcase those actions in desirable work settings. Inclusion of these words will definitely have a favorable impact on the reception of your electronic job search correspondence. Read the profession-specific nouns for your field, and ask yourself: Have I done work in this area? If the answer is yes, ask yourself: Is it detailed in my resume?

If you possess experience in an area not captured on your resume, describe that experience. The goal isn't to create a resume that includes lots of keywords at the expense of an accurate description of your background; you are simply making sure that your resume is the most powerful it can be. Once online, the important thing is to have the screening software work for you, pulling your resume back from cyberspace into the hands of employment managers—where it actually matters. Remember, you can always add keywords to the keyword/skill set area of your resume, and it takes only a little effort with no need to reformat.

Administration

administration
administrative
   infrastructure
administrative processes
administrative support
back office
budget administration
client communications
confidential correspondence
contract administration
corporate record keeping
corporate secretary
customer liaison
document management
efficiency improvement
executive liaison
executive officer support
facilities management
front office operations
government affairs
liaison affairs
mail and messenger services
meeting planning
office management
office services
policy and procedure
product support
productivity improvement
project management
records management
regulatory reporting
resource management
technical support
time management
workflow planning/
   prioritization

Association and Nonprofit Management

advocacy
affiliate members
board relations
budget allocation
budget oversight
community outreach
corporate development
corporate giving
corporate sponsorship
education foundation
educational programming
endowment funds
foundation management
fundraising
grassroots campaign
industry association
industry relations
leadership training
marketing communications
media relations
member communications
member development
member-driven organization
member retention
member services
mission planning
not-for-profit
organization(al) leadership
organization(al) mission
organization(al) vision
policy development
political affairs
press relations
public policy development
public relations
public/private partnerships
regulatory affairs

research foundation
speakers bureau
special events management
volunteer recruitment
volunteer training

Banking

asset management
asset-based lending
audit examination
branch operations
cash management
commercial banking
commercial credit
consumer banking
consumer credit
correspondent banking
credit administration
credit analysis
debt financing
deposit base
depository services
equity financing
fee income
foreign exchange (FX)
global banking
investment management
investor relations
lease administration
letters of credit
liability exposure
loan administration
loan processing
loan quality
loan recovery
loan underwriting
lockbox processing
merchant banking
nonperforming assets

portfolio management

receivership

regulatory affairs

relationship management

retail banking

retail lending

return-on-assets

return-on-equity

return-on-investment

risk management

secondary markets

secured lending

securities management

transaction banking

trust services

unsecured lending

wholesale banking

workout

Customer Service

account relationship
  management

customer communications

customer development

customer focus groups

customer loyalty

customer management

customer needs assessment

customer retention

customer satisfaction

customer service

customer surveys

field service operation

inbound service operation

key account management

order fulfillment

order processing

outbound service operation

process simplification

records management

relationship management

sales administration

service benchmarks

service delivery

service measures

service quality

telemarketing operations

telesales operations

Engineering

benchmark

capital project

chemical engineering

commissioning

computer-aided design (CAD)

computer-aided engineering
  (CAE)

computer-aided
  manufacturing (CAM)

cross-functional team

customer management

development engineering

efficiency

electrical engineering

electronics engineering

engineering change order
  (ECO)

engineering documentation

environmental engineering

ergonomic techniques

experimental design

experimental methods

facilities engineering

fault analysis

field performance

final customer acceptance

hardware engineering

industrial engineering

industrial hygiene

maintenance engineering

manufacturing engineering

manufacturing integration

methods design

mechanical engineering

nuclear engineering

occupational safety

operating and maintenance
  (O&M)

optics engineering

plant engineering

process development

process engineering

process standardization

product design

product development cycle

product functionality

product innovation

product life-cycle
  management

product manufacturability

product reliability

productivity improvement

project costing

project planning

project management

prototype

quality assurance

quality engineering

regulatory compliance

research and development
  (R&D)

resource management

root cause

scale-up

software engineering

specifications

statistical analysis

systems engineering
systems integration
technical briefings
technical liaison affairs
technology development
test engineering
turnkey
work methods analysis

**Finance, Accounting,
and Auditing**
accounts payable
accounts receivable
asset disposition
asset management
asset purchase
audit controls
audit management
cash management
commercial paper
corporate development
corporate tax
cost accounting
cost avoidance
cost reduction
cost/benefit analysis
credit and collections
debt financing
divestiture
due diligence
employee stock ownership
   plan (ESOP)
equity financing
feasibility analysis
financial analysis
financial audits
financial controls
financial models
financial planning

financial reporting
foreign exchange (FX)
initial public offering (IPO)
internal controls
international finance
investment management
investor accounting
investor relations
job costing
letters of credit
leveraged buyout (LBO)
liability management
make/buy analysis
margin improvement
merger
operating budgets
operational audits
partnership accounting
profit/loss (P&L) analysis
profit gains
project accounting
project financing
regulatory compliance
   auditing
return on assets (ROA)
return on investment (ROI)
revenue gain
risk management
shareholder relations
stock purchase
strategic planning
treasury
trust accounting
work papers

**General Management,
Senior Management,
and Consulting**
accelerated growth

acting executive
advanced technology
benchmarking
business development
business reengineering
capital projects
competitive market position
consensus building
continuous process
   improvement
corporate administration
corporate communications
corporate culture change
corporate development
corporate image
corporate legal affairs
corporate mission
corporate vision
cost avoidance
cost reduction
crisis communications
cross-cultural
   communications
customer retention
customer-driven
   management
efficiency improvement
emerging business venture
entrepreneurial leadership
European economic
   community (EEC)
executive management
executive presentations
financial management
financial restructuring
global market expansion
high-growth organization
interim executive
leadership development

long-range planning

management development

margin improvement

market development

market-driven management

marketing management

matrix management

multifunction experience

multi-industry experience

multisite operations
    management

new business development

operating infrastructure

operating leadership

organization(al) culture

organization(al)
    development

participative management

policy development

performance improvement

process ownership

process reengineering

productivity improvement

profit & loss (P&L)
    management

profit growth

project management

quality improvement

relationship management

reengineering

reorganization

return-on-assets (ROA)

return-on-equity (ROE)

return-on-investment (ROI)

revenue growth

sales management

service design/delivery

signatory authority

start-up venture

strategic development

strategic partnership

tactical planning/leadership

team building

team leadership

total quality management
    (TQM)

transition management

turnaround management

world class organization

Healthcare

acute care facility

ambulatory care

assisted living

capital giving campaign

case management

certificate of need (CON)

chronic care facility

clinical services

community hospital

community outreach

continuity of care

cost center

electronic claims processing

employee assistance
    program (EAP)

emergency medical systems
    (EMS)

fee billing

full time equivalent (FTE)

grant administration

healthcare administrator

healthcare delivery systems

health maintenance
    organization (HMO)

home healthcare

hospital foundation

industrial medicine

inpatient care

long-term care

managed care

management service
    organization (MSO)

multihospital network

occupational health

outpatient care

patient accounting

patient relations

peer review

physician credentialing

physician relations

practice management

preferred provider
    organization (PPO)

preventive medicine

primary care

provider relations

public health administration

quality of care

regulatory standards
    (JCAHO)

rehabilitation services

reimbursement program

risk management

service delivery

skilled nursing facility

third-party administrator

utilization review

wellness programs

Hospitality

amenities

back-of-the-house operations

banquet operations

budget administration

catering operations

club management

conference management

contract F&B operations

corporate dining room

customer service

customer retention

food and beverage operations (F&B)

food cost controls

front-of-the-house operations

guest retention

guest satisfaction

hospitality management

inventory planning/control

labor cost controls

meeting planning

member development/ retention

menu planning

menu pricing

multiunit operations

occupancy

portion control

property development

purchasing

resort management

service management

signature property

vendor sourcing

VIP relations

Human Resources

American with Disabilities Act (ADA)

benefits administration

career pathing

change management

chief talent officer (CTO)

claims administration

college recruitment

compensation

competency-based performance

corporate culture change

cross-cultural communications

diversity management

equal employment opportunity (EEO)

employee communications

employee empowerment

employee involvement teams

employee relations

employee retention

employee surveys

expatriate employment

grievance proceedings

human resources (HR)

human resources generalist affairs

human resources partnerships

incentive planning

international employment

job task analysis

labor arbitration

labor contract negotiations

labor relations

leadership assessment

leadership development

management training and development

manpower planning

merit promotion

multimedia training

multinational workforce

organization (al) design

organization (al) development (OD)

organization (al) needs assessment

participative management

performance appraisal

performance incentives

performance reengineering

position classification

professional recruitment

regulatory affairs

retention

safety training

self-directed work teams

staffing

succession planning

train-the-trainer

training & development

union negotiations

union relations

wage & salary administration

workforce reengineering

Human Services

adult services

advocacy

behavior management

behavior modification

casework

client advocacy

client placement

community-based intervention

community outreach

counseling

crisis intervention

diagnostic evaluation

discharge planning

dually diagnosed

group counseling

human services

independent life skills
   training

inpatient

integrated service delivery

mainstreaming

outpatient

program development

protective services

psychoanalysis

psychological counseling

psychotropic medication

school counseling

social services

social welfare

substance abuse

testing

treatment planning

vocational rehabilitation

vocational placement

vocational testing

youth training program

**International Business
Development**

acquisition

barter transactions

channel development

competitive intelligence

corporate development

cross-border transactions

cross-cultural
   communications

diplomatic protocol

emerging markets

expatriate

export

feasibility analysis

foreign government affairs

foreign investment

global expansion

global market position

global marketing

global sales

import

intellectual property

international business
   development

international business
   protocol

international financing

international liaison

international licensee

international marketing

international subsidiary

international trade

joint venture

licensing agreements

local national

market entry

marketing

merger

multichannel distribution
   network

offshore operations

public/private partnership

technology licensing

start-up venture

strategic alliance

strategic planning

technology transfer

**Law and Corporate
Legal Affairs**

acquisition

adjudicate

administrative law

antitrust

briefs

case law

client management

contracts law

copyright law

corporate by-laws

corporate law

corporate record keeping

criminal law

cross-border transactions

depositions

discovery

due diligence

employment law

environmental law

ethics

family law

fraud

general partnership

intellectual property

interrogatory

joint venture

judicial affairs

juris doctor (JD)

labor law

landmark decision

legal advocacy

legal research

legislative review/analysis

licensing

limited liability corporation
   (LLC)

limited partnership

litigation

mediation

memoranda

mergers

motions

negotiations

patent law

personal injury

probate law

risk management

shareholder relations

signatory authority

strategic alliance

tax law

technology transfer

trade secrets

trademark

transactions law

trial law

unfair competition

workers' compensation
   litigation

Law Enforcement and Security

asset protection

corporate fraud

corporate security

crisis communications

crisis response

electronic surveillance

emergency planning &
   response

emergency preparedness

industrial espionage

industrial security

interrogation

investigations management

law enforcement

media relations

personal protection

public relations

safety training

security operations

tactical field operations

white collar crime

Manufacturing

asset management

automated manufacturing

capacity planning

capital budget

capital project

cell manufacturing

computer integrated
   manufacturing (CIM)

concurrent engineering

continuous improvement

cost avoidance

cost reductions

cross-functional teams

cycle time reduction

distribution management

efficiency improvement

environmental health and
   safety (EHS)

equipment management

ergonomically efficient

facilities consolidation

inventory control

inventory planning

just-in-time (JIT)

kaizen

labor efficiency

labor relations

lean manufacturing

logistics management

manufacturing engineering

manufacturing integration

manufacturing technology

master schedule

materials planning

materials replenishment
   system (MRP)

multisite operations

occupational health & safety
   (OH&S)

on-time delivery

operating budget

operations management

operations reengineering

operations start-up

optimization

order fulfillment

order processing

outsourcing

participative management

performance improvement

physical inventory

pilot manufacturing

plant operations

process automation

process redesign/
   re-engineering

procurement

product development and
   engineering

product rationalization

production forecasting

production lead time

production management

production plans/schedules

production output

productivity improvement

profit & loss (P&L)
   management

project budget

purchasing management

quality assurance/quality
   control

quality circles

safety management

safety training

shipping and receiving
operation

spares and repairs
management

statistical process control
(SPC)

technology integration

time and motion studies

total quality management
(TWM)

traffic management

turnaround management

union negotiations

value-added processes

vendor management

warehousing operations

work in progress (WIP)

workflow optimization

workforce management

world class manufacturing
(WCM)

yield improvement

Public Relations and Corporate Communications

advertising communications

agency relations-directed

brand management

brand strategy

broadcast media

campaign management

community affairs

competitive market lead

community outreach

conference planning

cooperative advertising

corporate communications

corporate identity

corporate sponsorship

corporate vision

creative services

crisis communications

customer communications

direct mail campaign

electronic advertising

electronic media

employee communications

event management

fundraising

government relations

grassroots campaign

investor communications

issues management

legislative affairs

logistics
management
communications

market research

marketing communications

media buys

media placement

media relations

media scheduling

merchandising

multimedia advertising

political action committee
(PAC)

premiums

press releases

print media

promotions

public affairs

public relations

public speaking

publications

publicity

sales incentives

shareholder communications

special events

strategic communications
plan

strategic planning

strategic positioning

tactical campaign

trade shows

VIP relations

Purchasing and Logistics

acquisition management

barter trade

bid review

buy vs. lease analysis

capital equipment acquisition

commodities purchasing

competitive bidding

contract administration

contract change order

contract negotiations

contract terms and
conditions

cradle-to-grave procurement

distribution management

economic ordering quantity
methodology

fixed price contracts

indefinite price/indefinite
quantity

international sourcing

inventory planning/control

just-in-time (JIT) purchasing

logistics management

materials replenishment
ordering (MRO)

purchasing

multisite operations

negotiation

offshore purchasing

outsourced

price negotiations

procurement

proposal review

purchasing

regulatory compliance

request for proposal (RFP)

request for quotation (RFQ)

sourcing

specifications compliance

subcontractor negotiations

supplier management

supplier quality

vendor partnerships

vendor quality certification

warehousing

Real Estate, Construction, and Property Management

acquisition

American with Disabilities Act (ADA)

asset management

asset valuation

asset workout/recovery

building code compliance

building trades

capital improvement

claims administration

commercial development

community development

competitive bidding

construction management

construction trades

contract administration

contract award

critical path method (CPM) scheduling

design and engineering

divestiture

engineering change orders (ECOS)

estimating

environmental compliance

facilities management

fair market value pricing

grounds maintenance

historic property renovation

industrial development

infrastructure development

leasing management

master community association

master scheduling

mixed-use property

occupancy

planned-use development (PUD)

portfolio

preventive maintenance

project concept-driven

project development

project management

project scheduling

property management

property valuation

real estate appraisal

real estate brokerage

real estate development

real estate investment trust (REIT)

real estate law

real estate partnership

regulatory compliance

renovation

return on assets (ROA)

return on equity (ROE)

return on investment (ROI)

site development

site remediation

specifications

syndications

tenant relations

tenant retention

turnkey construction

Sales/Marketing/ Business Development

account development

account management

account retention

brand management

business development

campaign management

competitive analysis

competitive contract award

competitive market intelligence

consultative sales

customer loyalty

customer needs assessment

customer retention

customer satisfaction

customer service

direct mail marketing

direct response marketing

direct sales

distributor management

emerging markets

field sales management

fulfillment

global markets

high-impact presentations

incentive planning

indirect sales

international sales

international trade

key account management

line extension

margin improvement

market launch

market positioning

market research

market share ratings

market surveys

marketing strategy

mass merchants

multichannel distribution

multichannel sales

multimedia advertising

national account
   management

negotiations

new market development

new product introduction

product development

product launch

product life-cycle
   management

product positioning

profit & loss (P&L)
   management

promotions

public relations

public speaking

revenue growth

revenue stream

sales closing

sales cycle management

sales forecasting

sales training

solutions selling

strategic market planning

tactical market plans

team building/leadership

trend analysis

Teaching and Education Administration

academic advisement

accreditation

admissions management

alumni relations

 e design

conference management

curriculum development

education administration

enrollment

extension program

field instruction

grant administration

instructional media

instructional programming

intercollegiate athletics

lifelong learning

management development

peer counseling

program development

public/private partnerships

recruitment

residential life

scholastic standards

student retention

student services

student-faculty relations

textbook review

training and development

Transportation

agency operations

cargo handling

common carrier

container transportation

customer delivery operations

dedicated logistics operations

dispatch operations

distribution management

driver leasing

equipment control

facilities management

fleet management

freight consolidation

freight forwarding

import operations

inbound transportation

line management

load analysis

logistics management

maritime operations

outbound transportation

over-the-road transportation

port operations

regulatory compliance

route planning/analysis

route management

safety management

terminal operations

traffic planning

transportation planning

transportation management

warehouse management

workflow optimization

INDEX

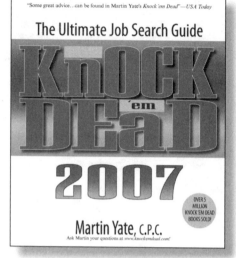
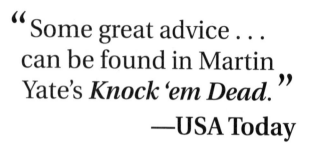